Essential Movement Experiences for Preschool and Primary Children

Victor P. Dauer
Washington State University
Pullman, Washington

426 South Sixth Street • Minneapolis, Minnesota 55415

Copyright © 1972 by Victor P. Dauer

All rights reserved. No part of this book may be reproduced in any form whatsoever, by photograph or mimeograph or by any other means, by broadcast or transmission, by translation into any kind of language, nor by recording electronically or otherwise, without permission in writing from the publisher, except by a reviewer, who may quote brief passages in critical articles and reviews.

Printed in the United States of America

Library of Congress Catalog Card Number 76-189382

SBN 8087-0422-2

1   2   3   4   5   6   7   8   9   0

This book was set in Helvetica by The Type House, printed by Colwell Press, and bound by A. J. Dahl & Company. The cover and text pages were designed by the Burgess staff. The editors were Robert E. Lakemacher and Dora Stein. Morris Lundin supervised production.

Action sequence illustrations were drawn by Bruce Frederick.

Preface

It has become quite obvious that physical education is being extended downward from the first grade even almost to the cradle. Since the majority of the learning experiences of young children are motor, making the most of these experiences becomes an educationally sound goal.

The author has already added kindergarten learning experiences to his earlier book, extending the original 1-6 range of activities to K-6. Now, the addition of material for preschool further extends the range of experiences at the preschool and primary levels.

Another fact became apparent. Teachers of young children have little need or interest in activities for intermediate children. So it seemed that a book especially for the lower level would be an excellent idea. Hence, the present manuscript, *Essential Movement Experiences for Preschool and Primary Children*, was born.

In assembling learning experiences for preschool children, it was evident that much flexibility should be incorporated in the approach, and the presentation reflects this posture. As the experiences move up the ladder through the kindergarten into the primary level, they become more definable as traditional physical education names.

While the range of activities and experiences has been extended into the preschool level, the convictions on which the original work, *Dynamic Physical Education for Elementary School Children*, is based still hold and merit restatement here.

First, a broad program of physical education should be the right of each child, with emphasis on rugged and demanding activities. Children need to be challenged if they are to move along the path of development. Enough physical education materials are available in this text so that a variety of learning experiences can be presented on each grade level. New and exciting experiences should face the children as they progress from grade to grade.

A second conviction is that a successful program for children occurs only through careful planning. The curriculum must be blocked out in enough detail that the year's work is outlined. Superimposed on the year's outline is the vital element of progression; progression from grade to grade, within grades, and within activities. A major purpose of this text is to present learning experiences allocated either by grade level or in progression within the activity descriptions. In some instances, the basic elements of an activity or area are presented in chart form to make apparent the progressions.

Third is the belief that the learning environment involving the teacher, the learner, and the activity will suggest the most appropriate method or approach, to attain the expected outcomes. At times experiences can be presented with a structured and directed approach, while at other times basic movement methodology will offer better results. Teachers differ in aptitude, personality, and background. To ask a teacher to restrict his efforts to one type of methodology is not sound. On the other hand, teachers must become familiar with basic movement techniques as these widen and broaden the learning potential of the material. Problem-solving, exploratory, and creative approaches enhance and enrich the movement experiences of children.

A fourth conviction is that physical fitness values for children come primarily from a program which is planned and administered with that end in mind. The attainment and maintenance of suitable levels of physical fitness can be neither happenstance nor casual. The child must be placed in a program in which the development and maintenance of fitness are regarded as important goals. Caution must be observed so that the emphasis on fitness does not become the dominant or overriding consideration.

Lastly, the conduct of the program must give consideration to the development of personal values (self-image) and make important contributions to the overall educational progress of the child. The key to this lies both in the kinds of learning experiences which are selected and in the manner in which they are conducted.

The author would like to give recognition to Mr. Robert Pangrazi, Supervisor of Elementary Physical Education for the Pullman Schools, who served as an associate in the Title III study and collaborated with the author in preparing this text. Many of the sequences and approaches presented in this edition were developed under Mr. Pangrazi's direction.

The illustration with regard to good and poor posture was adapted by permission from one of the curriculum guides of the Seattle Public Schools. The material on Rope Jumping is also from the Seattle Public Schools and was developed by Dennis Meyer. This was adapted from original material compiled by Paul Smith, Director of Physical Education for Shoreline Public Schools, Seattle, Washington. The author is also indebted to many other teachers and supervisors too numerous to mention for the many ideas incorporated into the book.

The teachers and children of the Pullman Schools, particularly Jefferson School, merit our heartfelt thanks for their cooperation and efforts as subjects for the many illustrations in the text.

Photography credits go to Robert Bullis, Staff Photographer, Washington State University, Pullman, Washington. Credits for selected drawings and illustrations go to Ron Smith and Paul House, Pullman, Washington. Action sequences were drawn by Bruce Frederick, University of Wisconsin at Superior.

Special acknowledgment is due Miss Dora Stein of the Burgess staff for her perceptiveness and guidance in editing the manuscript.

Pullman, Washington
March, 1972

Victor P. Dauer

Contents

Chapter 1 THE CHILD AND PHYSICAL EDUCATION 1
What Is Physical Education?, 1   Educational and Cultural Forces Affecting Physical Education, 2   Modern-Day Educational and Sociological Trends, 4   The Approach to Physical Education, 6

Chapter 2 THE BASIS FOR THE PROGRAM 2
Basic Urges of Children, 7   Characteristics, Interests, and Needs Important in Program Planning, 8   The Purposes of Physical Education, 10   Physical Fitness, 10   Movement Excellence — Useful Physical Skills, 11   The Social Goal, 12   Safety Skills and Attitudes, 13   Wholesome Recreation, 14   The Self-Image and Self-Concept, 14   Personal and Educational Values, 15   Physical Education as a Tool in the Education of the Disadvantaged, 15   How Can These Purposes Be Attained?, 16

Chapter 3 THE PHYSICAL EDUCATION PROGRAM 17
Guidelines for Program Planning, 17   Planning in Terms of Broad Program Areas, 19   The Allocation of Specific Activities to Grade Level, 19   Physical Education Programs for Each Grade Level, 21   Planning the Year's Program, 25   The Weekly Unit Schedule, 26

Chapter 4 FACILITIES, EQUIPMENT, AND SUPPLIES 31
Facilities, 31   Equipment and Supplies, 32   Outdoor Equipment, 32   Indoor Equipment, 33   Supplies, 35   Care and Repair, 38   Storage and Marking, 39

Chapter 5 ORGANIZING FOR EFFECTIVE TEACHING 40
The Community, the Administration, and the School, 40   Patterns of Teaching Responsibility, 40   Consultant and Supervisory Services, 41   Scheduling, 42   Policies for Health and Safety, 42   Safety Procedures, 44   Operational Policies, 46   Promotional Ideas and Public Relations, 47   Pageants, Demonstrations, and Assembly Programs, 48

Chapter 6 MOVEMENT EDUCATION 49
Movement Competency, 49   Defining Movement Education, 50   Basic Movement, 51   The Skills Instructional Program, 53   Posture and Body Mechanics, 54   Perceptual-Motor Competency and the Slow Learner, —

Chapter 7 EFFECTIVE CLASS MANAGEMENT 63
The Role of the Teacher, 63   Guiding the Learning Process, 64   Instructional Procedures, 66   Teaching Aids in Physical Education, 75

Chapter 8 LESSON PLANNING AND INTRODUCTORY ACTIVITY 77
The Physical Education Lesson, 77   The Design of the Written Lesson Plan, 78   Introductory Activity, 81

Chapter 9 THE PHYSICAL DEVELOPMENT GOAL 84
What Is Physical Fitness?, 84   Guidelines for Achieving Physical Fitness, 85   Physical Developmental Activities, 87   Fitness Routines for Grade 3, 90

Chapter 10 BASIC MOVEMENT 102
Purposes of Basic Movement, 102   Processes in Basic Movement, 102   Factors for Securing Variety of Response, 104   Instructional Procedures, 105   Problem Development, 108   Stressing Quality in Movement, 112   Formations for Movement, 112   Developing Ideas for Unstructured Movement, 114   Developing Ideas for Structured Movement, 115   The Movement Suggestion Box, 117   Perceptual-Motor Activities, Manipulative Activities, and Apparatus Activities, 118

Chapter 11 PERCEPTUAL-MOTOR COMPETENCY 119
Characteristics of the Underachiever or Slow Learner, 120   How Are These Individuals Discovered?, 120   Implications for Physical Education Programs, 121   Special Activities for Perceptual-Motor Programs, 124   The Perceptual-Motor Team, 126

Chapter 12 STORY GAMES, FINGER PLAYS, AND DRAMATIC PLAY 127
Stories, 127   Finger Plays, 129   Dramatic Play With Poems, 130   Other Experiences as a Basis for Dramatic Play, 134

Chapter 13 MANIPULATIVE ACTIVITIES 137
    Activities Utilizing Beanbags, 137   Basic Ball Skills, 139   Bowling, 143   Paddle and Ball Activities, 144   Parachute Play, 145   Wands, 148   Hoops, 150

Chapter 14 APPARATUS ACTIVITIES 152
    Return Activities, ___   Multiple Activity Organization, 153   Apparatus Types, 153   Rope Climbing, 153   Horizontal Ladder and Climbing Frames, 156   Exercise Bar, 158   Balance Beam, 158   Activities on Benches, 160   Activities on Jumping Boxes, 162   Magic Ropes, 164   Individual Mats, 165   Balance Boards, 166   Bounding Boards, 166   Gym Scooters, 167   Combination Sets, 167

Chapter 15 STUNTS AND TUMBLING 169
    The Stunts and Tumbling Program, 169   Progression and Grade Level Placement, 170   Presenting Activities, 171   Instructional Procedures, ___   Additional Considerations in Methodology, 175   Preschool and Nursery School Emphasis, 177   Kindergarten Program, 177   First Grade Program, 180   Second Grade Program, 188   Third Grade Program, 193

Chapter 16 RELAYS 201
    Instructional Procedures, 201   Selected Relays, 202   Kindergarten and First Grade Approach, 202   Second Grade Relays, 202   Third Grade Relays, 203

Chapter 17 GAME-TYPE ACTIVITIES 205
    Introducing Variations, 206   Safety Suggestions for Games, 206   Maintaining Balance in Games, 207   Instructional Procedures for Conducting Games, 207   Exploration with Games, 208   The Games Program for Preschool and Kindergarten, 208   The Games Program for the First Grade, 213   The Games Program for the Second Grade, 217   The Games Program for the Third Grade, 224

Chapter 18 RHYTHMIC ACTIVITIES 234
    Rhythmic Accompaniment, 234   Characteristics of Rhythmic Background, 236   The Program of Rhythmic Activities, 236   Fundamental Rhythms, 237   Rhythmic Beat Repetition and Reproduction, 237   Fundamental Movement Patterns to Rhythm, 238   Creative Rhythms — Identification, 243   Creative Rhythms — Dramatization, 244   Singing Games, 245   Folk Dance and Other Dance Activities, 246   Singing Games and Folk Dances, Preschool, Kindergarten, First Grade, Second Grade, Third Grade, 248   Rope Jumping to Music, 274   Games Using Rhythmic Background, 276

Chapter 19 INDIVIDUAL AND DUAL ACTIVITIES FOR ALL GRADES 279
    Individual Rope Jumping — Without Music, 279   Long Rope Jumping, 280   Other Activities, 281

Chapter 20 CLASSROOM AND LIMITED AREA ACTIVITIES 283
    Guides for Conducting Classroom and Limited Space Activities, 284   Suggested Classroom Activities, 285

Chapter 21 INTEGRATION WITH OTHER SUBJECTS 291
    Art, 291   Geography, 291   Health and Safety, 292   History, 292   Language Arts, 292   Music, 292   Number Concepts — Mathematics, 293   Projects, 293

Chapter 22 INTRODUCTORY SPORTS UNITS 294
    The Sports Unit, 294   Basketball, 295   Skills in Basketball, 295   Soccer, 297   Soccer Skills, 297   Softball, 298   Softball Skills for the Third Grade, 299

    APPENDIX I   DIAGRAMS FOR CONSTRUCTING PHYSICAL EDUCATION EQUIPMENT AND SUPPLIES 301

    APPENDIX II   SOURCES FOR RECORDS FOR THE RHYTHMIC PROGRAM IN THE ELEMENTARY SCHOOL 311

    APPENDIX III   BIBLIOGRAPHY AND RELATED MATERIALS RESOURCE 313

    INDEX 321

1

The Child and Physical Education

What Is Physical Education?
Educational and Cultural Forces Affecting Physical Education
Modern-Day Educational and Sociological Trends
The Approach to Physical Education

The results of good physical education are not limited to the body alone, but they extend even to the soul itself. —ARISTOTLE, 350 B.C.

The general goal of education *and* physical education is two-fold: (1) the greatest possible development of each individual, and (2) education for responsible democratic citizenship. Physical education provides an important educational medium which can make a significant contribution toward this goal. Basically, it makes use of the activity drive of children who, even the most timid, enjoy movement. The principal aim of physical education, then, should be to satisfy this insatiable appetite for movement, help them to enjoy it more, and guide them so that they may build lasting values. The aim of each teacher should be to assist in attaining the maximum development possible for each child.

These broad values can be achieved only if children like, enjoy, and appreciate physical education. A child will derive little value from the program if he has learned from traumatic experiences to detest his physical education classes and physical activity. The dignity of the individual must be preserved in his physical experiences, and each child must meet some measure of success in his own activities and activities with his peers. From this base, the full potential of physical education as an educational tool can be realized. To achieve high success in personal development, children need to become totally involved in the program and what they are doing.

The Elementary School Physical Education Position Paper* expresses this so adequately:

In a very real measure, the degree of success the elementary child experiences in his work and play is influenced by his ability to execute movement patterns effectively and efficiently. For the child, movement is one of the most used means of nonverbal communication and expression. It is one of the most important avenues through which he forms impressions about himself and his environment.

To make important contributions to the growth and development of children, a quality program, well-planned and well-taught, is needed in our elementary schools. Physical education must be an integral part of the total education program for the child.

WHAT IS PHYSICAL EDUCATION?

Physical education, then, is education of, by, and through human movement. It is that phase of general education which contributes to the total growth and development of the child primarily through selected movement experiences and physical activities.

*Essentials of a Quality Elementary School Physical Education Program—A Position Paper (Washington, D. C.: AAHPER, 1970).

Today's emphasis on physical education centers on its educational potential, its power to contribute to more than just the development of physical fitness, skills, or desirable social qualities. Educators are looking to physical education for more than just lip service to total child development. Increasing evidence appears to demonstrate that physical education can effectively expand its function as an educational tool by focusing on exploration, creativity, thought and problem-solving processes, concept formation, and concomitant learnings, leading to self-confidence and the establishment of a good self-concept and self-image.

That physical education can make significant contributions to total child development and learning is becoming increasingly more evident. Nevertheless, the concept of total development must include adequate attention to physical fitness and neuromuscular skills, which are the unique contributions of physical education to the child's well-being.

Health, vitality, and vigor are a basis for excellence in living. Physical education should be concerned with contributing to physical welfare and vigor, which are basic to a balanced life. If physical education does not provide the child with experiences to realize these attributes, no other area of the school curriculum will compensate for this loss.

Important too are basic skills and perceptual-motor competencies, which evidently have a bearing on academic progress in the lower grades. Studies by Kephart* and others have revealed that these competencies are of critical importance in the primary grades, particularly with respect to reading readiness and achievement. It is reasoned that as children learn to move effectively, handle their bodies in a variety of situations and challenges, and react favorably to their physical environment, a competency base is built upon which academic concepts and learnings can function more effectively.

EDUCATIONAL AND CULTURAL FORCES AFFECTING PHYSICAL EDUCATION

It is important that all educators recognize

---
*Newell C. Kephart, *The Slow Learner in the Classroom* (Columbus, Ohio: Charles C. Merrill Co., Inc., 1960).

and appreciate the quality and depth of the changes which have taken place in elementary school physical education under the impact of educational and cultural forces, particularly during the last decade. In a sense, the emphasis in physical education curriculums has been cycloidal in that educators have embraced new ideas and approaches enthusiastically when they first appeared, subsequently retaining only their best features as the glamor of the "New Look" wore off.

The Foreign Influence — Prior to World War I

Up to the outbreak of World War I, no single strong movement in physical education held dominance in the United States. A number of European systems, particularly German and Swedish, had their advocates, with no strong American system appearing to challenge these imports. European programs were rigid and militaristic in nature, with mind and body considered separate entities. This dichotomy, labeled "dualism," spawned a program which was pointed primarily toward the physical aspects of an individual.

The emphasis was largely on an exercise program, with dissenting voices from advocates of the German system favoring a gymnastic approach. In many of our schools, the physical education program consisted primarily of a series of exercises which could be done in the classroom while each student stood alongside his desk.

The Games and Sports Emphasis — World War I to 1930

Early in World War I it was determined that physical training programs for soldiers based on the prevailing calisthenic approach were unsuitable for military purposes, and a shift toward the utilization of games and sports for developmental purposes occurred. Dualism also continued in the new programs with mind and body still separated, but physical educators slowly became aware of the educational possibilities of physical education and its contributions to total development of the individual. The games and sports program appeared to be appropriate for the development not only of the physical goals, but also for the attainment of desirable social qualities.

On the elementary level, the program centered on the games and sports, strongly influenced by the athletic emphasis of the secondary and college sports programs. Literally, it was a program which could be described by answering the question, "What games are we going to play today?"

The Depression Years — 1930 to 1940

While physical education received strong impetus from the games and sports emphasis during the Roaring Twenties, it sank to a low level during the depression years. This was particularly true in the elementary schools, where the "frills" in education, i.e., art, music, home economics, shop, and physical education, were relegated to secondary roles, or in many cases eliminated entirely.

Gradually, dualism was being rejected and physical education began to center on the development of the total individual. Concern was still given to the physical aspects, but only within the concept of the total development of the child; physically, mentally, socially, and emotionally.

The Reawakening — World War II

Men and women accepted in the Armed Services in World War II were subjected to rigorous training programs, particularly in flyer and commando corps. The cream of American physical educators labored in both physical fitness developmental and hospital reconditioning programs, which provided an opportunity for much experimentation in methodology and new approaches.

The new approaches would argue that an improvement in the quality of American physical education might have been expected after the war, but little effect was evident in the quality of elementary school programs. It seemed that American physical education on the elementary level reverted back to "business as usual" routines, with emphasis on simple games with some sports added for good measure.

The Surge of Physical Fitness — 1954 to Present

Although physical fitness has always been considered an important goal in physical education, at times a renewal of the emphasis has occurred, dependent upon the social forces dominant at the time. Such a renewal occurred in 1954 following the publication of the comparative fitness levels of American and European children, based on the Kraus-Weber Tests. A study by Dr. Hans Kraus, comparing certain strength and flexibility measurements of 4000 New York area school children with a comparable sample of Central European children, had far-reaching results. The American press became aroused concerning the comparative weaknesses of American children, and with this concern, the present fitness movement was born.

One result of the furor over physical fitness was the establishment of the President's Council on Physical Fitness, a potent force in promoting good physical fitness not only among school children, but also among citizens of all ages. The President's Council on Physical Fitness and Sports, as it is now named, through its many publications, services, and promotions, has had a major influence on school programs leading to the development of better levels of physical fitness among children.

The results of this new emphasis on fitness have been evident in the elementary schools. Programs are of improved quality, and many have been established where none existed formerly. Administrators have become increasingly aware of the contributions which physical education can make to the growth and development of children. Other apparent effects are increased time allotment for physical education, better facilities and equipment, and provision for consultant service and specialized teachers. The Council's national seven-item physical fitness test has widespread acceptance and affords fitness comparisons on a country-wide basis.

Movement Education — 1960 to Present

Movement education brought a fresh new approach, a new methodology, and a new way of providing learning experiences for children. With its emphasis on the individual child, it features the problem-solving and exploratory approach.

Movement education has its origins in England and reached this country directly or through Canadian programs. At present it has become an indispensable and fully accepted part of American physical education. Movement education centers on the indirect (exploratory) method of teaching as opposed to the direct (command) approach. In practice, the degree to which indirect teaching is employed varies, giving rise to many choices of methodology.

There is confusion concerning the meaning of terms and definitions in movement. These will be clarified in later discussions.

Perceptual-Motor Competency — 1960 to Present

Based on the theories of Montessori, Luria, Piaget, and others, the importance of motor experiences in the normal learning process of children was recognized. Delacato and Kephart were among the leaders in developing a practical school approach based on the theory that children deficient in certain academic competencies could be helped with a structured perceptual-motor program, so as to achieve better in their academic pursuits.

Perceptual-motor theory holds that each child normally must pass successively through stages of neuromuscular development during childhood. If one or more of these stages is omitted or underdeveloped, then the child will have trouble with appropriate motor reponses, which may cause him difficulty in normal academic progress, specifically with reading, speech, spelling, and writing. The theory is that a program of selected perceptual-motor activities can help develop the missed stages, thus providing a better basis for normal academic achievement.

Evidence is strong that a certain stage of neuromuscular development is necessary for optimum academic development. Research is lacking pertaining to identification of the perceptual-motor qualities, and a good scientific basis for programs is not available. However, it is established that the thinking mind is rooted in the physical being, and all cognitive learning is based on physical and sensory input.

MODERN-DAY EDUCATIONAL AND SOCIOLOGICAL TRENDS

A number of trends and influences, some from education in general, are having and will have a profound effect on elementary school physical education. Their full impact has not yet been manifest, but they merit attention.

There is a trend toward extending education downward and upward. The downward aspects are of importance to the elementary school physical educator with the appearance of preschool education and child care centers. It is necessary to revise our thinking downward to provide movement experiences for these children. Head Start programs are another extension of the educational system. Since much of the instruction is motor and physical, there must be concern with providing appropriate and effective movement experiences for preschool children.

Physical education becomes a time for learning rather than a respite from lessons. Physical education can do more than develop the learning of which young children are capable — it can show them *how* to "learn."

Education now centers on the individual, with instruction and progress determined by how fast each child can absorb what the school has to offer. In physical education, more attention is focused on individual activities, with less on competition between teams or individuals. A child should be allowed to progress at his own rate.

In keeping with educational individualism, the development by each child of a proper self-image and self-concept is of vital importance. It is necessary to offer the type of programs where each child can meet success and not be discouraged by failure.

Conceptual understanding, i.e., the application of abstract ideas drawn from experience, also plays an important part in physical education today. Thus in the process of movement the child learns to distinguish between near and far, strong and weak, light and heavy, high and low. He should be given the opportunity to experiment and thereby establish an understanding of such other terms as curve, stretch, twist, turn, balance, and bounce, and so on. He should also be enabled to learn to work purposefully toward a designated goal or to be self-critical. Thus the learning environment of physical education becomes an extension of the educational activities of the classroom.

The role of physical education in working with disadvantaged and culturally deprived children needs to be re-evaluated. While the problems and relationships are complicated and deep, physical education can nevertheless help youngsters achieve status, enjoy respect, and succeed through improved peer regard.

A potent influence for educational experimentation and dissemination of results is found in the many research programs sponsored by the U. S. Office of Education under the legal provisions of such vehicles as the Elementary and Secondary Education Act and the Education Professions Development Act.

Modern international travel and interchange of educational personnel have provided fruitful exchanges of program ideas and equipment, broadening and enriching American programs. Such items as the balance-beam bench, climbing ropes on tracks, wall-attached climbing frames, and floor apparatus have now found their way from European programs into American schools.

An event of far-reaching importance affecting elementary school physical education programs was the establishment in the AAHPER of a consultant in elementary school physical education. This reflects a trend to recognize elementary school physical education as an entity in itself rather than as hanging on to the coattails of secondary school physical education. The consultant at the time of this manuscript, Dr. Margie Hanson, has been able to weld together many varied factions working toward common goals by scheduling national institutes and regional workshops, forming commissions, and publishing philosophical and explanatory material in the field.

Another trend appearing is toward the employment of the specialist in physical education on the elementary level. Where previously classroom teachers handled the physical education instructional chores, there is recognition that quality programs are possible only with quality teaching by specially trained instructors. Since this involves some added expense to school districts, total acceptance of specialist teaching has not yet arrived.

With the increased employment of specialists, a necessary adjustment of college teacher-training programs is indicated to provide a product that can function effectively in the elementary school physical education environment. Where formerly education of the elementary teacher was merely an extension of secondary training in physical education, appropriate programs in teacher education are now being structured, with particular emphasis on movement theory.

A type of school organization which will have implications for elementary school programs is the nongraded school. To fit into this philosophy, a physical education program will need to have many alternatives so that individual differences can be met. No longer will intact classes be scheduled for physical education. Groups of students will appear for physical education experiences, or children may even come and go as individuals on a varied schedule. This may mean chronological age differences greater than seen in the present program geared to the classroom schedule.

More attention is being centered on programs for special students, which include both the physically and the educationally handicapped. Federal funding has generated much interest and experimentation in programs labeled "Special Education."

It is interesting to note, too, that the American Medical Association, representing the entire medical profession, has recognized the value of physical education in a statement adopted at its national convention in 1960.

> Resolved, That the American Medical Association through its various divisions and departments and its constituent and component medical societies do everything feasible to encourage effective instruction in physical education for all students in our schools and colleges.*

The 1960 resolution was reaffirmed in 1969, strongly supported by the AMA Committee on Exercise and Physical Fitness, a body which was not in existence at the time of the 1960 resolution.

In the final analysis, the great change has been in the kinds of learning experiences now being provided for children in physical education. Programs have been expanded and broadened to include activities and experiences which were unknown a decade ago. Administration of such a program demands not only skilled instructors, familiar with a broad range of activity, but also sufficient supplies and equipment to conduct such a program. School boards must assume the responsibility for providing administrative support to finance and staff a modern program.

Another educational trend which some physical educators favor is the expression of expected outcomes in behavioral terms. A behavioral objective is expressed in terms of observable human behavior, is predictable, and is measurable. But not all elements of movement can be reduced to easy mathematical terms. Thus, reducing the accepted physical education objective that each child should demonstrate the ability to manage his body effectively in all situations to measurable mathematical terms would be a formidable task, and differentiating between the performance standards expected from different grade and age levels would be difficult.

Another variable is the instructional dimension. Who is directing the learning experiences, the specialist or the classroom teacher? If it can be reasoned that the physical education specialist should be able to accomplish more in terms of pupil progress, then two levels of performance outcomes must be considered to take care of the instructional dimensions.

The mere task of setting valid behavioral objectives is complex, and they are of value only if they are measured. For the teacher to evaluate all the pertinent cognitive, affective, and psychomotor variables after a period of instruction would demand an inordinate amount of teaching-learning time.

The physical fitness objective is actually the one most easily expressed in terms of pupil performance. Projected goals are available for all fitness tests. But some have objected that set standards in physical fitness do not consider individual differences, i.e., since each child should progress at his own rate, one standard for all is unsound. This raises the question of how this principle of consideration for individual differences could be incorporated effectively into behavorial objectives. Flexible standards would be necessary, further complicating the procedure. While behavioral objectives stated in precise performance expectations are undoubtedly of value to the teacher, their application presents difficulties which need solution before it can be effectively implemented.

THE APPROACH TO PHYSICAL EDUCATION

Some physical education people hold that modern educational theory has relegated the traditional approach to elementary school physical education to the sidelines. The rigid traditional (sometimes called the direct) approach, specifying conformance of all children to the same manner, is now considered by some to be an inferior approach. Little attention was given to creative aspects, the varied interests of children, the difference in capacity, and the opportunities for movement exploration.

On the other hand, in the opinion of the author, the pendulum has swung too far the other way *in some cases* in complete use of what is termed the indirect approach. This is a fresh approach to child-centered education in which the child has opportunity to explore, create, and move according to his desires and capacities. There are those who feel the term "Physical Education" is no longer apt and should be replaced by "Movement Education," since movement is the key to the new methodology. It takes a skilled and resourceful teacher to make the most of the indirect approach so that objectives are met, and the result is not merely a variety of free play.

It can be reasoned that if the present program has achieved something good, we must be doing some things right. The problem is to retain from our programs what has value and to prune some of the out-of-date ideas and deadwood from our methodology. Movement education has much to offer, and we should adopt those learning experiences which offer a better potential than what we now have to achieve optimum development of the child. Development is the key to the learning situation, and the teacher should employ those learning experiences which he feels offer the best chance of achieving this development. Prudent teachers will examine new ideas and try them out, rejecting those which are impractical, and retaining those which are found successful.

On a scientific basis, changes in methodology should be based only on appropriate research. Caution is indicated not to make abrupt and sweeping changes without an adequate basis. Empirical experiences, however, are providing some indications and direction for physical education in the wake of changing concepts. The right of the teacher to employ the approach he considers the most appropriate is affirmed.

2

The Basis for the Program

> Basic Urges of Children
> Characteristics, Interests, and Needs
> The Purposes of Physical Education
> Physical Fitness
> Movement Excellence — Useful Physical Skills
> The Social Goal
> Safety Skills and Attitudes
> Wholesome Recreation
> The Self-Image and Self-Concept
> Personal and Educational Values
> Physical Education as a Tool in the Education of the Disadvantaged
> How Can These Purposes Be Attained?

In selecting the purposes and content of the program for elementary school children, the characteristics, capacities, needs, interests, and basic urges of children should be given utmost consideration. The broad concept of basic urges applies to all age groups and is relevant to most children from nursery school to sixth grade. A basic urge is an intense drive, which the child seems to have in his natural makeup, toward certain goals or levels of achievement. A good program will provide opportunity so that these basic urges can be satisfied.

BASIC URGES OF CHILDREN

Basic urges will vary somewhat among children, but for most are important reasons for living and being. It is difficult to rank them in importance, and no attempt is made to do so here, as children will evaluate them differently.

The Urge for Success and Approval. Children not only like to achieve, but also desire recognition of this achievement. They wilt under criticism and disapproval, whereas encouragement and friendly support promote growth and maximum development. Failure can lead to frustration, lack of interest, and inefficient learning. In extreme cases, failure can lead to an antipathy to physical education which can have a profound effect on later physical participation.

The Urge for Physical Fitness and Attractiveness. Every teacher should understand how eager boys and girls are to be physically fit and possess bodies that are agile and attractive. To be strong is both a joy and a glory. It gives dignity and confidence. Teachers should understand the humiliation suffered by the youngster who is weak, fat, crippled, or abnormal in any way.

The Urge to Contest. This is tied up with the first urge and refers to the child's desire to match physical skill and strength with his fellows. It means the urge to wrestle, to hit a ball, to pit one's skill, to overcome the other, to take joy in competition, and to be successful in situations of stress.

The Urge for Social Competence. The child would like to be accepted, respected, and liked by others. He doesn't want to feel awkward or embarrassed in his movement achievements. He wishes to appear to an advantage not only with his peers, but also in the world of adults.

The Urge for Adventure. This is the urge to participate in something different, romantic, or unusual. The child desires to climb to the heights, to be able to do something different, and to participate in activities which of themselves are interesting. It means a change from the "old stuff" to something new and exciting.

The Urge for Creative Satisfaction. Children like to try out different ways, experiment with different materials, and see what they can do creatively. Finding different ways of expressing themselves physically satisfies the urge for creative action.

The Urge for Rhythmic Expression. Every boy and girl basically likes rhythm. The program should offer a variety of rhythmic activities which every boy and girl should learn well enough to give them many pleasant, satisfying hours. Rhythm is movement and children like to move. Dancing, rhythmic movements, rope jumping skills, ball bouncing and dribbling routines, and similar activities are pleasing and exciting experiences under competent leadership.

The Urge To Know. Young people live in a world of curiosity. They are interested not only in what they are doing, but they want to know why. The "why" is a great motivator. Lasting habits are established only if the individual is convinced they are worthwhile.

CHARACTERISTICS, INTERESTS, AND NEEDS IMPORTANT IN PROGRAM PLANNING

PRESCHOOL (NURSERY SCHOOL)

Characteristics	Program Needs and Implications
Inability to sit still for more than a brief period.	Utilize movement experiences for learning activities.
Awkward — inefficient movement.	Keep within the maturity level.
Fear of heights, falling.	Provide successful experiences in climbing and jumping off boxes — moderate height.
Binocular vision slowly developing.	Provide hand-eye, object handling experiences.
May walk well but have difficulty with other locomotor skills.	Wide variety of motor challenges needed. Stress hopping, skipping, galloping, etc.
Climbing skills need development.	Climbing over low, inclined planks, packing boxes, jungle gyms, stairs are needed experiences.
Balance skills developing.	Activities involving simple balancing important.
Fear of failure can be strong.	Allow to progress at own rate, but encourage experimentation.
Begin to develop throwing patterns.	Allow for hand-eye experiences with appropriate balls, beanbags, etc.
Like rhythmic activities.	Gross motor activities to rhythm. Simple rhythms. Marching.
Self-conscious.	Avoid sarcasm, ridicule, laughing at children. Seek emotional satisfaction.
Learning to use the hands.	Handle and guide objects such as scooters, little cars, building blocks, etc.
May have trouble with eye control.	Need low-level hand-eye experiences.
Loves to explore.	Allow for creative effort.
Toilet routines may need control.	Get children to accept this responsibility.
May be shy.	Bring out through participation and acceptance. Encourage to "show."

THE BASIS FOR THE PROGRAM 9

KINDERGARTEN AND FIRST GRADE

Characteristics	Program Needs and Implications
Noisy, constantly active, egocentric, exhibitionist. Imitative and imaginative. Wants attention.	Vigorous games and stunts. Games with individual roles — hunting, dramatic activities, story plays. Few team games or relays.
Large muscles more developed, game skills not developed.	Basic movement. Fundamental skills of throwing, catching, bouncing balls.
Naturally rhythmical.	Music and rhythm with skills. Creative rhythms, folk dances, singing games.
No sex differences in interest.	Same activities for both boys and girls.
Short attention span.	Change activity often. Short explanations.
May become suddenly tired, but soon recovers.	Use activities of brief duration. Provide short rest periods or include activities of moderate vigor.
Sensitive and individualistic. The "I" concept is very important. Accepts defeat poorly.	Needs to learn to take turns, share with others. Learn to win, lose, or be caught gracefully.
Is interested in what his body can do. Curious.	Movement experiences. Attention to basic movement.
Eye-hand coordination developing.	Needs opportunity to handle objects such as balls, beanbags, hoops, etc.
Perceptual-motor areas important.	Needs practice in balance, unilateral, bilateral, and cross-lateral movements.
Likes small group activity.	Use entire class grouping sparingly. Break into small groups.
Sensitive to feelings of adults.	Needs praise and encouragement.
Can be reckless.	Stress sane approaches.
Enjoys rough-and-tumble activity.	Include rolling, dropping to the floor, etc., in both introductory and program activities. Stress simple stunts and tumbling.
Pelvic tilt can be pronounced.	Give attention to posture problems. Provide abdominal strengthening activities.

SECOND AND THIRD GRADES

Characteristics	Program Needs and Implications
Still active but attention span longer. More interest in group play.	Active big muscle program, including more group activity. Begin team concept in activity and relays.
Like physical contact and belligerent games.	Dodgeball games and other active games. Rolling stunts.
Enjoy rhythm.	Continue creative rhythms, singing games, and folk dances.

Characteristics	Program Needs and Implications
Developing more skills and interest in skills. Want to excel.	Organized practice in a variety of throwing, catching, moving, and other skills. Basic movement work.
Improved hand-eye and perceptual-motor coordination.	Opportunity for handling hand apparatus. Movement experiences. Practice in perceptual-motor skills — right and left, unilateral, bilateral, and cross-lateral movements.
Becoming more social-conscious.	Learn to abide by rules and play fair. Learn social customs and courtesy in rhythmic areas.
Becoming more sports interested.	Introduce sports skills and simple lead-up activities.
Are curious to see what they can do. Love to be challenged.	Various challenges with movement problems. More critical demands in stunts, tumbling, and apparatus work.
Like to do things well and be admired for it.	Begin to stress quality somewhat. Provide opportunity to achieve.
Essentially honest and truthful.	Accept their word. Give opportunity for trust in game and relay situations.

THE PURPOSES OF PHYSICAL EDUCATION

While the general goal of physical education, and, for that matter, all education — well-rounded development of our children and youth as responsible citizens — is of a general nature, learning experiences should be provided to help the child attain more definable purposes or objectives. To be judged effective as an educational tool, physical education should help each child to:

1. Develop and maintain a suitable level of physical fitness.

2. Become competent in management of the body and acquire useful physical skills.

3. Acquire desirable social standards and ethical concepts.

4. Acquire needed safety skills and habits.

5. Enjoy wholesome recreation.

6. Acquire a desirable self-concept and an effective self-image.

7. Derive personal and educational benefits from the program.

An examination of basic urges and characteristics of children will show that each of the above objectives contributing to total development can be substantiated as meeting some portion of the basic growth and development needs of children.

PHYSICAL FITNESS

Purpose: *The physical education program should provide each child with the opportunity to develop and maintain a level of physical fitness commensurate with his individual needs.*

While physical education must be a means of expression through movement, it must be more than that. Physical education in our society must provide a developmental experience. Call it what you will — "physical fitness," "physical development," "organic development," — the name is not important, but the concept is. The physical education program must provide a planned, progressive environment of activity which will make sufficient physical demands on an individual during the seven growth years of the kindergarten and elementary school. In fact, this principle extends back even into the preschool years.

The child must have vigorous physical activity based on good physiological principles as a part of his regimen to assure proper development. This activity should be of sufficient intensity to make these demands on the body. Development occurs when the child has worked harder and longer than he has previously. Bones become stronger, musculature improves, and ligaments and tendons are strengthened to meet the demands of activity. The cardiorespiratory system, as well as other body systems, derives benefit from activity demands. The benefit from regular and systematic exercise in relation to the prevention of heart disease is a concept that should be established early in the child's education.

Physical fitness is a unique and important contribution which *can* be made by physical education as contrasted to other subject matter fields in the curriculum. If physical education cannot or does not provide fitness development, no other area of the curriculum will. A child who is deprived of, or who has an insufficient amount of, activity fails to reach his growth potential.

Fitness has other values. There is evidence that peer status and relationships, particularly for boys, are better for those possessing suitable levels of physical fitness. Desirable fitness levels seem to lead to better social adjustment and a more buoyant, action-minded, optimistic personality.

A more detailed analysis of physical fitness and its implementation in the school program is found in Chapter 9.

MOVEMENT EXCELLENCE — USEFUL PHYSICAL SKILLS

Purpose: *The physical education program should be so structured that each child can become competent in management of his body and acquire useful physical skills.*

More and more we are becoming a nation of skill seekers. Every elementary school boy and girl should have an opportunity to develop excellence in many kinds of movement and useful skills, so that they can enjoy activities and develop a desire to participate in them. This includes:

Competency in Management of the Body. Management of the body refers to physical control of the body in a variety of movement situations in relation to environmental demands. Basically, proper management of the body is needed to counteract the forces of gravity in normal activity. This is the maintenance of good posture. The child should understand, appreciate, and employ simple postural skills.

Other concerns in body management are control and balance of the body in different positions, rhythm of movement, coordination, and efficient movement. A child should be able to manage his body effectively on the floor (as in balance or flexibility stunts), moving across the floor, in the air (off the floor), and suspended on apparatus. Also, body management includes efficient use of force in such tasks as pushing and pulling, as well as weight-support tasks.

Perceptual-motor competency is an important body management goal. Included is the concept of laterality, which has a correlation with children having learning difficulties. The ability to control the two sides of the body separately and simultaneously must be developed. Good body management implies that the child can make unilateral, bilateral, and cross-lateral movements with ease and in good balance.

Basic Movement Skills and Patterns. These are the fundamental skills relating to body movement which are useful for the basic activities of living and playing. A child should become proficient in locomotor skills (walking, running, jumping), nonlocomotor skills (twisting, turning, forming shapes), and manipulative skills (throwing, catching, striking, kicking). Hand-eye and foot-eye coordination activities are important.

Special and Sports Skills. Included here are the more specialized skills of rhythmics, sports, stunts and tumbling, and similar activities.

The relationship of the elements of physical fitness and motor learning must be understood. The common elements of physical fitness — strength, endurance, and power, among others — are needed for optimum development of physical skills.

Movement Skills and Competency in the Total Program

Body management competency and the development of basic skills should be the emphasis at the preschool, kindergarten, and primary levels. The more precise sports and special skills have their foundations on these skills and as entities in themselves have introductory elements in the third grade. An examination of the introductory sports skills as presented in the suggested sports units for the third grade (Chapter 22) will bear this out. Sports and special skills receive progressive treatment throughout the intermediate grades.

The following chart illustrates the entire continuum of skills for the elementary school with competency in managing the body serving as the base. The range of skills covers all levels from preschool through the sixth grade. By the time the children finish the third grade, they should have progressed into introductory sports and special skills. Higher skill attainment in these areas beyond those introductory phases is reserved for the intermediate grades.

CONTINUUM OF PROGRAM DEVELOPMENT
BASED ON SKILL DEVELOPMENT AND ATTAINMENT

Higher Skill Attainment
Interschool Competition, Intramurals, Playdays, Sports Days, and Clubs

Special and Game Skills
Large Apparatus, Hand Apparatus Rhythmics (dance), Games and Sports, Stunts and Tumbling, Aquatics, Fitness Activities

Basic Skills
Locomotor: Walk, run, hop, skip, slide, leap, jump, gallop
Nonlocomotor: Bend, twist, reach, lift, raise, lower, turn.
Manipulative: Balls, beanbags, jump ropes, wands, hoops, etc.

Competency in Managing the Body
Control of the Body
On the floor, across the floor, through the air, on apparatus
Emphasizing
Balance, coordination, laterality, directionality, spatial judgments, identification of body parts, rhythmic movement, postural efficiency.

THE SOCIAL GOAL

Purpose: *The physical education environment should be such that children can acquire desirable social standards and ethical concepts.*

Physical education is concerned with the development of desirable standards of ethical behavior and social and moral conduct. Many terms, such as good citizenship and sportsmanship, can be used to describe this goal. A child needs to be able to get along with others, to take turns, to win and lose gracefully, to work for the common good, and to respect the personality of his fellows. He should learn to exercise self-control in activities which are often emotionally intense. He can be helped to act wisely with courage and resourcefulness in situations of stress.

For younger children, the teacher should think first in terms of helping them with their problems in the social world. However, there will be problems which they cannot solve and their measure of security therefore depends on their capacity to find either satisfactory solutions or accept the situation and learn to live with it. An individual needs to develop a variety of ways of adjusting to social living, otherwise he will just withdraw or indulge in fantasy. A child needs to feel that he is an active, accepted participant in his own peer group.

Since successful living demands the ability and willingness to lead skillfully and to follow intelligently, the child should be afforded opportunities to develop these capacities. One can develop the powers of judgment, observation, analysis, and decision through the medium of complex physical activities.

Physical education can aid the child in developing respect for facilities and equipment and an appreciation of the opportunity that is his through physical education. He needs to learn to be at ease in a variety of social situations and to accept the consequences of his own actions. He can learn to appreciate the concept of competition as life itself is competition.

Nowhere in the curriculum are the opportunities for give and take as high as they are in physical education. As life is governed by social rules, customs, and traditions, so are the activities on the playfield and gymnasium floor. Fair play, honesty, and conformance with the rules can be stressed through physical activities.

Basically, the teacher's task is to help children to discover the difference between acceptable and unacceptable ways of expressing feelings, and to guide behavior on this basis. This should include establishing and enforcing limits of acceptable behavior.

Proper attitudes of boy-girl relationships can be furthered through properly conducted coeducational activities. The group method, so often used in physical education, provides numerous opportunities for social and emotional growth.

In addition, peer relationships indicate that physical skills are of such importance that much social interaction centers around them, particularly in the intermediate grades. The child who does not possess the movement competencies to participate successfully in play activities which occupy and interest his classmates is likely to have a lonely time.

It must now be concluded that skill achievement is a much more important factor in personal and social adjustment than we have been led to believe. Teachers should strive to provide learning experiences for and give attention to those low-skilled and inept children who are in need of help to improve their skills. Giving them a better basis for peer relationships is important in good social and emotional health.

The school is an agent for establishing an attitude complex. The children may forget facts, but will retain values, concepts, and behavior patterns. Children need to learn how to live effectively and harmoniously in our society.

SAFETY SKILLS AND ATTITUDES

Purpose: *In physical education, each child should have the opportunity to acquire safety skills and habits and to develop a high degree of awareness regarding safety for himself and for others.*

In the child's world today, attention to safety factors is of utmost importance. The capacity for safe living is not an automatic value but must be sought. The ability to use equipment safely, to consider oneself and fellow students in the light of safety, and to handle one's body efficiently in times of stress are attributes which are important for safe living. The teacher needs to explain the techniques of an activity in the light of the consequences from unsafe procedures. While all necessary precautions should be taken to develop habits of safety, consideration also must be given to avoiding fear and overcautiousness in activity. Young children can at times become reckless, and this drive needs to be channeled into desirable learning directions. Rules are needed to eliminate unsafe procedures, and children need to understand and recognize the importance of these practices.

The teacher should be so familiar with the activities that the program can be carried out in a safe environment, and that the youngsters will learn safe procedures.

Water safety is an important facet of physical education. Although few elementary schools provide opportunity for aquatic instruction, students should be encouraged to seek swimming instruction. Communities should look for cooperation among the various agencies to see that a swimming and water safety program is a part of the educational opportunities for the child. This can be done variously and not necessarily as a part of the school physical education program. Each child of elementary school age should have the opportunity to participate in such a program, and communities should take steps to see that this is realized. Attainment of this goal should begin at the late primary level.

WHOLESOME RECREATION

Purpose: *Through physical education, each child should be stimulated to seek participation in and derive enjoyment from wholesome recreation during his leisure.*

Since children will play many hours beyond the opportunity afforded them in physical education, the program should aim at making this a fruitful experience. Part of this preparation can be met by teaching a variety of skills *well enough* so that the child has the tools for his leisure-time activities. In addition, the youngster should develop knowledge, attitudes, and appreciations which will guide him in his free play. Some of the ways physical education can contribute to the recreational ideal are:

1. Provide the child a wide variety of activities which are of use to him in his play time. This should include active games and movement experiences suitable for the home and backyard.

2. Give him experience in playing with and accepting other children in physical activities. Children should seek the company of other children of their ages and interests and not play alone.

3. Lay the basis for enjoyment of physical activity, as children who have fun and can achieve success in movement experiences tend to participate more than those to whom physical challenges have been unhappy experiences.

4. Provide opportunity for each child to develop simple motor skills, particularly in throwing, catching, and propelling balls so that children can participate successfully and competitively with their peers.

THE SELF-IMAGE AND SELF-CONCEPT

Purpose: *Each child should acquire a realistic self-image and develop a desirable self-concept through relevant physical education experiences.*

Not only is it essential to understand the learner, but it is important for the learner to understand himself. Each child brings into the world his own basic characteristics, limits of intelligence, body structure, energy drive, and sensitivity to external stimuli. He needs to make some assessment of what his abilities are and how they can be utilized to achieve what he is capable of.

This means that he must have an opportunity in physical education to expand, to extend, to develop, to create, and to mature. To express himself and seek self-enhancement are important goals for the individual. To become a fuller self and a more complete individual stimulates learning.

The concept of himself which a child develops is vital in the learning process, as it can make it possible for him to learn or it may prevent or block his ability to learn. If a child can feel he "belongs," that he is loved and respected, and that his successes outweigh his failures, then he is well on the way to establishing a desirable self-concept. Nothing succeeds with a child like success. Security gives him a basis for the development of a healthy personality.

The urge to grow must not become lost in personal problems and concerns. It must not become buried under layers of psychological defenses. The candle of learning must not be smothered under a blanket of emotional blocks.

Physical education can do much to bring out the child and give him an opportunity to express himself, be creative, and achieve success, stressing comfortable physical experiences well within the emotional, physical, and intellectual limits of the child. Children will retain substance from those experiences which hold personal significance and personal value. Each child needs to consider that in the educational process he is of value, worthy in his own right.

While certainly some competition in educational circles is essential, physical education can provide individual experiences where the child can work at his own rate without pressure of peer performances or competition. Children naturally compete against their peers, as they would like to do as well as, if not better than, their classmates. Each child should achieve success within himself and not be judged according to whether or not he can come up to the performance of his peers.

On the other hand, life itself is competition and children need to recognize this fact. Much of what is learned does take place in group situations, even if its emphasis is purportedly individual. Children do learn from each other and fundamental values are involved in group learning experiences. Achieving success in a learning situation is basically not determined on whether the approach is individual or group, but that progress is evaluated on an individual basis, with recognition, acceptance, and utilization of individual differences an important feature of the instructional process.

Physical education can not only be a medium for some measure of success for all children; it can also be particularly valuable to the child who performs at a lower level academically but can achieve his higher measure of success in physical activities. This may be the place where he blossoms.

PERSONAL AND EDUCATIONAL VALUES

Purpose: *Each child should be able to acquire personal and educational values which are within the developmental potential of a quality physical education program.*

There are many values of personal adjustment which can be gained from a sound program of physical education. It is often said that a school with a good physical education program is a happy school. The simple ability to have fun and take part freely and joyously in physical activities has high value in adjustment for the child. The relief from tension and anxiety through activity is important to his future well-being. Finding satisfaction and release in play is a goal for each child.

Developing creativeness and imaginative play should be an outgrowth of activity experiences. Development of reasoning powers can be furthered if the child is challenged with movement problems which reach a satisfactory and adequate solution. Such qualities as self-confidence, initiative, and perseverance can be given opportunity for development through problem-solving experiences.

Physical education should also tap levels of the child's conceptual thinking. Good teaching should concern itself with conceptual understandings, as these are the ingredients for thinking. Selected concepts as they relate to movement are important inclusions in the teaching process in physical education. Guidance should be given to the child in his concept growth and in the personalized interpretations which he has made along the way. The child should show not only versatility in movement, but also that he has established basic understandings of his movement.

A sound program will emphasize movement factors known to have relevance to perceptual-motor competency. Children should have opportunities for a broad range of movement in which activities stressing balance, coordination, identification of body parts, spatial judgments, and laterality are stressed. While valid evidence is lacking, there is indication that activities of the nature described can help some children achieve a level of movement competence which will contribute to their achievement in the classroom.

PHYSICAL EDUCATION AS A TOOL IN THE EDUCATION OF THE DISADVANTAGED

In addition to the aforementioned basic purposes, physical education can function as a tool of education and social relevance in the education of disadvantaged children. First of all, a physical education program can give the disadvantaged child a chance to achieve and a chance to compete with his peers. This may be the area in which he can first attain a measure of success and gain the respect of his peers. To gain in self-concept and in self-image is an important goal for the disadvantaged child. He needs to be brought out of the devastating feeling of uselessness.

A second line of attack can be made through the social relationships manifest in a physical education program. This is a two-way street. The disadvantaged child can be given opportunities to act in his own interests while avoiding intrusion on the rights of others. The peer group, on the other hand, can through properly structured approaches accept the child on his own personal worth as an individual and minimize racial, class, or ethnic bias.

A corollary to this is an opportunity for each child to share in democratic decisions in group associations and be a participant in leader-follower situations.

Physical education in no sense is to be regarded as a panacea for the ills of society, nor is it assumed that any of the above approaches can be easily and effectively implemented. Because of the uniqueness of the physical approach, teachers who are sensitive and perceptive can capitalize on the inherent potential of physical education for the betterment of human relations and recognition of the dignity of the individual.

HOW CAN THESE PURPOSES BE ATTAINED?

Basically, to attain these purposes and objectives, physical education must be a planned developmental program which takes into consideration the needs and interests of each child in the school. The following attributes characterize such a program:

1. There must be movement. There must be something happening. Movement is the basis of physical education, and one way to judge the quality of a physical education program is to evaluate the degree of movement which each child experiences. Children learn by doing and skills are taught by repetition. If there is practice, for example, in bouncing a ball, a child profits in direct relationship to how many times he is able to handle and bounce the ball. What the child does to the ball is important, but what the ball does to the child is more important.

Physical education implies activity. The child profits little from an experience which is characterized by too much standing around waiting for equipment to be arranged, lengthy explanations by the teacher, and domination of activity by one or two children.

2. The selection of the activities must be based upon the needs and interest of the youngsters and geared to their level. This means preplanning and not just a "what-shall-we-do-today" type of program. If desirable learnings are to result, the activities must be suited to the developmental level of the child.

3. The activities need to be directed and conducted in such a manner that the purposes of physical education will be attained. The values of physical education are not gained automatically or accidentally. Physical activities need to be skillfully taught by understanding teachers who like children and have faith in their own ability to help children develop through this medium. This implies the application of educationally sound methods of teaching and the evaluation of the teaching process in terms of progress to the goals. Values in activity are not inherent in the activity but rather in the method of presentation. If a child is to achieve his potential in skilled movement, he must have quality teaching.

Mere participation does not mean that the child will attain the developmental level he should. The activities must be planned and directed by qualified leadership. This cannot be stressed too strongly. If quality of movement is to result, the learning process must be directed toward this end.

3

The Physical Education Program

Guidelines for Program Planning
Planning in Terms of Broad Program Areas
The Allocation of Specific Activities to Grade Level
Physical Education Programs for Each Grade Level
Special Programs
Planning the Year's Program
Proportional Weekly Scheduling for Grades K-2
The Weekly Unit Schedule

Basically, a school- or district-wide approach in planning the program of physical education is needed. A practical curriculum guide which will give good direction but at the same time permit some flexibility should be developed. The following guidelines are important in establishing an educationally sound physical education program.

GUIDELINES FOR PROGRAM PLANNING

1. The basic goal of planning is the formulation of a program which will serve as the basis of a school curriculum guide. The program should be outlined in sufficient detail to provide necessary direction.

2. The program should be based on the needs, characteristics, abilities, and basic urges of children. It should allow the child to be a child and not rob him of his childhood.

3. A balanced and varied program covering many experiences should be presented. It should be balanced with proportional emphasis on basic movement, rhythmics, physical developmental activities, stunts and tumbling, games, and relays. It should be varied in that children meet with a variety of experiences, approaches, and activities. Childhood is a time for experimenting, sampling, and choosing. A broad range of activity opportunity makes this possible.

4. Program content should be based on the concept of value for *all* children — the highly skilled, the moderately skilled, and the low achiever. In addition, appropriate consideration for exceptional children and other special needs must be included in the program planning.

5. The selection of program activities should relate to the basic purposes of physical education, i.e. it should cover (1) vigorous physical activity which will promote growth and development and the attainment of an appropriate level of physical fitness; (2) the development of a broad range of movement competency and motor skills; (3) a variety of activities useful in leisure play; and (4) safety attitudes and practices as associated with the selected activities.

6. The program content should be constructed so that it can serve as a vehicle for the achievement of desirable behavioral changes, associated educational values, and personal benefits. It is true that many of the desirable changes in children and the values they receive from participation are determined more by instructional procedures than by the program *per se.* However, the selection of activities should be such that the aforementioned changes and values *can* be achieved with appropriate methodology. For example, a program relying chiefly on exercises, games, sports, and relays will do little for the individual child in terms of self-direction, creativity, self-reliance, and individual level of progress.

7. Program content should rest on a foundation of efficient body management and basic movement skills, geared to the developmental needs of the child. This implies an instructionally oriented program, leading toward a goal of reasonable skill and concept acquisition. The program should set aside sufficient time for skill instruction and practice. Practice should be systematically organized and based on good concepts of motor learning. The emphasis on instruction should be intense enough to lead to reasonable mastery of skills.

8. Progression is an essential element in program planning. The program must reflect progression from grade to grade, within each grade, and within activities. It is a major purpose of this guide to provide orderly learning sequences upon which instructional procedures can be based.

9. The learning experiences at any one grade level should be planned on a year's program outline, with consideration for seasonal activities. Such planning gives unity to the experiences and allows the teacher to center attention with proportional emphasis on the more important aspects of the program.

10. An extended physical activity interest program, the basis of which is provided by physical education, should be established within the school. Play days and special interest clubs are possibilities. In addition, cooperative municipal recreation departments may provide extended opportunity with scheduled recreation programs after school, on Saturdays, or during holiday periods.

11. The physical education program must have appropriate administrative support if it is to achieve its educational goals for children. The administration has an obligation to provide:

a. Competent instruction.
b. Adequate indoor and outdoor facilities to permit adequate time allotment and scheduling of classes.
c. Adequate budget for the purchase of supplies and equipment.
d. Appropriate storage space for supplies and equipment.
e. Dressing rooms and showering facilities.

The latter point merits some explanation. Dressing rooms are needed for changing clothing. Showers give added flexibility to the facilities and permit them to be used for evening and Saturday activities. Generally, showering is not an accepted practice for preschool, kindergarten, and primary school children, although a few schools begin this practice with third graders.

The degree of administrative support will have a profound effect on the program. Proper support will set high standards for the offerings and provide the means by which the learning activities may be accomplished.

Climatic and Geographical Factors

It is recognized that the weather is an important factor in planning. Whereas physical education should be an outdoor experience when possible, the vagaries of the weather in some sections of the country have a profound effect on the planning of an adequate program. Where the weather is consistent, few alternate programs are needed. Where the weather is uncertain, teachers must modify their overall plans from day to day.

The length of the seasons determines the emphasis within the program. In temperate climates, children can play outdoors well into December and are able to be on the playground again in late February. This means an indoor program of only eight to ten school weeks as contrasted with the possibility of perhaps double this figure in other localities.

Considerations by the administration for adequate facilities would involve such items as covered outside areas (shed types) and hard-surfaced areas which dry quickly. Where the climate permits, thought should be given to the installation of basketball goals and volleyball standards in areas large enough to sustain a wide number of children.

For those who lack facilities, inclement weather means that the teacher must provide physical experiences in the classroom setting, with its attendant problems.

The practice of teaching health instead of physical education during inclement weather when the children cannot go outside leaves a bad taste for health instruction. The motivation to better health is doubtful when taught under these circumstances.

PLANNING IN TERMS OF BROAD PROGRAM AREAS

A varied physical education program can help provide the interest and motivation to encourage lifelong habits of vigorous exercise. The time allocated to the various broad categories of activities appropriate to the interests and needs of the children at each level should be carefully balanced, and one way to accomplish this is on a percentage basis. This is the first step. This method will provide an answer to the questions of parents and administrators relative to the activity emphasis of the program.

However, it is difficult to delineate preschool programs with labels and percentage allotments. For this reason the program for that age level is discussed separately, followed by a percentage chart for K-3 grades.

Preschool Program

The program for children of nursery school age should consist primarily of movement experiences, simple challenges on floor apparatus, and rhythmic experiences. The schedule should be free and flexible, allowing for good variety of and emphasis on gross motor experiences.

PHYSICAL EDUCATION PROGRAMS
Grade Level Emphasis and Suggested Yearly Percentages

Primary Grades	K	1	2	3
Movement Experiences and Body Mechanics	40	35	35	20
Fitness Routines, Activities				10
Rhythmic Activities	30	25	25	20
Apparatus, Stunts, Tumbling	15	20	20	20
Simple Game Activities and Relays	15	20	20	20
Introductory Sports Skills and Activities				10
Swimming and Water Safety				(a)

(a) Swimming and Water Safety is a recommended area of instruction for elementary school children. The amount allocated to this area would depend upon the facilities and instruction available. If swimming is included in the school program, it should proportionately reduce the percentage of time allotted to other activities.

THE ALLOCATION OF SPECIFIC ACTIVITIES TO GRADE LEVEL

After the broad categories have been determined, the activities within each should be designated. Grade level placement of the specific activities within the broad categories is somewhat regulated by arbitrary selection. Adjustment upward or downward with respect to grade level should be made on an empirical basis, after a period of class trial.

Another factor enters the picture. A skilled specialist usually has more success in achieving higher skills at a lower grade level than does a classroom teacher with a more limited background. However, as a starting point for program planning, the following chart is presented. What it says is simply that a certain activity should be part of a particular grade level program. The elements to be included, the approaches to be followed, and the instructional procedures to be utilized are discussed in later sections of this guide.

SUGGESTED ALLOCATION OF SPECIFIC ACTIVITIES ACCORDING TO GRADE LEVEL

Activity

Movement Experiences and Body Mechanics	P	K	1	2	3
Basic Movement — Locomotor, Nonlocomotor	P	K	1	2	3
Stretch Ropes					3
Basic Movement — Manipulative	P	K	1	2	3
Beanbags	P	K	1	2	3
Yarn or Fleece Balls	P	K	1	2	3
Playground Balls (8½")	P	K	1	2	3
Small Balls (sponge, softball size)					3
Paddles and Balls					3
Hoops		K	1	2	3
Jump Ropes	P	K	1	2	3
Parachutes		K	1	2	3
Wand Activities					3
Rhythmics (see chart page 236)	P	K	1	2	3
Rope Jumping to Music				2	3
Apparatus	P	K	1	2	3
Bounding Boards	P	K	1	2	
Balance Boards		K	1	2	3
Balance Beams	P	K	1	2	3
Benches				2	3
Climbing Ropes		K	1	2	3
Climbing Frames		K	1	2	3
Floor Apparatus	P	K	1	2	3
Individual Mats	P	K	1	2	3
Jumping Boxes	P	K	1	2	3
Ladders and Bars			1	2	3
Stunts and Tumbling		K	1	2	3
Simple Games		K	1	2	3
Relays				2	3
Story Games, Poems, Quiet Play	P	K	1	2	
Sports Skills and Activities (Introductory)					3
Basketball					3
Soccer					3
Softball (mostly skills)					3

On examining the chart it will be noted that no breakdown (except for rope jumping) has been presented for the rhythmic activities. Rope jumping has been shown here because this activity (without music) is listed under the manipulative area and its inclusion under rhythmics serves to clarify its place in the recommended allocations. Apart from this, an explanation of all aspects of the rhythmic program would demand too much space at this point and be out of context. The program breakdown for rhythmic activities is included in Chapter 18 and for that reason does not appear here.

PHYSICAL EDUCATION PROGRAMS FOR EACH GRADE LEVEL

The material which follows will present descriptions of the type of program recommended for each grade level. Correlation should be evident between the recommended programs and (1) the needs of children, (2) program guidelines, (3) broad category percentages, and (4) grade placement of specific activities.

The Preschool-Nursery School Movement Program

Several guidelines are of particular relevance to the program for young children.

1. Programs should be staged in an environment which includes sufficient space, allows for freedom of movement, and possesses the amount and types of equipment and supplies needed for movement.

2. The program should allow for exploring, experimenting, and practicing all types of movement skills in a variety of movement situations.

3. Rhythmic movement is important, but the program must not be restricted to this.

4. Perceptual-motor elements should be included in the regular program of activities. Special help and remedial type programs should be in addition to the general movement experiences for all children.

5. The emphasis should be on the whole child and his responses, rather than on segmented attention to various skill movements.

6. The movement experiences, while showing some concern for the academic, cognitive aspects of learning, should focus heavily on nonverbal learnings. The program should provide an unstructured, noncognitive approach in the main with emphasis on creative, sensory, and motor responses.

The program should be flexible and free. Activities should be of three general classifications:

1. **Gross Movement Experiences.** A wide variety of movement experiences should be experiences either free or to rhythm wherein the child learns to manage his body efficiently and to acquire basic skills. Consideration for readiness is most important. The capability of each child must be challenged but not overtaxed.

2. **Manipulative Skills.** The child should be given opportunity to handle various play objects suitable for his age, such as balls, beanbags, and articles of this nature. He should also have put-together toys, block or construction sets, rhythm sets, "ride-em" toys, and toss games.

3. **Floor Apparatus.** Climbing, balancing, sliding down or jumping down, going through openings, and bouncing are the kinds of experiences toward which apparatus play is pointed. Any kinds of combinations of boxes, planks, boards, ladders, and things of this nature can be utilized for valuable experiences. Children should go over, under, through, and around various pieces of apparatus. Gym sets combining climber-slide units are recommended. Old tires, both bicycle and automobile, enhance the opportunities for movement. Things to tunnel through hold the children's interest. Mats to receive the weight from jumping and to be used for simple stunts are needed.

The activities classed as perceptual-motor should be utilized where appropriate. Establishing right-left discrimination and laterality are important goals.

The Kindergarten Program

There is a strong awareness of the characteristics of the learner at this level, resulting in more attention being focused on the learning process and the child. Play type activities are highly important in the kindergarten program, as young children are naturally active and learn best when they enjoy what they are doing. For some, kindergarten is a medium of adjustment, an attempt to ease the difficult transition from the security of the home to the uncertainty of the educational world. A child comes from a home where he is the center of attention to the classroom, where he is just one of a group of children his own age.

The large majority of suggested activities for kindergarten children are individual in nature, centering on movement experiences (40%) and rhythmics (30%). Some emphasis is given to simple stunts (15%) and to simple games (15%). While there is accent on cooperation with others, there is little emphasis on group or team play. The types of activities are such that the child has good opportunity to explore, try out, and create. He learns to express himself through movement and continues to develop the skills of verbal communication — speaking and listening.

In movement, he begins to lay the foundation of body management and basic skills, with attention to laterality, directionality, balance, and coordination. He seeks to further eye-hand coordination with simple manipulative activities. His fitness needs are taken care of within his movement experiences. Perceptual-motor competency theory has strong application to methodology on the kindergarten level.

The First Grade Program

The first grade program embraces the same four general areas as the kindergarten program, with some shift of emphasis to the apparatus, stunts, and tumbling areas. The largest portion of the first grade program is devoted to movement experiences (35%), which includes attention to physical development through selected movement. As in kindergarten, there is emphasis on basic skills and efficient management of the body, stimulated through challenges to elicit a wide variety of movement. Locomotor skills are of prime importance, with some application to non-locomotor movements. Manipulative skills are stressed, with a foundation being laid for the important play skills of throwing and catching. Beanbags, yarn balls, and playground balls (8½"), are important tools for experimentation. Hoops and jump ropes also are included.

Good body mechanics and posture are important, with attention to specific movements leading to the development of the arm-shoulder girdle and the abdominal region. Emphasis should be on both the how and why of activity. Perceptual-motor factors are an important consideration in conducting activities for the first grade child.

The rhythmic program (25%) should provide an extension of movement to rhythm, reinforcing and relating to basic movement experiences. The creative aspects of rhythmic activities have a prominent place in the first grade. In more structured numbers, singing games are stressed more than folk dance, although both are included.

The apparatus, tumbling, and stunts program is of material import (20%). Each school should possess apparatus in sufficient numbers to have a rounded program in this area, including climbing ropes, climbing frames, fixed or moveable ladders, balance beams, bounding boards, benches, and individual mats. Floor and mat stunts give the children an opportunity to react to directions and achieve a specific movement pattern. Methodology in apparatus, stunts, and tumbling should be based on basic movement principles, seeking a wide and flexible response to the tasks.

The games program (20%) has its proportional place in the program, but has yielded its traditional importance to movement experiences. In addition to the usual gymnasium-playground games for this level, story games, poems, and dramatic play have a place.

The Second Grade Program

In essence, the second grade program follows the pattern of the first grade, with the exception of the introduction of simple relays based primarily on locomotor skills. Children are still encouraged to move in their own way, to experiment, and to explore, but specific patterns of coordination begin to appear. Continued practice in the basic locomotor, non-locomotor, and manipulative skills (35%) is provided. Children should also be made aware of and encouraged to develop good posture. A few simple forms of systematic exercise may be introduced, but not to the extent of the more formal fitness routines.

The rhythmic area (25%) moves toward more emphasis on folk dances, but singing games, creative rhythms, and basic rhythms receive good coverage. Ball bouncing and dribbling skills to rhythm are well accepted on this level, as the children begin to improve their manipulative competency.

Apparatus, stunts, and tumbling (20%) as an area receives continued attention. Youngsters begin to take pride in achievement and lay the basis for future activities.

Play is increasingly structured into some forms of group games (20%). The basic locomotor and ball handling skills are combined with lines, circles, and other patterns to provide group experiences and an introduction to team play. This concept is furthered by the introduction of simple relays. The seeds of sports interest, which comes into its own in the third and fourth grades, are found in the late second grade program.

The Third Grade Program

Movement experiences (20%) still have an important function on this grade level. However, the emphasis on body management is secondary to improvement of basic skills, particularly of the manipulative type. It is here the child begins to find himself in skills. The third grade program provides a transition between the simplified activity program of the lower grades and the sports interests and more advanced emphasis of the intermediate level.

The third grade level is suggested for the introduction of the more precise fitness routines (10%), such as exercise programs, circuit training, and the like. It is here the child begins to absorb the concept of needed work if he is to realize good dividends from his fitness potential.

In the rhythmics (20%), a transition from the casually organized dances of the previous grades to the concept of dancing with a partner is now stressed, as the children have opportunity to coordinate their own movements more precisely with those of a partner. The application of rhythm to ball skills and rope jumping is an important outlet for creativity, in addition to the retention of some emphasis on basic locomotor skills done to rhythm.

The stunt area (20%) becomes more complicated and more precise with increased demands on balance, strength, and coordination. There is a shift toward more inclusion of what are regarded as the standard tumbling stunts. Apparatus work should stress a wide variety of movements, built upon the foundation of the previous grades.

Simple games and relays (20%) become increasingly important to challenge the child with his newly acquired skills.

A major difference in activity for the third grade is the introduction of simple sports skills and activities (10%). Balls are rolled, bounced, kicked, batted, dribbled, thrown, and caught using reasonable technique. Attention is directed to specific sports skills in softball, basketball, and soccer. Selected lead-up games provide a useful laboratory for the evaluation of the achievement of these simple skills.

If swimming and water safety are to be included in the school program, the third grade is a likely level for this introduction. Ten percent of the allotted yearly time should probably be apportioned to this activity, with the time spent in the other activities reduced proportionately.

Special Programs

Several programs merit special discussion to bring out their relationships to the overall curriculum in physical education. Considered here will be the program of swimming and water safety, the adapted program, and the program for the physically underdeveloped child.

Swimming and Water Safety

Swimming and water safety form a most important area of instruction, one which should be made available to each child. A community-wide approach is needed, in which the school may or may not have a part. The crux of the matter is that someone must get the job done. If the responsibility falls to the schools, then a number of decisions need to be made.

The first is to seek facilities. Cooperation can generally be secured from the municipal recreation department or the YMCA for the use of a pool. In some cases the program can utilize recreation facilities during the month of May, before the heavy use of summer. Weather is of course a factor. The pool should have a means of raising the water temperature to comfortable levels.

Portable pools are another possible solution. Commercially built pools which can be

24 THE PHYSICAL EDUCATION PROGRAM

Portable Swimming Pool. Courtesy Port-A-Pool (Universal Bleacher Co.) and Los Angeles City Schools.

set up by a crew in one day are now available. Pool size varies, but a great deal can be accomplished so far as water skills are concerned in a pool 24′ by 24′ with a depth of 3′. The pool can be placed in one location for four to six weeks and then moved to another school. Some states are recognizing the utility of the pool by authorizing in new construction the installation of both water valves and a drainhole connected with the sewage system.

Certified instruction is needed, and the instructional procedures of the Red Cross can be followed. It is suggested that the school swimming instructional program begin in the third grade, with a second program scheduled in either the fifth or sixth grade. Much attention should be directed toward helping the nonswimmer.

The Adapted Program

In many classrooms there will be children who cannot participate fully in the regular program in physical education. Frail children, those often absent due to illness, and others with identified handicaps need special consideration. The restriction may be permanent or it can be on a temporary basis as for children who have not fully recovered from injury or recent illness. It needs to be emphasized that a physician should be the determining factor in the recommendation for limited activity. Parents sometimes tend to be overly protective and set restrictions which are not in the best interests of the child.

A basic principle for children with restrictions is that they participate in the regular program within the limits of the restrictions. They need to be included in the group so that the concept that they are "different" is minimized. They need to be urged to become more self-directive with limitations rather than constantly having prescribed activity. In much of the activity program, the disabled or less able can profit by being in the regular program. Goals for them need to be adjusted and are not the same goals as for the rest of the children.

In the physical fitness elements, the physically handicapped child should develop an optimum degree of physical fitness for his condition. This means a selection of individual activities which the child can do on his own or with the aid of another student. It is important that the child learn to live with and within his physical condition. There is a great need to have the handicapped child gain status. If some accomplishment or knowledge can be achieved, this will be an important factor in creating a better self-image.

The teacher should give personal attention to the problems of the handicapped child. The practice of "excusing" him or shunting him to one side is no longer tenable. In some instances, where he cannot enter the regular program of activities modified for himself, he can be utilized as a monitor, official, or scorekeeper. However, this should not be overworked, as the other children may not react favorably to these appointments. He should have his turn and perhaps some special consideration.

If the school has a developmental program for the low-fit child, the handicapped person can take part in this. Homework and special tasks within his capacity are meaningful to him.

The key to the approach is integration into regular program activities and consideration for those who are beyond him. If the child is able to participate in the school as a learning environment, then he can take part in the majority of the activities, which may need to be modified for him.

The attitude of the other children toward those with handicaps is important. Children should invite and urge the handicapped child to participate within the limits of his handicap. They can take turns working with him in special activities. Tolerance and understanding are excellent social values which can be an outgrowth of such a program.

Teachers need to remember that physical education has values for everyone, not just the skilled or the so-called normal child. The wants and desires of the restricted child are the same as those of the normal child. His needs are realized in different ways.

The Special Program for the Physically Underdeveloped Child

Observation and test scores will reveal that a number of children have fitness levels indicating a need for special attention, which is not possible in the regular class setting. A special program for the physically underdeveloped child (sometimes called the "low-fit" child) should be administered if these children can be identified. Encouragement and special attention will do much to help children with physical problems.

PLANNING THE YEAR'S PROGRAM

Planning for the year's program for children from preschool level through the third grade demands consideration of a number of approaches. The first is the flexible approach needed in preschool experiences. Secondly, a proportional weekly schedule is presented for kindergarten, first, and possibly the second grade. Thirdly, a weekly schedule is presented for use for second and third grade programs. No matter what the schedule plan, there should be an overall list of activities to provide direction for the learning experiences.

PLANNING FOR THE PRESCHOOL PROGRAM

Since most of the learning experiences for preschool children are motor in nature, the play period provides an extension of the overall program pointed more to physical and motor goals. The program must be kept simple, flexible, and challenging, with the emphasis on body management competencies, selected basic skills, and hand-eye manipulative experiences. Relevant cognitive goals can be included in the movement experiences.

The teacher should draw up a list of appropriate and recommended learning experiences and then use a check list system for recording those stunts in which the children have participated. Each activity should be carried on long enough to have educational value, with changes or variations being introduced to provide the children with a wide range of movement experiences, including those which are for them new and exciting. The exploratory approach should dominate when activities are first introduced, with later emphasis given to broadening the experiences and giving attention to developing quality in movement.

PROPORTIONAL WEEKLY SCHEDULING FOR GRADES K-2

A plan that is more structured than the one for preschool children can be employed for grades K-2. Activities are still general in nature and the program is not complicated by the need to schedule special fitness developmental activities. In this plan, the overall percentages for the broad categories are maintained in a weekly schedule. Each week then conforms in percentages to the overall pattern. As an illustration, let us take the first grade program and base the calculations on a minimum of 150 minutes per week.

FIRST GRADE PROGRAM

Activity Category	Percentage (Yearly)	Total Minutes (Weekly)
Movement Experiences	35	52.5
Rhythmic Activities	25	37.5
Apparatus, Stunts, and Tumbling	20	30
Simple Games	20	30
Totals	100%	150 Minutes

ILLUSTRATIVE PROPORTIONAL FIRST GRADE WEEKLY PROGRAM

Day	Monday	Tuesday	Wednesday	Thursday	Friday
Activity	Movement 18 Min.	Rhythms 18 Min.	Movement 18 Min.	Rhythms 18 Min.	Movement 18 Min.
	Games 12 Min.	App.-Tumb. 12 Min.	Games 12 Min.	App.-Tumb. 12 Min.	Choice Games and/or App-Tumb. 12 Min.

This does not come out to the *precise* percentages listed above, but the percentages are at best an approximation. Adherence to this weekly schedule does assure a broad, balanced inclusion of activity content.

Within activity categories, allowance can be made for the short attention span. The teacher can vary the time schedule on any one day, dependent upon the response of the children to the instructional sequences.

To assure overall coverage, each of the activity categories should have a master list of suggested learning experiences, preferably in order of progression. This is not meant to be a rigid format, but one which can give direction to the list of experiences. Some teachers find it helpful to have a list of basic activities which are to be covered with another list of electives which can be utilized once the basic experiences have been covered.

A weekly format can be run off on a ditto or mimeograph, making it easy for the teacher to fill in with appropriate experiences under the various categories. As the experiences are taught in the program, they can be checked off from the master list.

THE WEEKLY UNIT SCHEDULE

For the third grade and possibly the second, a different kind of a schedule can be considered. This is the weekly schedule, wherein the same kinds of experiences are carried out during the entire week. Since the children are a little older, they can absorb the more concentrated and sequential instructional approach.

The advantages of the weekly plan are several. First, the teacher needs only one lesson plan for the week. The lesson plan should include sufficient material for the week. The teacher's objective in the lesson is to move the children along the path of learning at a comfortable rate. In a sense, what we don't quite cover today can wait until tomorrow.

A second point is that little orientation is needed after the first day. Safety factors, instructional techniques, stress points, and concepts need only brief review in the day-to-day plan during a week. Equipment needs are quite similar from day to day.

The third advantage is that progression and learning sequences are quite evident, as both the teacher and the children can see progress. The teacher can begin a unit with the basics of an activity and progress along to a point where instruction and skill practice are again indicated. This procedure provides needed review and adapts the activity to the group. The sequence of activity for each day is built upon that of the prior lesson. If the teacher has difficulty or needs to investigate an approach, he has time between lessons to clear up questionable points. Children may also be referred to resource material to study the activities for the next day or to clarify a point of difficulty from the past lesson.

The objection some have to a weekly unit program is that it does not have enough variety, and children tend to become tired of the same activities over a protracted period of time. Activities should be spaced so not more than two or three weeks at the most of the same type of activity are practiced in successive weeks. The games and relay area can provide a change of pace when this seems to be indicated.

Some other combinations in weekly planning are in vogue. One is to have one type of activity on Monday, Wednesday, and Friday of a week, and another type on Tuesday and Thursday. Another is to reserve the games and relays for Friday of each week, utilizing the first four days for more sequential material. Both of these arrangements will show good elements of progression.

The least desirable plan is to have a different program each day of the week, burdening the teacher with five different lesson plans each week. Also, this plan does not favor good elements of progression or allow ample time for practice.

Developing the Weekly Unit Plan

To develop a weekly unit plan based on percentage allocations from the chart on Physical Education Programs (page 19), the third grade program has been selected and a step by step procedure is outlined.

Step 1

The starting point for the year's program is the suggested percentage allocations for grade three.

Movement Experiences and Body Mechanics	20%
Fitness Routines, Activities	10%
Rhythmic Activities	20%
Apparatus, Stunts, and Tumbling	20%
Simple Game Activities and Relays	20%
Introductory Sports Skills and Activities	10%
Total	100%

Step 2

The second step is to calculate the number of minutes which would be devoted to fitness activities as these activities need to be scheduled over the entire year and not by weeks. For the entire year, the overall total of time for physical education is 5,400 minutes calculated on a base of 36 weeks, with a daily program of 30 minutes. Fitness activities comprise 10 percent of this total, or 540 minutes.

A day's lesson of 30 minutes can include a 5-minute period of physical fitness activities on selected days. By dividing the total time of 540 minutes by 5, one arrives at the total of 108 days during which the fitness activities can be scheduled. By scheduling fitness activities on three days per week over the entire year of 36 weeks, the fitness allocation of 10 percent time is met.

The following schedule is suggested for the kinds of activities which will be included in the overall area of fitness, given three times per week.

Weeks 1-4, 13-16, 25-28	Exercises
Weeks 5-8, 17-20, 29-32	Circuit Training
Weeks 9-12, 21-24, 33-36	Astronaut Drills

The activities are explained in Chapter 9.

Step 3

Let us assume now that, in any one week, fitness activities will be scheduled on Monday, Wednesday, and Friday, regardless of the other activity schedule. Looking back at the chart under Step 1, by inspection one can divide up the 36 weeks in the following fashion to meet the relative allocations.

Movement Experiences and
   Body Mechanics .... 8 weeks
Rhythmic Activities .... 8 weeks
Apparatus, Tumbling, and Stunts ... 8 weeks
Simple Games and Relays .... 8 weeks
Introductory Sports Skills and
   Activities .... 4 weeks

Step 4

The next step is to determine the specific activities for each week, similarly to what was done with fitness. Each area of activities will be treated in turn.

Movement Experiences

It is an excellent scheduling practice to combine a game or games with movement experiences. This could be a focal game or relay growing out of the related movement patterns. Arbitrarily, let's add two weeks of games to the eight weeks of movement experiences to total ten weeks of combined movement experiences and games. This means that approximately three-quarters of any one lesson would be devoted to instructional procedures in selected movement experiences and the remainder allocated to a game or relay.

The following breakdown is suggested for the kinds of activities to be included under movement experiences, keeping in mind that time for a game will be reserved daily.

Basic Skills — Locomotor and
   Nonlocomotor; Stretch Ropes ... 2 weeks
Hoops .... 1 week
Playground Balls .... 2 weeks
Paddles and Balls .... 1 week
Parachutes and Jump Ropes ...... 2 weeks
Wands .... 1 week
Small Balls .... 1 week
   Total ....10 weeks

Rhythmic Activities

The same approach as with movement experiences is appropriate with the area of rhythmic activities. One week's allocation of games will be attached to the rhythmic program so that games can finish up a number of the rhythmic lessons, advancing the rhythmic allocation from its original 8 weeks stipend to 9 weeks. This in the weekly program will not be broken down beyond the general designation of rhythmics.

Apparatus, Stunts, and Tumbling

Games are also to be combined into the apparatus, stunts, and tumbling program. A two-week's allocation of games is to be added to the original eight weeks' total in the area, making a total of ten weeks for the combined apparatus, stunts, and tumbling-games area. These are broken down into the following activity emphasis:

Stunts and Tumbling .... 4 weeks
Balance Beams .... 2 weeks
Benches .... 2 weeks
Climbing Ropes, Ladders,
   Climbing Frames .... 2 weeks
   Total — Apparatus, stunts,
     Tumbling-Games ....10 weeks

Introductory Sports Skills and Activities

In the four weeks that are allotted to sports skills and activities, these are to be allocated as follows:

Soccer .... 1 week
Basketball .... 2 weeks
Softball .... 1 week
   Total — Sports Skills
     and Activities .... 4 weeks

Games and Relays

Of the original eight-week allocation to games and relays, the equivalent of five weeks' time has already been assigned as follows: to movement experiences — two weeks; to rhythmic activities — one week; and to apparatus, stunts and tumbling — two weeks. This leaves three full weeks of games and relays unassigned and available for weekly units. It generally is good practice to open up the year's work with a week of games, out of which some organizational time must come. Some teachers like to have the last week reserved for games, stressing a low-key and fun finish of the year's program.

Step 5

Adjusted Schedule

After combining games and relays, allocations with three areas, the adjusted schedule has this appearance:

Movement Experiences and Games   10 weeks
Rhythmic Activities and Games ....   9 weeks
Apparatus, Stunts, Tumbling,
   and Games .... 10 weeks
Games and Relays ....   3 weeks
Introductory Sports Skills
   and Activities ....   4 weeks
      Total .... 36 weeks

Step 6

The Weekly Unit Schedule by Weeks

The assignment of activity preference to the particular weeks of the year is governed by seasonal choices and the need for block time. Activities like basketball which cover more than one week probably should be scheduled on consecutive weeks. This is also true of stunts and tumbling, although the four-week allocation could be scheduled with two two-week blocks. Rhythmic activities also could follow similar scheduling. An activity should be carried on long enough on consecutive days so that there is progressive learning, but not to the point of tiring the children of the activity. Other activities such as apparatus and manipulative activities could have a week during one part of the year and the second week at another time period. The schedule which follows reflects the above schedule preferences.

SUGGESTED YEAR'S PHYSICAL EDUCATION PROGRAM BY WEEKS
Third Grade Level

Week 1
Orientation (1 day)
Exercises
Games and Relays

Week 2
Exercises
Playground Balls
Game

Week 3
Exercises
Soccer

Week 4
Exercises
Balance Beams
Game

Week 5
Circuit Training
Parachutes
Jump Ropes

Week 6
Circuit Training
Rhythmics
Game

Week 7
Circuit Training
Benches
Game

Week 8
Circuit Training
Wands
Game

Week 9
Astronaut Drills
Games and Relays

Week 10
Astronaut Drills
Basic Movement
Stretch Ropes
Game

Week 11
Astronaut Drills
Rhythmics
Game

Week 12
Astronaut Drills
Rhythmics
Game

Week 13
Exercises
Basketball

Week 14
Exercises
Basketball

Week 15
Exercises
Rhythmics
Game

Week 16
Exercises
Rhythmics
Game

Week 17
Circuit Training
Balance Beams
Game

Week 18
Circuit Training
Stunts and Tumbling
Game

Week 19
Circuit Training
Stunts and Tumbling
Game

Week 20
Circuit Training
Climbing Ropes —
Frames
Game

Week 21
Astronaut Drills
Rhythmics
Rope Jumping to
Music

Week 22
Astronaut Drills
Rhythmics
Rope Jumping to
Music

Week 23
Astronaut Drills
Stunts and Tumbling
Game

Week 24
Astronaut Drills
Stunts and Tumbling
Game

Week 25
Exercises
Benches
Game

Week 26
Exercises
Climbing Ropes
Game

Week 27
Exercises
Rhythmics
Game

Week 28
Exercises
Rhythmics
Game

Week 29
Circuit Training
Basic Movement
Stretch Ropes
Game

Week 30
Circuit Training
Paddles and Balls

Week 31
Circuit Training
Parachutes
Parachute Game

Week 32
Circuit Training
Playground Balls
Game

Week 33
Astronaut Drills
Hoops
Game

Week 34
Astronaut Drills
Small Balls
Game

Week 35
Astronaut Drills
Softball Skills

Week 36
Astronaut Drills
Games and Relays

4

Facilities, Equipment and Supplies

Facilities
Equipment and Supplies
Outdoor Equipment
Indoor Equipment
Supplies
Care and Repair
Storage and Marking

It is essential that sufficient facilities and adequate equipment and supplies be present so that an effective program can be operated. Standards should be established and adhered to. In setting up a building program, it is important to decide first the type of program desired and then plan the play facilities to meet the needs. In building, be sure to build the gymnasium large enough for maximum enrollment, as physical education facilities are difficult to enlarge. Planning may also need to consider community use during non-school hours.

FACILITIES

Facility planning must consider climate and geographical conditions with respect to both indoor and outdoor play space. In geographic areas where weather conditions require adequate indoor facilities a minimum of one indoor teaching station for each ten classrooms is needed. Beyond ten and up to twenty classrooms, a second teaching station is needed.

All children should change to play clothing, including gym shoes. Provision must be made for the storage of play clothing. Such storage space for the kindergarten and first and second grades can probably be arranged in the classroom, thus enabling the teacher to make sure that each child has the necessary items when the class starts for the play area. Dressing rooms should be provided and shower facilities sufficient to take care of community needs should also be present.

Adequate storage room should be planned for supplies and portable equipment. In view of the trend toward employment of the physical education specialist, it is desirable to have an office in the facility, since often no assigned space is available elsewhere in the school. Such an office should contain a shower and a toilet.

The combination gymnasium-auditorium-cafeteria facility leaves much to be desired, creating more problems than it solves. Labeled a "multipurpose room," a better term probably would be "multiuseless." The cafeteria is a particular problem. The gymnasium must be vacated prior to the lunch hour for setting up chairs and tables, and is not available for activity until the facility has been cleaned, which usually involves mopping. This eliminates any noon-hour recreational use, leaving little play area for children during inclement weather. In extreme cases, the lack of help takes the gymnasium out of use during the early part of the afternoon until the custodian has completed his cleaning chores.

Play and special event practice is hardly compatible with the free atmosphere of physical education activities. Special programs, movies, and other events necessitating chairs also complicate the situation.

The indoor facility should be planned as a

physical education facility in which athletic contests may be scheduled at times, not predominantly as an athletic facility with consideration for spectators. The latter approach is not in error if the physical education needs do not suffer.

Outdoor planning should include provision for sufficient field space, hard-surfaced areas, apparatus areas, and other needed space. Play area standards should meet the minimum of 5 acres, with one additional acre for each 100 pupils. Automobile and bicycle parking areas should be in addition to play space standards.

Outdoor areas should be suitably turfed, surfaced, leveled, and drained. An automatic sprinkler system is desirable, but the sprinkler heads should not prove to be safety hazards. The hardtop surface should be suitably marked for movement patterns and games. Areas for court games are also desirable. Separate areas should be established where various groups of children may play in safety without interference from other groups of children. Good standards of maintenance and sanitation should prevail in both indoor and outdoor facilities.

EQUIPMENT AND SUPPLIES

Equipment refers to those items of a more or less fixed nature. Supplies include those nondurable materials which have a limited time of use. To illustrate the difference — a softball is listed under supplies while the longer-lasting softball backstop comes under the category of equipment. Equipment needs periodic replacement, and budgetary planning must consider the usable life span of each piece of equipment. Supplies are generally purchased on a yearly basis.

It is important not only to have adequate financing for equipment and supplies, but also to expend funds wisely.

If the objectives of physical education are to be fulfilled, there must be an adequate amount of equipment and supplies. It is difficult to envision children learning skills or acquiring physical fitness when they handle objects only infrequently or are limited to an occasional turn on the mat. Since physical education is activity, there must be sufficient materials to keep the children active. Special attention to policies involving purchase, storage, issue, care and maintenance records, and inventory are necessary if maximum use and return from the allotted budget is to be realized. It is important to decide what the boys and girls need in the program, and then base the purchasing plan upon this list.

Purchasing Policies

The purchase of supplies and equipment involves careful study of needs, prevailing prices, the quality of workmanship, and satisfactory materials. Safety and protection of the participants are also of vital concern.

Quantity buying by pooling the needs of the entire school system generally results in better use of the tax dollar. However, there may need to be compromise on the type and brand of materials in order to satisfy different users within a school system. If bids are asked, there is need to make careful specifications for materials. Bids should be asked only on those items specified, and "just as good" merchandise should not be permitted as substitutes.

One individual within a school should be designated as responsible for the keeping of records of equipment and supplies and for the purchase of these items. Needs vary from school to school, and it becomes practical for the school district authorities to deal with a single individual within a school. Prompt attention to repair and replacement of supplies is more likely under this system.

Constructed or home-made equipment should receive strong consideration. However, quality must not be sacrificed. Articles from home such as empty plastic jugs, old tires, milk cartons, and the like should be regarded as supplementary and enrichment materials. Care must be taken that administrators do not look for the cheap, no-cost route for supplies and sacrifice valuable learning experiences if an appreciable cost is indicated.

Outdoor Equipment

Two criteria are important in selecting equipment for the outdoor setting for physical education. The first is that the piece of equipment must contribute to the development of the child. For this reason items which involve only "sit and ride" experiences such as swings, teeters, and merry-go-rounds are not recommended. In addition, the slide is questionable, but some feel that there is value in the climbing part, and that the slide is a challenge to overcome fear. The second criterion is the safety factor. Many of the circular, hanging types like the giant stride are prone to cause accidents.

The following are suggested as items of outdoor equipment.

Climbing Structures. There are many names and many good varieties. Various types such as jungle gyms, castle towers, and similar items have value in physical fitness. For preschool and kindergarten children these are important and should be present in sufficient number and variety to absorb reasonable numbers of children.

Horizontal Ladders. Horizontal ladders are valuable pieces of equipment on the playground. They come in a variety of combinations and forms. Arched ladders are quite popular, as they allow children to reach the rungs easily. Uniladders, consisting of a single beam with pegs on each side, offer good challenge for children. A set comprising two arched ladders, crossing each other at the center at right angles, offers the potential for many types of movement experiences.

Arched Ladders

Climbing Ropes. In some climates where the weather is not too severe, schools are installing climbing ropes outside. These should not be over 12' to 14' in height and should be equipped with a circular stop at the top.

Balance Beams. Beams made from 4" x 4" beams can be put in permanent installations. These can be arranged in various patterns as indicated, but should not be more than 12" to 18" above the surface. Outdoor balance beams provide an extension of the instructional activities of the program.

Turning Bars. Turning bars made from 3" galvanized pipe offer exciting possibilities for children. The bars can be from 6' to 10' in length and positioned 30" to 36" above the ground.

Horizontal Bar Combinations. The set of three horizontal bars together at different heights is a valuable piece of apparatus for physical education.

Basketball Goals. These may or may not be combined with a court. Youngsters play a great deal of one-goal basketball, and a regulation court is not needed for this game. These should be in a surfaced area, however.

Softball Backstops. Softball backstops can be either fixed or portable.

Tetherball Courts. Tetherball courts should have fastening devices for the cord and ball so that these can be removed from the post for safe keeping.

Indoor Equipment

A shortcoming of many schools is the lack of suitable developmental equipment in the indoor physical education facility. As the basis for a good program, it is imperative that the gymnasium be equipped with overhead support equipment, climbing structures, climbing ropes, balance beams, and mats, in addition to the usual basketball goals and volleyball standards. Boxes for jumping and vaulting should also receive strong consideration in planning. Overhead support equipment includes horizontal ladder sets, exercise (horizontal) bars, and chinning bars. Climbing sets may be fixed or portable. Climbing ropes are particularly valuable tools for physical education. Suggested items for consideration in equipping an indoor facility follow.

Balance Beam Benches. This item has a double use. It can be used as a regular bench for the many types of bench activities, or when turned over becomes a balance beam. It should be of sturdy construction to stand up under the various demands. Wooden horses or other supports can be used to provide inclined benches. Six benches are a minimum for class activity.

FACILITIES, EQUIPMENT, AND SUPPLIES

Balance Beams. A wide beam (4") is recommended for the preschool, kindergarten, and the first grade. Otherwise, the usual 2" beam should be used. Balance beams with alternate surfaces (2" or 4") can be constructed of normal building materials. Construction details are found in the appendix.

Chinning Bar. The chinning bar is especially useful in the testing program for physical fitness, as well as providing body support activities. The portable chinning bar to be used in the doorway of the gymnasium is a substitute.

Climbing Ropes. Climbing ropes are essential to the program. At least eight should be present, but more allow for better group instruction. Climbing rope sets on tracks are the most efficient method of handling these pieces of equipment. With little effort and loss of time, the ropes are ready for activity. Ropes are available in a variety of materials, but good quality manila hemp seems to be the most practical. Ropes should be either 1¼" or 1½" in diameter.

Portable Climbing Structures. These are portable sets usually based on wooden or metal horses and include supported bars, ladders, and other equipment for climbing. (See diagram in the appendix.)

For preschool and kindergarten children, a wide variety of common materials should be utilized for climbing. Wooden boxes, ladders, beams, and steps-slide devices represent possibilities to extend movement experiences. (See Appendix for diagram of a step-slide device.)

Portable Climbing Sets

Tumbling Mats. Mats are basic to any physical education program and at least six should be present. Enough mats must be available to provide safety flooring for climbing apparatus. Mats should be 4' wide and 6' to 8' long. Light folding mats, while not as soft as some of the others, have the advantage that the children can handle them with ease. Folded mats also stack better. Mats should have fasteners so that at least two may be coupled together. Plastic covers are more suitable, as the old canvas mats are most difficult to keep clean.

Bounding Boards. These are 2' by 6', generally made of ¾" marine plywood. Knots in poor plywood will cause the boards to break. Useful in the primary program, four boards should be constructed. (See appendix.)

Balance Boards. Four to six balance boards of different types are a desirable extension of apparatus experiences. (See appendix.)

Record Player. A good record player with a variable speed control is a must for the

Climbing Ropes on Tracks

FACILITIES, EQUIPMENT, AND SUPPLIES

Types of Balance Boards

program. Pause control is also helpful. The physical education program should have its own record player, as there is enough demand to justify this. Access to a tape recorder is also helpful.

Supply Cart. A cart to hold supplies is quite desirable.

Jumping Boxes. Small boxes used for jumping and allied locomotor movements have good value in extending the opportunities for basic movement skills. For kindergarten and first grade, boxes should be 8″ and 16″ in height. For the older children, boxes of 12″ and 24″ offer sufficient challenge. The box with the lesser height can be 16″ by 16″ while the taller box can be 18″ by 18″ in size. The smaller box can be stored inside the larger box.

The top of the box should be padded with carpet padding and covered with leather or durable plastic. Holes drilled through the sides will provide finger holds for ease of handling. Eight boxes, four of each, are a minimum number for the average size class.

Horizontal Ladder Sets. Horizontal ladders which fold against the wall make an excellent addition to indoor equipment. The ladder may be combined with other pieces of apparatus in a folding set.

Climbing Frames. Climbing frames, mostly of European origin, are becoming increasingly popular and available in this country. The author has found excellent success in his program with a particular type of frame popular in Holland.

Another type of frame which has good acceptance in this country is the Hampton Frame, a type popular in England.

Klimraam — Holland Climbing Frame

Supplies

The basic rule for supplies is that they should be in sufficient amount so that no child has to wait too long for a turn because there is insufficient quantity. For some items there should be one for each child. The list is divided into two sections: basic items and additional supplies.

First Grade Children Using 16″ Jumping Boxes

FACILITIES, EQUIPMENT, AND SUPPLIES

English Climbing Frame — The Hampton Frame

Basic Items

Jump ropes (one for each child). Length: 7' or 8'.
Beanbags, assorted color (2 for each child).
Long jump ropes, 14'-16' (1 for each five children).
Small balls, assorted colors (1 for each child).
Yarn or fleece balls (for K-1, 1 for each child).
Rubber playground balls (mostly 8½", but have variety. One for each child).
Sports balls (football, basketball, soccer — 6 of each).
Wooden paddles for paddle tennis and similar games (1 for each child).
Softball equipment, including masks.
Indian clubs (12 or more).
Wands, 36" or 42" (1 for each child).
Pinnies or other team markers (1 for each two children).
Gym scooters (4 for relays, or 1 for each two children for games).
Measuring tape, 50' (1).
Jump-the-shot ropes (3).
Rubber traffic cones for boundary markers, 12" (24).
Records.
Tom-tom or drum with striker (1).
Hoops, 36" (1 for each child).
Wire baskets for storage (6 or more).
Ball inflator with gauge (1).
Eyeglass protectors (4).
Whistles (6).
Individual mats 18" x 36" or 20" x 40" (1 for each child).
Magic or stretch ropes (8).
Parachute, 24'-28' (1).
Tetherball sets.

Additional Supplies

In addition to the items specified as basic, a number of the following should be considered:
Deck tennis rings.
Rubber horseshoes.
Bongo boards.
Stilts (6 pair).
Table tennis equipment.
Pogo sticks.
Lummi sticks.
Broom handles (8).
Bicycle or auto tires.
Oversize inner tubes.
Rubber balloons (12).

Storage Plans

When a teacher takes a class into the gymnasium for physical education, he has the right to expect and be assured of sufficient supplies to conduct his class. A master list stipulating the kinds and quantities of supplies which should be in storage should be established. A reasonable turnover should be expected, and supply procedures should reflect this. One teacher should be placed in charge of the supply room, with responsibility for maintenance and replacement. The supplies from this source should be used for physical education and after-school events. It should not be a source of recreational issue for recess or free play periods. Each classroom should have its own supplies, marked for classroom identification, for this purpose.

Available supplies should be arranged in such a fashion that an easy count can be made. There should be a particular spot or bin to which the supplies should be returned. Off-season items should be removed to a "dead" storage area. Good housekeeping procedures should be followed and the supply room kept orderly. Selected students or squad leaders could take some responsibility for helping to maintain a tidy storage area.

Some schools have found it helpful to use small supply carts of the type pictured below.

Equipment Cart — Home Constructed

The cart holds the articles in more frequent use. It does take up space, but it is quite a time-saver. Carts can be built inexpensively to a personal plan or an equipment carrier can be purchased. A second cart to hold the record player and records is also suggested.

The principal or physical education supervisor should inspect storage areas at regular intervals. An established routine of taking care of repairs and replacement of supplies must also be instituted.

A few schools dispense with a central storage area and place the responsibility for supplies in each classroom.

This plan keeps a sufficient supply of physical education materials in each classroom for participation of that class. Advantages of the plan are:

(1) Less time is wasted. (2) The supplies available are known. (3) Definite responsibility may be fixed for loss or damage. (4) Children have a sense of responsibility for "their" materials. (5) There is no competition or overlap in demands for supplies by different classes.

Disadvantages given for this plan are that it is initially expensive, storage facilities are needed for each classroom, and equipment must be marked carefully to ensure its being returned to the right classroom.

Recommendations for Supplies

Some supplies are designed especially for children. Junior-size footballs and basketballs are available and should be used. Rubber-covered balls generally prove more satisfactory than the leather variety for use in the elementary school, particularly during wet weather.

Smaller children can use rubber playground balls for volleyball-type games. When playground balls are used for soccer skills, they work more satisfactorily when slightly deflated.

When children are working on simple bouncing skills, it is desirable for each child to have a ball. The supply of balls can be augmented by tennis or sponge balls. Discarded tennis balls from the high school tennis team are a good source. Sponge balls are inexpensive and with care last indefinitely.

For jump ropes, ⅜" sash core is suitable. The ends should be whipped or dipped in some type of hardening solution in order to prevent unraveling. Adhesive tape may also be used to bind the ends of the ropes. The new plastic link jumping ropes are particularly attractive and should be considered. With care, these last indefinitely.

Another good source for jump ropes is ⅜" yellow plastic (not nylon) rope of a *hard weave* variety. The ends can be melted with a match or burner.

Beanbags can be made easily. Good quality, bright colored muslin is suitable. Some prefer a beanbag with an outer liner which snaps in place to allow for washing. Another idea is to sew three sides of the beanbag permanently. The fourth side is used for filling and has an independent stitch. The beans can be removed through the side when the bag is washed. Beanbags should be about 6" by 6" and can be filled with dried beans, peas, wheat, rice, or even building sand.

For games requiring boundary markers, pieces of rubber matting can be used. In addition, small sticks or boards, painted white, are excellent. A board 1" by 2", 3' or 4' in length makes a satisfactory marker.

Empty gallon plastic jugs filled halfway with sand and recapped, make fine boundary markers. Clorox or similar plastic jugs can be cut down to make ball catchers.

Softballs can be purchased without stitching (concealed stitch) which eliminates the problem of broken stitches and consequent repair.

A jump-the-shot rope can be made by using an old, completely deflated volleyball tied on the end of a rope.

Old tires, even those from bicycles, can be used for throwing targets.

Schools in and near ski areas may contact lift proprietors for discarded tow ropes. These make excellent tug-of-war ropes.

Indian clubs can be turned in the school woodshops. However, many substitutes can be made. Lumber of size 2" by 2" cut off in short pieces (6" to 10" long) will stand satisfactorily. Lumber companies generally also have available round poles from 1" to 1½" in diameter. Sections of these make satisfactory Indian clubs. Broken bats also can be made into good substitute clubs.

Bases can be constructed from heavy canvas. The canvas should be folded over three or four times and then stitched together. Bases may be made from outdoor plywood and should be painted. Heavy rubber matting also is suitable material for bases.

Handles from old brooms or mops can provide the needed wands and sticks. These come in various diameters, but this is not an important factor.

Deck tennis rings can be made from heavy rope by splicing.

Deck tennis rings and hoops can also be made from plastic water pipe. However, the color selection is limited and uninspiring. (See appendix.) Garden hose can also be used to make deck rings.

White shoe polish has numerous uses and will come off the floor with a little scrubbing. Marking lines and making designs are some of the uses for this marking device.

Individual mats can be made from indoor-outdoor carpeting that has a rubber backing. Mats of this type can be washed readily.

Coffee cans (3 lb.) can be used as targets.

Empty half-gallon milk cartons also have a variety of uses.

Paddles can be made from ⅜" to ½" plywood. Handles can be augmented with the use of plastic tape. (See appendix.)

Play scooters can be constructed, but care must be exercised in selecting swivel wheels which will not mark the floor.

Magic or stretch ropes can be made by stringing together twenty-five to thirty large size rubber bands. Common clothing elastic, ½" or ¾", also makes excellent stretch ropes. (See appendix.)

Yarn balls can be made by older children or by the PTA. Wool yarn has the advantage of shrinking after washing, tightening into an effective ball. (See appendix.)

Blocks with a groove on the top and one of the sides are excellent for forming hurdles with wands. A 4" x 4" timber cut into various lengths, 6", 12", and 18", gives a variety of hurdles. Grooves can be cut with a dado or a regular table saw. Grooves should be ¾" wide and about ½" deep. (See appendix.)

Old bowling pins can be obtained from most bowling alleys free of charge. Since they are too large for the children to handle easily, cut off the top 6" to 8". Parallel cuts through the body of the pin will provide hockey pucks and shuffle board disks. Bowling pins can be turned down on a lathe in the woodshop to resemble Indian clubs.

Care and Repair. There must be a definite system established for repair of supplies and equipment. If the central storage system is used, the repair materials can be kept in this location. Children and teachers tend to become discouraged if the repair process is lengthy and, rather than be deprived of an item, may continue to use it until it is no longer worth salvaging.

An important social objective for children is respect for and care of school property. Proper development of attitudes and habits in the care of physical education materials will help achieve this goal.

Balls need to be inflated to proper pressures. This means an accurate gauge and periodic checking. The needle should be moistened before it is inserted into the valve. Children should not sit on balls and should kick balls made specifically for kicking (soccers, footballs, and playground balls).

Softball bats and wooden paddles should not be used for hitting rocks, stones, or other hard materials. Neither should bats be knocked against fences, posts, or other objects that will cause damage. Broken bats should be discarded, as they are unsafe even if taped around the break. Children should learn to keep the trademark up when batting. Bats should be taped to prevent slippage.

Cuts, abrasions, and breaks in rubber balls should be immediately repaired. In some cases this repair can be handled by means of a vulcanizing patch as used for tire tube repairs. In others, the use of a hard-setting rubber preparation is of value. However, some repairs are beyond the scope of the school, and the ball should be sent away for repair.

Storage and Marking.

A systematic procedure should be established for the storage of equipment and supplies. A place for everything and everything in its place is the key to good housekeeping. A principal certainly is more favorably inclined toward purchase requests when he observes the good care that the supplies are receiving.

Mats are expensive and care is needed if they are to last. A place where they can be stacked properly should be provided or there should be handles for hanging them up. A mat truck is another solution, provided there is space for storing the truck. The newer plastic or plastic-covered mats should be cleaned with a damp, soapy cloth.

For off-season storage, balls should be deflated somewhat, leaving enough air in them to keep their shape. Leather balls should be cleaned with an approved ball conditioner.

For small items, clean ice cream containers (2-gallon) make adequate storage receptacles. Most school cafeterias have these and other containers which may be used in the storage room to provide order. Small wire baskets also make good containers for small physical education materials.

An area should be established for the equipment needing repair so that the articles for repair are evident at a glance.

Equipment that will warp should be laid in a flat place.

All equipment and supplies should be marked. This is particularly important for equipment issued to different classrooms. Marking can be done with indelible pencils, paint, or stencil ink. However, few marking systems are permanent and re-marking at regular intervals is necessary. Sporting goods establishments have marking sets available for this purpose.

An electric burning pencil or stamp is also useful but must be used with caution so as not to damage the equipment being marked.

Rubber playground balls come in different colors, and an assignment to a classroom can be made on the basis of color. A code scheme can also be used with different color paints. It is possible to devise a color system by which the year of issue can be designated. This offers opportunities for research into equipment use.

5

Organizing for Effective Teaching

The Community, the Administration, and the School
Patterns of Teaching Responsibility
Consultant and Supervisory Services
Scheduling
Policies for Health and Safety
Safety Procedures
Operational Policies
Promotional Ideas and Public Relations
Pageants, Demonstrations, and Assembly Programs

THE COMMUNITY, THE ADMINISTRATION, AND THE SCHOOL

With physical education fast approaching the milestone of acceptance as a partner in education, school administrators are now more concerned with the type and quality of their overall school programs. This program in turn will reflect the degree of confidence which the school administration has in physical education as an educational tool. A quality physical education program will convince school officials that physical education is worthy of the effort and support it requires.

It is vital that the administration accept the fundamental concepts that physical education is a developmental and instructional program which is an important part of the child's educational experience, and that this teaching area merits suitable consideration in planning. It is also important for the administration to understand the relationship which exists between perceptual-motor competency and certain academic skills. Whether or not physical education is a teaching period or a glorified recess period, where the chief purpose seems to be for youngsters to let off steam, is largely determined by the administrative approach.

The community climate for physical education must be positive. If parents are made aware of the existence of a quality physical education program and know what it can do for their children, pressures on schools to provide better physical education experiences will result. PTAs can become effective lobbies. Physical educators should never underestimate the power of parents and should welcome every opportunity to work with parent groups through displays and effective dissemination of informational materials.

Two administrative decisions with regard to personnel must be made at the beginning to set the basis for the program. The first is the decision as to who is to teach the classes — specialist, regular teacher, or other pattern. The second specifies the kind of consultant or supervisory aid to help the teacher.

PATTERNS OF TEACHING RESPONSIBILITY

The patterns of teaching physical education vary with respect to staff assignments from school district to school district. Larger school districts have more flexibility in selecting an appropriate pattern, but many small districts have solved the problem of providing quality teaching. Some of the plans by which physical education teaching is organized today are as follows:

1. Full Responsibility by the Classroom Teacher with No Consultant or Supervisory Services. Often in this administrative arrangement no curriculum guide is available. This kind of format does not generally result in a quality program. In many cases the program becomes no more than a supervised play period. This is not a recommended teaching pattern for physical education.

2. Specialist Teaching in Physical Education. This plan produces the best results in terms of child progress toward the objectives of physical education. A major objection to specialist teaching is that it requires extra teachers. A second reservation about this program is that the classroom teacher loses contact with the students during the physical education classes and thus misses a valuable opportunity to work with and observe the children in this setting. Some of this objection can be overcome by having the classroom teacher present during the physical education lesson.

The most prevalent practice is to assign the specialist the responsibility for the intermediate level classes and have the classroom teacher handle the kindergarten and primary grades.

3. Teaching Responsibilities Shared by the Classroom Teacher and the Special Teacher. This must be a partnership of effort between the two teachers or it will fail. The ideal arrangement is to have the special teacher introduce units and teach the more difficult elements, with the classroom teacher providing follow-up lessons. The logistics of this arrangement are difficult. In some instances, the specialist teaches only one day per week and the classroom teacher the remainder. When the special teacher comes the following week, he has little knowledge of what has transpired between his visits. The special teacher has a difficult time learning personality characteristics of the children; in fact, he may not even be able to learn their names from his meager contacts.

4. Teaching by the Classroom Teacher With Consultant Aid. To implement this plan, it is necessary to have a program of inservice education. The classroom teacher basically does the teaching, but there could be demonstration teaching by the consultant. Curricular materials and lesson plan formats need to be provided. Classroom teachers generally are willing to follow a prescribed curriculum if the demands of paper work are not excessive.

CONSULTANT AND SUPERVISORY SERVICES

In the era of rapid change, with new ideas, activities, and teaching approaches coming to the fore, some plan for consultant or supervisory services is essential. Careful selection of the individual who is to function as a consultant or supervisor is important. Not only should he be qualified, but he should possess the confidence and enthusiasm to work successfully with teachers. He must be a superior teacher himself.

Working relationships with the principal and the teachers must be clarified. The pattern of inservice meetings, the frequency of consultant visits, and other relevant working procedures must be established.

He must be both knowledgeable and available. His office should be a center for resource materials, and he should produce instructional aids for the teacher as needed and requested. Paper work for teachers must be kept to a minimum.

The human relationships with his educational community are also of high importance. A "help" attitude based on constructive criticism is much more effective than a posture of supervision. A good rapport with the teaching staff is important.

A sound philosophy and an effective and functioning curriculum, based on good educational standards, serve as the basis for this type of program. A curriculum guide should be in the hands of all teachers working in the program. The practice of placing one or two curriculum manuals in the principal's office means that little use will be made of them.

The importance of the principal in the educational scheme must be recognized in the relationships the supervisor maintains with the school. The principal should be kept informed and should be consulted as indicated. He should receive a copy of all announcements and directives for his teachers. An effective procedure is to route all equipment and supplies through his office, so that he will know what has been received.

The consultant should be a participating member of local, state, regional, and national professional associations. As a function of this professional involvement, he should interpret new trends to his school community and incorporate into his program desirable changes and additions which are of proven value.

SCHEDULING

A definite schedule for physical education classes should be established at each school, based on instructional time of at least 150 minutes per week, exclusive of recess or other supervised play. The standard is for instructional time and does not include time needed for moving to and from class, changing to gym clothing, visiting the washroom, and cleaning up.

The recommendation by most national bodies is that physical education be scheduled on a daily basis. Younger children profit more from a daily period of activity rather than, for example, longer periods three days per week.

Where sufficient teaching stations exist, the scheduling problem is minimized. Caution is urged with outdoor scheduling where equipment is to be shared and conflicts can arise with limited supplies. Problems occur when too many classes are scheduled using the physical education materials available.

Class size should not exceed the normal limits of one class. The practice of sending out two or more classes with one teacher for physical education results in little more than a supervised play period.

The substitution of band, chorus, play practice and other programs for physical education is not a recommended procedure. Teachers too frequently take the physical education period to practice special events for part or all of the children. Neither should health instruction be counted as a part of the physical education requirement. Health instruction is an important area in its own right and should be so treated. Confusion exists because often the terms health and physical education are coupled in literature.

POLICIES FOR HEALTH AND SAFETY

The school has both a moral and a legal responsibility toward its students. The moral responsibility is part of the school's broad educational purposes, namely to provide a school setting in which each child may develop an optimum level of personal health. The legal responsibility arises out of the public's assumption that the school cannot escape the legal obligation to provide a healthful and safe environment for the child.

Periodic Health Examination

A first concern for the student is the provision of a periodic health examination. This should determine, among other things, the extent of a child's participation in physical education. Ideally this examination would be held yearly and would include all health factors having a bearing on the child's educational experience. In practice, however, examinations should be scheduled on entrance into school.

The examination should classify students in one of three categories: (1) normal participation in physical education; (2) participation subject to certain adaptations or restrictions; and (3) severe limitations or nonparticipation. The teacher must have access to the results of the examination in order that each student may receive the consideration stipulated in the examination.

An examination form approved by the local medical society makes for more consistent information. Agreement can also be reached with the local medical society with respect to a standard fee for the examination.

Excuses and Readmittance

If a child is to be excused from physical education for a day or two for health reasons, the teacher can accept a note from the parent. If the excuse involves a significant length of time, it should be accepted only on the recommendation of a physician. Readmittance of children who have been out for a period of time should also be subject to a physician's recommendation. If there is a school nurse, excuse and readmittance cases should be routed through her, and she will in turn discuss the problem with the physical education teacher. In the absence of recommendations from both physician and nurse, consultation with the principal and the parent is probably the best solution.

Students who have been absent because of illness or some other condition should be observed closely for signs which might suggest that they are not ready to participate in unlimited physical activity.

Good rapport between the physicians and the schools is important in handling the health problems related to excuses and readmittance. One physician from the medical society should be designated to provide liaison among those responsible for physical education and the medical profession.

Screening by the Teacher

Periodic health examinations will not uncover every health problem related to physical activity participation. Some conditions may appear only after exercise. In other instances, the condition may develop between examinations or even shortly after an examination and have an important bearing on the health status of the individual.

The task of screening children who respond poorly to exercise is not difficult, as it involves primarily noting certain observable conditions which are an indication of an abnormality. The Committee on Exercise and Fitness of the American Medical Association lists these observable signs which may accompany or follow exercise and which are indications for referral and further investigation:

Excessive Breathlessness. Some breathlessness is normal with exercise, but breathlessness that persists long after exercise is cause for medical referral.

Bluing of the Lips. Except in a cold wet environment, bluing of the lips or nailbeds is an unnatural reaction to exercise. Its occurrence in the ordinary exercise setting is cause for medical referral.

Pale or Clammy Skin. Pale or clammy skin or cold sweating following or during exercise is not a normal reaction to physical activity within the usual temperature ranges of the gymnasium or playing field. Again, medical referral is recommended.

Unusual Fatigue. Excessive fatigue, as evidenced by unusual lack of endurance or early failure to maintain moderate activity, also suggests the need for medical referral. It is dangerous to attribute such reactions to malingering until possible organic causes have been ruled out.

Persistent Shakiness. Unusual weakness or shakiness that continues for more than ten minutes following vigorous exercise is cause for medical referral. Normally, recovery will be reasonably prompt.

Muscle Twitching or Tetany. Muscular contractions such as twitching or tetany, whether localized or generalized, sometimes occur as an unusual reaction to exercise. It may be abnormal and warrants medical investigation.

In addition, such medical symptoms as headache, dizziness, fainting, broken sleep at night, digestive upset, pain not associated with injury, undue pounding or uneven heartbeat, disorientation, or personality changes are contraindications of normal functioning. The Committee cautions that an occasional episode need not alarm the instructor, but recurring or persisting patterns of any of these symptoms, particularly when related to activity, indicate the need for medical review.

The instructor needs to be sensitive to these possible reactions of the children and note them in stride. He is further cautioned to remind himself that *unusual* reactions are not necessarily *abnormal* reactions.

The specialist, with his scientific and health background, is in a better position to assess such health indications than is the classroom teacher. However, with concentration and practice the classroom teacher can make effective use of the physical education period as a part of the daily health screening of the children.

Healthful Environment for Physical Education

A healthful environment for physical education requires attention to standards for school safety, hygiene, and sanitation. In addition, the physical education setting should emphasize good standards in cleanliness, ventilation, and heating. Ventilation should be sufficient to remove objectionable odors. Temperatures, depending upon the extent of the activity, should range from 65 to 68 degrees. Generally, a temperature comfortable for an elderly teacher is too high for active youngsters.

Healthful environment also includes attention to mental hygiene factors. Proper student-teacher relationships in activity areas are important. Students should be able to relieve tensions through activity. Physical education should be a period where students lose rather than acquire tensions.

Cleanliness of the gymnasium floor is particularly important in the present-day physical education program, as many of the movements require the children to place their hands or bodies on the floor. The floor should be swept in the morning just prior to the classes. In addition, it should be swept as often as needed between classes. A wide dust mop should be handy for this purpose, as children can perform this chore.

Ideally, all children should change to play clothing for physical education classes. It is particularly important that girls wear something other than dresses.

The solution to the problem of changing clothing for class is not easily found. Some teachers find it practical to have youngsters change when convenient, wearing the play clothing during class sessions. Changing in washrooms has drawbacks, but at least accomplishes the task.

The problem of storing the children's play clothing if lockers are not available needs a positive approach. The cooperation of the classroom teacher must be gained to establish some kind of a system. The system should preserve the ownership of each child's things, not be time-consuming, and be a child-handled system.

As a basic minimum, children should wear gym shoes during the physical education class. The practice of having children "skate" around in stockinged feet limits the children greatly in their responses to activity challenges. It would be better to have the children in bare feet, rather than in stocking feet. The teacher should also be in appropriate clothing and footwear.

Some authorities hold that children should participate in bare feet, as this is more beneficial in terms of proper foot development. This complicates the cleanup problem and is not suitable for much of the outdoor play.

Adequate facilities should be available for cleaning-up after class, and enough time should be allowed for the finishing-up procedure.

SAFETY PROCEDURES

It is often said that proper safety is no accident. Safety education should be positive in terms of what approaches and considerations are needed and not based on the "scare" approach. A school safety committee is desirable to set safety regulations, policies, and procedures. The committee should be composed of students, faculty, the school nurse, and perhaps representatives of the PTA. A school safety code should be established and a written compilation, including all policies, regulations, and procedures, should be in the hands of all teachers. Regulations affecting the students should be posted. The committee should be open-minded and receptive to safety suggestions from students, faculty, and others. An important function would be to review accidents for the purpose of determining appropriate preventive measures to be taken.

The school safety program consists of three aspects: (1) a safe school environment; (2) safety education; and (3) safety services. Each is discussed in turn.

Safe Environment

The school must be certain that the school environment meets all the criteria for safety. This involves a number of aspects.

1. Health Status.

As previously discussed, the health status of the children must be ascertained through a health examination so no child may be placed in a physical environment beyond his capacity.

2. Provision for a Safe Teaching Place.

This is both quantitative and qualitative. There must be sufficient room for the activity, and the area must be suitable for the intended purpose. The character of the activity will determine the amount of space needed for safe play, including sufficient boundary clearance from walls, fences, and other obstructions. The area should be free from posts, wires, holes, and other hazards. The presence of broken glass, along with miscellaneous junk, is a source of accidents. Sprinkler heads and pools of water can also cause serious injury.

3. Safety in Equipment and Supplies.

The equipment and supplies provided must be suitable for the level of the children and the selected activity. The equipment should be in good functioning condition or removed from use.

4. Regular Inspection of Facilities and Equipment.

Inspection of facilities should be made on a regular basis, perhaps monthly. This can be a shared experience by the principal, custodian, and physical education specialist. Items needing attention should be noted. Where indicated, equipment should be taken out of service until properly repaired.

5. Supervision of Activities and Play Periods.

All school-sponsored activities must be supervised, including recess, noon-hour recreation, and after-school play. Much of this can be assigned to qualified teacher aides, releasing the teacher for instructional duties. Under law, a class may not be turned over to high school students or cadet teachers, as supervision must be supplied by a certified individual.

6. Proper Selection of Activities

The selected activity must stand up under scrutiny as a proper educational medium for the group involved. Teachers should avoid highly specialized or difficult games beyond the ability of the children. The principal who sets rules for snowball fighting is encouraging an activity which is questionable and may cause injury.

Safety Education

The term *safety education* as it relates to instructional procedures will be used in a limited sense in this discussion. The physical education teacher has a responsibility to instruct children in the skills needed in an activity so that they may take part in it safely. The instruction should cover the basic essentials in sequential order.

A second phase of safety education involves considering the inherent safety hazards of each activity and taking whatever measures are necessary to meet the challenge. The teacher must provide the leadership in seeing that the safety precautions for each activity have been met. An instance of this is the placement of mats under climbing ropes. The children must be made aware of safety practices and taught them along with the instruction. They must be motivated to accept responsibility for their own safety and that of others. They should ask for and be willing to provide help as needed.

Safety Services — Emergency Care

In spite of all precautions, accidents will occur in various phases of the school program. The school has a responsibility to arrange a system of emergency care, so that prompt and appropriate measures will be taken to protect the child who has been injured. Emergency care procedures should follow this sequence:

1. The administration of first aid is the first step. The problem of proper care is solved if a school nurse is present. If not, at least one person in the school should have first aid certification. Some principals like to have the school secretary with such certification, because she is readily available. If a teacher has first aid responsibilities, proper supervision must be supplied for his class when he is called to the scene of the incident. First aid procedures will indicate if the child can be moved and in what fashion.

2. Unless the injury is such that the child needs to be taken to a doctor without delay, the parents should be notified. The school should have on hand sufficient information pertaining to each student to give direction in case of an emergency. This would include telephone numbers of the parents, both at home and at place of employment. In addition, it is well to have written permission from parents to refer the child to the family doctor for treatment. Sometimes the name of a neighbor or close friend to whom the child can be taken in case the parents cannot be contacted is helpful.

3. The third step is to release the child to his parents or other person designated by them. Policies for transportation should be established.

4. A report of the accident should be filled out promptly, generally on a form adopted by the school system. The teacher and the principal should each retain copies, the additional specified copies being forwarded to the administration. The report should contain all necessary details with respect to full names of the child and witnesses; details of the accident including place, time, activity, circumstances, and possible causes; and disposition of the child.

5. Follow-up procedures should be instituted to eliminate the causes of the accident and prevent future occurrences.

The Medicine Chest

Whether or not to have a medicine chest is a debatable point. The medical association for the area (local or county) should help make such a decision. Only those medications and materials approved by the association should be in the medicine chest and approved directions for use of the contents should be prominently posted.

Student Insurance

The school should make available accident insurance providing compensation in case of accident to a child. If a parent rejects the option of school accident insurance, in case of an accident he has little basis for objection to expenses which could have been partially or fully covered by insurance. Physical education insurance for young children is relatively inexpensive.

Other Safety Considerations

Dogs and other animals should be kept from the schoolyards. Children can trip over the animals and the possibility of being bitten is always present. Whenever the skin is broken from an animal bite, the possibility of rabies must *always* be considered. The animal must be caught and held for the authorities. Only by observing the animal for a period of two weeks or so can the possibility of rabies be rejected.

The rubbish burning area should be protected from the children. Children are naturally attracted to fire, and they love to handle burning materials.

Throwing stones and snow balls needs to be controlled. Other habits of rowdyism having possibilities of injuries need to be controlled also.

Special rules need to be established for procedures in various areas, particularly in the use of various pieces of apparatus on the playground. These should be discussed with the children and posted.

Legal Responsibility

Since the child is subject to compulsory attendance laws, the school has the legal responsibility of providing a safe environment. Teachers, as individuals, share this responsibility. While the teacher cannot be held responsible for all accidental occurrences in activities under his supervision, he can be held legally responsible for the consequences of his negligence which has proven injurious to one of the children.

Liability occurs when the teacher is held responsible for a given situation. It is always a court action, and negligence by the teacher must be established. Negligence is a basic factor involved in all liability. A person is deemed negligent when he has failed to act as a reasonably prudent person would act under the circumstances. Foreseeability is the key to whether or not there is negligence. If the teacher could have foreseen the causes leading to the injury, and failed to take action as a prudent person would, then the ruling of negligence can result.

Each teacher needs to ascertain that the child is in an environment that meets all the criteria of safety. In addition, it would be well to consider liability insurance, which is available quite reasonably in conjunction with memberships in some educational societies. However, schools should have liability insurance to cover adequately all teachers and other staff members.

OPERATIONAL POLICIES

Coeducational Activity

Coeducational activity is activity in which boys and girls participate together. If the social and emotional objectives of physical education are to be realized fully, boys and girls should have the opportunity to play together in activities on each grade level.

On the primary level, there is little need for separation of sexes in any activity. Boys and girls of these ages are very much alike in development and almost all activities may include both sexes. The types of activity where separation is recommended are the contact and rougher activities.

The Supervised Play Period

Commonly called recess, the supervised play period provides a time for relaxation and relief from tensions for youngsters. Adequate supervision is necessary to ensure that safety practices are being followed and that youngsters have proper consideration for each other. Children must be reminded that they are under self-discipline and must follow established rules.

Supervision should be positive and in terms of helping youngsters make the most of their free play. Teachers must recognize that supervisory duties of this type are a regular and important part of the teaching duties. Assignments are generally handled on a rotation basis.

The Noon-Hour Play Period

The noon-hour period can be both educational and recreative. The first part must be devoted to a supervised, happy, restful lunch. After this, the children should be allowed to play, in the main, in quiet games. There should be plenty of time allowed for attending to personal needs.

Each child should have an opportunity to enjoy an activity of his interest. Individual games, quiet games, table-type activities, and semiactive sports are recommended. Adult supervision is needed.

Children who eat lunch at home should not return to school before the designated time for afternoon classes.

Clubs

Club work can be encouraged. Clubs for tumbling, hiking, swimming, skiing, skating, and other activities increase the motivation for activity. Opportunities for informal physical recreation in the school should be encouraged and sponsored.

Playdays

A playday is a festival-type setting where children of a school or different schools meet to take part in physical education activities. The emphasis is on the social values rather than competition. Yet competition is important in that teams made up from different participating schools can play against each other.

A playday may be entirely within a particular school. However, the usual pattern is for a playday between schools. It may be carried on during the school day, after school, or on a Saturday.

The program may include the more simple games, relays, and contests. Stunts, individual athletic events, and even rhythms are the basis of activities in some meets. The programs vary according to the size of the schools and the grade level of the children. They usually involve both boys and girls.

PROMOTIONAL IDEAS AND PUBLIC RELATIONS

The marked changes in physical education over the last decade create a necessity for public understanding if the physical education program is to receive its measure of support. In the minds of some, physical education means a sports program. Others regard it as simply a time to play games. Since the philosophy, educational approach, instructional methods, and content differ markedly from what was the experience of the adult population, a positive program of public relations, primarily informative, should be instituted so school patrons can be made fully aware of the education possibilities of physical education. Such measures should include a variety of approaches.

A Quality Program

The most effective public relations instrument for physical education is a quality program. The informal reports of the children to the parents on the satisfaction, interest, and value the program holds for them is a most effective means of creating a climate of parental regard for the program.

Parent Involvement

Parents can be involved actively as participants or in a passive manner as spectators. One approach is to schedule a Parents' Night, which may take the following directions: (1) parents participating along with the children in regular class work; (2) parents observing a regular schedule of classes; (3) Achievement Night to show special attainments; (4) demonstrations interpreting the main features of the year-round physical education program.

The PTA should serve as a vehicle for interpreting the program. Discussions, panel presentations, outside experts, and selected visual presentations are effective program elements. Parents should be given the opportunity to ask questions and resolve debatable points.

School-Affiliated Methods

Many promotional ideas can utilize elements of the school program. The physical education program can contribute to assembly programs. Playdays can be scheduled. Special events involving some competition, such as Junior Olympics, free throw contests, gymnastic-type competition, demonstrations, and the like have value.

Community-Oriented Informational Measures

Public informational media should be utilized. Newspapers should be supplied with articles of special interest or action. Pictures are important. At times, feature articles or sections can be assembled.

Television and, to a lesser extent, radio should be exploited. Events of special interest provide a second jolt of publicity through television coverage. Radio panel discussions have good value also.

The support of service clubs should be enlisted through speeches, films, demonstrations, and other approaches. Service clubs are often anxious to provide material support in the form of sponsorship of some special event or the purchase of a special piece of equipment, beyond the fiscal capacity of the school.

Brochures covering yearly summaries, program descriptions, philosophy, and educational values are effective instruments toward better understanding.

The physical educator should take part in community affairs, joining such clubs and groups as feasible. He should be willing to help groups seeking the kind of school services for which he is responsible.

PAGEANTS, DEMONSTRATIONS, AND ASSEMBLY PROGRAMS

Classroom teachers are asked at times to organize demonstrations for assembly programs, parents, and other groups. These are excellent mediums of public relations and dispel some of the false notions regarding physical education. If such programs are requested, the following may be helpful:

1. The activities should grow out of and be typical of the physical education program.

2. The activities should not require a long period of preparation so that the physical education period becomes a training period for the demonstration.

3. Children should be properly dressed for the activity, but elaborate and intricate costuming should be avoided. Simple costumes that can be made by the children are most acceptable.

4. The demonstration should generally include numbers of children. Programs can be designed so that all children participate in some phase of the exhibition. However, recognition can be given to superior ability by specialty numbers.

5. It is important to avoid tests of strength and skill which would lead to embarrassment of those defeated.

6. While a high degree of performance is not needed, the activities should be done reasonably well within the level of the children.

7. The program should be fast-moving and contain activities of good audience appeal. Music is indispensable, and a well-balanced program will contain several numbers with music.

8. The program should call attention to physical fitness, and some elements should be devoted to this area. A demonstration of physical fitness activities is always well-received.

9. Some part of the program can include a demonstration of instructional procedures rather than centering all attention on accomplishments.

6

Movement Education

Movement Competency
Defining Movement Education
Basic Movement
The Skills Instructional Program
Posture and Body Mechanics
Perceptual-Motor Competency and the Slow Learner

Movement education as a term is a fairly recent addition to the conceptual framework of physical education. In the past, physical educators spoke about each child having the opportunity to develop skills. Today, we think more in broader terms of helping an individual acquire movement competency. The process by which the child is helped to acquire movement competency is called movement education.

MOVEMENT COMPETENCY

A better understanding of movement education can be achieved if one can look ahead at the behavioral changes in children which are its goals. Traditionally, physical education directed its efforts in motor learning toward two skill goals, namely, basic skills and specialized skills. Basic skills refer to those simple skills which relate to a broad spectrum of activity, important to the child's play and daily living. They have wide application to many situations.

Specialized skills is a term reserved for skills having application to a particular sport or activity. Many are intricate and specific, with clear-cut points of technique.

Added to these traditional concepts is the human capacity known as competency in the management of the body. Recognition of the area of body management competency as important in elementary school physical education has provided new educational significance to programs. A deeper look into body management competency, basic skills, and specialized skills will serve to pinpoint the place of each in movement competency and demonstrate the interrelationships among them.

Competency in Body Management

Body management involves the body as a whole. Learning to manage the body leads to greater control and skill over gross movements. The child controls his body in a non-locomotor or fixed location, in movements across the floor, through space, or when on apparatus. To secure good body management skill is to acquire, expand, and integrate elements of general motor control through wide experience in movement, based on an exploratory and creative approach. The child needs to learn what his body can do and how he can manage his body effectively in a variety of movement situations and challenges.

Good body management practices are also related to the body's resistance to the forces of gravity. We want children not only to be able to manage the body with efficiency and ease of movement, but also to accept good standards of posture and body mechanics as meaningful constituents of their movement patterns.

In addition to posture and body mechanics, another consideration in body management skill is perceptual-motor competency. The principles and concepts basic to perceptual-motor competency have strong relationship and application to the area of body management. Good motor control requires sufficient neurological control and development, which can be aided by attention to perceptual-motor approaches and activities. Perceptual-motor approaches which are considered relevant to physical education include those which give attention to balance, coordination, laterality, directionality, awareness of space, and knowledge of one's own body and body parts.

Basic Skills

Basic skills can be divided into three categories, each of which can be considered separately for clarification. It is possible for a child to isolate and perform a selected skill from a category. On the other hand, a movement pattern may include a number of skills from different categories. For example, a child may shake his body (a nonlocomotor activity) while running across the floor (a locomotor skill). Or, he may combine throwing and catching a beanbag (a manipulative skill) while hopping in various directions (a locomotor skill).

Locomotor Skills

Locomotor skills are those used to move the body from one place to another, or project the body upward, as in jumping or hopping. In addition to jumping and hopping, locomotor skills include walking, running, skipping, leaping, sliding, and galloping.

Nonlocomotor Skills

Nonlocomotor skills include those which the child does in place or without appreciable movement from place to place. Nonlocomotor skills are of a wider variety and not as clearly defined as locomotor skills. Nonlocomotor skills include bending and stretching, pushing and pulling, raising and lowering, twisting and turning, shaking, bouncing, circling, and others.

Manipulative Skills

Manipulative skills are defined as those skills employed when the child handles some kind of a play object. Most of these involve the hands and feet, but other parts of the body can be used also. Manipulative objects lead to better hand-eye and foot-eye coordination.

Propulsion (throwing, batting, kicking), volleying (redirecting an object that already is in flight), and receipt (catching) of objects are important elements to be developed using beanbags and a variety of balls.

Control of an object such as a wand or hoop also has a place in manipulative activity. Manipulative activities are the basis of the related game skills, so important in the lives of children.

Specialized Skills

These are the skills related to the various sports and other physical education areas such as apparatus, tumbling, dance, and specific games. In the development of specialized skills, progression is obtained through planned instruction and drills. Many of the specialized skills have critical points of technique, with a heavy emphasis on conformance. Specialized skills are of little importance in the K-2 program and begin to appear in the third grade.

DEFINING MOVEMENT EDUCATION

The term "movement education" is subject to different interpretations and definitions. Some people hold that the term refers to the newer methodology employing problem-solving techniques emphasizing individual response and stressing exploration, choice, and creativity. Such terms as "basic movement," "movement education," "movement exploration," and "educational movement" can, therefore, be used interchangeably. Others hold that "movement education" has a broader meaning. The author agrees with those who define movement education broadly, as the sum of all the child's experiences in movement.

Movement education has also been defined as learning to move and moving to learn. This makes it somewhat synonymous with the term "physical education."

If one accepts the broad concept of movement education, then another term must be applied to the problem-solving approach or the "indirect method," as it is sometimes called, since this can now be regarded as a part of the overall concept of movement education. While the designation "the indirect method" has some acceptance, a better and more appropriate term would be "basic movement."

What, then, is included in the "sum of all

the child's experiences in movement"? What instructional approaches can be effectively utilized in helping a child attain movement competency as defined earlier? What can each approach contribute to the functional whole of movement education?

Movement education can be divided into four instructional approaches, each of which has a unique and important function in the attainment of overall movement competency. These are:

1. Basic Movement.
2. The Skills Instructional Program.
3. Posture and Body Mechanics.
4. Perceptual-Motor Competency.

Each has its place in the program of physical education, depending upon the particular kind of skill or type of body management competency to be developed. In practice, the methods are often combined to arrive at the most effective instructional procedure. The following analysis of the purposes of each will indicate how each relates to the whole of movement education:

Basic Movement

Provide opportunity for the child to explore, create, and consolidate.

Structure an environment which stimulates the child to think. Develop the child's versatility in movement, including the development of good body management skills.

Allow each child the element of self-direction so he can work at his own pace governed by the limits of his own potential. Provide a foundation of basic movement skills, upon which specialized skills of later years are built.

The Skills Instructional Program

Provide sequential instructional procedures with drills and repetition of movement leading to the acquisition of both basic and specialized skills.

Provide a means by which children can learn critical skills of sports and games with emphasis on the "how" and "why" of known techniques.

Posture and Body Mechanics

Stimulate the child to the achievement of good body alignment and carriage.

Give opportunity for correct body mechanics as the child goes about his daily living tasks.

Perceptual-Motor Competency

Provide consideration in the physical education program for such perceptual-motor competencies as balance, laterality, directionality, and others considered important qualities for children.

Further discussion of each of the above four terms follows.

BASIC MOVEMENT

The key to the entire approach of basic movement is the incorporation somewhere in the methodology of the factor of self-selection, the opportunity for the child to be creative. If choice is eliminated, then the process becomes direct teaching, the traditional approach to teaching. The degree of choice, the degree of opportunity for self-discovery, indicates the extent to which basic movement concepts are employed in the learning experiences for the child. True and pure basic movement would permit the child to select for himself the activity in which he would like to participate, the apparatus (hand or large) he would like to use, and the movement experiences he would like to undergo.

At times this approach of broad choice may be of value, but for more practical purposes the teacher must place certain limitations on the type of activity the child experiences. While in movement language this is termed as "setting a limitation" for the problem to be solved, in actuality this is a direct command (direct teaching) establishing the extent to which the child may move. Within the limitation so set, the child has the opportunity for self-discovery, self-education, exploration, and problem-solving. Within the goal of the teacher to assist each child attain the maximum development possible for that child, the teacher may use methods ranging throughout the entire spectrum of direct to indirect teaching. The question for the teacher is not whether or not basic movement should be employed, but the degree to which learning experiences should be so organized. Whenever possible, the child should be encouraged to experiment, create, and explore. He should be directed to apply his knowledge in many different situations in movement.

Characteristics of Basic Movement

The element of self-selection is paramount in basic movement. An opportunity for experimentation, exploration, and self-discovery must be included. This ranges from exploration within precise and narrow limitations to opportunity for children to make choices of activity and the approach they wish to follow. It is the responsibility of the teacher to set the stage and create situations which challenge the child to develop his resources of movement. The teacher no longer dominates the lesson, but stimulates the children to use their ideas to plan different ways to carry out the movement experiences. Each child is encouraged to make what contributions he can to the whole. Since children have a desire to express themselves physically, as well as in other ways, satisfaction of this desire can only be obtained if the children have a measure of choice and an opportunity to exercise individuality.

Because the child expresses himself individually in movement, he can achieve a satisfactory measure of success *for himself* as opposed to teacher-dominated or group standards. The child progresses according to his innate abilities, stimulated by the teacher and the learning situation. No child need feel awkward or self-conscious because he doesn't measure up to predetermined standards. The fact that children differ in size, shape, maturity, and motor ability does not preclude success and satisfaction. The child makes progress according to his own rate and to his satisfaction.

There is deeper aim in basic movement in that it seeks to develop the child's awareness not only of *what* he is doing, but also of *how* he is moving to do it. By this it is hoped to have the children appreciate their own ability and make better interpretation of their movement patterns. The process then becomes the acquisition of movement experiences rather than an accumulation of knowledge or subject matter. Each child should be given the opportunity to succeed in his own way according to his own capacity. There is value not only in the accomplishment of the child, but also in the manner by which he reaches this accomplishment. The teacher attempts to establish a learning experience by which the child is stimulated to think.

Basic movement methodology is presented in Chapter 10 on page 102 together with suggested movement experiences.

Some Observations About Basic Movement

It should be emphasized that a great deal of the teacher must go into the process of basic movement. To make movement purposeful and guide children toward maximum growth and development so that desirable progress can be made requires a knowledge of children and of the learning process. The teacher who labors under the misconception that he can retire into the background after the children have chosen the activity has completely missed the point of movement methodology. This practice will not bring out good variety, let alone quality in movement. It is necessary for the teacher to approach the lesson with a plan concerning the kinds of things which are to be done; the tasks, problems, or approaches to be used; and the methods of guidance, together with stress factors of importance to be considered. The lesson plan should include consideration not only for providing variety of responses, but procedures for improving the quality in movement.

Another point of contention in movement methodology is the question of how much direction should precede the introduction of a movement pattern. Some hold that every child must *first* have a chance to try out the movement pattern or skill in his own way until he has gotten the feeling of it and has experienced the difficulties and the challenges. How strictly this rule might be applied probably should be governed by the type of activity or skill. A blanket rule is not educationally sound because it deprives the teacher of his right of individual approach.

This premise is supported in the national position paper, *Essentials of a Quality School Physical Education Program.**

"To deal effectively with the whole child, many styles of teaching must be brought to bear on the learning situation. These include both teacher-directed and self-directed learning. If learning is to be personalized and con-

---

*AAHPER (Washington, 1970), p. 12.

cerned with the cognitive and affective domains, problem-solving as a teaching strategy becomes vital."

The maturity level of the children has a critical effect on the choice of method. The lower the age of the children, the more dominant the problem solving, exploratory approach should be.

Today so much emphasis is placed on the basic movement method as the "educational method" and on the benefits of choice, self-discovery, and exploration that some teachers feel they are out-of-date and wrong if they are not employing basic movement, at least in part. Emphasis should be placed upon the right of the teacher to *determine* the best approach.

A question arises about the relationship of basic movement to the development of physical fitness. When a child chooses his activity and how he will carry out the problem, how can it be assured that there will be sufficient vigorous big-muscle activity so that the major elements of physical fitness (strength, power, and endurance) will receive proper attention? In addition, how can it be assured that all areas of the body, particularly the arm-shoulder girdle and the abdominal wall, will receive proper development? It is unsound to substitute movement exploration with its stress on choice, variety, and educational concepts for developmental activities pointed toward the physical development of the child. *Both* developmental activities and basic movement can and should be included in the program.

One problem in the guidance and directive process leading to quality in movement is that group instruction becomes difficult if the children are engaged in different activities or on different pieces of apparatus. With a variety of activities, instruction becomes an individual process, limiting the effectiveness of the teacher. He can hardly center his attention on one or two children when all should be considered. This becomes even more difficult when the teacher feels that he must center his efforts on the one piece of apparatus which needs attention because of potential safety hazards.

An element of basic movement which is of concern to a number of educators is the premise that children are free to choose and free to respond in the manner they wish and at their own rate. It is postulated that allowing children to do only those things they choose and in the manner they choose is not desirable social training. Few real life situations are based on this premise. To counterbalance this attitude, the teacher can include certain required activities regardless of whether or not the children approve. Children from homes where they are permitted considerable freedom often meet with problems in the school situation where more conformance is required.

Movement Exploration

Some clarification of the term "Movement Exploration" is needed. Exploration implies a degree of choice of response, experimentation, and exploration. It refers to a type of methodology and not to an area of content in physical education. The employment of exploratory activity is most important in basic movement. It has an application even in direct teaching techniques when an appropriate opportunity is used for experimentation and exploration. The idea of trying out this or that to discover which is more valuable or useful is an excellent reinforcement of learning.

Some physical educators tend to regard movement exploration as a different kind of physical education, while in reality it provides another valuable method of attaining the goals of physical education. Within the framework of instruction, it is important that children have an opportunity to try out different ways and approaches to learning skills.

THE SKILLS INSTRUCTIONAL PROGRAM

The skills instruction program provides instruction in both basic and specialized skills. The approach is more concerned with direct (command) teaching, with predetermined goals in mind as a result of the teaching process. This does not rule out exploratory activity, as experimentation and exploration should be utilized within the concept of good technique.

This latter concept of flexibility and freedom is important. A combination of direction and freedom of movement response, labeled by the English as the "Limitation Method," is an important directive in the instructional process.

The emphasis is on the "how" and "why" of the known techniques, with drills and repetition of specific movements as the basis of the learning process. Skills should be based on sound techniques. It is important to avoid simply exposing the child to a skill and trusting to providence for results. Instructors need to know well the skills they are teaching. Demonstration is important in the skills teaching process, in contrast to basic movement, where the ideas originate mostly from the children.

POSTURE AND BODY MECHANICS

Posture and Body Mechanics have an important part in movement education.

Posture refers to the habitual or assumed alignment and balance of the body segments while standing, walking, sitting, or lying. In good posture, these parts are in proper relation to each other, and their good balance is reflected in ease, gracefulness, poise, and efficiency of carriage and bearing.

Correct use of the body is called good body mechanics and has its basis in good posture. How to lift and carry objects, open windows, go up and down stairs, climb ladders, and pull or push are examples of simple activities which need application of good principles of body mechanics.

Consideration of posture and body mechanics in movement education should be from two standpoints. First, direct instruction in posture and body mechanics should at times be included in the program. Secondly, good standards of posture and body mechanics should be an overriding concern for all physical activity and movement. No matter how the child moves, postural considerations should be a guiding factor.

Posture is dependent primarily upon the strength of the muscles which hold the body in balance against the force of gravity. These muscles work continually and require sufficient strength and energy to hold the body in correct alignment.

However, in good posture from a mechanical standpoint, the musculature must be balanced and hold the bones and joints in proper position and provide a basis for efficient movement. Faulty alignment can cause undue strain on supporting muscles and ligaments, leading to early fatigue, muscle strain, and progressive displacement of postural support. In extreme cases, pain may result and the position and function of vital organs, primarily abdominal, can be impaired.

It needs to be recognized early by the teacher *and* child that the maintenance of good posture is a positive act and has its basis primarily in the practice of good postural habits. The teacher needs to be concerned not only with faulty posture, but also with the causes underlying this condition. Physical abnormalities such as poor vision and hearing, deformities, and even disease cause postural problems. Children who lack energy and fatigue easily become prone to postural slumps. Proper clothing and shoes are a consideration for good carriage. Emotional factors are important, as the bearing of an individual reflects his emotional outlook.

Anatomical and Physiological Principles Affecting Posture

A better understanding of postural conditions can be established with an examination of some basic physiological facts which have bearing on posture problems.

The body, the wonderful mechanism it is, adjusts to the exterior forces applied to it. Unfortunately, this is true with regard to poor posture. With elementary school children, poor posture may just be a habitual position. But, as the child matures, this becomes a growth characteristic. The result is that the muscles which activate the joints, of necessity, adapt both in length and function to the faulty positions of the body segments.

Further breakdown occurs when the body is slumped continuously. The vital organs are compressed and crowded out of position and bones are forced out of alignment. Postural conditions which were once remediable in the elementary school now become structural, with more difficult correction. Early attention to posture will yield large dividends.

For every set of muscles having a specific movement, there is another group with an opposite action. There must be balance to the power of these antagonistic muscle groups, particularly in those keeping the body in alignment. If one set of muscles is markedly stronger than the other, the resultant elastic pull and possible shortening causes an imbalance at the joint concerned. An example of this is in the muscle groups governing the position of the shoulders. The chest muscles exert force to pull the shoulder blades forward, tending to round shoulders, and the upper back postural muscles must counteract this influence with sufficient development. A second example concerns the lower back curve which can be kept in check with a strong abdominal wall working against the lower back muscles.

In addition to the opposing muscle pull, the postural muscles have the force of gravity to overcome. If posture is poor, this gravitational force becomes stronger, and, coupled with the opposing muscle pull, causes the muscles holding body alignment to weaken and stretch.

Flexibility should be sufficient to permit the child to assume good postural positioning without excessive effort or strain. A short, tight muscle group, lacking enough flexibility, can exert sufficient pull at a joint to make it difficult for the child to assume good posture.

Muscles exhibit another characteristic important in postural considerations. This is the development of muscle tone, defined as a slight degree of tension or contraction. Muscle tone is important because it aids in holding the body in correct skeletal alignment. If muscles are weak, flabby, and underdeveloped, tone is lacking and posture suffers. Good tone is a characteristic of a healthy, conditioned muscle.

From the standpoint of body structure, the slope or tilt of the pelvis is a critical point. The vertebral column is composed of small bones, called vertebrae, which form a number of natural curves governing body contour. The foundation of the vertebral column rests on the pelvis, forming a joint with very little movement. With correct tilt of the pelvis, the body contours can be natural and graceful. If the front of the pelvis is tilted down, the lower back curve becomes exaggerated, causing swayback which can vary from slight to pronounced. Some curvature in the lumbar region (lower back) is natural. Correct tilt will aid in flattening both a protruding abdomen and a prominent seat. Incorrect tilt in the standing position of an individual has a tendency to force the upper legs back, with attendant hyperextension of the knee joint.

However, some caution must be observed in interpreting this relevant to preschool children. Many preschool children exhibit a prominent abdomen and an exaggerated lumbar curve (lumbar lordosis), which can be regarded as normal. Some knock-knees may be carried over from early childhood growth patterns. The teacher must work on the basis that good posture is the result of a healthy, vigorous child, and these characteristics of childhood will mediate with a good program as the years pass. Lack of physical vigor may cause them to become undesirable growth attributes in later years of the elementary school.

Young children during early development tend to point the toes out to afford a more stable base. The child should have attention directed in his early years of movement experiences to the values of having the feet pointed forward in standing posture, walking, and assuming different postures in work and play. This principle is reflected in the descriptions and instructions which follow.

What the Teacher Can Do

Teachers must include in their lesson plans and administrative practices specific attention to good body mechanics and posture. Careful planning is needed if good posture is to result. But, in this area, teachers are not to regard themselves as corrective specialists. They can, however, help children form desirable postural patterns and acquire good habits in the many postures assumed. There are a number of factors to which the teacher can give attention in working with youngsters for better posture and body mechanics.

1. The first and most important objective is to provide motivation for good posture. There must be a development of understanding and appreciation of good posture through pictures, posters, demonstrations, and other media so that the youngster consciously develops within himself the desire for a body in good alignment.

2. A program of vigorous physical activities to strengthen muscles that hold the body correctly is needed. The program should include especially designed muscular development (fitness) activities and broad movement experiences, as well as rugged, demanding games, stunts and tumbling, and rhythmics.

3. A planned program of instruction in the basic skills of locomotion, work, and play should be instituted as a part of the physical education program with definite time apportionment and definite goals on each grade level.

4. A healthful school environment is needed with particular attention to proper seating, good lighting, avoidance of overfatigue, and elimination of tension.

5. The removal and correction of health conditions which contribute to poor posture are a necessity. Cooperation between home, school, and physician in this program is essential.

6. The teacher must give attention to such emotional factors as discouragement, feelings of inferiority, consciousness of an unattractive appearance beyond the power of the individual to change. Children with fears, timidities, and other feelings of insecurity often reflect these inner states in postural positions.

7. The teacher needs to accept the concept that good posture is a practice and not a subject. Even in the most simple movements and position, postural problems are continuously present. The teacher should introduce and teach good postural habits, particularly as related to activities the children are learning. Children should be given a word of encouragement or advice as reminders for good practice. The teacher needs to be able to recognize good posture and deviations from the normal.

8. The rigid military type of posture is not the goal of normal living. While the service academies at West Point, Annapolis, and Colorado Springs find this useful, it has little part in the posture picture of the elementary school child.

9. The teacher should be an example of good body mechanics and posture. It is important not only that the children have a good example to follow, but also that the teacher be able to endure the demands of classroom teaching with less fatigue.

10. The teacher should refer the student to the nurse, physical education specialist, principal, or other appropriate agencies for help in problem posture cases. After a corrective program has been set up, the teacher's part is in cooperating with the program and guiding the youngster in fulfilling his prescribed corrective work.

What Is Good Posture?

Posture varies with the individual's sex, age, and body type, and what is proper posture for one individual may not be suitable for another. However, the basic components for posture are much the same for all children. These are illustrated by the following chart.

POSTURE TYPES

GOOD POSTURE

FAIR POSTURE

POOR POSTURE

MOVEMENT EDUCATION 57

Good Posture	Fair Posture	Poor Posture
Head up, chin in, head balanced above the shoulders with the tip of the ear directly above the point of the shoulders	Head forward slightly	Head noticeably forward, eyes generally down
Shoulders back and easy with the chest up	Chest lowered slightly	Chest flat or depressed
Lower abdomen in and flat	Lower abdomen in but not flat	Shoulder blades show winged effects
Slight and normal curves in the upper and lower back	Back curves increased slightly	Abdomen relaxed and prominent
Knees easy	Knees back slightly	Back curves exaggerated beyond normal
Weight properly placed with toes pointed forward	Weight a little too far back on heels	Knees forced back in back-kneed position
		Pelvis noticeably tilted down
		Weight improperly distributed

Directions for Assuming Good Posture in Standing Position

Feet. Toes are pointed straight ahead, weight evenly distributed on balls of feet and the heels. Cue by saying "Feet forward! Point feet straight ahead! Feet parallel! Weight off heels!" The feet should be parallel and from 2" to 4" apart.

Knees. Knees should be relaxed and easy. Avoid the back-kneed position where the knee joint is held forcibly back as far as it can go. Remind the children: "Knees easy! Knees relaxed!"

Lower Back and Abdomen. The abdominal wall should be flattened but relaxed. The lower back curve should be natural and not exaggerated. Children can be told: "Tuck your seat under! Flatten your tummy! Push the body up, tummy in! Flatten lower back! Hips under!"

Upper Body. The shoulders should be back and relaxed and the shoulder blades flat. Chest should be up and raised. Give them directions like: "Shoulders easy! Shoulder blades flat! Lift chest! Chest high!"

Neck and Head. The head should be up and chin in. Neck should be back. The ear should be directly over the point of the shoulder. Say: "Chin in! Head high! Stand tall! Stretch tall! Chin easy!"

Lateral Deviations in Posture

The discussion of posture to this point has been concerned mostly with the forward-backward plane of movement. The body must also be in balance in the lateral plane. From a structural standpoint, when viewed from the front or rear, a perpendicular line should divide the body into two symmetrical or equal halves. If parts of one-half of the body cross over this line, there is an unnatural curvature. Again, habit plays a part. The position may be due to faulty practices. A shift of the head may be caused by either visual or hearing problems or both. Uneven shape or size of the bones, particularly the leg bones, will cause the pelvis to tilt laterally, with a compensating curvature of the spinal column.

The presence of lateral curvature can be determined by a check on the level of the pelvis, whether or not the shoulders are even, or if the head has a tilt to either side. It is estimated that about 50 per cent of the population have a lateral tilt to some degree.

Faulty habits contributing to this condition are standing on one leg, leaning against a support, and sitting improperly.

Lateral deviations which need attention are generally beyond the scope of the teacher, even the physical education specialist. Referral to proper medical attention is the recommended procedure.

Good Walking Posture

Good walking posture begins with proper use of the feet. It is vitally important that the feet point forward and stay nearly parallel for best functional use. A person who walks with toes pointed out is subject to considerable strain in the arch and lower ankle, leading to a breakdown of the arch and lower leg structure. The heel should touch first in a step, with the weight transferred quickly to the balls of the feet and to the toes for a push-off.

The legs should swing freely from the hips with the knees bent enough to clear the feet from the floor.

The arms should swing in opposition to the legs, the body should retain the properties of good standing posture, and the eyes should be focused on a point on the floor 50' to 60' ahead.

Proper Sitting Posture

The knee joint should form a right angle, the feet flat on the floor and pointed generally forward. The hips should be back against the chair and the body erect. Forward movement in a working position should occur mostly from the hip joint, with the head, upper body, and pelvis remaining in good balance.

Evaluating Posture

Since it is a responsibility of the elementary school teacher to detect and refer bodily conditions needing attention, some program of posture evaluation must be established. Evaluation can be done through observation, both formal and informal, and measurement devices. The discussion will cover only those methods which classroom teachers can find practical and usable.

Formal Observation. Posture screening can be accomplished through a rating device which allows the teacher to check segments of the body and note the condition with respect to postural standards. The following simplified rating sheet is useful for making checks.

POSTURE CHECK SHEET

Name_____ Grade_____ School_____
Date_____ Check made by_____

SIDE VIEW
Head
    Erect, chin in_____ Somewhat forward_____ Markedly forward_____
Upper Back
    Shoulders back_____ Slightly rounded_____ Round shoulders_____
Lower Back
    Slight natural curve_____ Moderate curve_____ Hollow back_____
Abdomen
    Flat_____ Slight protrusion_____ Protruding_____
Knees
    Relaxed_____ Slightly back_____ Hyperextended_____
Feet
    Pointed ahead_____ Somewhat out_____ Pointed out_____

FRONT AND BACK VIEW
Shoulders
    Level_____ Slightly uneven_____ Considerably uneven_____
Hips
    Level_____ Slightly uneven_____ Considerably uneven_____
Back of Ankles and Feet
    Heel and ankle straight_____ Turned out somewhat_____ Pronated_____
Remarks

The individual form lends itself better to interpretation by parents and administrators. The class form is more adaptable for class analysis and comparisons. Each item can be rated 1, 2, and 3 on an ascending scale. By averaging the rating numbers, it is possible to come out with a mean rating for each child.

Some formal type of organization is needed.

The teacher may prefer a single sheet including all of the class. Such a sheet could be organized as follows.

POSTURE CHECK

Class_____ School_____
Date_____ Teacher_____

		Side View					Front and Back View			
Code		Head and Neck	Upper Back	Lower Back	Abdomen	Knees	Feet	Level of Shoulders	Level of Hips	Feet and Ankles	Remarks
Meets good postural standards	1										
Slight but definite deviation	2										
Marked deviation	3										
Name											
1.											
2.											
3.											

Children can be examined five or six at a time. While it does present some difficulties, a better posture evaluation can be made if the children are in gym clothing or swim suits. Any formal posture evaluation is an analysis of an assumed posture and not necessarily the one the child uses in daily living.

Informal Observation. Postural checks can be made of young people when they are participating in classroom and physical education activities. How does he walk, stand, or sit when he is not conscious of an observer? The teacher can make notes and supplement the formal posture check.

The Plumb Line Method. A plumb line can be used for a practical check of body alignment. The plumb line should hang freely. The student stands so the plumb line is between him and the observer, positioned so the line bisects the instep. The plumb line should go through the tip of the ear, the point of the shoulder, the point of the hip, just back of the knee cap, and the middle of the instep. Divergencies from the line can be checked and noted.

The Ear-Shoulder Method. The ear-shoulder method is based on the plumb line method and the principle that if one part of the body is out of line, another part compensates in the opposite direction to provide body balance. This would mean then that if the head were forward, there would be other parts of the body protruding to counterbalance the first poor alignment. If we measure the degree the head is forward, then we have an estimate of general posture.

Other Methods. The use of pictures or silhouettes to check posture is expensive and time-consuming, but is effective. It has more use on the high school and college level because of the availability of specialized physical education personnel and facilities.

The Feeling of Good Posture

Every child needs to "feel" when he is in good posture. The wall or door method provides an easy check which the child can use at home. The child places himself with his heels against a flat wall which has no floor molding. A flat door can also be used. The child stands with his heels, calves of the legs, seat, elbows, shoulders, and back of the head touching the surfaces. He walks away maintaining this position without tenseness or

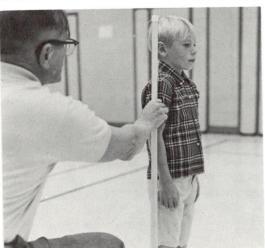

strain. The wall position is exaggerated but has value in aiding the child in getting the feeling of proper alignment.

A posture walk can be done by using the wall position. A tom-tom can give the signals. When the tom-tom begins to beat, the children walk away from the wall in good walking posture. On a loud thump the children abruptly change direction, continuing the walk. When the beat is changed to a fast beat, the children shuffle rapidly to the nearest wall and stand in the wall posture position.

A second method of providing a kinesthetic feel is to have the child take a deep breath, lifting up his chest while at the same time tucking the pelvis under. Have him release the air but maintain the lifted position without tenseness.

A method to aid the shoulders to be back in proper position is to rotate the thumbs outward (arms at the sides) as far as they will go, at the same time bringing the shoulders back and flattening out the abdominal wall. Release the contraction in the arms but keep the shoulders back and the abdomen flat.

Exercises for Posture

A rounded program of vigorous activities coupled with hanging, climbing, and other activities which use the arms to support the body weight is helpful in strengthening the antigravity muscles of the body. However, at times, the teacher may wish to use special exercises, strengthening areas which generally need attention from the standpoint of body alignment.

HEAD-SHOULDER-UPPER BACK DEVELOPMENT

SWAN EXERCISE

Position: Prone lying (face down), arms extended sideward with palms down.

Movement: Raise upper back, head, and arms in an exaggerated swan dive position. The chin is kept in and the movement is limited to the upper back. Hold for two counts. Repeat 8 or 10 times. Confine movement to upper back *only*.

TAILOR EXERCISE

Position: Sit tailor fashion (cross-legged) with trunk erect and locked fingers on middle of back of head, elbows out.

Movement: Force head and elbows back slowly against pressure. Repeat 10 to 15 times. Be sure that there is no change in the erect body position.

ABDOMINAL MUSCLES

PARTIAL CURL-UP

Position: On back with feet flat and knees bent, with hands flat down on top of thighs.

Movement: Leading with the chin, slide the hands forward until the fingers touch the kneecaps, lifting the head, shoulders, and upper body from the floor. Hold for two counts and then return to position. Repeat 10 to 15 times.

CURL-UP

Position: On back with feet flat and knees bent. Instep should be held by a helper. Hands are placed at side with palms down.

Movement: Rise to sitting position with arms extended at shoulder height. Keep head well back. Hold for four counts. Repeat 10 to 15 times.

ROWING

Position: Lie on back with arms overhead.

Movement: Sit up, bringing knees to chest and holding firm. Arms are parallel to the floor and pointing beyond the knees. Repeat 10 to 15 times. Use slow rhythm.

CURL-UP WITH TWIST

Position: On back with feet flat and knees bent. Toes should be held by a helper. Fingers are clasped behind the head.

Movement: Curl-up and touch the right knee with the left elbow. Repeat, alternating elbows. Repeat 10 to 15 times. The movement should be in the abdominal region.

FEET

FLOOR SCRATCHING (Sand Scraping)

Position: Sitting or standing, feet flat on floor.

Movement: Using the toes, scratch the floor by bringing the toes toward you forcibly on the floor. Repeat 10 to 15 times.

MARBLE TRANSFER

Position: Sitting on a chair or bench. A marble or a wadded piece of paper is needed.

Movement: Pick up the marble with the right foot and bring it up to the left hand. Transfer the marble to the right hand and bring up the left foot to put the marble back on the ground. Repeat 8 to 12 times.

KNOT TYING WITH FEET

Position: Standing.

Movement: Lay a jumping rope on the floor. Tie a knot in the rope using one foot only. Repeat with the other foot.

FOOT CARRY

Position: Standing.

Movement: A piece of rope or narrow felt tied in a loop about 1' in diameter is to be carried. The child grasps the loop with the toes of one foot and hops a short distance. He repeats changing the loop to the other foot.

Perceptual-Motor Competency and the Slow Learner

During the last decade, the growth of perceptual-motor programs for the slow learner has made an important impact on physical education programs. The programs were originally for the slow learner and the neurologically handicapped, but, if the theories are valid, they have value for all children, whether or not they have learning disabilities.

Good scientific basis for the perceptual-motor programs has not been forthcoming, but substantiation of program effectiveness comes from empirical judgments and observation. However, there is enough indication from current programs to warrant consideration of perceptual-motor principles as they affect the physical education program.

It is not the purpose of this guide to discuss perceptual-motor programs as separate programs or entities. Discussion will concern only how physical education programs can benefit from accepted perceptual-motor principles and activities. This discussion is found in Chapter 11.

7 Effective Class Management

The Role of the Teacher
Guiding the Learning Process
Instructional Procedures
Teaching Aids in Physical Education

The purpose of effective class management is to structure an efficient and effective instructional environment so that the child may realize his potential in educational progress and achieve educational outcomes deemed appropriate for him. In relation to physical education, this concept can be broken down into three broad outcomes.

The Acquisition of New Elements of Learning

The child has opportunity to acquire new movement skills, knowledges, attitudes, and concepts.

Improvement and Consolidation of Learned Elements Deemed Desirable

What the child has that is good should be reinforced, consolidated, and expanded so it becomes a part of his personal heritage.

Lessening and Elimination of Undesirable Learned Elements

In this area, the teacher needs to aid the child to rid himself of things which get in the way of his learning and cause conflict in his personal living. Substitution of the desirable for the undesirable is the key to this learning situation.

It is quite obvious that physical education activity not only is an end in itself, but also is a learning environment for the achievement of other educational outcomes. It is equally apparent, then, that the teacher is the key factor in implementing the achievement of a broad range of objectives now thought to be within the potential of physical education.

THE ROLE OF THE TEACHER

It is the teacher's responsibility to develop an instructional atmosphere that will be in keeping with the stated purposes of the school physical education curriculum. First and foremost, the teacher must possess the conviction that physical education is an important educational medium for the child's optimum development not only in the physical area, but also in many other aspects of learning. To believe in physical education is the first essential for successful teaching.

Closely allied to this viewpoint is a second basic premise. The teacher needs to recognize that physical education is largely an instructional program and as such needs planning. A well-executed lesson is a joy for the children and a source of pleasure for the teacher.

The role of the teacher is that of a leader, not a dictator. Helpfulness, friendliness, respect for the dignity of the individual are qualities needed to assure that children will derive maximum benefit from their experiences. The teacher needs to talk with and listen to children in contrast to merely talking to them. The democratic process can be an instrument of direction in physical education.

This is even more true in today's physical education with its "new look," where the teacher teaches the child and not the activity. Children demonstrate much variation in their rates of progress and derive different sets of values from activity. However, in some ways they are very much the same and travel a common path of growth and development. This allows the teacher to select activities of a central core for the class, but consideration for individual differences remains important. It is not a sound practice to set the same standards for all children.

The interaction of children with their peers in an activity situation provides a fruitful opportunity to observe them in the interchanges with each other in a social setting. Helpful knowledge can be garnered about children. Intelligent observation is also needed to assess the learning situation and inject hints, suggestions, and guidelines, stimulating the child to greater variety and better quality of movement.

The teacher can learn from the students. Rather than attempting to provide all the guidelines for activity development, the teacher should seek the aid of the children to expand development in an activity area or help provide direction for the lesson.

The teacher should be a reasonable example of the health and physical fitness dictums that the school is attempting to promote. Elderly teachers may feel that this would be a difficult standard to meet. However, the teacher should be free of glaring departures from what are considered good healthful practices.

Children tend to imitate those whom they admire and respect. The teacher needs to be certain that his personal example will not lay the basis for improper habits or attitudes. Teachers should be appropriately dressed for physical education teaching, at least to the extent of having proper footwear.

The teacher is the key to the learning situation. The degree of control, the quality of the instructional procedures, and the response of the children are inherent in the personality of the teacher. Whether physical education is a quality educational experience or just glorified free play is determined by the teacher's approach.

GUIDING THE LEARNING PROCESS

Having elaborated on the elements of learning, the role of the teacher, and other physical education conceptual factors, we can now turn our attention to the task of teaching the child. This will involve a discussion first of general principles of education designed to promote optimum learning, and then of more class-related instructional procedures in physical education, categorized into a number of subdivisions.

General Educational Considerations

Three requisites are important in the learning process. The first is that the child be capable of learning what is presented. The second is that the child have the level of motivation necessary so learning can be accomplished. The third is that the environment be so structured that learning can follow an orderly process and take place.

Capability

Capability simply means that the learning task is within the capacity of the child, that he is capable of doing what he is expected to do. Many factors affect capability, among them maturation level, physique, state of physical fitness, previous experience, and personality factors. The physical and neural levels of competency should be such that the child can achieve a good measure of success in performing the tasks with which he is presented.

Capability can be modified by appropriate experience in movement. A child should move from one level to another with experiences which are consistent and progressive. It is not educationally sound to teach children softball when their throwing and catching skills are not up to the level required for the game.

Good body management skills lead to good basic skills, which in turn are the basis of specialized skills. The teacher may need to "back up" in the activity until a point is reached where the children can handle the prescribed chores. Expansion *within activity* may be the indicated approach rather than too much progression up the ladder of challenge. The teacher must start at the children's level of competence and move forward from that point. If the lowest level of the activity does not meet this criterion of capability, then the activity is not a suitable educational experience.

If a child can handle the activity and meet with success, he is capable of progress. If he experiences intense frustration, learning will either move in undesirable channels or be cut off almost entirely. It is frustrating and a waste of effort to attempt to teach children on a level which is beyond their capacity.

However, with very young children, there is another factor involved in the concept of capability. For preschool children we need not only to foster the learning they are capable of, but also to "learn" them to learn.

Motivation and Readiness to Learn

Capability infers that the child can learn. Being motivated means that he wants to and is ready to learn. Capability has both a physical and neural basis, while motivation centers on psychological drives. The learner must have a need, some kind of a drive to action, or little learning will take place. Children must want to learn.

Motivation comes from within. The task must hold personal significance for the child; he must have a "stake" in it. He must feel the necessity to become involved, and that involvement must be of sufficient depth.

Physical education itself carries motivation for the child. The teacher can see the faces of the children light up when he tells them it is time for physical education period. They go to the activity area with an aura of expectancy. To satisfy this drive for activity and skim off some of the energy, introductory activities (Chapter 8) are educationally sound.

Another critical motivational factor is the teacher-image projected to the children. If the teacher is prepared, enthusiastic, and positive in his approach, some of this feeling is bound to rub off on the children. The teacher needs to demonstrate in his behavior many of the characteristics he expects from the children. The process of identification with an appropriate model, in this case the teacher, is a mechanism of high importance.

The children should be included, at times, in the planning, capitalizing on the premise that those who participate in the planning are more likely to support the activities. This forms a preset-in expectancy, as they know what they will receive in the lesson which follows. This, however, can cause children to react negatively, as they may reject a program prematurely which they feel they will not like.

The eagerness and expectancy that our young people have for physical education should be exploited. This initial motivation and readiness should be maintained through appropriate reinforcement and feedback.

Maintaining Readiness to Learn — Feedback and Reinforcement

Feedback and reinforcement can be effective in modifying the learning process and maintaining receptiveness to learning. Unfortunately, detrimental effects can appear if feedback is unpleasant or negative. Feedback refers to the impressions, feelings, or concepts a child derives from the learning experiences in which he engages. Reinforcement implies a strengthening, a consolidation, a shoring-up of learning, as a result of feedback.

First of all, children should find enjoyment and pleasure from participation in physical education. Learning is facilitated when children enjoy what they are doing.

The child should experience the consequence of his actions, that is, accomplish something. The learner builds confidence when he meets with success and is ready to move to higher achievements. The learning situation should be such that each child can attain a measure of success. Success should vary with children, as they progress at different rates and attain success differently.

A related postulate is that reasonable goals should be set for the child which are within his power to reach. Children are stimulated when they have a target goal which is both challenging and attainable. Somewhere the child needs to get the feeling that he has met the challenge and "I did it!"

Include in instruction the reason for doing things; teach not only the "how" but also the "why." Children learn more readily when they know the "why" of an activity. This attaches significance to the procedure and gives it a personal value to the learner.

Children thrive on praise and encouragement, as the positive approach is more meaningful to them than negative comments. With students who have problems involving confidence, this becomes increasingly important. The feedback comes from the child's urge to seek status through approval, which is reflected in the comments of the teacher. Encouragement can help the child to progress by indicating to him that he is on the right track. It can overcome fear of failure. This is particularly important in programs for young children.

From a negative viewpoint, children sometimes react violently to a traumatic experience in physical education to the point of strong antipathy or even withdrawal. Deep psychological hurt can be caused by sarcasm, biting comments, slurs, and embarrassing situations.

INSTRUCTIONAL PROCEDURES

Some reference has been made to teaching procedures in the preceding material, particularly with respect to feedback and reinforcement. Instructional procedures applicable to a broad range of activities are presented here. Procedures relevant to specific activity areas are treated in the respective sections for each activity area.

Working with Children

1. See that each child has an opportunity to be active in the learning situation. Self-activity is the basis of physical learning and — for that matter — all learning. There should be sufficient equipment so that there can be individual activity. In group work, the children should be divided into small enough groups so there is little waiting for turns. Standing, watching, and waiting should be kept to a minimum.

2. Involve all children in the program, including the handicapped, the overweight, and the unskilled.

3. The child who does not participate, who is not accepted by the group, or whose ineptness does not allow him much success needs special consideration to help him find himself. Give him tasks in which he can succeed or can achieve status in the eyes of his fellow students.

4. Beware of activities which tend to eliminate slow or unskilled children. Those eliminated usually are the ones who need the activity the most. Get eliminated children back into activity fast. Use this type of organization sparingly.

5. Give children opportunity for exploratory and creative activity. Children need an opportunity to try out their own ideas, solve some of their own movement problems, and bring forth movement of their own origin. Teachers need to take advantage of this drive by providing opportunity for the child to come up with his own movement ideas.

6. Get children into activity as quickly as possible.

7. Children love to run at times for the sheer zest of activity. Provide time in the program for this basic drive.

8. If children are assigned as leaders, give them an actual opportunity to lead. Give children all the responsibility they can assume.

9. A class should be organized into squads, each with a leader. These are convenient groups to use for activity. Change squad composition and leaders frequently, giving all children a chance to lead if possible.

Squad Organization

10. In selecting squads or groups, use methods of selection which will not embarrass a child chosen last. In no case should this be a "slave market" type of selection, where the leaders look over the group and visibly pick whom they wish.

11. Have a designated place and formation for squad assembly. When the teacher says, "Get into squad formation," four squad columns are formed with the leader in front of his squad, and the assistant leader next. The children should be seated cross-legged with the columns far enough apart so children cannot reach each other. The formation is con-

venient for instruction and strengthens the concept of squad organization.

12. Teach respect for equipment. Children should take care of equipment as if it were their own.

13. Have a system for issuing and returning equipment. Children should handle this whenever possible.

14. Teach children to wait for instruction before using equipment they have been issued. They should receive this instruction promptly. In some cases it is well to tell the child what to get and what to do with it at the same time so that he can immediately begin to practice.

15. Devise ways of moving children easily and efficiently from one activity to another.

16. Have respect for the dignity of the child. Avoid laying hands on him, or pushing or placing him in position when he does not understand the directions.

17. Avoid overstimulation with children, particularly with younger children.

18. If facilities permit, children should change to gym clothing for activity. Better health practices result when children can also clean up properly.

19. Rubber-soled shoes or sneakers should be a requirement for indoor play, except for preschool children. Children in kindergarten and first grades may need instruction and practice in tying shoe laces. Shoes may also have to be marked so that children can distinguish right and left. One suggestion is to place the shoes flat on the floor with the inside edges together. A mark can be placed on each shoe so that the marks will come together when the shoes are placed alongside each other. This avoids the right shoe being on the left foot and vice versa.

20. Consideration for proper storage of the gym shoes is important. The child's name should be on the shoes, preferably on the outside where it can be read easily. Also, a routine for orderly arrangement of street shoes should be established, so that after the class the child can find his own shoes quickly without unnecessary scrambling.

The cooperation of the classroom teacher should be sought in helping to solve the shoe storage problem.

21. Each child should be expected to work at or near his potential. It is important that children gain the concept that success can be achieved only through good effort. The child that doesn't "put out" is selling himself short. If a teacher expects poor effort and work from a child, he will certainly get them. Children should learn to "give it a good try."

22. Have some kind of predetermined means of selecting partners, when such is indicated. Partners can be set for a period of time, with children matched according to size or some other factors.

Directing Activities

1. The teacher should use the daily lesson plan as the basis of the instruction. For the experienced teacher this can be brief. Proper coverage of material is assured only through planned lessons.

2. A major technique to be acquired is the ability to change and vary an activity so that the most value can be secured from what is chosen for learning experiences. The various ways of securing variety in movement experiences are important. Basic movement provides many ideas for extending the potential of activity. Games, relays, and stunts are activities which can be enhanced by an enterprising teacher with changes and modifications offering additional challenge to the children. Teachers should be alert for changes which can increase interest and make more physical demands of the children. The children should be a source of suggestions for change and variations.

3. Use the whistle sparingly. Give one sharp blast and insist on the courtesy of attention. Early attention to this will pay off later in the dividends of time saved.

The whistle should be used only to halt activity. Starting commands for activities can be given with verbal signals. The whistle should mean, "Stop, Look (at the teacher), and Listen."

4. Whether to teach by the whole or part method must be decided. The whole method is the process of learning the entire skill or activity in one dosage. The part method is to learn parts separately until all parts are learned and can be combined into a unified whole. The choice of the whole or part method depends upon the complexity of the skill or

activity. The teacher needs to decide whether or not the activity is simple enough to be taught wholly or if it should be broken down into parts.

5. Use the more formal methods of organization only when needed. Stunts and tumbling are examples of activities in which good selection of formations is needed for safety and good teaching.

6. Techniques of evaluation should be a part of the program. Only through evaluative procedures can the degree of progress toward the objectives of the program be ascertained.

7. At times, allow choice of activity.

8. If the classroom teacher has the responsibility for the physical education instruction, maximum use of activity time can be derived by giving time-consuming explanations in the classroom prior to the scheduled time for going to the play area. Rules can be explained, procedures and responsibilities outlined, and formations illustrated on the blackboard.

9. Teachers should analyze each activity from the standpoint of how maximum movement can be a part of the activity. Teachers must realize that activities are a means of development through movement and that as much movement must be coaxed from them as possible.

10. Avoid too rigid an approach with young children. Allow for experimentation and exploration by the children. The teacher may find it appropriate to give basic instruction in the topic or skill and then allow for exploration and creative activity based upon the material just presented.

11. When giving instructions in activity, be explicit. If there are different, acceptable ways to perform, show these and discuss with the children the reasoning behind the various difference in technique. Explain enough to get the activity underway successfully.

12. Set up your procedures so that when the explanation is completed, the activity will begin promptly.

13. Know and emphasize the stress points in an activity. These are the critical points which are important to success in an activity.

14. The prevention of fear in young children in handling play objects should be a consideration. Use a soft ball or beanbag in introductory phases. When the children work as partners, begin with short distances, using the simplest activity first. Begin in a stationary position before progressing to moving skills.

15. A physical education class needs to be a happy medium between quiet and boisterousness. Youngsters should be able to let off steam but be under control. Two types of noise should be differentiated. The first is the noise growing out of purposeful activity, interest, and enjoyment. The second is noise that springs from disorder, disinterest, rowdyism, and lack of control.

16. While desirable learnings can result in a proper learning atmosphere, these are not automatic for activities but are the result of planning. Relays can be used as an example. In a good learning atmosphere, a child can learn to cooperate, to observe rules, and to abide with the capacities of his teammates. On the other hand, in a poorly conducted class, he can learn to cheat, to become intolerant of the shortcomings of the members of his team, and to put winning over all other goals.

17. The development of courtesy, fair play, and honesty are important goals to be achieved by children. In discussion and evaluation, children need to bring out what constitutes proper conduct in various situations.

Teachers should note in their lesson plans where opportunities exist for introduction of these social concepts. Their development must not be left to chance.

The Vocal Side of Teaching

1. When there is instruction, the teacher should have the attention of the students. Be brief and to the point. Avoid excessive verbalization.

2. Speak in terms consistent with the maturity of the children. Gradually develop the child's vocabulary, but avoid technical terms which will not be understood. In working with disadvantaged children, be sure the terms are appropriate and relevant to the group.

3. Use a voice with enough "carry" to cover the group, but do not shout.

4. Stand where you can see all the children. Avoid the center of the circle. Position the children so you, the teacher, are facing the sun or the light source.

5. In phrasing instructional points of the lesson, accent the positive. Instead of saying, "Don't land so hard," say rather, "Land lightly."

6. Avoid excessive repetition and reliance on certain words and phrases, such as "OK," "All Right," and that irritating "and-uh."

7. Avoid rhetorical questions which in reality are meant to be commands, such as "Shall we go in now?" or "Would you like to . . . ?"

8. Use appropriate methodology for questions and answers.

a. Phrase questions in such a manner that they stimulate a child to a thoughtful answer and not just a "yes" or "no" response.

b. In asking questions, select an individual child, as a question thrown at a group will get a chorus of responses. The teacher will then need to designate a child to be heard, a procedure which should have been instituted in the first place.

c. Children should wait to be recognized before answering, usually by raising a hand.

d. Try to stimulate a free flow of ideas by expanding the answer with probing phrases, such as, "What are other points?" and "Let's have another reason."

9. If a child does not respond to directions, an assessment needs to be made as to whether the difficulty is in communication or a lack of ability.

Disciplinary Factors

Several points are important in maintaining a good instructional climate. If disciplinary trouble develops, one must look first at the teacher and the program, that is, is there any reason for the deviant behavior? After this has been determined, attention can be turned to the children. With children, some aggression is normal, but it must be channeled into proper outlets.

The selection of membership for squads offers an opportunity to minimize certain problems of association. It offers a chance to separate children who might cause trouble by being in too close association.

The class clown is a nuisance and sometimes a disturbing problem. His chief aim in life is to get the other children to laugh. Care should be used in asking such an individual to demonstrate. His antics should receive no support from the teacher. Acceptable response should be encouraged.

Because of the attractiveness of physical participation, classroom teachers on occasion use the exclusion from physical education as a disciplinary measure for breaches of conduct not related to physical education. This cannot be regarded as a sound educational practice, as the child has a right to the learning experience. However, within the physical education class framework, temporary exclusion is effectively practiced by some teachers. Children who do something naughty are told, "You go over to the sidelines and sit down. You tell us when you are ready to come back and play according to the rules."

The best antidote for discipline problems is a teaching climate of warmth, understanding, friendliness, and firmness.

Basic Principles Important in Movement Experiences and Skill Performance

Skill includes both basic and specialized skills. Specialized skills need more precise and definitive approaches than basic skills, which can be taught through the exploratory approach of basic movement. For this reason, the instructional procedures for skill learning are more applicable to the specialized skills, but still have a firm place in basic movement methodology.

To move more effectively and reach a better level of skill performance, the elementary school child should apply certain established principles to his movement patterns and skills. First of all, he should be made aware that there are such principles; and, secondly, he should learn how to apply these in his learning experiences. It is also important that the teacher utilize the principles in coaching and helping youngsters with their skills.

If effective patterns and correct techniques are established early in the learning process, the child will have little need to make a difficult adjustment later from an undesirable habit which has been allowed to be established in his skill patterns.

The principles are mostly general in nature, covering a variety of skills. A few, however, are specific and refer to certain types of skills. For children, the following principles in the performance of skills should be considered.

Body Position

In a normal, ready position for an activity, the feet should be at shoulder width. For some skills one foot may be forward of the other. The knees are loose, toes pointed forward, and weight carried on the balls of the feet. There is a readiness so that the legs may move easily in any direction as desired. The back should be reasonably straight, the head up, and the hands ready for action (as in catching).

If a fast start is needed, the feet are brought together more (less than shoulder width), and a body lean in the direction of the proposed movement should be made. The center of gravity is lowered somewhat by the body lean and more bend at the knees.

For the powerful movements of pulling or pushing, the base (the feet) should be widened, the knees bent, and the center of gravity dropped with the lower base.

Visual Concentration

Visually, the eyes should be focused on some fixed or moving point in keeping with the skill. In catching, the child should watch the ball. In throwing or bowling, the fixation should be on the target. In kicking, he should keep his head down and watch the ball.

Follow-Through

Follow-through refers to a smooth projection of the already-initiated movement. The principle is vitally important in throwing, striking, batting, and kicking skills. In kicking, the movement is to kick through the ball, not at it. In batting, the normal swing must be fully completed, not arrested.

Relaxation

The child should be relaxed in his movements. To be relaxed means to use just enough muscular effort to perform the skill, but avoid an overuse, generally called "tightening up," causing a distortion of the skill. This principle has particular application to target skills such as shooting baskets or pitching.

Opposition

Opposition refers to the coordinated use of the arms and legs. In throwing right-handed, the forward step should be made with the left foot. In walking or running, the movement of a leg is coordinated with that of the arm on the other side of the body. A step with the left foot means a forward swing with the right arm.

Total Body Coordination

Many skills require the entire body to be brought into play to perform the skill effectively. A child who throws primarily with his arm should be taught to bring his whole body into play.

Development of Torque

Torque means to bring to bear together a combination of body forces employing twisting and rotating motions. It is related to the foregoing point of total body coordination. In throwing or batting, the child should start with a forward motion of the hip and rotation of the body, thus adding force to the throw or batted ball.

Weight Transfer

A transfer of weight from the back to the front foot is a critical element in throwing, batting, striking, and rolling skills. The initial weight of the body is on the back foot, with the transfer occurring during the execution of the skill.

Visualization

The mental review of a skill with emphasis on the key points to be done in sequential fashion is called visualization. A performer thinks through the execution of the skill with a mental performance before actually performing the skill. The value comes in concentrating on the key points which make for better success in the skill. Visualization has application mostly to the more complex skills.

Pads of the Fingers

The pads of the fingers are the controlling elements in many manipulative skills, particularly in ball skills. A ball should be handled with the pads of the fingers.

Effective Motor Learning

Methods of teaching depend upon the level of the children and the skill being taught. Some considerations are given in motor learning on the elementary level.

1. There must be sufficient repetition to establish good retention. This involves the

principle of overlearning. Correct form must be practiced until it becomes fixed. The more complex the skill and the higher the performance level, the more need for practice to maintain the level. Repetition is effective only if it does something beyond what it did previously.

2. A child must participate to learn. He should have an opportunity to explore, try out, and experiment with different ways of performing skills as opposed to the autocratic "this is the way you do it" teaching.

3. Teachers should be able to verbalize skills. This means to break a skill down verbally into its component parts so the children can follow the pattern of instruction.

4. Skills should be practiced with as small a group as possible consistent with the skill and the equipment available. Whenever possible and practical, *each* child should have a piece of equipment.

5. Relatively short practices (in time or in number of repetitions) make for more efficient learning than do longer practices.

6. Older children can derive more benefit with longer practice than is possible with younger children.

7. The "start-and-expand" technique should be the basis for skill learning. This means that the skill level is started low enough so that all children meet with success and then expanded to more challenging skill performance.

8. Children should follow sound mechanical principles, but to expect all to perform skills in an identical manner is an error, not in keeping with the principle of individual differences.

9. A teacher should emphasize the "best" way to do things and what constitutes correct technique in a specific skill. However, he should point out to the student that there are performers who are successful even when using what is considered poor form. Such performances should be regarded as exceptions developed only after a long period of practice and participation.

10. Provide effective demonstration and visual aids when teaching specialized skills. Children learn by example, and effective demonstrations can show youngsters how to perform skills. Many techniques lend themselves to slow motion demonstrations. Selected children, properly directed, can provide suitable demonstrations. In addition, slides, film strips, motion pictures, pamphlets, posters, and other visual aids can be obtained from different sources. Loop films are of particular value in teaching skills.

11. Mimetics have a place in skill teaching. Students can be in mass formation and follow the directions of the leader. Many can practice at one time, good form is emphasized in a short time, questions can be answered, and gross errors can be discovered at the earliest period. Since the student can concentrate on the skill without the implement (ball, bat, or object), kinesthetic feeling for the skill can be acquired. The child gets the feel of the movement.

12. Teachers need to be able to coach youngsters to good levels of skill, by analyzing and making corrections. Students expect an intelligent answer to the question, "What am I doing wrong?" Coaching depends on good powers of observation and the development of keen recognition ability. Coaching involves two aspects. The first is the application of the basic principles important in movement and skill performance. The second involves items of technique which are important to the skill itself.

13. After a period of skill practice, the teacher may hold a critique with the students for discussion of the stress and critical points of the skill. It can be based on a question such as, "What are the important things we must remember to do this skill efficiently?"

14. Speed in relation to performance has several aspects. Children learn well at a speed which is just slightly less than the normal speed of a skill, moving up to normal speed as soon as feasible. In other cases, too much speed in a game or relay before the child has absorbed the skill hardly helps learning.

15. Competition can enhance learning and performance. However, when competition becomes too heated, performance deteriorates. When excessive emotions are involved, learning ability goes down.

16. Teachers should not assume that the youngsters will learn the skill elsewhere. While some may learn from parents, brothers, sisters, and older children, repetition and prac-

tice will improve the level of performance. If errors in execution are present, the skill session can establish correct form.

The Teacher Who Cannot Demonstrate

There are teachers who, because of physical limitations, cannot demonstrate effectively. Few teachers, who are not physical education specialists, can do all physical activities well. Even the relatively skilled teacher will, at times, need to devise substitutions for an effective demonstration. For the teacher who has difficulty in demonstrating activities, the following suggestions should prove helpful.

1. Through reading, study, analysis of movement, and other devices, arm yourself with an understanding and knowledge of the activities which you have difficulty demonstrating. Even if you cannot perform, know how the activity is to be done.

2. Select skillful children to help demonstrate.

3. Be able to verbalize the skill so you can coach the students and correct their errors.

4. Secure and use effective visual aids at appropriate points in the unit of teaching.

5. Place more reliance on the squad leaders and use the squad formation in skill drills.

Safety in Instruction

Policies for health and safety have been introduced in Chapter 5 as they relate to administrative responsibility. Additional safety suggestions of an instructional nature are offered here. Safety precautions and considerations with respect to the various activity areas are presented with the instructional sequences and procedures of the separate activities. For example, softball has definite need for safety rules such as not throwing the bat, and having the waiting batters stand in a safe area. These items relate only to softball and are discussed under that unit.

There is nothing automatic about establishing a good safety climate. Instruction in safety must be taught along with the other elements of the activity, and the lesson plan should reflect appropriate emphasis. The positive approach should be stressed with emphasis on how we can play safely, in contrast with the scare approach of possible injury.

Once the rules have been established, good supervision and observation are needed to insist on correct and safe application of the rules. Some important general considerations for safety are as follows:

1. The first responsibility is to see that the playing area is a suitable and safe environment. A quick assessment by the teacher will note the presence of obstructions and articles which might prove hazardous and merit removal. The area should be of sufficient size.

2. Next, the teacher *must* consider the forthcoming activity and what is needed for safe participation. The children should know the basic and lead-up skills well enough for safe participation. They should be instructed in needed safety procedures and rules. The teacher needs to make sure the safety regulations are followed.

3. Where the children are in two or more groups, leave sufficient space between them. The activity should not demand that the children of different groups run toward each other, as nasty collisions can occur. Also, where throws are employed, as in dodgeball, distances should be such that the throw has lost its force or hits the ground before entering the territory of another group.

4. In ball activities, teach children to keep eyes on the ball, not to throw the ball to another child unless he is watching.

5. Traffic rules in games and drills are important. Children should pass to the right when coming toward each other in games. Establish the time or distance when children follow each other, such as consecutive turns on a mat. One-way patterns should be established for other activities.

6. Set up rules about recovering balls. One child only should go after a ball. Have stringent rules regarding procedure in recovering balls that go into streets, areas of other groups, apparatus areas, etc. A stop-and-look pause should precede any action for recovery.

7. Shoelaces should remain tied. Stop the play and see that this is done. Children should be required to wear shoes for outside activity. In some races and contests, children like to remove shoes because they feel they can travel faster, but this should not be permitted.

8. Maintain the instructional climate by not permitting horseplay and unnecessary roughness. Viciousness, such as vindictive tagging, has no place in physical education.

9. Children should be cautioned against bringing pencils or pens to the physical education class, nor should they be allowed to chew gum or munch on suckers.

10. For rough activity, glasses should be removed or glass guards made available. If glasses are removed, establish a safe place for them to protect against breakage.

11. Rules governing different activities and pieces of apparatus should be developed among the teachers as a whole, so the children have uniformity in direction. It is well to have regulations posted.

12. Teach children to keep their hands off other children, as this not only is annoying, but can lead to trouble.

In no sense is this meant to be an all-inclusive list of safety considerations for all activity. The teacher is referred to the specific activity section for others.

Leadership Experiences

Some leadership experiences, centered more in the primary grades, can be provided. The jobs assigned should be realistic and definite and within the capacity of the children. There should be rotation so that all children have an opportunity to share in these experiences. The following should be considered.

1. Equipment Manager. Obtains and arranges equipment for the day's activities. A list of equipment needed and a diagram of how the things are to be arranged are helpful.

2. Squad Leader. Supervises the activities of his squad. Acts as a leader when squads are the basis for activity arrangement.

3. Monitor. Leads the class to the play area, turns the lights on and off, supervises (within limits) the washup after class. Helps put away the shoes and other personal equipment to the proper storage place in class.

Evaluation

Evaluation is the process of determining the extent to which the program in physical education meets its stated objectives. It would provide more valid information if all evaluative techniques could be based on measurement procedures, but not all objectives lend themselves to measurement. Physical educators are attempting to build greater precision into the evaluative process by zeroing in on behavioral objectives. These objectives attempt to specify in more precise and definite terms, for example, discarding "acquiring a satisfactory level of skill" in favor of the more limited measurable and precise behavioral objective of "attaining a distance of 72" in the standing long jump. However, until behavioral objectives have been fully developed and refined to the point of practicality, other means of assessment must be employed. The means by which evaluation can be made is divided into three areas: (1) general standards for the program, (2) teacher observation, and (3) pupil expression and opinion.

General Standards

General standards set the pace for the entire program, and because of this are examined first:

Evidence of Planning. The program should be based on good planning procedures. Available as evidence should be an overall year's program from which the weekly and daily programs are drawn. Instruction should be based on lesson plans.

Time Element. Is there a daily program totaling at least 150 minutes per week?

Facilities, Equipment, and Supplies. Are these sufficient for the particular situation so that they do not provide detrimental limitations in the experiences for children?

The Program. Does the program meet good education standards? Is it geared to the needs, interests, and capacities of the children?

The Direction. Is the instruction in the capable hands of a trained and interested teacher? Does the teacher keep up-to-date through current literature and inservice or college workshops or courses?

Health and Safety. Are there good standards of health and safety? Is the participation based upon a regular medical examination? Is there proper provision for emergency care?

Is there consideration for the child who cannot participate fully?

Observation by the Teacher

The teacher can make reasonable judgments of the progress toward the goals of physical education by observing certain signs of desirable progress.

Physical Fitness. How well does a youngster meet the strength and endurance demands of activity?

How smoothly and adequately can he handle his body?

How does he respond physiologically to the demands of activity? Is there dizziness, nausea, shortness of breath, unusual paleness or redness, weakness, depressed mental or emotional states, or anxiety states?

How well does the child recover from activity? After ten minutes, does the pulse return to normal? Is he still overly tired? Is there marked stiffness or soreness that evening or the next day? Has he recovered the next day from the activity?

Is his posture and bearing satisfactory?

What about arm and shoulder girdle development? Can he perform on the ladder and horizontal bar with reasonable success?

Does he enjoy and thrive on vigorous activity?

Competency in Body Management. Can he manage his body in a variety of movement situations? Does he move with ease? Can he go over, around, and under apparatus and obstacles?

Useful Skills. Has he mastered the basic skills of locomotion? Can he do these successfully to rhythm?

Does he show good form in specialized skills? Is he making satisfactory progress for his size and maturity?

Has he mastered throwing, kicking, and batting skills well enough to take part successfully in game type activities.

Can he perform on apparatus the activities appropriate for his age?

Does he know and apply the appropriate mechanical principles to skill learning? Does he have the desire to practice for better performance?

Does he have a wide appreciation of skills rather than concentration in a narrow area?

Social Learnings. Does he act democratically by entering wholeheartedly into activities chosen by group process?

Do children play together well and comfortably as boys and girls with wholesome boy-girl relationships? Are social graces the rule in the rhythmic program?

Is there evidence of good leadership and followership patterns? Do the children accept the proper decisions of the leader?

In competitive games, is there evidence of good sportsmanship in observing the rules, accepting the decisions of officials, and following the captain's suggestions? Can the youngsters win or lose in a sportsmanlike manner?

Can the child share with others and not try to dominate the play?

Safety. Have the children developed a safety consciousness?

Are they considerate of other children in safety situations?

Do they spot hazards and unsafe conditions and tend to correct them?

Recreational Objective. During free play, can the child organize his own play either individually or with other children?

Does he learn the rules of activities so he can enjoy these on his own time?

Can he play with assurance on various pieces of apparatus?

Does he know modifications of rules so that he can adapt games to small-group play and places?

Is he motivated to take part in activity for activity's sake — that is, the maintenance of fitness?

Developing a Realistic Self-Image and Acquiring a Desirable Self-Concept. Does he "belong" to the group? Is he accepted by his peers? Is he achieving success in his play activities? Does he seem secure in his physical education experiences? Does he have a realistic self-image in terms of his capabilities.

Personal and Educational Values. Does he take part joyously in play and find satisfaction in movement experiences? Can he react creatively when the call is for free rein to the imagination?

Does he approach problems with assurance and confidence? Does he give evidence of reasoning powers during problem-solving situations?

Is he learning terminology, acquiring understandings, and learning concepts as he participates in movement experiences? Does he understand the reasons behind what he is doing?

Student Opinion and Discussion

After a class period or the completion of a unit, the teacher can organize an evaluating session with the children for the purpose of critical discussion of the merits of the experience. Discussion should be in terms of what was accomplished and how well they enjoyed the activity. Suggestions can be made on what needs to be done and how it can be accomplished.

TEACHING AIDS IN PHYSICAL EDUCATION

Film Strips, Motion Pictures, Slides

In addition to the regular class work in physical education, the teacher should consider enriching the program demonstration with the use of loop films, motion pictures, film strips, slides, and opaque projector. Good audio-visual procedures need to be followed.

The visual aid should fit in with the learning situation and be appropriate for the level of the children. Since the rental charge covers the use of the film for a period of time, coordination with other classes should be arranged for additional showings. Programs ought to be projected far enough ahead so films may be scheduled for correct placement in the program.

Visual aids emphasizing skill techniques should be shown early in a skill learning unit.

Loop films have become an important medium of instruction. A wide variety of topics is available, including basic movement techniques. New projectors utilizing plastic cartridges have made this an effective aid for instruction. Schools can make their own loop films using Super 8 film and a tourist type camera.

Sound films and sound strips generally need to be shown completely through without interruption. Discussion can be permitted in a slide presentation or with a film strip without sound.

Teachers should give some thought to the use of the 35 mm slide as a teaching tool. Critical skills probably cannot be too well illustrated, but formations, game boundaries, and field layouts lend themselves to the home slide projector.

The Opaque Projector

Another useful tool to consider is the opaque projector. This device, like the old magic lantern, will throw on the screen an enlarged version of the material. A teacher who uses a card system for games, rhythms, or other activities will find this an effective and useful time-saver. If a new game is scheduled, the teacher can flash the card on the screen or blackboard and go over the details with the children.

Bulletin Boards

The class bulletin board should devote a proportionate space to physical education. It is well to select a theme for the board and change it often. A theme could illustrate fitness, a unit, a sport, physical education in other states or countries, posture, or health practices. A particular skill can be selected for illustration. Pictures from magazines, newspapers, and other sources can be used for illustrations.

The board can be constructed of wall board or beaver board which will hold thumb tacks or staples. A backdrop made of colored paper or colored muslin makes a nice display. The color scheme can be tied up with the theme and changed with the display. Some materials that can be used are listed:

1. Pictures and diagrams lend life to the display. Snapshots also can be included. Newspaper materials should be pasted or stapled to sturdy paper for better display.

2. Colored paper of all kinds and colors is needed. Construction paper provides an excellent source for these materials.

3. Stickmen can be made from pipe cleaners. These are interesting and provide an outlet for creative talent.

4. Yarn or string can make field outlines or provide borders for the displays.

The character of the bulletin board is limited only by the imagination of the children. The responsibility for the board could be assigned to groups of children on a rotative basis. An interesting bulletin board program also offers possibilities for integration with other subject matter fields.

It is important that the bulletin board be of, by, and for the children. Too often, the character of the board is determined by the standards of the teacher and becomes an adult project with minor assistance by the children.

Displays

Displays offer possibilities similar to bulletin boards. However, the display is generally done in three dimensions. The display should have the material organized around a theme.

A display may be put in a showcase in the school hall. It could be arranged on a table in the classroom.

Bibliographical Materials

Physical education is not static and the collective written materials provide a wealth of ideas for enriching a program. Materials can be classified as follows:

1. Texts in Elementary School Physical Education. Works offering an overall treatment of physical education in the elementary school are available in considerable number. It seems that each year one or two new manuscripts are offered. While there is considerable duplication among texts in the basic material presented, each text emphasizes certain ideas and activities.

2. Curriculum Guides in Physical Education. Curriculum guides have been assembled on a number of different levels. Many states, counties, cities, and school systems have developed guides for their own situations. The guides are not generally advertised but are available reasonably from the various agencies.

3. Specialized Subject Area Books. For more intensive treatment in a particular area of physical education, a number of good books are on the market. These treat only a portion of the physical education program, but develop the area to a much greater extent than the written works covering the entire program. Books dealing with games, sports, rhythmics, posture, classroom activties, testing, and similar topics are available from publishers.

4. Magazines and Periodicals. There are magazines devoted to physical education in general, but no periodical which gives its entire emphasis to the elementary school physical education program is on the market. The *Journal of the American Association for Health, Physical Education and Recreation* is probably the one best source for up-to-date materials in physical education on the elementary level.

5. Card Files. Available today are card files for various physical education activities. Card files* can be secured in the area of games, rhythmics, relays, and stunts. These are convenient teaching aids and good time-savers. Cards include the description of the activity, teaching suggestions, safety considerations, and variations.

6. Miscellaneous Materials. Posters, pamphlets, mimeographed material, convention reports, and research reports are indicative of the vast amount of material which is available to the teacher today. Some system of filing is necessary for the teacher. Materials can be filed under the general topic (like rhythmics) and be available for handy reference.

A successful and enterprising teacher will keep up-to-date in his materials.

---

*Card files are obtainable from Burgess Publishing Company, 426 South Sixth Street, Minneapolis, Minnesota 55415.

8

Lesson Planning and Introductory Activity

The Physical Education Lesson
The Design of the Written Lesson Plan
Introductory Activity

THE PHYSICAL EDUCATION LESSON

The physical education lesson for a particular class period should grow out of a unit of instruction, which in turn is a part of the year's plan. Each lesson should be a part of a sequence based on the work of previous lessons. It is most important that each lesson follow a written plan, especially for a beginning teacher. A written lesson plan will vary in form and length dependent upon the activity and the background of the teacher. A written lesson plan ensures that thought has been given to the lesson before the children enter the activity area. It avoids spur-of-the-moment decisions, losing unity and progression of the material. This does not mean that a teacher cannot modify the lesson as needed, but it does keep the central core and purpose of the lesson intact.

Progression is more likely to occur in the forthcoming lesson if the teacher has the previous lesson plan for a guide. In future years, the teacher can also refer to his collection of lesson plans for suggestion and improvement.

A lesson can be divided into the following parts, each of which is discussed:

1. Introductory Activities (1-3 minutes)
2. Developmental Activities (4-8 minutes)
3. The Lesson Core
   a. Review of Previously-Presented Material
   b. New Learning Experiences
4. Closing Activity (2-5 minutes)

Except for the lesson core, any of the parts can be omitted as indicated by a particular lesson. In some cases, developmental activities serve as introductory work.

Introductory Activity

Introductory activity accomplishes in the lesson just what the designation implies. Children come to the physical education class eager for movement, and the first part of the lesson is designed to meet this sheer appetite for movement. Once this is satisfied, the lesson can proceed toward the achievement of its specific objectives. A secondary purpose of introductory activity is to serve as warm-up activity, preparing the body for the movements which are to follow.

Generally, some type of gross, unstructured movement is used for introductory activity, usually based on locomotor movements. An enterprising teacher can employ many different activities and variations effectively as introductory activity. Examples are found later in this chapter.

Developmental Activities

Developmental activities are defined as those activities which have as a major objective the development of the various qualities of physical fitness — strength, power, endurance, agility, and flexibility, among others.

Some activities, such as circuit training, involve the entire body. Others, such as exercises and gross movement, involve development of a specific part of the body. Rope jumping, astronaut drills, and other general fitness activities can also be used.

The developmental activities should show a progression of increasing demands. The work demands must be gradually and consistently increased as the program develops.

The development of physical fitness is presented in Chapter 9.

The Lesson Core

The lesson core is the heart, the meat of the lesson. Presented here are the learning experiences growing out of the overall instructional unit. The first consideration is to review and work with the activities of the previous lesson, until a satisfactory level of learning has been reached. In some instances the entire lesson core would be taken up with a repeat of the work of the previous lesson.

After sufficient time has been given to the review, the new learning experiences are presented. Skill instruction, participation in a rhythmic activity, or a progression of stunts and tumbling are the kinds of things which are in the lesson core.

The amount of time to be devoted to the lesson core is determined by the time demands of the other three parts of the lesson. After introductory and developmental activities have been done, the remainder of the time, less that needed for the closing activity, can be devoted to the lesson core.

The Closing Activity

Closing activity can take many different forms. The lesson can be completed with a game or other fun activity for the purpose of finishing up with something the children know and enjoy. The game should be simple in nature and one in which all the children have a vigorous part, so that a pleasurable feeling is taken away to the next class after the physical education class.

A consideration in closing the lesson is returning equipment, apparatus, and supplies to their proper storage places. This should utilize student responsibility with definite assignments. Squads under the direction of leaders can assume this responsibility.

The closing activity could take the form of group evaluation, with suggestions for future procedure. This is reinforcement of learning and contributes to a better learning climate.

In some lessons, the closing activity may be minimal or deleted entirely. This might be the case when a game or other activity as the core of the lesson demands as much time as possible.

THE DESIGN OF THE WRITTEN LESSON PLAN

A written lesson plan should be made out for each physical education lesson. The plan should contain all information needed for the teacher to ensure progression, unity, and completeness. Some teachers find it helpful to have a form which saves time and effort and includes all necessary information. The format given as an example provides the following data:

General Information

Name of school, classroom or class involved, date, activity.

Expected Outcomes of the Lesson

A short description of the specific things the lesson is trying to accomplish.

Supplies and Equipment Needed and the Initial Arrangement of These

A list of the materials needed, indicating the specific number of each item.

The Lesson Description

This should be divided into the four parts of the lesson — introductory activities, developmental activities, the lesson core, and the closing activity. Under each should be listed the time allotment for the activity, the specific learning experiences, and the organizational and teaching procedures. Under the heading of "Hints, Stress Points, Safety" should be included hints for performance or form, points to be stressed as important to the activity or skill, safety factors, and concepts to be brought out. Organizational and teaching procedures specify how the children will be arranged for the various learning experiences and how the teaching process is to proceed.

The Evaluation

During and after the lesson, the teacher should note what was covered and with what success. The teacher should make notes to himself for directions for future lessons.

Some teachers may question the feasibility of writing out lesson plans, reasoning that it takes too much time and effort, and is not really needed. From the standpoint of length, a lesson plan should be precise enough to be an effective guide for the learning experiences. The length of a lesson plan would depend upon the background of each instructor. Beginning teachers necessarily will need to provide more detail than a more experienced instructor. A lesson plan should be understandable as a functional tool. Some teachers may need only a word or a phrase to suggest an idea or a procedure, while others may need more written directions. This understanding should be apparent at the time of teaching and also when it is necessary to refer to a lesson already given.

A specimen lesson plan is detailed for a lesson in simple ball skills on the third grade level. The plan illustrates the four parts of the lesson.

LESSON PLAN FOR PHYSICAL EDUCATION

School: Washington   Classroom: 3rd — Jones   Date: 10/3/72   Teacher: Sweeney

Activity: Bowling at Pins — Gym

Materials Needed

Expected Outcomes of This Lesson

Introduce bowling at clubs.

Learn reasonable form.

12 playground balls — 8½"
12 Indian clubs

Initial Arrangement of Equipment

None

Time Min.	Specific Activity	Organization and Progressions	Hints, Stress Points, Safety
2	Introductory Activity	1. One-half scattered, down on hands and knees. Others standing — scattered. Go over person — leap, jump, hop, step over. Groups change on whistle.	Use any order. Watch out for others. Stress being high enough and landing lightly.
		2. Down children form high bridges. Change to going under bridges.	Avoid touching the "bridge." Make bridges high.
5	Developmental Activity	1. Scattered at floor positions, bent-over position. Practice swimming strokes — crawl, breast, dolphin.	Shoulders kept up and back, eyes forward. Change time factors—slow, fast, slow to fast, fast to slow. Change body levels, raising and lowering.
		2. Face down on floor. Same movements.	Try not to touch the floor with the moving arms or hands.

LESSON PLANNING AND INTRODUCTORY ACTIVITY

Time Min.	Specific Activity	Organization and Progressions	Hints, Stress Points, Safety
		3. Supine position. Touch hands and feet: Right to right Left to left Right to left Left to right Both to both Touch foot out to side. Reach high with one foot. With one foot, write name, make figures.	Bring designated foot and hand up, touching as high as possible. Reach as far as possible. Alternate right and left feet.
2	Lecture and Demonstration	Group in semicircle. With ball, explain bowling. Demonstrate.	Face forward, feet together. Right hand under, left hand over ball. Bring both hands back to side, roll ball. Slight twist at waist. Follow through. Weight transfer. Eyes on target. Lower body by bending knee.
4	Dry Run Practice	Scattered. Repeat the directions. Go through mimetic rolling.	Use "Ready, back, roll" (3 counts).
5	Skill Practice	Shuttle turn-back formation by squads. One ball per squad. Demonstrate with Squad #1. All practice.	Need four balls. Move around, coaching. Stress controlled rolling.
5	Continued Practice	By pairs, across the room. Roll back and forth. One partner get a club, roll at club.	Stress accuracy. Roll with the other hand. Caution about controlled rolling.
5	Game — One-Step	One partner rolls at club until he misses. Step back on each successful hit.	Score one point when child reaches back line (stepping) without missing.

2	Evaluation, Closing	Seated in semicircle. Discuss important points of technique.	Bring out:
			  What are the important points to remember?
			  What is "follow-through"?
			  With which foot do we step?

INTRODUCTORY ACTIVITY

The chief characteristic of introductory activity is its vigorous nature. Gross movements, generally locomotor activity, are employed, but the activity can take many forms. It should challenge every student with movement, should not be rigidly structured, and should allow considerable freedom of movement.

Introductory activity should require only brief instructions, as its purpose is to get the children into activity quickly. Abrupt changes in direction, in the kinds of movements, and in the pace of activities predominate. Moving and stopping is another pattern often used. The first activity presented is European Rhythmic Running, which represents a strong bias of the author for inclusion.

European Rhythmic Running

Some type of rhythmic running is done in many countries of Europe to open the daily lesson. Essentially, this is light, rhythmic running to the accompaniment of some type of percussion, usually a drum or tom-tom.

Much of the running follows a circular path, but it can follow other patterns. To introduce a group of children to rhythmic running, have them stand in circular formation and clap to the beat of the drum. Next, as they clap, they can shuffle their feet in place, keeping time. Following this, have them run in place, omitting the clapping. The children should now be ready to move in a prescribed path with the run. It is essential that the run be light, bouncy, and rhythmic, keeping strict time with the beat.

A number of movement ideas can be combined with the rhythmic running pattern.

1. On signal (whistle or double beat on the drum), runners freeze in place. Resume running when the regular beat begins again.

2. On signal, make a running full turn in four running steps. Lift knees high while turning.

3. Have children clap hands every fourth beat as they run. Instead of clapping, sound a brisk "hey" on the fourth beat, raising one arm and fist on the sound.

4. Run in squad formation. Follow the path set by the squad leader.

Rhythmic Running, Circular Fashion

Gross Locomotor Movements and Changes

Most of these patterns involve either a change from one locomotor movement to another, a change in direction, or a stop in a specified position. Some examples of variations in free locomotor movements are:

1. Free running. Run in any direction, changing direction at will. Or, run and do giant leaps as you wish.

2. Running and changing direction. Run in any direction, changing direction abruptly on signal. Change levels on signal.

3. Running and changing the type of movements. On signal, change to a different type of locomotion. The change could be free choice or specified. Change of direction and a change of the locomotor movement could be combined.

4. Running and stopping. Run and, on signal, freeze.

5. Running and assuming a specified position or pose. Run and on signal assume a pose such as push-up position, a balance task, or a specified shape.

6. Running, stopping, and doing a task. Run and on signal stop and do a specified task such as exercises, jumping in place, or a stunt.

7. Different locomotor movements to the beat of the drum. Most of the above ideas can be incorporated with rhythmic accompaniment.

8. Tortoise and Hare. Run in place slowly (tortoise), and on signal change to a very rapid run (hare), but still in place.

9. Combinations of movements. A flow of several movements can be specified, such as run, skip, and roll. Or, jump, twist, and shake.

Most of the routines use two signals. The first signals the change, and the second tells the children to revert to the original pattern (running). Running has been used in most of the routines, but other locomotor movements can be substituted.

Partner or Group Activities

Partner or group activities offer excellent opportunities for introductory work.

1. Marking. The children can do what the English call "marking." Each child has a partner, somewhat equal in ability. One partner runs, dodges, and tries to lose the other partner, who must stay within one yard of him. On signal, both stop. The chaser must be able to touch his partner to say he has "marked" him.

2. Follow Activity. One partner leads and performs various kinds of movements. The other partner must move in the same fashion. This idea can also be extended to squad organization.

3. Partner Carry. One partner carries the other. On signal, reverse positions. This activity should be confined to the upper primary level.

4. Group Over and Under. One-half the children are scattered. Each is in a curled position. The other children leap or jump over the down children. On signal, reverse the groups quickly. Instead of being curled, the down children form arches or bridges, then the moving children should go under these. A further extension is to have the children on the floor alternate between curled and bridge positions. If a moving child goes over the curled position, the floor child immediately changes to a bridge. The moving children react accordingly.

5. New Leader. Squads run around the area, following a leader. When the change is signaled, the last person goes to the head of the line and becomes the leader.

6. Manipulative Activity. Each child has a beanbag. The children move around the area, tossing the bags upwards and catching them as they move. On signal, they drop the bags to the floor and jump, hop, or leap over as many bags as possible. On the next signal, they pick up any convenient bag and resume tossing to themselves. One less beanbag than children adds to the fun. Hoops can also be used in this manner. Children begin by using hoops in rope jumping style. On signal, the hoops are placed on the floor, and the children jump in and out of as many hoops as they can. Next, they pick up a near hoop and resume jumping. The activity can also be done with jumping ropes.

Tambourine-Directed Activity

The tambourine can signal changes of movement because of its ability to produce two different kinds of sounds. The first sound is a tinny noise made by vigorous shaking. The second is a percussion sound made by striking the tambourine as a drum, either with the knuckles or the elbow. Movement changes are signaled by changing from one tambourine sound to the other. Suggestions are listed according to the types of sound:

Shaking Sound

1. Children remain in one spot but shake all over. These should be gross movements.

2. Same movement, but children gradually drop to the floor (level change).

3. Children scurry in every direction.

4. Children run very lightly with tiny steps.

Drum Sound

1. Jerky movements to the drumbeat.
2. Jumping in place or covering space.
3. Locomotor movements in keeping with the drumbeat.
4. Using three beats of the drum — collapse (beat one), roll (beat two), and form a shape (beat three).

To form a combination of movements, select one from each category. When the shaking sound is made, the children perform that movement. When the change is made to the drum sound, the children react accordingly.

Games

Selected games are quite suitable for introductory activity, provided they keep all children active, are simple, and require little teaching. A familiar game saves organization time. Some appropriate games are listed:

Stop and Start, page 223.
Circus Master, page 214.
One, Two, Button My Shoe, page 215.

Miscellaneous Approaches

Children can run laps around a field or gymnasium for introductory activity.

Certain pieces of manipulative equipment, such as jump ropes, balls, hoops, and wands can be put out. Children can be directed to practice as they wish for a few minutes.

Climbing ropes, climbing structures, mats, boxes, balance beams and/or benches can be arranged so the children may have practice on a selected piece of equipment as they wish.

9

The Physical Development Goal

What Is Physical Fitness?
Guidelines for Achieving Physical Fitness
Physical Developmental Activities
Fitness Routines for Grade 3

Few children, left to their own devices, will engage in systematic and demanding exercise sufficient to satisfy the body's basic need for physical activity. It is granted that some children are quite active and seem to be in perpetual motion. But what about the masses of children whose living habits have been influenced by the ease of modern living and the benefits of modern technology? Gone now are the chores and the physical demands of the homes of the past. The school literally and actually has inherited the task of keeping America's children physically fit.

The discussions which follow stress physical fitness as an important goal in physical education. In no sense do we imply that it is the only goal worth seeking, nor is it the most important goal. Some American programs can be justly criticized for going overboard on fitness. The viewpoint that should be established is that physical fitness is an important goal of physical education, and that a positive approach in action must be taken or the goal will not be realized. On the other side of the picture, it should also not be regarded as a concomitant goal growing out of a program employing a particular kind of methodology or approach. Some strong proponents of educational movement regard physical fitness developmental activities as unsuitable learning experiences because of the direct teaching approach, labeling them as "training activities" rather than educational experiences.

WHAT IS PHYSICAL FITNESS?

A person who is physically fit possesses the strength and stamina to carry out his daily tasks without undue fatigue and still has enough energy to enjoy leisure and to meet unforeseen emergencies. The definition can be broken down into a number of concepts:

1. A person should possess enough strength, power, endurance, flexibility, agility, coordination, balance, and speed to do easily and effectively the routine duties and maximum tasks that the day may bring.

2. He should be free from disease and removable handicapping disorders.

3. He should possess a sturdy physique, which means a well-developed body with proper proportions of bone, muscle, and fat tissue. His posture should be acceptable and evidence of good nutritional habits should be present.

4. At the end of the day he should be sleepy, but not overly tired. He should be able to sleep well and feel recovered in the morning from the activities of the preceding day.

The Health Appraisal and Physical Fitness

The first step in establishing a firm foundation for physical fitness is the identification of pupils with correctable orthopedic and other health problems and subsequent referral to medical authorities. A child's health status is determined by medical evaluation in the form of a periodic health appraisal. Correctable defects and health problems should be referred for professional attention. After such measures have been taken to bring up the level of the child's health to the highest standard possible, the child can then effectively benefit from the school physical education program. The appraisal may also uncover in a few children certain permanent health conditions or handicaps which demand special consideration in the form of adapted programs tailored to the child's difficulty.

An ideal, but not practical, standard is that each child undergo a health appraisal each and every year of his school career. A more practical standard is to have the child examined at the beginning of different stages of his school career, i.e., kindergarten-primary, intermediate school, junior high school, high school, and college. In addition, health appraisals should be scheduled when health conditions need clarification.

The health appraisal becomes a meaningful procedure under two conditions. The first is that information from the health appraisal is available to and utilized effectively by the teacher to consider appropriate measures for the physical limitations of certain children. The second is that referral is made for health conditions needing attention. A large majority of the children will have no restrictions placed on participation. A few may need special consideration in their activities. These special considerations must be known and followed.

GUIDELINES FOR ACHIEVING PHYSICAL FITNESS

An important guideline for conducting the physical education program is recognition that physical fitness can be acquired only through the medium of muscular effort and is maintained only through continued activity. A second guideline, closely related to the first, is that, to raise levels of fitness, the child must exercise regularly and must participate in a progressive program. Motivation is important and progression must be incorporated so students will be taxed at the level of effort necessary for development. A third guideline is that the type of activity must be geared to the age, sex, and physical condition of the child. Flexibility must be built into the program, to take care of the needs of all children.

A fourth guideline involves viewing physical fitness in the light of its components. If each of the respective components is given emphasis, then collectively the development of physical fitness will be accomplished. The most important measurable components of physical fitness are strength, power, and cardiorespiratory endurance. Agility and flexibility rate only slightly less in importance, followed by such qualities as speed, balance, and coordination. It should be noted that balance and coordination, while of secondary importance *as components* of physical fitness, are of high importance in the perceptual-motor competency area. These are related more to movement competency than to physical fitness, but still are considered a part of fitness.

The development of each of the components of physical fitness is discussed in turn.

1. Strength. Strength refers to the ability of a muscle or muscle group to exert force. Among the child's learning experiences in physical education, there must be sufficient big muscle activity over a wide range of activities done regularly and with enough intensity to develop strength. The improvement of strength is a basic necessity to the development of physical fitness. Muscles can be developed only through stress and the tension applied during activity demands. We need to make our children work progressively harder if strength is to be developed.

Strength is necessary in skill performance, since without strength a low standard of performance can be expected, as muscles give out before they can reach their skill potential.

2. Power. Power implies the process of using strength to apply force for effective movement. Power is based on strength and its application to movement. Teaching youngsters how to move effectively in situations demanding an application of force will develop the ability to apply powerful movements when needed.

3. Endurance. Endurance refers to the ability to carry on muscular effort over a period of time. It has a basis in strength in that the stronger person is able to keep up muscular effort longer than one without adequate strength. However, there are other involvements in the body. Primarily, this is a postponement of the stages of fatigue so that muscular work can be carried on. A person with good endurance has a conditioning involving the cardiorespiratory system and other deep body mechanisms.

4. Agility. Agility refers to the ability to change direction swiftly, easily, and under good control. A particularly agile person is one who is hard to catch in a tag game. He can dodge and change direction well.

Agility is a needed safety quality. Many persons today are alive and free from injury because they were agile enough to get out of the way of a moving object.

5. Flexibility. Flexibility is a person's range of movement at the joints. A flexible child can stretch farther, touch his toes, bend farther, etc. He has more freedom of movement and can adjust his body to various movement challenges more readily. Youngsters need movement experiences where they can stretch, reach, bend, hang, and otherwise force the joints into maximum ranges of movement.

6. Speed. The ability to move quickly and rapidly is a needed skill in many physical activities. While there are inherent limitations of ultimate speed, each youngster should have the opportunity to develop efficient speed with respect to his potential. Among fitness qualities, speed has a high prestige factor, as illustrated by track stars and the ultimate Olympic winners.

7. Balance. Balance is the ability to maintain control of the equilibrium in a variety of positions and movements. The control of balance is of particular importance in kindergarten and first and second grades, but has value at all levels. Program elements should cover three aspects of balance: (1) *Static Balance,* the ability to maintain equilibrium in a fixed position; (2) *Dynamic Balance,* maintaining balance while moving or engaging in action; and (3) *Rotational Balance,* the ability to maintain or regain balance after turning, rolling, or other maneuvers while not in contact with the floor or apparatus.

8. Coordination. Coordination refers to the harmonious functioning of muscles in producing complex movements. Generally, a movement of high skill well done demands a high degree of coordination. A characteristic of many people with high levels of physical fitness is their graceful carriage, fluidity of motion, and ability to meet the challenge of more complex movements.

Program Activities and Physical Fitness

The types of activities included in the physical education program should be selected *and* conducted with the physical fitness goal in mind. There should be a rugged and demanding program, measured by the criterion of how much physical work the individual child receives during the lesson. Children should be kept active.

Many of the usual physical education activities involve primarily the use of the legs, lower back, hands, and arms. A good program will include hanging and arm-support activities, which are generally used insufficiently in programs. The inclusion of rope climbing, ladder work, horizontal bar stunts, and similar hanging activities is important in making sure that the upper torso is developed proportionately to other parts of the body.

Another approach to upper body development is the principle of including activities during which the children get down on the floor in movements and positions where the body is partially supported by the arms. Care must be taken to include a variety of positions, including the crab position, where the body is supported by the hands and feet, but faces the ceiling.

The trend toward more stunts and tumbling activities in the program will pay off in total body development. These activities also provide ample opportunity for the exercise of balance control.

To achieve endurance, the program must make demands on the individual in the form of muscular effort which causes accelerated breathing. Generally, this involves activities including running or other sustained movement. No activity should be carried on to the point where the participants are breathless. However, the children need to push themselves beyond the first inclination to cease.

Rope skipping to music, rhythmic running (European style), and similar movements contribute to the development of endurance.

Agility can be developed in many games, relays, and similar activities. The development is not automatic, however, and children need to be taught how to stop, start, and change direction properly.

Flexibility can be furthered by stimulating children to extend the limits of joint movement in twisting, bending, and rotational movements, particularly in the stunts and tumbling program. Children need to be urged to extremes in joint movements by such directives as, "See how far you can stretch," or "How far can you bend?"

Relays and simple games provide opportunities to practice speedy movement. Chase and tag games are particularly valuable in this respect, as well as for reinforcing agility. Instruction in proper running techniques should be accomplished.

PHYSICAL DEVELOPMENTAL ACTIVITIES

Developmental activities are those carried on primarily to develop physical fitness with little consideration for the other goals of physical education. Two developmental approaches are suggested for children. The first is to use movement experiences based on basic movement methodology, with emphasis on gross body movements, leading to total body development. The second is to use selected fitness routines of a more formal nature, which include exercises, simple circuit training, and astronaut drills.

Probably the most appropriate place to begin formal fitness work of this type is in the third grade. Some instructors have found first and second grade children quite receptive to these drills. However, caution must be exercised in the use of these routines for young children.

Movement Experiences for Fitness (K-2)

Many big-muscle movement experiences can be structured for children, assuring demands on all, or at least most, parts of the body. Included in the consideration for gross body development is the introductory activity for each lesson.

Each lesson should begin with introductory activity, which also has fitness implications. This is generally, but not necessarily, some type of gross locomotor activity. Much of this involves heavy demands on the lower limbs and serves as an introductory and warm-up activity for the fitness activities to follow.

The approach for total body development in movement experiences is to center attention on three general areas of the body, the trunk, the arm-shoulder girdle, and the legs. Furthermore, the development of the various fitness qualities (strength, flexibility, agility, etc.) should also be a consideration.

Methodology

In working with the three categories, it is recognized that many movements will contribute to more than one body area, and in some cases to all three divisions. This is understandable, but the emphasis on gross movement fitness work during any one daily lesson must be such that all three body areas receive appropriate work demands.

In all three categories, movements can be locomotor or they can be in place. If the movement is locomotor, the children must be directed to move in such a fashion that the desired area of the body will be exercised.

If the movements are done in place (non-locomotor), generally two elements are necessary. The first is to put the student into some kind of a position and proceed from this base. The second is to provide a number of challenges or directives so movements having fitness values for that area of the body will occur. Inventiveness and imagination on the part of the teacher or leader are essential ingredients to successful movement work.

The formations for basic movement (page 113) can be employed for locomotor movements. Nonlocomotor movements are generally done with the children scattered or in extended squad formation.

The amount of physical effort that the children are to undergo probably becomes a question of instructor judgment. If development is to occur, the children must be challenged and in turn be stimulated to exert sufficient effort so that development can occur. This is someplace between working them "hard enough" and "not too hard." Considerable reliance must be centered on the children to accept responsibility for their own progress.

Trunk Development

Movements which include bending, stretching, swaying, twisting, reaching, and forming shapes are important inclusions here. No particular continuity exists, except that a specified approach should move from the simple to the more complex. However, challenge to the abdominal muscles should be included in each developmental session.

The most logical approach is to select one or more of the above movements and use it or them as the theme for the day. Vary the position the child is to take — standing, lying, kneeling, sitting, etc. From the selected position, stimulate the child to varied movement based on the theme for the day. Examples follow with regard to how the different types of trunk movements can become both fitness and learning experiences for youngsters.

Bending

Bend in different ways.
Bend as many parts of the body as you can.
Make different shapes by bending two, three, and four parts of the body.
Bend the arms, knees in different ways and on different levels.
Try different ways of bending the fingers and wrist of one hand with the other. Use some resistance. Add body bends.

Stretching

Keeping one foot in place, stretch your arms in different directions, stepping as you move with the free foot. Stretch at different levels.
On the floor, stretch one leg different ways in space. Stretch one leg in one direction and the other leg in another direction.
Stretch slowly as you wish and then snap back to original position.
Stretch with different arm-leg combinations in diverse directions.
See how much space on the floor you can cover by stretching. Show us how big your space is.
Combine bending and stretching movements.

Swaying and Twisting

Sway your body back and forth in different directions. Change the position of the arms.
Sway your body bending over.
Sway your head from side to side.
Select a part of the body, twist as far as you can in opposite directions.
Twist your body at different levels.
Twist two or more parts of the body at the same time.
Twist one part of the body while untwisting another.
Twist your head to see as far back as you can.
Twist like a spring; like a screwdriver.
Stand on one foot and twist your body. Untwist.
From a seated position, make different shapes by twisting.

Forming Shapes

Children love to form different shapes with their bodies, and this interest should be utilized to aid in trunk development. Shapes can be formed in most any position — standing, sitting, lying, balancing on parts of the body, and moving. Shapes can be curled or stretched, narrow or wide, big or little, symmetrical or asymmetrical, twisted or straight.

Abdominal Emphasis

The best position to ensure exercise of the abdominal muscles is to have the child lying supine on the floor or mat. Challenges should direct him to lift the upper and lower portions of the body from the floor either singly or together. The following are examples of directives to a child lying on his back on the floor:

Sit up and touch both toes with your hands.
Sit up and touch the right toe with the left hand. The other way.
Bring up your toes to touch behind your head.
With hands to the side, bring your feet up straight and then touch them by the right hand. By the left hand.
Lift your feet up slowly an inch at a time. Without bending your knees.
Pick up your heels about 6" from the floor and swing them back and forth. Cross them and twist them.
Lift your head from the floor and look at your toes. Wink with your right eye and wiggle your left foot. Reverse.

Arm-Shoulder Girdle Development Activity

Movement experiences contributing to arm-shoulder girdle development can be divided roughly into two groups of activities. The first includes movements where the arms are free of any body support function. In the second the arms support the body weight either wholly or in part.

In the first group, where the arms are free, movements such as swinging, pulling, pushing, lifting, and reaching can be exploited for development.

Swinging and Circling

Swing one limb (arm or leg) at a time, different directions and levels.

Combine two limb movements (arm-arm, leg-leg, or arm-leg combinations) in the same direction and in opposite directions. Vary levels.

Swing arms or legs back and forth and go into giant circles.

Swing arms as if swimming—bent-over position. Try a backstroke or a breaststroke. What does a sidestroke look like?

Make the arms go like a windmill. Go in different directions.

How else can you circle your arms?

Pretend a swarm of bees is around your head. Brush them off and keep them away.

Reaching and Pulling

Reach high into the sky and pull stars toward you.

Using both hands, pull something high, pull something low. Pull from different directions.

Reach out and grab snowflakes. Did you get one?

Pull from different positions — kneeling, sitting, lying.

Reach out in one direction as far as you can and then reach out with the same hand in the opposite direction. Reach out high in one direction and low in another.

With your hands clasped behind your head, pull your head forward. See if you can make wind by waving your elbows back and forth.

From a sitting position, pull on your knees and legs. Can you pull your big toe up to your nose? Try it with the other foot.

Reach up and climb a ladder to the sky. See how high you can reach.

Pushing

Pretend to push something heavy with both hands. Push it at a high level. Push it at a low level.

Push up the sky slowly. Hold it up with your feet on tiptoes.

Push with one hand then the other. Alternate hands back and forth.

From a kneeling position, push yourself up to a stand.

Lie on your tummy. Push yourself backwards with your hands. Push yourself right and left.

Sit on the floor with legs outstretched. Place your hands alongside your seat and lift your seat off the floor.

Lifting

Lift your arms as high as you can. Extend them out wide. Bring them close.

Kneel down. Start your arms low and lift them high. See how many different ways you can lift them.

Pretend you are lifting and throwing logs. Throw in different directions. How high can you lift your log?

Developmental Activities Based on the Push-Up Position

Each child is asked to assume the push-up position, which he uses as a base of operation. The challenges require a movement and then a return to the original push-up position.

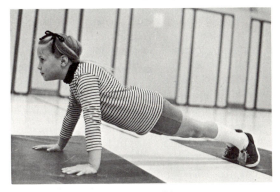

Push-Up Position

From this position we ask the children if they can —

    Lift one foot high. Now the other foot.

    Bounce both feet up and down. Move the feet out from each other while bouncing.

Inch the feet up to the hands and go back again. Inch the feet up to the hands and then inch the hands out to return to the push-up position.

Reach up with one hand and touch the other shoulder behind the back.

Lift both hands from the floor. Try clapping the hands.

Bounce from the floor with both hands and feet off the floor at the same time.

Turn over so the back is to the floor. Complete the turn to push-up position.

Lower the body an inch at a time until the chest touches the floor. Return.

Inch the hands (one at a time at first) out to the sides. Return.

There is value in maintaining the push-up position for a length of time. The various tasks to be done provide interest and challenge to the youngsters. The informal and individual approach stimulates the child to good effort in muscular work.

The crab position should also be utilized in a similar fashion. The side leaning rest position is another which may be employed. Many of the same directives listed above for the push-up position can be used with modification for that position.

Leg Development

A first consideration is to decide whether or not the introductory activity has contributed sufficient activity for the legs. If this were rhythmic running, for example, no further leg demands probably would be needed. Activities for the legs can be considered in two broad categories. The first are erect movement patterns with the body supported entirely by the legs. In the second the body is in a position other than erect. This could be on all fours or in a seated or lying position.

Erect Position. The running patterns described later under Basic Movement (page 116) can be employed.

The Tortoise and the Hare Routine has value. On the command "Tortoise," the children run slowly in place. On the command "Hare," they speed up the speed of the stationary run.

Jumping and hopping patterns in place or moving can be used.

Partner-pulling movements can be utilized involving one partner pulling the other with one or both hands and the other providing passive resistance.

Jump rope activity either with or without music is of value.

Have the children run laps inside the gymnasium or around a prescribed course on the playground.

Marching either in place or moving has good value. Music should be the basis for the activity.

Other Leg Movements. These, of course, will involve demands on other body areas, but do provide leg developmental possibilities.

In an all-fours or crab position, move forward, backward, sideward, turn around.

On the back with the feet in the air, "ride the bicycle."

Do the same from a seated position, by picking up the heels and "pedaling."

Using a sprinter's position wherein one knee is under the chest and the other leg is extended straight back, change the position of the legs rapidly. (See page 98.)

FITNESS ROUTINES FOR GRADE 3

In contrast to the developmental program of movement experiences, the fitness emphasis for Grade 3 can shift to more formalized fitness routines as an introduction to those generally employed in the intermediate grades. It has somewhat of an ego approach in that the children now feel they are shifting to more grown-up procedures and doing things like the older children.

A well-executed exercise program should be the basis for the fitness activities. Exercises must be learned — and learned well — as they are basic to the other two suggested routines — circuit training and astronaut drills. Movement experiences from the earlier years should still be a part of the developmental experiences of third grade children. The type of developmental activities should be changed every three or four weeks to provide variation and to maintain interest. Alternating them from day to day is not recommended, as this makes increased dosages difficult and leads to learning time wasted in making the different presentations each day. Once a drill or routine is learned, little instructional time is needed until a change occurs.

Exercises

Exercises, or calisthenics, as they are sometimes termed, have much to offer and can make the following contributions to the physical education program:

1. Developing and Maintaining Specific Muscle Groups. Emphasis should be on those muscle groups which give support to the body in the matter of posture. The important muscle groups include those of the feet, the abdominal wall, the back muscles, and those holding the shoulders and head in normal position of good posture.

2. General Overall Physical Activity. Vigorous exercises involving most or many of the large muscle groups in the body are used for this purpose.

3. Carry-Over Activity. Providing exercises in the program enables the youngsters to learn their value and develop the basis for desirable activity in later life when the vigorous games and activities are not recommended.

4. Loosening and Stretching Muscles. Preliminary to such activity areas as stunts and tumbling, apparatus, and track and field, the children can be put through a series of stretching exercises to loosen and prepare muscles for the activities which follow. Bending, stretching, and twisting exercises are the most commonly used for this purpose.

5. Particular Attention to Selected Fitness Components. Exercises can be selected to contribute particular fitness attributes such as flexibility, coordination, power, strength, and agility. Endurance is not developed through an exercise program to a great degree, nor is balance. No categories for endurance or balance are included in overall exercise groups.

Cautions in Giving Exercises

Certain cautions should be observed in giving exercises. These also apply to other physical education activities.

1. Good postural alignment should be maintained. In exercises where the arms are held in front, to the side, or overhead, the abdominal wall needs to be tensed and flattened to maintain proper position of the pelvis. In most activities, the feet should be pointed reasonably straight ahead. The chest should be kept up, and the head and shoulders kept in good postural position.

2. Some care should be taken in using exercises requiring a straight leg position with no bending at the knee joint, such as forward-bending exercises. These activities tend to force the knee back in a hyperextended position, which contributes to posture faults. Some stretching of the leg muscles is excellent for flexibility, but the knee joint should be relaxed slightly rather than forced back to a back-kneed position.

3. Repeated deep knee bending (full squats) is regarded by some as injurious to the knee joint. While an exercise or activity which demands an occasional deep knee bend causes little harm, an activity which calls for repeated full knee joint bending should be avoided. It is interesting to note that Japanese physical educators dispute the danger element of deep knee bending. Their claim is that the Japanese people have sound and strong knees, in spite of the many squatting positions which are assumed as part of their living habits.

4. The activity known as the "Bicycle Ride" or the "Bicycle" should be used only if there is no overstretching of the muscles in the back of the neck. In the "Bicycle" the child is on the back of his neck and shoulders with his feet going in circles as in riding a bicycle. The exercise should be done with the weight mostly on the back of the shoulders, not high on the back of the neck.

5. In each set of exercises, there should be an exercise for the arm-shoulder girdle and one for the abdominal wall.

6. The Curl-up, with the legs in a bent-knee position and feet flat on the floor, should be used in preference to the sit-up, where the legs are extended on the floor with the knees straight. The Curl-up tends to isolate the abdominal muscle group from the psoas muscle group. The straight leg sit-up develops the psoas muscle group, which can lead to increased lower back curve, the opposite of the desired effect of strong abdominal muscles.

In addition, when the upper part of the body comes up, as in the Curl-up, the movement should begin as a roll-up, with the chin moving to touch or come close to the chest as the initial movement. This also helps to flatten out the lower back curve.

7. In exercises using leg raising, such as marching in place or running in place, the knees should be lifted to the point where the thigh is parallel to the floor. By lifting the knees high, more and different muscles are brought into play, which ordinarily would not be true with a moderate knee lift.

8. Exercises in themselves do little to develop endurance. Additional activity in the form of running, rope jumping, or other such vigorous activity is needed to round out fitness development and take care of this component.

9. The tempo with which an exercise is done is important. Most exercises have an effective rhythm which should be employed. Experimentation is needed to determine which speed of cadence is best for a particular exercise.

Setting Formation

In giving exercises to a class, the first task is to get the students into an appropriate formation quickly. This can be done in a number of ways:

1. In an early session of the class, set up a formation for the exercise program. Upon a signal, the students take their places in this prearranged formation. Spots or numbers can be painted on the floor.

2. Have the students simply scatter, allowing sufficient room for the activity.

3. Use squad formation and extend the formation to the rear, with the students far enough apart so as not to interfere with each other.

Introducing Exercises

Once the students are in formation, the instructor proceeds with a description of the exercise. He can follow the procedure outlined below:

1. "The first exercise we are going to do is the Side Straddle Hop."

2. "Starting position is the position of attention. It is a two-count exercise."

3. "On count one, jump to a side straddle position with arms overhead." (Illustrate.)

4. "On count two, recover to starting position." (Illustrate.)

The instructor now has the class go through the exercise slowly (by the numbers) with him until he is satisfied that he can put them through the activity in cadence. Exercises are usually performed in four or eight-count rhythm. The number of repetitions will vary according to the fitness level of the group.

After the instructor has given his description and has had the group go through the exercises slowly, he is ready for class activity. This introductory procedure is satisfactory for most exercises.

Leading Exercises

1. After the exercise has been named or described (if necessary), the leader can emphasize the stress or critical execution points. For example, he can say for the Rowing Exercise, "Remember to squeeze tight with the knees and point the arms out level to the front." Attention to proper execution is important in exercises, particularly in new exercises, so that the purpose of the exercise can be realized.

2. Put the group in starting position. This can be done informally by simply directing the children to assume the starting position.

3. The next command gets the group off together in rhythmic execution. The starting command can be "Ready — exercise," or "In time — exercise." This should be given in approximately the same cadence as the exercise rhythm.

4. The count now continues and the exercise should be done in unison. The count goes (for example) "1-2-3-4, 1-2-3-4." To halt the group together, slow down the count, change the tone of the voice, and command "1-2-and halt."

5. The number of repetitions is a consideration. Begin the program with around five repetitions for each exercise. The counting can include the repetitions in this fashion: "1-2-3-1, 1-2-3-2, 1-2-3-3," etc. Or, it could be: "1-2-3-4, 2-2-3-4, 3-2-3-4," etc.

6. The exercise should be followed by a brief period of relaxation. Give the group, "At ease" or "In place — rest."

There are times when it is best to allow the students to set their own limits informally. This works well with Curl-ups, Push-ups, and similar exercises where the limits can be based on individual capacity. The instructor simply requests the child to do as many repetitions as he can.

Another method of counting can be employed for such two-count exercises as the Curl-up and Push-up, where a specified number of repetitions is desired. For the Curl-up, the cadence count can go, "Up — one, Up — two, Up — three," etc. For the Push-up, it can go, "Down — one, Down — two, Down — three," etc. This allows an accurate count so the specified number can be administered. The children can be involved in the counting by having the leader give the initiating command, "Down" or "Up," and the children count in unison as they complete each movement.

Securing Progression

Progression is essential in the exercise program, and each lesson plan should specify the number of repetitions. If development is to occur, what is known in physical education as the overload principle must be applied so that the child works harder each exercise period.

Increasing the number of repetitions is only one way of providing progression by means of the overload principle. A second way is to change to a more demanding type of exercise of a similar nature. A third method is to increase the speed of the repetitions, and a fourth is to lessen the resting time between the exercises. Combinations of the above may also be used to increase the work load.

SELECTED EXERCISES

The recommended exercises in this section are presented under the following categories.
1. Flexibility.
2. Arm-Shoulder Girdle
3. Abdominal
4. Leg Agility
5. Trunk Twisting and Bending

For the primary level, a set of six exercises seems to be about the right number. Included in each set should be two exercises from the Arm-Shoulder Girdle group and at least one from each of the other categories. Specific exercises should be changed at times, and a minimum of twelve to fifteen exercises should be included in the overall year's experiences.

Several approaches are used to insure a variety in exercise selection. One system is to select a basic or fundamental group of exercises. Let's assume that twelve exercises are selected. These could be divided into two sets of six each, with the selection meeting the standards of category coverage as previously discussed. Some teachers like to alternate the sets day by day. Others prefer to have one set in effect for a week or two before changing.

As a timesaver, teachers can make up sets of exercises on cards, using a different colored card for each of the categories. In this manner, the teacher can be assured of full developmental coverage by selecting a card from each color, with the stipulation of two from the Arm-Shoulder Girdle group.

Variety in exercise selection is desirable. It is not sound to stay with a narrow, inflexible set of exercises through the entire year.

Recommended exercises are presented under each of the five categories. Stress points or points critical to execution are presented where appropriate under the exercises. Teachers can supplement the listed exercises with those of their own choice, provided the exercises are fundamentally sound. Some exercises which have value as corrective activities in posture work have already been presented and reference is made to them in the exercise program.

FLEXIBILITY EXERCISES

Many exercises in general can contribute to the development of flexibility. However, the main goal of those included in this section is the development of flexibility. Flexibility exercises feature forceful stretching of joints or muscle groups well toward their limits. The exercises may be accompanied by a rhythmic cadence or not, at the option of the teacher.

BEND AND STRETCH

Starting Position: Standing erect, hands on hips, feet shoulder width apart and pointing forward.

Cadence: Slow.

Movement:

1. Bend forward, touch the knuckles to the floor three times.
2. Return to starting position.

The knees should be relaxed slightly, if needed, to prevent a hyperextended knee position.

SITTING STRETCH

Starting Position: Sitting on the floor with legs extended forward and feet about a yard apart. Hands are clasped behind the neck, with the elbows pointed forward and kept close together.

Cadence: Slow.

Movement:

1. Bounce down with the upper body, bringing the elbows as close to the floor as possible.
2. Recover slightly and bounce again.
3. Repeat (2).
4. Recover to sitting position.

Variation: Instead of bouncing straight forward, bounce first toward the left knee, then straight forward, then toward the right knee, and recover to sitting position on the fourth count. Next sequence, reverse the direction.

Stress Points: Because the legs are against the floor, there is little chance for a hyperextended knee position, so the bouncing can be quite forceful.

HURDLE STRETCH

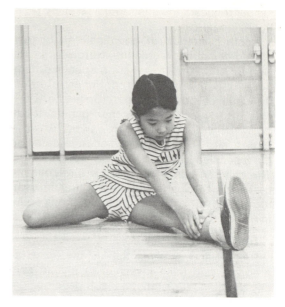

Starting Position: One leg is pointed forward and fully extended. The other thigh is to the side, with the knee bent and the leg pointing to the rear. The position resembles that of a hurdler going over a hurdle. Both arms are pointed forward toward the extended foot.

Movement:

1. Bounce forward with the upper body and reach the hands toward the forward foot.
2. Recover slightly and bounce forward again.
3. Recover slightly and bounce again.
4. Recover to original position.

Stress Points: Attempt to keep the movements in an erect forward-backward movement, avoiding a tendency to lean away from the side of the back leg. The leg position should be reversed after about four exercise patterns (4 counts each).

ARM-SHOULDER GIRDLE EXERCISES

PUSH-UPS

Starting Position: Front leaning rest. The body is straight from head to heels.

Cadence: Moderate or at will.

Movement:

1. Bend elbows and touch chest to ground, keeping body straight.
2. Straighten elbows, raising body in straight line.

Modification: If student is unable to perform the activity as mentioned above, have him start with knees or hips in contact with the floor.

Stress Points: The only movement should be in the arms. The head should be up and the eyes looking ahead. The chest should touch the floor lightly without receiving the weight

THE PHYSICAL DEVELOPMENT GOAL 95

of the body. The body should remain in a straight line throughout, without sagging or humping.

Variations: (1) After the children have some competence in doing push-ups, have them try the following four-count sequence:

(a) Halfway down
(b) All the way down
(c) Halfway up
(d) Up to starting position

(2) For kindergarten classes, this can be called a "Flat Tire." The teacher can start the movement with a "bang," and the children can lower themselves slowly to the accompaniment of the sound of air escaping from a tire.

ARM CIRCLING

Starting Position: Erect, feet apart, arms to the side with palms up.

Cadence: Moderate.

Movement:

1. Five forward 12" circles, moving both arms simultaneously, palms up.

2. Five backward 12" circles, moving both arms simultaneously, palms down.

The number of circles to be made before changing to the opposite direction can be varied.

Stress Points: Good posture position should be maintained with the abdominal wall flat and the head and shoulders held back.

CRAB KICKING

Starting Position: Crab position — the body is supported on hands and feet with the back to the floor. The knees are at right angles.

Cadence: Moderate.

Movement:

1. Kick as high as possible toward the ceiling, alternating the feet.

2. Extend one leg forward so the heel touches the floor. Alternate the legs.

3. Begin with both feet flat on the floor with knees bent in normal crab position. Thrust both feet forward so the legs are straight and the weight is on both heels. Recover.

4. Have the children move forward, backward, sideward on all fours, maintaining crab position. Turn in a small circle, right and left.

Stress Points: Children must maintain a high hip position. The tendency is to drop the seat. A method of getting children to maintain proper body position is to have them watch the ceiling.

WING STRETCHER

Starting Position: Stand erect; raise elbows to shoulder height, fists clenched, palms down in front of the chest.

Cadence: Moderate.

Movement:

1. Thrust elbows backward vigorously. Be sure to keep the abdominal wall flat and the head erect. Keep elbows at shoulder height.
2. Return to position.

Variation: Alternate the backward elbow thrust with a full backward swing of the arms. This makes it a four-count exercise.

Stress Points: The abdominal wall should be kept flat and the head and shoulders held in good postural position.

Other Exercises

In addition to the preceding exercises, the following exercises included with the discussion of posture development should be considered:

The Swan (page 60)
Tailor Exercise (page 60)

ABDOMINAL EXERCISES

For most exercises stressing abdominal development, the child lies on his back on the floor or mat (supine position) as a basic starting position. To secure abdominal muscle involvement from this position, the child can bring his legs up, his upper body up, or both the legs and upper body up at the same time. If the upper body is brought up, the movement should begin with a roll-up by moving the head first so that the chin makes contact or near contact with the chest, thus flattening and stabilizing the lower back curve. The bent-knee position of the legs, either originally or in the execution of the movement, places more demands specifically on the abdominal muscles.

Isometric principles of utilizing held position can be applied efficiently to abdominal exercises. The position should be held without movement for 4 to 8 seconds at the point of the greatest contraction specified for the particular exercise.

An excellent exercise for abdominal development which does not use the supine position is the *Leg Extension*.

HEAD AND SHOULDER CURL

Starting Position: On back with hands clasped, palms down, behind the small of the back. Knees are up and soles of the feet flat on the floor.

Cadence: Moderate.

Movement:

1. Lift the head and pull the shoulders and elbows off the floor.
2. Hold the tensed position for 5 counts.
3. Return to starting position.

The verbal count for the exercise can be: "Up (lift), 2-3-4-5 (hold), down (return)."

Variation: The arms are extended so the hands are palms down on the thighs. When the upward lift of the shoulders is made, the hands slide to the knees.

KNEE RAISE (Single and Double)

Starting Position: On back with knees slightly flexed, feet flat on the floor, and arms out to the side.

Cadence: Moderate.

Movement:

1. Raise one knee as close to the chest as possible.
2. Return.
3. Raise the other knee.
4. Return.

The exercise should be done later with both knees coming up at once and returning.

Other Exercises

Abdominal exercises included under the discussion of posture should also be included here.

    Curl-Up (page 60)
    Rowing (page 61)
    Curl-Up with Twist (page 61)

LEG EXTENSION

Starting Position: Sitting on floor with legs extended and hands on hips.

Cadence: Moderate.

Movement:

1. With a quick, vigorous action, raise the knees and bring both heels as close to the seat as possible. The movement is a drag with the toes touching lightly.
2. Return to position.

LEG-AGILITY EXERCISES

Leg-Agility exercises should feature rhythmic, graceful motion with emphasis on control. Cadence should be regular and even.

RUNNING IN PLACE

Starting Position: Standing with arms in loose thrust position.

Cadence: Slow, fast, slow.

Movement: Stationary run. Begin slowly (counting only on left foot). Speed up somewhat, raising knees to height of hips, then run at full speed, raising knees hard, then slow down. Run should be on the toes.

Variations:

1. *Tortoise and Hare.* Jog slowly in place. On the command, "Hare," double the speed. On the command, "Tortoise," slow the tempo to original jogging speed.
2. March in place, lifting knees high and swinging the arms well up.

SIDE STRADDLE HOP

Starting Position: At attention.

Cadence: Moderate.

Movement:

1. On count one, jump to a straddle position with arms overhead.
2. On count two, recover to starting position.

Side Straddle Hop is also a coordination exercise.

Variations:

1. Begin with the feet in a stride position (forward and back). Change feet with the overhead movement.
2. Instead of bringing the feet together

when the arms come down, cross the feet each time, alternating the cross.

3. On the completion of each set of 8 counts, do a quarter turn right. After four sets, the child will again be facing in his original direction.

THE TREADMILL

Starting Position: Push-up position except that one leg is brought forward so that the knee is under the chest.

Cadence: Moderate.

Movement:

1. Reverse position of the feet, bringing the other leg forward.
2. Change back with original foot forward. The exercise is continued rhythmically with feet alternating. The *Treadmill* is one of the test items in the New York State Physical Fitness Test.

Stress Points: Head should be kept up. A full exchange of the legs should be made with the forward knee coming well under the chest each time.

TRUNK EXERCISES

These activities are primarily twisting and bending exercises which cover a variety of movements with emphasis on trunk development. Some involve either bending or twisting movements. A few include both twisting and bending motions. Twisting and bending should be done to forceful limits. Movements should be large and vigorous.

SIDE FLEX

Starting Position: Lie on side, lower arm extended overhead. The head rests on the lower arm. Legs are extended fully, one on top of the other.

Cadence: Moderate.

Movement:

1. With a brisk action, raise the upper arm and leg vertically. Attempt to make contact with hand and foot, without bending elbow or knee.
2. Repeat for several counts and change to the other side.

TRUNK TWISTER

Starting Position: Standing with feet about 2' apart sideward, hands clasped behind head, elbows held backward, chin in.

Cadence: Slow.

Movement:

1. Bend and bounce downward, knees straight. Recover slightly. Do this vigorously.
2. Bounce downward, but simultaneously rotate trunk sharply to left.
3. Same to the right.
4. Return to original position, pulling head back and chin in strongly.

The *Trunk Twister* reaches and strengthens all muscles of the trunk. It has excellent postural benefits. It results in greater flexibility of the lower back region.

BODY CIRCLES

Starting Position: Feet shoulder-width apart, hands clasped behind the head, body bent forward.

Cadence: Moderate.

Movement: The movement is a complete circle done by the upper body in 4 counts. A specified number of circles should be made to the right and the same number to the left. The right circle is described:

1. Circle upper body a quarter turn to the right.
2. Another quarter turn to the back.
3. Another quarter turn to the left.
4. A final quarter turn ending in original position.

This exercise can be done in free movement by directing the children to circle in one direction until told to stop. Direction is then reversed.

TURN AND BOUNCE

Starting Position: Erect, with feet shoulder width apart and arms out to the side, level, with palms down.

Cadence: Moderate.

Movement:

1. Using the lower body as a fixed base, twist the upper body as far as possible in one direction, carrying one arm as far backward as possible.
2. Recover slightly and twist again (bounce).
3. Recover and bounce again.
4. Recover to original position.

Repeat to the opposite side.

Stress Points: Abdominal wall should be kept flat and upper body in good postural position throughout. The hips must be kept in place, with the vigorous twist on the hips as a base.

CIRCUIT TRAINING

Circuit training is an exercise program consisting of a number of stations arranged in the form of a circuit. Each of the stations demands an exercise task from the child, as he moves from station to station in sequential order.

Basic Theory

The exercise tasks composing the circuit should contribute to the development of all parts of the body. In addition, the activities should contribute to the various components of physical fitness, i.e., strength, power, endurance, agility, flexibility, and others. Thus, circuit training can be a valuable tool in the development of physical fitness.

Methodology

Each station should provide an exercise task which is within the capacity of the children. The type of activity at each station should be one that the child can learn and do without the aid of another child. As the child moves from one station to the next, the exercises which directly follow each other should make demands on different parts of the body. In this way the performance at any one station does not cause local fatigue which could affect the ability to perform the next task.

It is important that sufficient instruction in the activities be given so that the children can perform correctly at each station. The children should be taught to count the number of repetitions correctly, if a system of counting is employed.

The class can be divided so that some start at each station. From the standpoint of supplying necessary equipment at each station, this method keeps the demands low. For example, if there are thirty children for a circuit of six stations, five children would start at each spot. The maximum equipment at each station in this case would be that necessary for five children.

Timing and Dosage

In general, a fixed time limit at each station seems to offer the best plan for circuit training on the elementary level. Each child attempts to complete as many repetitions as he can during the time limit at each station. Increased work load can be accomplished by increasing the number of repetitions (by the child) and increasing the amount of time at each station. A suggested progressive time schedule to be used as a guide for timing the circuit is as follows:

Introduction	15 seconds at each station
First 2 weeks	20 seconds at each station
Second 2 weeks	25 seconds at each station
After 4 weeks	30 seconds at each station

Keeping in mind that children must be challenged, the above schedule should be modified accordingly. Children need to be "pushed" and the time limit is adjusted to accomplish this. A circuit that is too easy will contribute little to the development of fitness.

A 15-second interval should be established to allow children to move from one station to the next. Later, this can be lowered to 10 seconds or even 5 seconds. Students may start at any station as designated, but must follow the established order of stations.

Circuit for Primary Children

While the number of stations can vary, six seems to be an appropriate number, with consideration for keeping equipment needs to a minimum. Signs are of value at different stations to provide direction and emphasize stress points. The six station circuit which is suggested uses little equipment and the activities are within the range of late primary children. It covers all areas of the body and gives attention to strength, agility, and flexibility. Cardio-respiratory endurance is accomplished by the activity in total.

SAMPLE CIRCUIT TRAINING COURSE

Six-Station Course

1 Running in Place	2 Curl-Ups	3 Arm Circling
6 Crab Walk	5 Trunk Twister	4 Agility Run

Supplies and Equipment: Mats for curl-ups (to hook toes).

Time Needed: 4 minutes — based on 30-second activity limit, 10 seconds to move between stations.

A description of the activities follows, together with a suggestion for an alternate activity at each station:

Station 1. Running in place

This should be done with high knee action and vigorous arm action.

Alternate Activity — Rope Jumping.

Station 2. Curl-Ups

A mat is needed so that the performers can hook the toes underneath and do these individually. Curl-Ups are described on page 61.

Alternate Activity — Rowing (see page 61).

Station 3. Arm Circling

Arm Circling is described on page 95. Good postural position should be maintained.

Alternate Activity — Push-Ups (page 94).

Station 4. Agility Run

Two lines are established about 15 feet apart. The child moves between the two lines as rapidly as possible, touching one line with the right foot and the other with the left.

Alternate Activity — Side Straddle Hop (page 97).

Station 5. Trunk Twister

This is described on page 98.

Alternate Activity — Bend and Stretch (page 93).

Station 6. Crab Walk

Two parallel lines 6 to 8 feet apart are needed. The child in crab position touches his hands on one line and then moves to the other line to touch with his feet.

Alternate Activity — Crab Kick (page 95).

The circuit presented includes exercises from the previously presented exercise list, which reinforces the principle that exercises are to be scheduled first during the year so that the activities can be used later in circuit training.

ASTRONAUT DRILLS

The children form a large circle and are spaced about 6' apart. The basic movement is a walk around the circle, not necessarily in step. The teacher gives various commands designating the activity to be performed. Most of these are locomotor movements which the children do while moving in the circle. The teacher may at times direct the circle to stop and do certain exercises. After the task has been done, the children continue the walk around the circle.

The following movements and tasks can be incorporated into the routine.

1. Various locomotor movements such as hopping, jumping, running, sliding, skipping, giant steps, high on toes, etc.

2. On all fours, moving in the line of direction forward, backward, and sideward. Repeat backward and forward using crab position.

3. Stunt movements like the *Seal Crawl, Gorilla Walk, Bunny Jump,* etc.

4. Upper torso movements and exercises that can be done while walking, such as arm circles, bending right and left, body twists, etc.

5. Various exercises in place. Always include an abdominal development activity.

Children who lag can move toward the inner part of the circle and allow more active children to pass them on the outside. Both clockwise and counterclockwise directions can be used, but not necessarily on the same day.

The following series of directives will provide an understanding of how the children's movements can be guided in astronaut drills. The directions should be timed and spaced to allow for appropriate responses by the children.

1. "Everybody walk."

2. "Let's Run." "Now with a high knee action."

3. "Walk." "Walk high on your toes."

4. "On all fours, head first."

5. "Walk again." "Now, take long strides."

6. "Stop! Face the center. Do as many push-ups as you can."

7. "Once more, walk." "Now, trot lightly."

8. "Face the center. Do any kind of a curl-up or rowing exercise you wish."

9. "Walk once more."

10. "Crab walk, feet first."

11. "Walk." "Circle your arms as you walk — forward and backward."

12. "On all fours facing the center. Move sideways to your right."

13. "Walk."

14. "On all fours with feet toward the center. Move sideways to your left."

15. "On your feet. Run lightly — high knees."

There is no set pattern, but instructors are cautioned to have the continuity planned so that the activity is instructionally sound. Judgment is needed to determine how much distance each of the activities should consume before the change back to walking.

10

Basic Movement

Purposes of Basic Movement
Processes in Basic Movement
Factors for Securing Variety of Response
Instructional Procedures
Problem Development
Stressing Quality in Movement
Formations for Movement
Developing Ideas for Unstructured Movement
Developing Ideas for Structured Movement
The Movement Suggestion Box
Perceptual-Motor Activities, Manipulative Activities, and Apparatus Activities

Basic movement is movement carried on for its own sake, for increased awareness and understanding of movement possibilities of the body, and for the acquisition of a good vocabulary of movement skills. The child, through guidance, uses basic movement as a way of expressing, exploring, and interpreting himself and of developing his capabilities. The experiences should be organized so that the child can learn about his movement possibilities.

Basic movement must be guided. Teachers must be prepared to introduce originality and something of their own personality into the teaching process. Invention is the key to the movement experiences. The problems are set up with instruction and demonstration kept to a minimum, to be used only as needed.

The emphasis in basic movement is on activity and movement of a *purposeful* nature. The teacher must be interested in promoting within the child *both* quantity and quality of movement. Only then does movement become an educational experience. Too often the children undergo movement experiences without guidance or insistence on their doing things as well as possible. Learning takes place primarily when a child reinforces a desirable motor pattern or concept, or acquires a new pattern or concept. Creativity means coming up with something worth saving, either because of its own intrinsic value or because it can be the basis for another movement pattern.

PURPOSES OF BASIC MOVEMENT

What are the objectives of the basic movement program? The following are considered basic and important:

1. Basic movement must structure a learning environment so that children learn to think for themselves and accept responsibility in a large measure for their own learning.

2. The program should offer a wide experience in movement, so that children will move with ease, coordination, fluency, and versatility to the limit of the body's potential.

3. The program should seek individual *creative* responses and should be structured so that the children have the opportunity to be creative and participate in self-learning.

4. The children should be made aware of their movement possibilities, so that in time they can move skillfully with sureness and confidence in a variety of situations, with emphasis on more efficient management of the body.

5. The children should develop a "movement vocabulary" of basic skills to serve as a foundation for the more complicated sports and dance skills.

6. The movement experiences should include gross movements so that developmental

demands will be made on the body. A variety of big-muscle activities should be a part of the program so fitness values can accrue for each child. (Page 87.)

7. The learning situation recognizes individual differences and allows each child to improve at his own rate and reach a measure of satisfaction in achievement.

8. It is postulated that a safer atmosphere is provided because children are not forced or urged to perform movements beyond their own capacity. They are led to a particular performance only when they themselves have established appropriate readiness.

9. The program should develop an awareness of the concepts of space, time, qualities of movement, flow, and body factors and their relationship and influence in movement.

10. Children should be able not only to move efficiently, but also to analyze critically their own movements and those of others.

PROCESSES IN BASIC MOVEMENT

Basic movement can be viewed as the summation of four different processes which cannot be taught in isolation but must be related.

What can the body do?

The teacher looks to basic movement to aid in four areas of movement competency, which in essence involves most human movement. Movements and skills can be selected from any of these areas.

a. *Efficient body management.* Body management involves the body as a whole. The child should gain body awareness, i.e., he must be aware of each part of the body as related to other parts or to the whole. This is an awareness of the individual (self) in the total physical environment.

b. *Basic skills.* Basic skills include specified locomotor movements (as opposed to general locomotor movements), nonlocomotor movements, and manipulative skills. In today's programs, manipulative skills have been broadened in number and scope so that they can be regarded as an entity in themselves. Manipulative skills are discussed in Chapter 13.

c. *Specialized skills.* These are the skills of the sports, specialized rhythmic activities, stunts and tumbling, and fitness. While most of the skills have techniques of a specific nature, their development can be enhanced through the application of basic movement instructional procedures.

d. *Apparatus skills.* Apparatus skills make up a special category, as they can serve as important tools of basic movement, particularly to develop body management competency. Like manipulative skills, apparatus activities have increased in number. They are presented in Chapter 14.

The kind of movement competency specified as the goal for a basic movement program will determine the approach. More freedom and exploration are required when the goal is good body management competencies, more specific instruction is needed to develop basic skills, and still more individual and specific instruction is demanded for specialized skills.

With what or with whom does he move?

The concerns here are the relation of the child and his movements to the physical environment (gymnasium, classroom, playground, or other area) in which he moves, whether large or hand apparatus is involved, and whether he works alone or with other children.

a. *Individual work.* The child first learns to move with competency and to manage himself and his piece of apparatus without interfering with other children.

b. *Partner work.* After he has learned to handle himself reasonably well as an individual, he can learn to work with another child.

c. *Participating in a group situation.* The child can develop sensitivity to others and learn to work effectively as a member of a group through this type of organization. Sharing experiences and judgments in a give-and-take situation leads to better social maturity.

Where can the body move?

This concerns the use of space. Spatial factors have two aspects, general and personal. In general space, the child moves with consideration for others in locomotor movements. In personal space, the child is concerned only with *self* in his movements. Spatial factors are direction, level, patterns, size, and plane of movement.

How can the body move?

Included in this concept are: time factors,

qualities of movement, flow, and the body factors involved in the movement. Time includes variation in speed, acceleration and deceleration, and rhythm. Qualities of movement, which some term *force,* include force of the movement and expressive movement. Flow can be either sustained (free) flow or interrupted (bound) flow. Body factors describe the body and its parts in relation to the prescribed movement problem.

FACTORS FOR SECURING VARIETY OF RESPONSE

The various factors of space, time, qualities of movement, flow, and body factors merit increased discussion and expansion, as they are most important in instructional procedures in basic movement. A thorough understanding of the factors is essential if the teacher is to stimulate the children to potential limits of variety and depth of movement.

Space — Space factors involve level, direction, size, plane of movement, and patterns.

Level — low, high, or in-between.

Direction — straight, zigzag, circular, curved, forward, backward, sideward, upward, and downward.

Size — large or small movements.

Plane of movement — horizontal, vertical, or diagonal.

Patterns — forming squares, diamonds, triangles, circles, figure eights, and other patterns.

Time — The time factor may be varied as follows:

Different speeds — slow, moderate, or fast.

Acceleration or deceleration—increasing or decreasing the speed of movement.

Even or uneven time — sudden, jerky, smooth, or even movement; variation in rhythm.

Flow — Establishing continuity of movement.

Interrupted flow (bound flow)—stopping at the end of a movement or part of a movement.

Sustained flow (free flow) — linking together smoothly different movements or parts of a movement.

Qualities of Movement

Force — light or heavy, strong or weak.

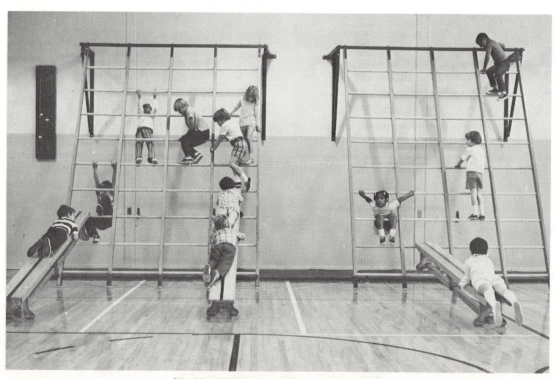

Climbing Frames Combined with Benches

Expressive movement — happy or sad, gay or restrained, angry, rough.

Imitative — imitating animals, personalities, machines, fictitious characters.

Body Factors — A number of considerations in the use of the body can add variety to movement.

Shape — can be long or short, wide or narrow, straight or twisted, stretched or curled, symmetrical or asymmetrical.

Weight bearing — different parts of the body supporting the weight, or receiving the weight; different number of body parts involved in a movement.

Execution — the movement may be done unilaterally (one-sided), bilaterally (both sides together), or cross-laterally (each side independently), performing with a different part of the body.

Body center-oriented — leading with different parts of the body, movements away from and toward the center of the body.

Variations Working on Apparatus

In addition to the variations just presented, variety in movement as the children work on large apparatus can be stimulated by the following considerations:

1. Apparatus can be arranged in different sequences, combinations, and numbers. Benches and balance beams, for example, can be placed on an incline, suspended higher than normal, or placed in combination with other equipment.

2. Variety can be promoted by viewing apparatus as a three-step process, and each step can be varied. Various ways to get on or mount the apparatus can be stipulated. Things to do on or with apparatus can be outlined. Different means of dismounting or getting down from apparatus can be specified.

3. Things to do on apparatus can be varied. The child can be challenged to go over, under, around, or through apparatus. He can support himself in different fashions, using a variety of body factors.

INSTRUCTIONAL PROCEDURES

The impression sometimes exists that we either have basic movement or we have direct instruction. This is a common misconception, as there are many shades or combinations of the two. There can be a heavy emphasis on command teaching with some exploratory activity included, or there might be a movement-centered approach with a modicum of direct teaching. The following diagram of methods of teaching* illustrates the range of teaching approaches.

METHODS OF TEACHING

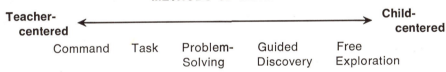

Teacher-centered				Child-centered
Command	Task	Problem-Solving	Guided Discovery	Free Exploration

*Tillotson, Joan and Staff, "Questions and Answers about Movement Education." *Selected Readings in Movement Education,* Robert T. Sweeney, Editor. (Reading, Mass.: Addison-Wesley Publishing Co., 1970), p. 168

Command methodology allows for no individualization. Children are told what to do and how to do it. *Task* approaches set up a type of task to do, but allow little variety in the method of doing it. *Problem-Solving* sets up a problem and guides the students toward the solution. There can be freedom of choice, but guided toward a desired solution. *Guided Discovery* is more open-ended than problem-solving and accepts more individualization of response. *Problem-Solving* can be used more for the development of skills, while *Guided Discovery* is more applicable to general body movement (body management) activities. *Free Exploration* without restrictions from the teacher is usually employed after a level of competency and background have been established to provide the child with sufficient experience on which to base his exploratory movements.

In this guide, the terms "problem-solving" and "guided discovery" are included under the broad term of problem-solving, with the recognition that problem-solving has broad ranges of application and at times can permit a wide and individualistic solution to the problem. Guided discovery, however, begins with a set of concepts toward which the instruction is pointed. Through experimentation and exploration, the child is guided toward these chosen concepts.

Movement patterns, however, can be roughly divided into two broad categories, depending upon the desired outcomes. The first is unstructured movement with the goal of body management competency. The second is structured movement, with the objective of the development of certain skills.

Unstructured Movement

Unstructured movement aims toward the development of body awareness and efficient management of the body in a variety of situations. The emphasis is on exploration, repetition, and creation. Movement tasks of this nature specify certain factors of movement to be included in the problem, but do not specify a precise skill or movement. For example, the child may be asked to move about the room using a quick, low movement in alternation with a slow, high movement. Or, the directive might be, "Find a way to make your ball travel around the floor." There is no right or wrong answer as long as the child solves the problem. The choice is the child's, and the teacher should accept the solution. Unstructured movement will elicit a wider response of movement than problems for structured movement. The instructional emphasis focuses on versatility and breadth of response.

Another approach, which is occasionally used in unstructured movement, is expressive and imitative movement. Expressive movement relies on feelings such as being happy, gay, sad, angry, contrite, etc. Imitative movement mimics animals, personalities, and other elements. Expressive and imitative movement add breadth to the movement possibilities, but should not be regarded as the main objective.

Unstructured movement can be based on broad themes which give meaning to the movement patterns. An entire lesson can be based on a theme which provides the central idea for movement, or two or more themes can be combined in a day's lesson. Many themes can be used. Here are some examples:

1. Learning to receive and transfer the weight.
2. Learning to take the weight on the hands (or other part of the body).
3. Shapes in the air.
4. Curling and stretching.
5. Leg work.
6. Over and under things.
7. Flight.
8. Lifting and lowering.
9. Symmetry and asymmetry.
10. Leading with different parts of the body.

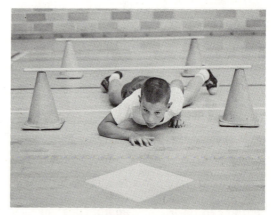

Developing the theme 6, over and under things, using wands and cones.

Many other themes, some broad and some narrow, can be used. Additional themes can be established using equipment and hand apparatus.

Structured Movement

Structured movement involves a specific skill which can be named and identified as opposed to general movements of a wide choice under unstructured movement. Children may practice such structured movements as walking, batting, bouncing, jumping, and pitching. A structured movement can be identified by the fact that it usually ends in the suffix "-ing." Included in structured movement are the basic skills, specialized skills, and the more precise skills on apparatus. Structured activity implies a limitation; the child must conform to the specified activity, but the activity can be accomplished or interpreted by various responses. The emphasis is on the development of a particular skill, which includes a concept of right and wrong with respect to technique, but the child should be allowed to arrive at or discover the best way or ways for him to do the skill, within reasonable limits.

The more precise the skill, the more critical the need to establish good techniques. Good techniques should prevail even if the child feels more comfortable with a known departure from accepted form. A child who throws right-handed and steps with his right foot as he throws should be induced to change to a left foot step, as the right hand, right foot throwing technique will establish an undesirable habit pattern which would need to be changed later. He should be encouraged to change, even if after exploration and experimentation he feels more comfortable in the right hand, right foot throw.

When dealing with structured movement, a different instructional approach than with unstructured movement is necessary. For structured movement, the range of acceptable technique needs to be known and adhered to. In some cases this can be broad, but in others, it can be quite narrow. The solution is to establish the basis in technique and then proceed with exploration, repetition, and creativity on this fundamental basis.

Organizing the Class

The objectives and nature of the movement experiences will indicate to the teacher how a class should be organized for activity. The amount and type of equipment and supplies will affect the approach.

There are many variations and subdivisions of the three basic schemes. In each case, the children may work as individuals, with a partner, or as a member of a group.

The Single-Activity Organization

All children are reacting to the same challenge, whether as individuals, partners, or with groups. The plan of organization is excellent for introductory work, because the children are all at approximately the same starting point. The plan allows the teacher to conduct the class with a planned lesson and the elements of progression. It is convenient for providing guidance (coaching), demonstrations, and evaluation at the completion of a segment of the lesson.

Multiple Groups

The class is divided into two or more groups, each working with a different movement problem, which could involve different large or hand apparatus.

Dividing the groups for work with different movement patterns is of value at times, particularly when supplies and apparatus are insufficient for the entire class to participate in the same activity at one time. In this way, equipment can be better utilized and waiting for turns is minimized. Some means of rotation should be established, either by signal or at will. Class control and guidance become more of a problem as it is not practical to stop the class to give instruction and guidance. The teacher must move from group to group, providing help as needed.

Another problem is the time element. Each group, ideally, should have sufficient opportunity in the activity for full development. In some activities, children may finish and run out of things to do, while in others the opposite may be true.

For effective movement the children should have some basis on which to superimpose new experiences if they are to be given a number of activities in rotation. Dividing into groups should be done usually after the children have had experience in the kinds of movement experiences designated for the groups. Introductory and initial work can best be accomplished through single-activity organization.

Individual Choice

Children select the movement experiences with which they choose to work and rotate at will. They can get their own equipment out, or can choose from selected pieces already placed. This should be done after the children have a good basis for further exploration and creativity. They should be encouraged to practice on needed areas or create beyond their present level. It should be a period of creativity, not just supervised free play.

Some teachers have found this effective as the introductory activity to a daily lesson. Occasionally, the teacher can give the following directions to a class upon entrance into the gymnasium. "For the first few minutes of our class period today, you may select and practice the movement pattern you wish." The teacher can qualify this by enumerating the possibilities with: "You may practice movements without equipment; you may select from the available balls, beanbags, wands, or hoops; or you may work on the climbing ropes, balance beams, or mats."

A choice period could also be used to finish up a daily lesson or a unit of work. The choice could be limited to the activities and movements of the lesson or unit.

PROBLEM DEVELOPMENT

The Approach to Problem Development

A number of guidelines should be considered in developing a problem with children.

Repetition. Repetition is the basis for learning, and sufficient repetition in particular patterns is necessary. The teacher must develop the sensitivity to determine when sufficient exploration and repetition have occurred at a particular stage so that children may move to the next progression.

Experimentation. Each child must be permitted free expression of movement within the limitations of the problem. His energies are to be directed toward the solution of the problem, and he must be allowed sufficient time to accomplish this goal working at his own rate according to his own ability.

Creative Opportunity. The child should have the opportunity to create and come up with movement patterns arising within himself, based on experimentation and exploration pointed toward the solution of the problem. His creativity should show that the movement patterns and concepts of the lesson have been absorbed, and that he can put to his use the factors from the movement experiences.

Creativity in this instance would mean coming up with something relevant and worth saving.

Focus on Potential. To help each child reach his full potential, high standards and a full effort should be demanded from each child.

Principles of Movement. Principles of movement governing the development of skills have strong application to movement work and should be an integral part of guidance and coaching. At times, they can be embodied in the instruction. (Page 69.)

Challenging Quality. As soon as children have responded and succeeded in meeting the demands of the problem in the introductory stage, they should be stimulated toward more efficient movement. Inept or sloppy performance should not be tolerated beyond the initial stages.

Perceptive Guidance. For the teacher, the lesson period is one of observation, analysis, and perceptive guidance.

Demonstrations. Demonstrations are important in basic movement procedures. They serve the purpose of illustrating variety or depth of movement, showing something unique or different, pointing out items of good technique or approach, illustrating different acceptable styles, and showing progress or accomplishments.

Demonstrations should be used only infrequently at the beginning of the lesson, as children should be given opportunity to develop individual approaches rather than imitating the style of another child. However, a few basics indicating the problem limits might be presented early in the lesson, or even in the introductory phases, to give direction to the activity.

The demonstration should be directed toward increasing the child's understanding and movement potential. A child needs to observe critically and analyze rather than just be entertained by the presented movements. In order that he may profit by what he has just viewed, the demonstration should be followed by a period of practice.

The demonstration may include an entire movement pattern or just some portion of it. The children selected for demonstration should be capable of presenting a reasonable model of what is desired. The teacher can ask for volunteers, or can pinpoint children who have proved capable of demonstrating what is wanted. The selection should be varied so that the chore of demonstrating does not fall too frequently on a few children. During the course of lessons, all children should be given the opportunity to demonstrate, with the caution that their self-concept and peer regard must be preserved.

The pattern of demonstrations may take several forms:

1. **The Single Demonstration.** In this pattern, one demonstration is presented at a time. It may be limited to one presentation, but it is well to have more than one individual successively provide demonstration, so that children may see varied approaches. If partner or small group work is undertaken, the same principle holds.

2. **The Multiple Demonstration.** In this a number of children (individually, by partners, or in small groups) are providing demonstrations simultaneously. One convenient way to organize this is to have squads demonstrate. In utilizing squads, the teacher may select one of the squads to demonstrate and then direct the children to return to activity. Other squads could have turns later. The teacher might even use this as a motivational device by telling the children: "After a period of time, I am going to select the squad to demonstrate which I feel has made the best progress."

Another means is to have one-half the class demonstrate, while the other half watches.

3. **The Achievement Demonstration.** This may use either of the two previous patterns, but is more likely to take the multiple method. At the end of a unit or sizeable portion thereof, a demonstration is held to show what has been accomplished. The squad provides a desirable unit for this purpose.

The question-and-answer technique has a place in the demonstration process, but must not dominate it. Questions can be directed toward such learning elements as what was good, what factors are important, and what directions the efforts should take. Care must be taken so that the demonstration period does not become too protracted due to a lengthy question-and-answer period.

Steps in Developing the Problem

After the initial, introductory activity, the development of the movement lesson can follow these steps:

1. Set the original problem, sometimes called the central problem. This follows the process of basic movement. The directives given to the child can be answers to these questions:

What is the child to do? (Jump, run, move to a certain spot, balance, etc.) How is he to work? (Individually, with a partner, or with a group.) On or with what apparatus? (A ball, wand, or hoop: on a balance beam, bench, or rope.)

Where is he to move? (What direction, level, or other factor?)

How is he to move?
  On, off, or across the floor?
  What body parts are used to execute the movement and how?
  What quality factors are involved?
  On apparatus, where does the body go?

An example of an unstructured problem following this format is: "Let's see you move across the floor, changing directions, with a quick movement on one foot and a slow movement on the other."

An example of a structured movement is: "Let's see you run across the floor in any direction you wish, changing the levels of the arms frequently." For structured movement, hints for technique may be added such as: "Remember to run lightly on your toes with a slight body lean."

The children are now introduced to the problem and initial movements occur.

2. The second step in the progression is to extend and challenge the creativity of the children, seeking to enhance their movement, to give depth to movement experiences around the problem, to encourage a variety of response, and to give attention to qualities of movement.

Securing a variety of response means that the teacher should be familiar with the factors which can elicit variation. These factors are time, space, flow, qualities of movement, and body factors and have been previously discussed.

3. After the children have exhausted the possibilities of variety, attention should be turned toward developing quality in movement. Have the children select and practice a movement with the objective of securing quality, doing it as well as it can be done under the circumstances. They may work on several movements, emphasizing good form and techniques, and such qualities as smoothness, lightness, coordination, and rhythm.

For structured movement and proper development of skills, this step should include stress on critical points of technique, which are important to the skill being practiced. This can be accomplished in a number of ways, such as by demonstration, discussion, or a question-and-answer period.

4. The fourth step is to put the movement patterns in sequence and combination, emphasizing sustained flow from one movement pattern to another. The child can select certain movements from those which have been practiced and put them together in sequence, with good transition from one movement pattern to the other. For example, he may be instructed to "put together a light run, a heavy run, and a body turn."

Practice can be extended to include different types of movement which demand from the child the ability to think how he might put these together most effectively. The problem emphasizing different movements could be: "As you dribble the ball, move with different locomotor movements in various directions. Select some definite combinations, and repeat several times before changing to a new combination."

5. The fifth step, which may or may not be employed, is to use the movement pattern in a relay or a game. This demonstrates the utility of the movement or skill and shows the child the practical application of what he has practiced. This generally is labeled the focal game or activity.

Another way to extend the experience is to have the child work with a partner or as a member of a group.

Working with a Partner

In partner work, the learning experiences should be the type which the child cannot do alone. Working with a partner is generally confined to later stages of movement patterns after practice has occurred on an individual basis. Teaching cooperation to children is an important social goal. It is generally better, depending upon the activity, to pair children of reasonably equal achievement, but at other times, size and weight might be governing factors.

How may children work together? A number of suggestions follow:

1. One child may be used as an obstacle and his partner devises ways of getting over, under, and around the "obstacle."
2. One child may support the weight of the other in part or wholly.
3. There can be matching, contrasting, or following movements.
4. Sequence building can be undertaken.
5. There can be critique of movement, with one child moving and the other providing the correction and critique.

Working as a Member of a Group

Group work in movement education is generally confined to small groups. This is not to be interpreted as a group of children working individually on similar movements, but a group of children working together on a movement task. The task of the group should be definite so that the interests are directed toward a common end. Examples of group work are finding different ways of making a human tower or finding different ways two children can bear the weight of two other children.

There is some difficulty in coordinating this type of activity, because activities are not balanced in length and interest and one group may finish before another. If the groups are too scattered, it is difficult for the teacher to provide proper help and guidance for each.

Phrasing the Challenge or Question

Stimulating an effective movement response from the children depends upon the manner in which the problems are phrased. Problems can be presented in the form of questions or statements, both of which should be of a nature to elicit and encourage variety, depth, and extent of movement. The teacher can secure ideas from the following directives, but will no doubt develop his own style and approach. The form is given first, and a specific application of the form follows. The directives are divided into those which initially define the problem to be solved and those which have value in stimulating variety or imposing a particular limitation.

Presenting a Problem

1. Show me how a . . . moves, or Show me . . . Show me how an alligator moves along the ground.
2. Have you seen a . . . ?
   Have you seen a kangaroo jump?
3. What ways can you . . . ?
   What ways can you hop over the jump rope?
4. How would you . . . ?, or How can you . . . ?
   How would you dribble a ball changing hands frequently?
5. See how many different ways you can . . .
   See how many different ways you can hang from a ladder.
6. What can you do with a . . . ?, or What kinds of things can you . . . ?
   What can you do with a hoop?
7. Can you portray a . . . ?
   Can you portray an automobile with a flat tire?
8. Discover different ways you can . . .
   Discover different ways you can volley a ball against a wall.
9. Can you . . . ?
   Can you keep one foot up when you bounce the ball?
10. Who can . . . a . . . in such a way that . . . ?
    Who can bounce a ball in such a way that it keeps time with the tom-tom?
11. What does a . . . ?
    What does a cat do when he is wet?

Securing Variety or Setting a Limitation

1. Try it again another way, or, Try to . . .
   Try to jump higher.
2. See how far (many times, high, close, low, etc.) . . .
   See how far you can reach with your arms.
3. Find a way to . . . or, Find a new way to . . . Find a new way to jump over the bench.
4. Apply . . . to . . .
   Apply a heavy movement to your run.
5. How else can you . . . ?
   How else can you roll your hoop?
6. Make up a sequence . . .
   Make up a sequence of previous movements, changing smoothly from one movement to the other.
7. Now try to combine a . . . with . . .
   Now try to combine a locomotor movement with your catching.
8. Alternate . . . and . . .
   Alternate walking and hopping.
9. Repeat the last movement but add . . .
   Repeat the last movement but add a body twist as you move.
10. See if you can . . .
    See if you can do the movement with a partner.
11. Trace (or draw) a . . . with . . .
    Trace a circle with your hopping pattern.
12. Find another part of the body to . . . , or, Find other ways to . . .
    Find another part of the body to take the weight.
13. Combine the . . . with . . .
    Combine the hopping with a body movement.
14. In how many different positions can you . . . ?
    In how many different positions can you carry your arms while walking the balance beam?
15. How do you think the . . . would change if . . . ?
    How do you think the balance we are doing would change if our eyes were closed?
16. On signal . . .
    On signal, speed up your movements.

Stimulating Effort

While stimulating variation will in a sense stimulate the children to better effort, it is important that the children extend themselves within the movement itself. This is the idea of including in the establishment of the movement problem incentives such as asking them to carry out tasks "as far as possible" or "with abrupt or definite changes." Although competition between individuals is not an accepted concept in movement education, some goals like "How far can you reach?" or "How far can you jump?" lend themselves to measurement. The number of floor boards covered or reached could be counted. There is also the idea of using beanbags or other markers and placing them "as far as you can." The device of having children stretch or reach until they pull themselves from their base makes them extend their limits.

STRESSING QUALITY IN MOVEMENT

Establishing quality is the vital part of movement education. Without this aspect, movement is mere activity. If the educational process can be viewed as experimentation, selection, modification, clarification, and repetition, guidance and direction fall into their proper perspective. If desirable learning is to occur, the child must be supplied with the basis to select from the many experiences those which he wishes to retain and develop. Thus retained and repeated, the movement pattern becomes a part of his being.

The guidance process of movement experiences first centers on securing a variety of response. The teacher must, however, be able to assess the child's performance in terms of suitability and quality. It is axiomatic that the teacher, in order to improve the quality of performance, must develop the ability to analyze movement and suggest the necessary adjustments to the children so that desirable learning proceeds toward the goal of individual development. The element of demonstration, primarily by the student, is also brought in. In the case of more precise skills, teaching aids would also be of value.

Guidance in movement can be roughly divided into two aspects. The first is in general terms of the quality of movement and the application of what is termed "Principles Important in Movement and Skill Performance." This is discussed in the text on pages 69-70. The principles are applicable to basic movement patterns as well as to skills.

In unstructured movement, where there is no "right" way to respond with a movement pattern, the concentration in guidance can be centered on general qualities of movement, lightness, smoothness, and coordination.

The second aspect of guidance occurs where structured movement is the basis of the lesson. There can be, and is in many cases, a correct way to perform the skill and there also are certain undesirable elements which should be avoided. In a lesson emphasizing or including walking, stress should be placed on the feet being pointed reasonably forward. Children should not be permitted to walk with their toes pointed out *even if they so choose*. Teachers must know the basic elements of skills so that proper techniques can be inculcated and undesirable habits avoided in the learning process. This means that the more precise and demanding the skill, the less room for movement education methodology and the more emphasis on direct instruction. Systematic progression is needed if skill is to improve. An increasingly difficult challenge must be presented, and effective repetition must be introduced. However, experimentation and exploration always have a place in the learning experiences for establishing skills. Often the performer will need to select the pattern he wishes to adopt by experimentation from among a number of good or accepted ways.

The question of how much form should be stressed is raised. Few elementary school children will reach perfection in form in any activity. On the primary level, form should be considered in a minor sense but should be consistent with the development of the child. Necessarily, the child should not be permitted to acquire a poor habit which will cause him difficulty later. Emphasis should be on doing things as well as possible, but this must not become an overriding consideration.

Proper postural habits must be emphasized throughout movement education, since these are related in many cases to quality of performance. Within the concept of maximum growth and development of the child, there should be stress on the possession of reasonable body alignment and the establishment of good postural habits. These also become factors in the guidance and directive process of movement education.

FORMATIONS FOR MOVEMENT

Instruction involving nonlocomotor movement involves little problem with the children, as they can take a place on the floor and undergo the movement experiences. In locomotor movement, however, a different situation presents itself with regard to the manner in which the children can be organized for movement. The number of the children, the space available, and the type of activity are factors which influence the choice of formation for effective teaching. The following formations can be considered for locomotor movement:

1. Individual movement in every direction. The children must be cautioned about collisions and the need to be courteous. Children should be directed to use all the available space and to move in various directions.

2. Around the area in a circular fashion. The objection to this is that it creates competition and generates conformity. However, collisions are not likely, and the teacher can observe the children effectively.

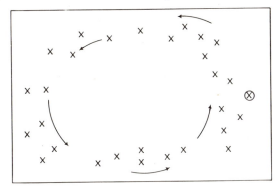

3. On opposite sides of the room, exchanging position. The children on signal cross to the opposite side of the area, passing through the opposite line.

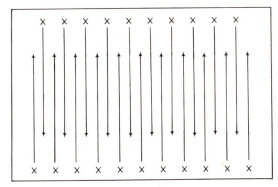

4. On opposite sides of the room, moving to the center and back. A line can be formed with ropes, wands, or cones to mark the center limit. Children move to the center of the area and then return to place.

5. On opposite sides of the room, one line moving across and back. The two sides alter-

nate in their turns. The line of children from one side crosses to a point near the other line and then makes a turn, returning to place. After these children have completed the movement, the other group takes a turn.

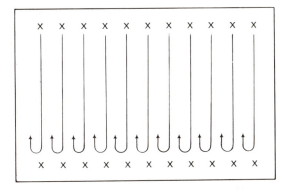

6. Squad formation, re-forming at the other end of the space. The leading child in each squad begins his movement across the floor. When he is about halfway, the next child starts. The squads re-form at the other end and get ready for another movement.

7. Squads in crisscross formation. Squads form as indicated, with two opposite squads

moving at a time. In effect, they exchange places. Members of each squad move in turn when the child in front is far enough ahead. After the first two squads have performed, the other squads move similarly.

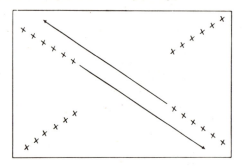

8. Children on four sides of the area, exchanging position. The children on one pair of opposite sides exchange first, and then the others exchange. They alternate back and forth in this manner.

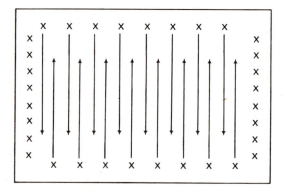

DEVELOPING IDEAS FOR UNSTRUCTURED MOVEMENT

The challenge to the child gives him the general directions of movement, but does not specify the precise skill or movement by which he meets the challenge or question. It should lead to a variety of response, which can later be refined or altered. The examples as given are stated as tasks to be done, but should be properly phrased using the guidelines for phrasing questions as previously discussed (page 110). These are divided into locomotor and nonlocomotor challenges, but could be combined in some cases.

Locomotor Challenges

1. Move about the room and in every direction with a rapid, low movement followed by a slow, high movement. Various other combinations can be specified.

2. Do a movement at regular speed, followed by the same movement in slow motion.

3. Use big, wide movements to imitate an elephant. Other animals can be imitated.

4. Be a giant, a dwarf, or a witch.

5. Go over (or along, or under) the benches using different movements and body shapes.

6. Move around the room using different swimming strokes.

7. Move around the room using any movement you wish. On signal, freeze. On the next signal try another movement.

8. One-half of the children are on hands and knees (or face down, or in curled position). The other half on signal go over all the other children, using various locomotor movements. Other factors can be added. After a period of movement, reverse the children.

9. Home-base activities can be used. Each child has a home spot on the floor. He is given tasks to do and returns each time back to his home base. Have him (1) pick out another spot, do a stunt, and return; (2) touch a wall or walls and return; (3) trace a particular pattern on the floor with his movement and return. Other tasks can be set.

10. Move so one foot is always off the ground.

11. Move around the room with a selected high locomotor movement, gradually lowering your body until you can do some kind of a roll. Begin anew.

12. Move around the room beginning with a low position, gradually raising until you propel yourself into the air. Drop to a low position and repeat.

13. Move around the room taking the weight on different parts of the body.

14. Travel around the room using bilateral movement of the hands and feet.

15. Travel around the room with your head lower than your waist.

16. Carry a wand around the room as you move. On signal, place the wand on the floor and jump or hop back and forth over it. Repeat using a beanbag, hoop, jumping rope, or other piece of hand apparatus.

17. Carry a piece of hand apparatus as you move around the room. On the first signal, place the piece of apparatus on the floor and

move over and around the pieces of apparatus on the floor. On signal #2, pick up the piece nearest you and again move around the room.

18. Move around the room in various directions touching different walls. After you touch a wall, try a new movement.

19. Each child has a partner. On signal #1, one of the two partners moves around the room with a movement of his choice, the other child imitating the movement. On signal #2, the other child leads with a new movement.

20. Move around the room, stressing taking the weight on different parts of the feet.

21. Practice different ways of moving the feet — singly, crossing, alternately, together, one foot leading.

22. Move around the room using movements like the different track and field events.

23. Move around the room making right angle turns. Each time you turn, change your type of movement.

24. Pick a sport and pretend you are playing that sport.

25. Choose a piece of small apparatus (ball, beanbag, etc.) and practice with that apparatus piece, sometimes standing still and sometimes moving.

26. Demonstrate different ways of rolling, utilizing different shapes, directions, and parts of the body.

27. Move sideways (backwards, or forwards) in as many different ways as you can.

28. Move around the room in different directions, experimenting with different parts of the body leading.

Nonlocomotor Challenges

1. Balance on one, two, or three parts of the body, or on a particular part of the body.

2. Stretch your body to full limits in different directions.

3. Make different body shapes to represent kinds of buildings, autos, trains, machines, etc.

4. Make different kinds of bridges with the body.

5. Show different ways and combinations in which you can twist the body to its limits.

6. Keeping one foot in place, show how far you can reach in different directions.

7. Alternate curling and stretching movements.

8. Make yourself big and small with various shapes.

9. Using various positions such as push-up, crab, sitting, lying (prone or supine), on hands and knees, on all fours, side-leaning rest, and others, react to challenges like these:
Lift various parts of the body off the floor.
With a part of the body, make a pattern, or write a letter or word in the air.
Draw a picture.
Reach out as far as possible in different directions with various limbs. Touch the floor.
Change positions of the limbs in various manners and combinations. Use unilateral, bilateral, and cross-lateral patterns.

10. Make big circles with various parts of the body. Use different planes — horizontal, vertical, and diagonal.

11. Show in different positions the different kinds of swimming movements that can be made.

12. From a wide straddle position, bend and twist in various directions, touching the floor as far out as possible. Touch with the hand out to the opposite side.

13. Practice different balances on one foot. On one hand and one foot.

14. With a partner, practice different ways of supporting each other wholly or in part.

15. Make one hand follow the other hand around the body.

16. Experiment with the different joints of the body and see what movements each can do.

17. Make different parts of the body move in patterned movements or tracing designs. This has wide application. The children can be standing, sitting, or in any of the various body positions. One, two, or even three of the body parts can move in tracing different designs. Geometrical designs, letters, words, and other ways of moving can be explored.

DEVELOPING IDEAS FOR STRUCTURED MOVEMENT

Locomotor Movements

These include walking, running, jumping, galloping, sliding, hopping, skipping, and leaping. Some general directions for all movements of this type can be made to secure variety of response.

BASIC MOVEMENT

1. Changes in speed — slow to fast, accelerate or decelerate.
2. Weight bearing on different parts of the foot — on the toes, heels, sides of the foot.
3. The length of the stride or jump — tiny to large.
4. Varied actions of the feet — pointed out or in, following (one foot catching the other), crossing front or behind, changing leading foot.
5. Changing directions.
6. Moving forward, sideward, backward. Using turns.
7. Tracing different patterns — squares, triangles, figure eights.
8. On and over objects.
9. Putting together sequences of various locomotor movements.

In addition, space, body, flow, and movement quality factors as previously discussed can be employed.

While variety is important, quality in movement is essential and must be sought in the instructional process. Each child should be encouraged toward the highest quality movement of which he is capable.

An Example of an Exploratory Approach in Structured Movement, Emphasizing Running, Leaping, and Stopping Techniques

The following routine illustrates how a locomotor movement like running can be combined with leaping and stopping to provide meaningful experiences for children. Although the approach is primarily direct instruction, children have the opportunity to respond in individual patterns within the tasks as set. There is good control and opportunity for instruction in having the movement performed by squads in squad column formation with the stipulation that each squad member follows when the member in front of him is halfway across the area. The children run across an area 20 to 30 yards in width, depending on their age level. When they have completed a run across the area, the squads re-form on the other side, awaiting directions to come back.

Cross your feet over each time as you run.
Run low, touching the ground on either side alternately.
Run low, touching the ground with both hands as you go along.
Run forward, looking back over your right shoulder.
The same, except look back over the left shoulder.
Run zigzag, that is — changing direction every few steps.
Run to the center, stop, and continue.
Run forward, stop with the right side forward, then another stop with the left side forward.
Run forward and stop. Come back three steps and stop again. Continue in original direction.
Try a two-count stop with a definite "one, two" slap on the ground with the feet.
Try a hop, step, and a jump and then continue.
Run sideways, leading the first time with one side. Next time, reverse the position.

The children can devise other combinations to try out. Be sure that the children understand and use good running form. Skipping, galloping, and other locomotor movements can be included in the combinations.

The following running variations can be done as the children run across the area:

Run as lightly as possible.
Run high on the toes.
Run on the heels.
As you run, bounce as high as you can.
Run with tiny, fast steps.
Run with giant strides.
Run with high knee action.
Mix in giant leaps with your run.
Run backward.
Run forward halfway and backward the rest.
Run backward halfway and forward the rest.
As you run across, turn around (right) completely and continue across.
The same, but turn to the left.
Run slowly and then suddenly change to running fast.
Run with an exaggerated arm movement.
Run with a goose-step movement.

Additional Suggestions for Jumping and Hopping Activities

Jumping and hopping activities should develop spring, lightness, balance, coordination, and control in activity. Some ideas for activities are presented.

1. Jump or hop in and out of various patterns and designs on the floor made by jump-

ing ropes, hoops, wands, benches, or balance beams.

2. Specific floor patterns can be marked on the floor or on sheets of vinyl or plastic by painting footprints on them. Right and left are marked and the children follow as indicated. Lines in different kinds of geometric figures and mazes can be painted on blacktop surfaces. Many basic locomotor movements can be done on these patterns.

Nonlocomotor Movements

Nonlocomotor movements include bending, twisting, turning (in place), movements toward and away from the center of the body, raising and lowering the parts or the body as a whole, and other body movements done in place. Nonlocomotor movements do not lend themselves as well to the distinction between unstructured and structured movement as do the locomotor and manipulative skills. Gross body movements to the limits of flexibility are important. Good control and a variety of body movement leading to effective body management are also important goals. Balance is another factor which should receive attention.

Structured movements have a place in the program when the teacher wishes to emphasize a particular movement and have the children explore this to its extent. Here are examples of structured problems:

1. "Take a comfortable position with your feet about shoulder width apart and pointed ahead. Bend forward without bending the knees, and see how far you can touch down in front of you, between your legs, and to the sides. Try it now with a wider position of the feet."

2. "From a wide straddle position with the arms out to the sides at shoulder level, twist as far as you can to the right and determine how far you can see around behind you, using a full twist of the body. Try it to the left side. See if it helps if you bounce the twist. Try it with your arms in other positions."

These are examples of a specific kind of a movement which the teacher wishes to have the children explore to the full extent of the body's range of movement. This increases their awareness of what the body can do. Similar challenges can be applied to other particular kinds of movement.

Combinations of Movement

The foregoing illustrations and suggestions of movement possibilities have generally been directed toward a single movement with little thought of combinations. Combining different kinds of movement opens extensive possibilities. Both locomotor and nonlocomotor movements can be put together in various combinations and sequences, such as the following:

1. Run, leap, and roll.
2. Run, collapse, and roll.
3. Twist and lift.
4. Twist and smile.
5. Lift and grin.
6. Hop, turn around, and shake.
7. Run, change direction, and collapse.
8. Hop, make a shape in the air, and balance.
9. Rock, jump high, and sit down.
10. Rock and twist.
11. Curl, roll, and jump.
12. Twirl and make a statue.
13. Make different letters of the alphabet.
14. Show us how waves come in on an ocean beach.
15. Kneel and balance.
16. Kneel and sway.
17. Stretch like a rubber band. Snap back to position.
18. Blow up like a balloon. Let the air out.
19. Blow up like a balloon. Let the balloon burst.
20. Squat and do a jump turn.
21. Twist and untwist. Slow one way and fast the other.
22. Click heels different ways. Add various kinds of hand claps.

Attention should be centered on following directions and doing movements as well as possible.

THE MOVEMENT SUGGESTION BOX

An idea which has been received enthusiastically by children is the Movement Suggestion Box. This box, which should contain enough cards for the whole class, can be used in two ways.

The first approach is to have movement challenges on the cards. Each child takes a card and responds to the challenge. This activity can be used well at the beginning of a lesson.

In the second approach the child is offered some choice of the type of movement he may select. Cards covering three or more areas can be in different compartments. Suggested are:

    Mat Activities
    Locomotor Movement
    Nonlocomotor Movement
    A Manipulative Activity

The child may choose a second area if he has finished his first task and there is still time left.

PERCEPTUAL-MOTOR ACTIVITIES, MANIPULATIVE ACTIVITIES, AND APPARATUS ACTIVITIES

The teacher is referred to the next three chapters for additional material on movement experiences. The focus in the present chapter was on locomotor and nonlocomotor activities. Manipulative and apparatus activities should be a strong part of basic movement. Perceptual-motor activities also have value, but some are in a different context. While some of these activities involve exploration to a degree, many are inflexible because they are a response to a command. They can serve to supplement activities of basic movement.

11

Perceptual-Motor Competency

Characteristics of the Underachiever or Slow Learner
How Are These Individuals Discovered?
Implications for Physical Education Programs
Special Activities for Perceptual-Motor Programs
The Perceptual-Motor Team

There is increasing evidence that an association exists between perceptual-motor competency and certain academic skills, primarily reading readiness and achievement. Some children, often normal or above normal in intelligence, fail to achieve satisfactorily because of a learning disability. Many of these children, who are classed as underachievers or slow learners, can be helped with a program of specific movements leading to perceptual-motor competency. A slow learner may possess such characteristics as poor balance, mixed or no lateral dominance, visual-motor problems, poor hand-eye coordination, and poor spatial body image.

The perceptual-motor educational concept is based on the theory that correlation of movement is centered in the brain stem and that reading, writing, spelling, and speech are controlled by this area of the neurological system. If the child has good perceptual-motor skills, then the motor-neural system has matured and developed to the point where it is not a negative factor in the learning process. Conversely, the theory holds that a child with deficient perceptual-motor development will exhibit disability or fail to reach the proper potential in one or more of the areas of reading, writing, spelling, and speech.

There is another aspect to academic achievement that merits consideration. Some educators hold that academic areas *per se* (reading, writing, etc.) are not directly improved, but rather certain personal qualities and study skills are directly involved, which in turn lead to improvement in the aforementioned areas. Such critical skills as effective listening, following directions, and reproducing as directed can be made more efficient through perceptual-motor activities and in turn have a beneficial effect on school work.

Another unresolved area confronts those employing the diverse perceptual-motor activities. While there is some agreement that a group of perceptual-motor activities together, carefully selected so that variety is present, has value in helping children, there is little evidence to substantiate and delineate the contribution which each of the separate activities makes toward the whole. For example, walking on a balance beam is considered to be of value, but no valid evidence is available to substantiate the value claim, nor is there comparative data to show the relative value of this activity with respect to other activities commonly included in the perceptual-motor area.

While the main emphasis to this point has been the correction of deficiencies, it can be postulated that a program of activities stressing good perceptual-motor training would also be of benefit to children with apparently satisfactory levels of achievement. If a program of perceptual-motor training can help raise the level of deficient children, then it should be of value in increasing the academic achievement potential of the so-called normal child.

CHARACTERISTICS OF THE UNDERACHIEVER OR SLOW LEARNER

What characteristics does a child with poor or deficient perceptual-motor development exhibit? The child may have trouble holding or maintaining his balance. He appears clumsy and cannot carry himself well in motion. He may appear to be generally awkward in activities requiring coordination.

He may show signs of dysfunction in lateral dominance. He can do things well or better with one side or one limb of the body. He does not know right from left readily and may have to hesitate or think carefully before being able to come up with a definite movement or answer to a direction. In locomotor skills, he does movements much more efficiently on one side than the other. He may reverse with regularity when such a reversal is not indicated.

Young children may not be able to hop or skip properly. They have difficulty making changes in or combinations of movement. After learning after a fashion to hop or skip, they cannot then hop or skip backwards, nor can they hop well for a period of time.

Spatial orientation is another area in which indications can appear. The child has difficulty in gauging space with respect to his body, and bumps and collides with objects and other children. He may be accident-prone. Hand-eye coordination may be poor. He has trouble handling the simple tools of physical education — beanbags, balls, and other objects that involve a visual-motor-perceptual relationship.

HOW ARE THESE INDIVIDUALS DISCOVERED?

While the teacher may believe from indications that a child has a perceptual-motor disability, definite testing measures can be employed to make this determination. A Perceptual Rating Scale has been devised by Newell C. Kephart and is presented in his book, *The Purdue Perceptual-Motor Survey.** Testing involves two aspects. The first is whether or not the child can do the task as specified, and the second is the assurance and confidence with which he does the task. The test includes not only physical skills, but also hand-eye skills in using the chalkboard. Two areas only from the test are presented for purposes of illustration.

Testing for Balance and Laterality

A walking board, on the balance beam principle, is made up of a 2" x 4" board 12' long. The 4" side is used for the test. The child is asked to walk forward, backward, and sideward (each way) without losing balance. Children should be able to move forward, backward, and sideward with ease and assurance. A child with a laterality problem will have difficulty moving one of the ways sideward, usually from left to right.

Skill Movements and Combinations

Combinations of hopping, jumping, and skipping movements on the floor are used in this part of the test. The child is given commands to demonstrate the following movements:

1. Put both feet together and jump forward one step.
2. Hop forward one step using the right foot only.
3. Hop forward one step using the left foot only.
4. Skip across the room.
5. Hop in place, first on the right foot and then on the left, continuing this pattern.
6. Same as the foregoing, but twice on the right and twice on the left.
7. Same procedure, but twice on the right and once on the left.
8. Same as (7) but twice on the left and once on the right.

The child is carefully observed to see that he can make the movements and the changes with a smooth, rhythmical motion and with ease and assurance. Failure indications would be a stiff, jerky motion, with pauses indicating that he has taken time to think before moving.

---

*Roach and Kephart. *The Purdue Perceptual-Motor Survey* (Columbus, Ohio: Charles E. Merrill Books, Inc. 1966).

IMPLICATIONS FOR PHYSICAL EDUCATION PROGRAMS

Testing and specialized remedial work in perceptual-motor training are within the province of specialists. Classroom teachers can cooperate with these programs, but generally the work is outside of the normal physical education program. If a child is low in reading readiness and reading achievement, testing should be accomplished to determine the possibility of perceptual-motor deficiency.

Since perceptual-motor development is located in the early primary years, activities which have the potential of development in this area should be stressed. The following guides are important:

1. Children should be given opportunity and practice in hand-eye and foot-eye coordination by frequent use of activities where they can handle balls, beanbags, hoops, ropes, rings, and the like.

2. The balance beam and its activities should be a part of the program.

3. A program emphasizing the development of basic locomotor skills should be instituted. This should be an instructional program.

4. Opportunity for management of the body in a variety of situations should be a part of the curriculum. Children should have activities on the floor, off the floor, across the floor, and on apparatus.

5. The concept of laterality should be included in all movement. The child should counter a move to the right with a similar move to the left. If he moves forward, stress a backward movement. No one side of the body nor direction of movement should dominate.

6. Movements should be further considered from the standpoint of unilateral, bilateral, or cross-lateral approach. Wherever possible, all should be used. A unilateral movement is one done by a single part or side of the body. Moving one arm forward would be a unilateral movement. A bilateral movement occurs when both arms or legs make corresponding movements. Moving both arms forward in a similar fashion is an example of a bilateral movement. A cross-lateral movement demands that parts of the body move in a different manner. Moving one arm forward and one backward at the same time would be a cross-lateral movement. This movement, however, is an opposed cross-lateral movement. An unrelated cross-lateral movement occurs when two corresponding parts move without relationship to each other. Lifting one arm up and the other arm forward would be unrelated movements.

7. A variety of movement and movement combinations should be presented as challenges to the child. The teacher needs the imagination and ability to take a simple movement and exhaust it completely with variety and combinations, thus giving play to many perceptual-motor-neural pathways.

8. Specialized activities designated particularly for perceptual-motor training should be included. These are the bounding board, Angels in the Snow, specialized movement sequences, cross-lateral crawling and movements, touching and naming body parts, left-right discrimination activities, and rope jumping.

There is evidence that perceptual-motor training can help deficient and mentally retarded children. Whether or not such training can help regular students in increasing their academic potential has not been resolved. However, the application of the movement principles of perceptual-motor work can enhance and give breadth to children's movement competencies. It is a new and exciting approach toward the concept of education for the whole child.

The movement experiences should begin simply, but increase progressively in complexity, offering more challenge. Throwing and catching to self, for example, should start with an "in place" practice. Later, the teacher should add locomotor movements and other requirements to the task. The basic tasks should allow success so that progress can be made from this base.

In discussing the inclusion of perceptual-motor considerations in the program for *all* children, two types of activities are presented. The first group is from the "normal" type of physical education activities which are part of a recommended program. The second group of activities are those which can be regarded as designed particularly for perceptual-motor objectives.

Regular Physical Education Activities Having Value in Perceptual-Motor Development

1. Ball skills stressing throwing, catching, bouncing, dribbling, volleying, striking, and others, using all sizes and varieties of balls in as many combinations as possible.
2. Individual rope jumping, using both feet, right and left feet in various combinations. Stress rhythm and timing.
3. Balance beam work.
4. Simple tumbling stunts.
5. Handling objects, such as beanbags, hoops, wands, and rings.
6. Climbing up, over, and around ropes and apparatus.
7. Fundamental skills to rhythm.
8. Basic movement competency.

Specialized Perceptual-Motor Activities
Crawling and Creeping Patterns

1. Unilateral crawling — Crawl forward on hands and knees, using the arm and leg on the same side together.
2. Bilateral movement — Move forward, reaching out with both hands and then bringing the feet up to the hands (Bunny Jump).
3. Cross-lateral crawling — Crawl forward, moving the right arm and the left leg at the same time, and vice versa.

Variations:

1. Move forward, backward, sideward, make quarter turns right and left.
2. Add turning the head first toward the leading hand and then opposite to it, coordinating with each step.

Command Movements Involving Jumping, Hopping, and Turning

1. Jump forward, backward, sideward. Jump in patterns.
2. Hop forward, backward, and sideward, stressing right and left.
3. Hop in various combinations: R-1, L-1; L-1, R-1; R-2, L-2; L-2, R-2; R-2, L-1; L-2, R-1. (The notation R-1, L-1 means to hop once on the right and once on the left.) In addition to the combinations listed, others can be devised.
4. Jump with quarter turns right and left, half turns, right and left.
5. Establish the directions (east, south, west, north) and call out directions with the children making jump turns.

Angels in the Snow — Command Movements

Children are on their backs with hands at the sides and feet together. On any command, the arms and legs as designated move out and then back along the floor. The directions are given as follows:

"Right arm, left leg — MOVE," (pause) "BACK."

Then alternate the words "Out" and "Back," repeating each movement 6-10 times.

The following movements are suggested:

Bilateral — both arms, both legs, both arms and both legs together.

Unilateral — right (or left) arm, right (or left) leg, right arm and right leg together, left arm and left leg together.

Cross-Lateral — right arm and left leg, left arm and right leg.

NOTE. The *Angels in the Snow* exercises were originally designed to be given by the examiner pointing to an arm or leg and saying, "Move that arm (or leg)." This, however, is individual activity and not suitable generally for group work. Children, conceivably, could work in pairs, and this type of Angels work could be done.

Command Movements — Standing

These movements follow the same command pattern as *Angels in the Snow* with the directive given first, followed by the execution command "Move." The position is held until the leader says "Back." Children should learn to exercise good control in waiting without preliminary movement until the command "Move" is given, at which time they make the prescribed movement. The initial movement is held until the teacher can check the accuracy of the response. Two approaches can be used. The first is to change from one pattern into another, without repetition of any pattern. The other is to repeat a pattern as when giving exercises. Repeat 6-10 times.

Types of movements which are effective are:

Right arm, right leg forward (unilateral).
Left arm, right leg forward (cross-lateral).
Both arms forward (bilateral).
Both feet forward — a jump (bilateral).

Add the turn of the head to the movements. The head is usually turned toward the arm which is moved forward, but can vary. Such a command would be, "Right arm and left foot forward, head right — MOVE."

Side steps left and right can be used, with arms still moving forward and head turning as directed.

Imitation of Movements

The children stand facing the teacher so that all can see the teacher. Feet are apart enough (6"-12") for good balance and arms are at the sides. The teacher makes definite movements with the arms first in various movements. Arm and leg movements in combinations are also to be imitated. Children imitate the movements on the same side (right for the teacher, left for the children). There should be emphasis on all three types of movement — unilateral, bilateral, and cross-lateral. A mixture of movements should be made. All movements are to the side first. Later, forward movements of the arms can be added.

Some games using imitation of movement are useful and fun for the children. *Do This, Do That* has its basis of fun in that the child imitates the movement as done when the leader says, "Do this!" When the leader says, "Do that!" no one is to move. Those caught can have points scored against them. The game, *Simon Says,* follows the same principles, with the children moving when the command is preceded by "Simon says."

Another similar game is that the leader attempts to confuse the children by giving directions, which they are to follow, and making a different movement. For example, he can say, "Touch your shoulders," and at the same time put his hands on his hips. The children are to follow the verbal directions.

Bounding Board (see appendix for diagram)

1. Simple bouncing — both feet, right foot, left foot, combinations.
2. Bouncing with quarter and half turns.
3. Begin at one end, jump along the board. Repeat using right or left leg only. Jump forward, backward, and sideward.
4. Sight fixation targets should be established so that the child fixes his gaze on a point and maintains the pattern of movement.

Bounding high on the bounding board.

The Balance Board (see appendix for diagram)

Balancing beanbags while on balance boards.

The child stands on the board with his feet separated and attempts to keep his balance. Try with one foot. Sight fixation targets should be used with the balance board. Pick spots high and low, right and left, and have the child hold this visually.

Obstacles

Wands and chairs can be used as obstacles. A wand over the top of two chairs makes an obstacle under which the children move. Move underneath without touching, backward or sideward as well as frontward. Another obstacle can be made by having a wand over the seats of two low chairs or over 12" hurdle blocks. The children step over this without touching. A hoop can be held by a partner, allowing the child to crawl through without touching.

An effective obstacle arrangement can be structured with traffic cones, blocks, wands, and a hoop or tire supported on a stand.

An Obstacle Arrangement

The child goes over the first wand, under the second, and through the hoop. Repeated efforts should employ variety in the different ways a child may meet the challenge of the obstacles.

SPECIAL ACTIVITIES FOR PERCEPTUAL-MOTOR PROGRAMS

The distinction between what might be termed regular activities with perceptual-motor implications to be included in the physical education program and those special activities generally labeled perceptual-motor is somewhat nebulous. It can be argued that any activity which is of value in a remedial program for children with perceptual-motor dysfunction can be helpful to the normal child. Probably, the choice between what activities are scheduled in the regular program and those which are allocated to specialized perceptual-motor programs is a matter of choice.

The activities presented in this section are those which the author has observed as designated perceptual-motor activities and used in programs with that name. The purpose of the list is to be illustrative of the kinds of things which are included in such programs and is not to be regarded as an all-inclusive list. One other thought needs to be expressed. There is little research evidence to support the value of each of the several activities presented. Many of them are established on face validity and on an empirical basis.

Blast-Off Launcher

A Blast-Off Launcher, of which commercial varieties exist, can be used to provide challenge for hand-eye coordination. The child places a beanbag on the launch pad and propels the bag into the air with a forceful stamp of the foot on the end of the launcher. He catches the bag. Challenge with different combinations of catching and employ either foot in the launching process.

Baseball Rebound Net and Stand

A rebound net-frame of the type used for baseball practice can be used with beanbags and balls to exercise hand-eye coordination. The child tosses or throws the object against the net, from which it is rebounded to him.

Balloon Keep-It-Up

The task for the child is to keep one or more balloons in the air by repeatedly striking them with a selected instrument such as a small paddle, wand, small bat, or baton. This should give exercise to ocular tracking and spatial estimates. Sufficient room is necessary and extra balloons are needed.

Balloon Keep-It-Up using a paddle, small wands, or the hands.

Identifying Body Parts

The purpose of this activity is for the child to learn and know the precise location of the named body parts and be able to touch them with both hands without looking at his body or securing cues from other children. Children stand and face the teacher, who says:

"Touch your shoulders."
"Touch your hips."
"Touch your head."
"Touch your ankles."
"Touch your ears."
"Touch your toes."
"Touch your eyes."
"Touch your elbows."
"Touch your knees."

Early in the activity, after each direction, children repeat the following, "I am touching my _____," inserting the correct term. The teacher may do the activity with the children during the initial phases, but should revert to verbal cues as soon as practical.

Stepping Stones

A number of red and black asphalt or vinyl tiles are needed. Twenty to thirty are sufficient to form interesting patterns. Involved in this activity are foot-eye coordination and right-left discrimination.

The tiles are arranged in a formation which should vary from the straight line so that children have a challenge of different stepping patterns. The object is for the child to step on red tiles with his right foot and black tiles with his left. Mark the child's feet with the appropriate color, using a ribbon, garter, crepe paper, or something similar. Give him the following instruction: "Your right foot is marked with a red ribbon and your left with a black. You are to walk down the pathway of tiles stepping on red tiles with your right foot and black tiles with your left. You must always step on the very next square and you are not to skip any tiles."

You can tell the child to say to himself, "I will step on the red tiles with my right foot and the black tiles with my left."

The pace should be definite but not hurried. After some practice, more difficult patterns can be laid out. The child can also walk to the beat of a drum or to the rhythm of music appropriate for walking.

Form Recognition and Sequence Building Employing Geometric Forms

Geometric forms of two sizes are needed in each of the following shapes: circle, triangle, square, and rectangle. A set of forms consists, then, of eight shapes, four large and four small. Sets should be painted in two colors, with random selection from large and small shapes. A support for each shape is made from a piece of wood.

Two kinds of activities can be employed with the shapes.

1. *Shapes placed flat on the floor.*

Challenges can be structured as follows:

a. Can you walk around the largest circle?

b. Jump three times inside the large circle, hop once inside the small triangle, and return.

c. Take the weight on the hands inside the red rectangle, balance on one foot inside the blue circle, and return.

Challenges of a similar nature can be made up.

2. *Shapes standing upright in supports.*

The purpose is to go through the shapes without touching them. Various means of going through can be specified, such as head first, feet first, on your back, etc. Sequence building is also important. Some challenge illustrations follow:

a. Go through the large circle and back through the small triangle.

b. Go through the small circle head first, through the large triangle feet first, and return through the large rectangle as you wish.

c. Crawl to the large triangle, then to the small circle, and then to the big rectangle.

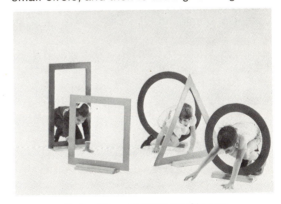

Going Through Different Shapes
Reprinted by permission of © J. A. Preston Corp., 1971

Floor Ladder Activities

A wooden ladder is placed on mats and used as a floor target for a number of activities. The child begins at one end of the ladder and performs while moving along the length. Activity challenges which are of value are:

1. Walk, run, hop, or jump between the ladder rungs, moving forward and sideward.
2. Walk on the rungs, balancing carefully on each. Do not touch the floor.
3. Do different movements on the hands and feet on the rungs and on the sides of the ladder.
4. Free choice of movement. Child creates his own patterns.

It is important that all movements be done under good control and that the child be given creative opportunity to come up with his own selection of movement.

Other Approaches

Specific activities designed to improve ocular pursuit are included in some programs. These involve a fixed position of the head and the eyes following a pattern of movement.

One method of exercising ocular pursuit is to have the children seated approximately 10 yards from a line. A ball is rolled moderately fast back and forth along this line by two other children for a distance of about 10 yards. The children exercising the eye muscles follow the ball back and forth along the line with their eyes.

Another method is to have the child hold out both arms forward with the thumbs up. The right thumb can be marked with a red tape. On command, the child switches his focus back and forth from thumb to thumb.

A third method is to have a small ball on the end of a three-foot string. The teacher holds the end of the string and allows the ball to swing back and forth with the children following the path of the ball with the eyes.

Another area of emphasis is chalkboard work. The most likely chalkboard patterns to be made are circles. These are made with each hand in turn and with both hands at once. Repetition and conformity to a selected pattern govern this procedure.

The question arises whether both ocular pursuit and chalkboard work are regular class activities or should they be confined to remedial situations. In addition, stressing ocular pursuit seems to trespass on optometry and the province of the oculist. Caution should be observed particularly in the conduct of ocular pursuit activities.

THE PERCEPTUAL-MOTOR TEAM

Although the emphasis in previous discussions is on incorporating perceptual-motor principles and instructional procedures into the *regular* physical education program, the physical education instructor should be a member of the perceptual-motor team which considers student problems of deficiency in this area. He can cooperate with special perceptual-motor programs and can also give encouragement and special help in the regular physical education program to individuals identified as needing such aid.

12

Story Games, Finger Plays, and Dramatic Play

Stories
Finger Plays
Dramatic Play with Poems
Other Experiences as a Basis for Dramatic Play

Story games, finger plays, and dramatic play have a part in the program of physical education for children, particularly the younger ones. The children love to interpret stories with gross body movements and dramatic movement patterns. The finger plays provide not only opportunity for expression, but also practice in manual dexterity.

Story plays and creative rhythms provide similar experiences, except that in the first case the children interpret the unfolding of the story in movement rather than take cues from the rhythm.

Finger plays allow the children to act out the poem, which it usually is, with fingers as the props and serving as the "wee men." Many are old familiar stories, from whence the fun comes in doing them over and over again. Finger plays are a little more structured in their movements than story plays, as many of them are done in a rather precise routine.

Story games, finger plays, and dramatic play should provide a variety of creative opportunities, be a satisfying experience, allow freedom of response, and encourage all to participate at a level of ability, regardless of the quality of performance. The activity should be conducted informally in such a way that it will allow children to investigate the range of body movement and give way to free response within the limits of the story. Story plays can give opportunity for each child to achieve status and find his place among his classmates.

Story games are so labeled because the children regard it as a game to match the words of the story with movement patterns. However, there should be no competition, nor should there be any elimination of children who do not achieve a certain standard or routine.

A skillful leader can do an effective piece of work in story games with comparatively simple materials. The old, familiar stories offer excellent material for stories. Then, too, many poems can be utilized as a basis for movement experiences. The leader should be able to draw out ideas from child and adult worlds.

Formations should be informal, with the children scattered or in a loose circle. All should be able to see and hear the leader. It is important that a good story basis be set for the stories, so probably the teacher would need to do the relating. However, if children are capable, they can be utilized.

STORIES

Children love to act out and dramatize many of the old, familiar stories. No doubt, both the children and the teacher have favorites. Some may be in the following list:

The Three Bears
The Three Pigs
Black Beauty

Cinderella
Rumpelstiltskin
The Shoemaker and the Elves
The Pied Piper
Mother Goose Stories
Henny Penny
The Sleeping Beauty
The Town Musicians
Peter Pan

The list is only a starting point, but is given to illustrate the kinds of stories that have possibilities.

Stories may need to be adapted and rewritten, using only the main points of the story to direct the movement.

As an illustration, the story, "Jack the Giant Killer" is given with the story in the left hand column and the suggested actions on right. It should be emphasized that the actions grow out of the discussions with the children with respect to the best way *they feel* the story should be interpreted.

JACK THE GIANT KILLER

Once upon a time a giant, called **Caramaran**, lived on top of a mountain in a cave. He was a very wicked giant, so the king of the country offered a large reward to the person who would kill the giant. So Jack, a country boy, decided he would try his luck.

1. One morning Jack took a shovel and pick and started toward the mountain. He hurried, as he wished to climb the mountain before dark.

2. Jack finally reached the foot of the mountain and started to climb up.

3. He came to a place where he had to use his hands to help him climb.

4. Just as it grew dark, Jack reached the top of the mountain. When he was sure the giant was asleep in his bed, he took his pick and began to dig a hole outside the cave entrance.

5. After he had loosened the dirt with his pick, Jack took the shovel and threw the dirt up on all sides of the hole.

6. Then Jack covered up the hole with some long straws and sticks he picked up.

7. After this was done, Jack waited until morning, when he called loudly and wakened the giant, who strode angrily out of the cave. As he was very tall, he took big steps.

8. The giant was so very angry he didn't look where he was going and walked right into the hole Jack had made. Down he fell and was killed.

9. Then Jack filled up the hole with the dirt he had taken out.

---

1. Picking up pick and shovel and running around in a circle.

2. Walking around in a circle with high knee movements.

3. Climbing with motions using hands and arms.

4. Vigorous digging movement with trunk twisting, standing with feet apart.

5. Vigorous shoveling movement, first right, then left, throwing the dirt in various directions.

6. Forward, downward bending, picking up straws, twisting alternately left and right.

7. Arms overhead, stretching up tall, walking around in a circle on tiptoes.

8. Stooping quickly as if falling.

9. Forward, downward movements, pushing dirt into hole, moving around in a circle, and doing the same thing over again.

10. Jack went into the cave, got the giant's treasure, and ran home to tell his mother about it.

11. When he got home he was so excited and tired he was all out of breath. Ever after this Jack was called the Giant Killer.

10. Running around circle in the opposite direction, carrying the treasure.

11. Deep breathing.

FINGER PLAYS

Finger plays are numerous and of a wide variety. None are long, and some are quite short. Many represent hand-me-downs from various cultures. They have long been used to interest and amuse children. Their use is usually confined to preschool and kindergarten children, but some may be carried into the first grade.

GRANDMOTHER'S GLASSES

Words	Action
Here are grandmother's glasses,	Make "glasses" with the thumbs and forefingers.
Here is grandmother's cap,	Hands come to a peak over the head.
And this is the way she folds her hands,	Fold the hands.
And lays them in her lap.	Lay the folded hands in the lap.

HICKORY, DICKORY, DOCK

Words	Action
Hickory, dickory, dock,	Raise left arm over the head and move it back and forth like a pendulum.
The mouse ran up the clock.	Run the right hand up the left arm with fast finger action.
The clock struck one, the mouse ran down,	Clap the hands overhead, run the right hand down with finger action.
Hickory, dickory, dock.	Move left arm back and forth.

JACK AND JILL

Words	Action
Jack and Jill went up the hill	Put the hands together with thumbs up and raise the hands in stages.
To get a pail of water.	Turn the hands over, thumbs down, and "pour."
Jack fell down and broke his crown,	Drop the right hand down to the lap and tap the head with the left hand.
And Jill came tumbling after.	Bring the left hand down in circular movements.

MY FINGERS

Verse	Action
I have ten little fingers, And they all belong to me. I can make them do things. Would you like to see?	Hold up the hands and wave the fingers back and forth. Continue opening and closing fingers. Hold fingers up opened wide.
I can shut them tight Or open them wide; I can put them together Or make them hide.	As indicated.
I can make them jump high; I can make them jump low; I can fold them up quietly, And hold them just so.	Follow actions as indicated.

LITTLE MISS MUFFET

Words	Action
Little Miss Muffet sat on a tuffet	Hold up the left hand with the thumb up to be Miss Muffet.
Eating her curds and whey.	Move thumb (Miss Muffet) back and forth.
Along came a spider	Bring the right hand forward toward Miss Muffet.
And sat down beside her,	As indicated.
And frightened Miss Muffet away!	Put left hand behind his back quickly.

DRAMATIC PLAY WITH POEMS

The field of poetry can be exploited to its fullest for source material for dramatic play. Mother Goose Rhymes are particularly suited for activity, and there are many others. Poetry has some advantages over stories because of the use of catchy phrasing, rhyming, and the "feeling" that is in much of it.

Poems have an appeal particularly for kindergarten and first grade children. Some examples of poems together with suggested actions follow.

THE ELEPHANT

Poem: The elephant's walk is careful and slow;
His trunk like a pendulum swings to and fro.
But when there are children with peanuts around
He swings it up and swings it down.

The poem is read line by line by the teacher. Sufficient pause should be made between lines so the children can react. Some prior discussion should be held to explain elephant actions and what is meant by a pendulum. Action can vary. Later, the children can recite as they move.

THE GIANT

The Words

1. Once a giant came a-wandering
2. Late at night when the world was still
3. Seeking a stool to sit on
4. He climbed on a little, green hill.
5. "Giant, Giant! I am under you,
6. Move or this is the last of me."
7. But the giant answered, "Thank you,
8. I like it here, don't you see."

Action

1. Children wander around the room in a swaggering, giant type of step and movement.
2. Children become quiet and put a finger up to the lips to indicate silence.
3. Giant swaggers around looking for a place to sit.
4. All children perform climbing movements to get to the top of the hill.
5. Children crouch down and pretend that they are stepped upon.
6. Children try to push the giant away.
7. Children walk around surveying the countryside.
8. Giant swaggers around with thumbs under armpits.

GIANTS AND DWARFS

The Words

1. Let us all be little men,
2. Dwarfs so gay and tiny, then,
3. Let us stand up straight and tall
4. We'll be giants, one and all.

Action

1. Walk around like dwarfs, with body in a hunched position and arms and legs bent.
2. Continue walking. Be gay.
3. Walk on tiptoes, arms stretched upward.
4. Continue walking, occasionally turning around.

HIPPITY HOP

Each child has a partner; inside hands are joined.

The Words

1. Hippity hop to the barber shop,
2. To buy a stick of candy.
3. One for you and one for me,
4. And one for cousin Andy.

Action

1. Partners skip around the room.
2. Stop. Face partner. Reach in pocket for money, holding up one finger.
3. Point to partner, point to self.
4. Join inside hands and skip around the room.

LITTLE JACK HORNER

Words

Little Jack Horner sat in a corner
Eating his Christmas pie.
He put in his thumb and pulled out a plum
And said, "What a good boy am I!"

Action

Crouch down in a sitting position.
Eat out of the left hand.
As indicated.
Put thumbs in the armpits and strut.

HOW TO MAKE A HAPPY DAY

Two eyes to see nice things to do,
Two lips to smile the whole day through,
Two ears to hear what others say,
Two hands to put the toys away,
A tongue to speak sweet words each day,
A loving heart for work or play,
Two feet that errands gladly run —
Make happy days for everyone.

Talk with the children about happiness and how we can help everyone be happy. As the verse is read or recited, the children point to the various parts of the body as they are mentioned. On the last line, everyone smiles!

JACK BE NIMBLE

Words	Action
Jack be nimble,	Move around in various ways.
Jack be quick,	Speed up action, change direction.
Jack jump over the candlestick!	Jump high into the air or leap over a "candlestick."

PAT-A-CAKE

Each child has a partner, partners facing.

The Words	Action
1. Pat-a-cake, pat-a-cake, baker's man,	Clap own hands, clap hands to partner. Repeat. Shake forefinger at partner three times.
2. Bake me a cake as fast as you can,	Stir the cake fast and vigorously.
3. Pat it, and mold it, and mark it with a "T,"	Follow words with patting, molding, and putting a "T" on top of the cake.
4. And bring it safely home to baby and me.	Walk around in good balance carefully so the cake will not be dropped.

Children find another partner during the walking and the poem is repeated.

RIPE APPLES

The Words	Action
1. Lovely ripe apples on branches so high,	With arms stretched upward, children sway back and forth.
2. I cannot reach them, way up in the sky.	Reach up high with one arm at a time.
3. I stretch up so tall, and I jump this way.	On tiptoes, stretch upward. Then jump upward to pick an apple.
4. I know when I've picked them, I'll eat them today.	Pretend to eat, raising hands alternately to mouth.
5. I'll sit down and rest, and eat them some more.	Sit down cross-legged and continue to eat.
6. "Um-m-m. Aren't they good?"	Shake heads, rub tummy while repeating in unison the last line.

ROW, ROW, ROW YOUR BOAT ACTIVITIES

The verse, Row, Row, Row your boat is easily learned and can supply the basis for many interesting creative activities. The verse is:

> Row, row, row your boat
> Gently down the stream
> Merrily, merrily, merrily
> Life is but a dream.

Let the children make up verses substituting other movements for "row." They can then act out the verses that they have created. They might come up with something like this, as one child did:

> Run, run, run around
> All around the room
> Merrily, merrily, merrily
> Zoom, zoom, zoom.

Other actions around which verses could be built are walk, march, hop, jump, fly, swim, ride, etc.

THREE BLIND MICE (Verse)

Words	Suggested Action
Three Blind Mice, Three Blind Mice	Children walk around with their hands over their eyes.
See how they run, see how they run.	Children run lightly in different directions.
They all ran after the farmer's wife,	Pretend to chase each other, or chase the teacher.
She cut off their tails with a carving knife,	Make cutting motions.
Did you ever see such a sight in your life	Stand up on tiptoes and look around.
As three blind mice?	Hands over the eyes.

THE WIND

The Wind is a more complicated poem and necessitates a little preparation. The children should be seated to hear the poem, discuss its contents, and plan appropriate responses. Different responses should be expected, dependent upon how each child interprets the poem. To stimulate an adequate response, the poem should be read with feeling.

> I saw you toss the kites on high
> And blow the birds about the sky:
> And all around I heard you pass,
> Like ladies' skirts across the grass.
>   Oh Wind, a-blowing all day long
>   Oh Wind, that sings so loud a song.

> I saw the different things you did
> But always you yourself you hid,
> I felt you push, I heard you call,
> I could not see yourself at all.
>   Oh Wind, a-blowing all day long
>   Oh Wind, that sings so loud a song.

> Oh you that are so strong and cold,
> Oh blower, are you young or old?
> Are you a beast of field and tree
> Or just a stronger child than me?
>   Oh Wind, a-blowing all day long
>   Oh Wind, that sings so loud a song.

First Verse:

1. Wind blowing very hard.

2. Birds being buffeted around in air.

Second Verse:

3. "I saw the different things you did." Blowing poplar trees.

4. Blowing a paper sack around.

5. "I heard you call."

Third Verse:

6. The wind is so strong and cold that the children have to stop play and get warm.

7. Still the wind blows on.

Action

1. a. Tossing up kites, holding the string, and skipping around the circle while the kites are in flight.
   b. Pulling the kites in hand over hand.

2. Little running steps with arms stretched sideways and swaying movements side to side in imitation of birds.

3. With the arms stretched overhead the children imitate tall poplar trees; they then alternate vigorous side bending with forward, downward bending.

4. Representation of empty paper sack, crouching on floor, then jumping up as high as possible, moving into the center of the circle.

5. Long drawn-out calls in imitation of the wind.

6. a. Jumping on toes with feet placed sideways and clapping of hands overhead and on thighs.
   b. Clapping arms around body.

7. Deep breathing.

It might be necessary to explain in this day and age how skirts used to billow!

WALLABY KANGAROO

The Words

1. Wallaby, wallaby, kangaroo,
2. How do you jump the way you do?

3. I'm sure if I tried for a year and a day,
4. I'd never be able to jump that way.

Action

Children have hands in front of shoulders to represent paws of the kangaroo. Look around from right to left but do not move.

Jump around like a kangaroo.

Continue to jump like a kangaroo.

OTHER EXPERIENCES AS A BASIS FOR DRAMATIC PLAY

Many everyday experiences from the childhood and adult world can form the basis for much dramatic play. The children can help the teacher plan the story to guide the play. A simple idea like the *Railroad Train* can be a good basis. It could be developed in the following fashion.

RAILROAD TRAIN

Each child is given the name of a part of a freight train. Several trains may be formed. The teacher tells a story in which the various parts of the train are mentioned in the telling. Several children are the engines, and the story usually begins with this portion of the train. After the story unfolds, the children form in line, one behind the other in the order named. After the trains have been assembled and all "cars" are on the train, the story continues by describing a train trip. The route is described in detail, with the train going slowly up and down grades, around curves, stopping at stations, and finishing up with a wreck. It is also possible to assemble the trains by having each of the parts of the train on "side tracks" and the train backing up to hook on the "cars."

Some attention should be given to the story, as the imagination of the teller is very important. Also, children can make suggestions for the train ride.

It is apparent that there is no dearth of material or ideas. Imagination plays a big part in widening the scope of dramatic play.

For another illustration of how an idea can be expanded, let us take the children on an imaginary hike.

THE HIKE

The Words	Action
1. Today we are going on a hike. What are some of the things we need to take?	1. Children will suggest various articles which should be included.
2. We are going to roll our packs into a nice, neat bundle. Put down your tarp first, next arrange your blankets, and put the rest of your things in. Now let's roll the pack and tie it up.	2. Children lay out packs, roll, and tie.
3. Off we go.	3. Children march two by two around the room carrying packs.
4. Time to rest.	4. All remove packs and sit down.
5. Off again.	5. Resume marching.
6. Make blazes so we can find our way back. Make trail markers.	6. Children make blazes in various manners. Arrange stones for markers.
7. Here we are. Pick out a good spot for the tent and put it up.	7. Cut stakes and poles. Drive stakes and put up tents. Arrange beds.
8. We need lots of wood for the campfire. Will you see what you can find?	8. Children go out and drag in logs and wood. Some cutting may be needed.
9. Build the fire and broil the steaks.	9. As directed.
10. Bugle call for "turning in."	10. Children go to one side, brush their teeth, wash up, and then turn in. They crawl in tent, cover themselves carefully, and go to sleep.

It should be noted that integration with other subject fields is possible. Conservation practices can be stressed. Safety in the woods can be emphasized.

Some suggestions of how other ideas can be used follow.

Playing
  In the leaves
  In the snow, making a snowman, sledding
  Riding a bicycle, wagon, tricycle, kiddie car, or other vehicle
  On the playground
  Flying a kite

Pretending to Be
  An animal — bear, deer, squirrel, giraffe, elephant, pony, etc.
  An imaginary creature — giant, witch, dwarf, troll, etc.
  An official or worker — conductor, policeman, engineer, etc.

Going to
- A circus
- A zoo
- A toy shop
- The farm

Doing Common Things Like
- Washing and hanging up clothes
- Washing dishes
- Trimming a Christmas tree
- Pitching hay
- Sowing grain
- Making a garden
- Shaking and beating rugs
- Cutting grain

Having Fun at
- Paddling a canoe, rowing a boat
- Playing baseball, football, track, basketball, etc.
- Skiing, ice skating, roller skating, water skiing.
- Swimming, using different strokes

Celebrating
- Holidays — Christmas, Halloween, Thanksgiving, Fourth of July
- Seasons — Fall, winter, spring, summer

Industries, Professions like
- Lumbering
- Fishing
- Construction
- Road Building

13

Manipulative Activities

Activities Utilizing Beanbags
Basic Ball Skills
Bowling
Paddle and Ball Activities
Parachute Play
Wands
Hoops

A manipulative activity is one in which a child handles some kind of a play object, usually with the hands, but it can involve the feet and other parts of the body. As basic skills, manipulative activities invite strong application of basic movement methodology, adding an important dimension to movement experiences. Manipulative activities can strengthen both hand-eye and foot-eye coordination, as well as develop dexterity in handling a variety of play objects. Activities utilizing beanbags, balls of various kinds, hoops, wands, paddles and balls, and a parachute round out a basic program. Deck tennis rings, toss items like rubber horseshoes, lummi sticks, and floor hockey equipment can enrich the offerings. Individual rope jumping is in a sense a manipulative activity, but is usually classed among individual and dual activities, where it has been placed in this guide (Chapter 19).

The supply factor is critical to a program of manipulative activities. For individual work, one item should be on hand for each child. In partner work, one item should be present for each two children. The demands for group work are less. However, most activity consists of individual and partner work, except, of course, for parachute play. One parachute is sufficient for a normal size class.

Beanbags, paper balls, and yarn balls provide the first throwing and catching skills for younger children. A softer object instills confidence and tends to eliminate the fear younger children have of catching a hard or unyielding object. After these introductory skills, other types of balls are added and more demanding skills are brought in.

Since early competency in handling objects provides a basis for later or specialized skills, basic principles of skill performance (page 69) should have strong application, particularly as related to throwing and catching skills.

The Start-and-Expand approach is sound for manipulative activities. Start the children at a low level of challenge so all can achieve success, and expand the skills and experiences from that base. In progression, most activities begin with the individual approach and later move to partner activity. Partners should be of comparable ability.

ACTIVITIES UTILIZING BEANBAGS

Activities based on beanbags provide valuable learning experiences for children at all levels in the elementary school. They provide a good introduction for throwing and catching skills for kindergarten and primary children and should precede instruction with inflated balls. All parts of the body can be brought into play with beanbag activity.

Instructional Procedures

1. Smaller beanbags (4″) are suitable for preschool and K-2 grades. A larger beanbag

(6") should be used with older children. The larger beanbag balances and can be controlled better on various parts of the body, offering a greater measure of success for upper primary children.

2. Throwing and catching skills involve many intricate elements. Emphasize the skill performance principles of opposition, eye focus, weight transfer, and follow-through. It is important that children keep an eye on the object being caught and on the target when throwing.

3. Stress laterality and directionality, and work at different levels.

4. Give some attention to targets when throwing. Children should throw about chest high to a partner, unless a different type of throw is specified. Teach all types of returns — low, medium, high, left, and right.

5. In early practice, stress a soft receipt of the beanbag when catching by "giving" with the hands, arms, and legs. Softness is created by having the hands go out toward the incoming beanbag and bring it in for a soft landing.

6. In partner work, keep distances between partners reasonable, especially in introductory phases. Fifteen feet or so seems to be a reasonable starting distance.

7. In partner work, emphasize skillful throwing, catching, and handling of the beanbag. Hard and difficult throwing, the purpose of which is to cause the partner to miss, should be avoided.

Recommended Activities with Beanbags

Activities are generally classified into individual and partner activities. A few games round out the suggested activities.

Individual Activities

1. In place, tossing to self. Toss with both hands, right hand, left hand. Catch the same way. Catch with back of the hands.

Toss from side to side, right to left, (reverse), front to back, back to front, around various parts of the body, different combinations.

Toss and catch at different levels. Toss and catch from seated position.

2. In place, adding stunts. Toss overhead to the rear, turn around and catch. Toss and do a full turn and catch.

Toss, clap hands, and catch. Clap hands more than once. Clap hands around different parts of the body and catch.

Toss, kneel on one knee, and catch. Try this going to a seated or lying position. Reverse the order, coming from lying or sitting position to a standing position to catch.

Toss, touch the floor, and catch. Explore with other challenges. Use heel clicks, or balance positions.

3. Locomotor movements. Toss to self, moving to another spot to catch. Toss forward, run, and catch. Move from side to side. Toss overhead to the rear, run back, and catch. Add various stunts and challenges previously described.

Vary with different locomotor movements.

4. Balancing beanbag on various parts of the body. Balance on head. Move around, maintaining balance of beanbag. Sit down, lie down, turn around, etc.

Balance the beanbag on various parts of the body and move around in this fashion. Balance on top of instep, between knees, on shoulders, on elbows, etc.

Use more than one beanbag for balancing.

5. Propelling beanbag with various parts of the body. Toss to self from various parts of the body — elbow, instep, between feet, between heels, knees, shoulders.

Sit and toss bag from the feet to self. Practice from a supine position. From a supine position, pick up the bag between the toes, place it behind the head, using a full curl position. Go back and pick it up, returning it to original place.

6. Manipulating with bare feet. The children are barefooted. The bag should be picked up by curling the toes. This has value in strengthening the muscles supporting the arch.

Pick up with one foot. Hop to another spot. Change feet.

Toss to self from either foot. Using a target (hoop), toss the beanbag into the target.

Partner Activities

1. Tossing back and forth. Begin with various kinds of two-handed throws — underhand, overhead, side, and over-shoulder. Change to one-handed tossing and throwing.

Throw at different levels, also at different targets — right and left.

Throw under leg, around the body. Center as in football. Try imitating the shot put and the discus throw. Try the softball windmill (full arc) throw.

Have partners sit tailor (cross-legged) fashion about 10' apart. Throw and catch in various styles seated in this fashion.

Use follow activities, where one partner leads with a throw and the other follows with the same kind of a throw.

Toss in various directions to make partner move and catch.

With one partner standing still, have the other partner run around him in a circle as the bag is tossed back and forth.

Games

Simple games can be devised like tossing through a hoop, tossing into a waste basket,

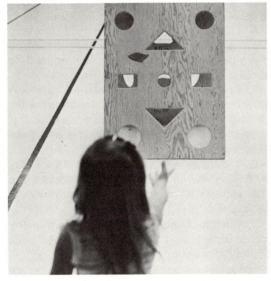

Target for Beanbags

and using a target board with cutout holes. Holes can be triangles, circles, squares, and rectangles, stressing form concepts.

Relay races can be organized with beanbags. Games like One Step (page 232) and Teacher Ball (page 217) have value in challenging the learned skills.

Beanbag Horseshoes

A toss game can be organized based on the principle of horseshoes. A spot is put on

Beanbag Horseshoes

the floor. Any beanbag nearer the spot than the opponent's nearest bag scores a point. If the beanbag covers the spot completely, it scores two points. Games can be 15 points. Player scoring the point or points leads off with the next tosses. Each player can have two beanbags and toss both before the partner tosses. A variation is to have the players toss the bags alternately.

BASIC BALL SKILLS

Included in this section are the basic ball skills in which the child handles balls without the aid of other equipment such as a bat or paddle. Ball skills are mostly of two types:

Hand-Eye Skills: throwing, catching, bouncing, dribbling (as in basketball), batting (as in volleyball), and rolling (bowling).

Foot-Eye Skills: kicking, trapping, and dribbling (as in soccer).

Other parts of the body are used on occasion, but the main emphasis centers on ball handling with the hands and feet.

Ball skills are of vital importance to children in their play experiences. A good basis for these skills must be laid in the lower grades, with continued development in the upper grades. Not only should the children acquire skill through varied experiences in handling balls, but they should also gain knowledge of skill principles essential to competency in ball-handling skills.

Type of Ball

Paper, yarn, and fleece balls are excellent for introductory skills on the preschool, kindergarten, and first grade level, as they help overcome the fear factor. Some teachers have found success with balls made from crumpled-up newspaper dipped in sizing. A design for yarn ball construction is in the appendix. Another type of ball that has value is a soft softball, a much softer version of the regular softball. It has advantages in catching thrown balls and fielding grounders but does not hold up well if batted.

The inflated rubber playground ball (8½") should be the predominant ball for most of the children's ball-handling experiences. Skill work should start with this size ball and move to smaller items later. Balls should be moderately inflated so that they will bounce well, but not to the point of overinflation, which causes difficulty in catching. Overinflation can also distort the spherical shape.

Individual, Partner and Group Organization

Instruction should begin with individual work and progress to partner and group activities. After the children have acquired some skill, a lesson can include both individual and partner activity.

In propelling the ball back and forth between partners, children can progress from rolling the ball to throwing the ball on first bounce, to throwing the ball on the fly. Be sure a disparity in skill between partners does not cause a problem for either partner. A skilled child can aid a less skilled child to better performance, but the more skilled individual may resent being restricted in more complex skills by an inept child.

Other Factors

Distance between partners should be short and gradually lengthened. The concept of targets is introduced by directing the children to throw the ball to specific points. Later, a change from a stationary target to a moving target maintains progression. Relays are useful in reinforcing skill learning, but caution is suggested that the skills are reasonably learned before being applied in a relay.

Instructional Procedures

1. The principles of skill performance (page 69) have strong application to ball skills, particularly visual concentration, follow-through, arm-leg opposition, weight transfer, and total body coordination. These principles should be incorporated into the instructional sequences and, in addition, be an important part of the coaching process. Balls should be handled with the pads of the fingers and should not be "palmed."

2. In catching, a soft receipt of the ball should be created by a "giving" movement with the hands and arms. Hands should reach out somewhat to receive the ball, and then cushion the impact by bringing the ball in toward the body with loose and relaxed hands.

3. In catching a throw above the waist, the hands should be positioned so the thumbs are together. To receive a throw below the waist, the catch is made by the hands with the little fingers toward each other and the thumbs out.

4. When throwing to a partner, unless otherwise specified, the throw should reach the partner about chest high. At times, a variety of target points should be specified — high, low, right, left, knee-high, etc.

5. A lesson should begin with simple basic skills within the reach of all children and progress to more challenging activities.

6. Laterality is an important consideration. Right and left members of the body should be given practice in turn in somewhat equal time allotments.

7. Practice in split vision should be incorporated into bouncing and dribbling skills. Children should learn to look somewhat forward, not at the ball, in bouncing and dribbling work.

8. Tactile senses can be brought into play by having the children dribble or bounce the ball with eyes closed, allowing practice in getting the "feel" of the ball.

9. Rhythmic accompaniment, particularly for bouncing and dribbling activities, adds another dimension to ball skills.

10. It is desirable that enough balls be present so each child may have a ball. However, in case there are only enough balls present so that two children need to share a ball, the first child does the prescribed routine and then bounces, tosses, or passes the ball as prescribed to the second child, who repeats the designated routine.

Recommended Ball Activities

Activities with balls are presented with the larger rubber playground ball (8½" or larger) in mind. Some modification is needed if the balls are smaller or are of the type which does not bounce, as in the case of yarn, paper, or fleece balls. Activities are presented under four headings: (1) individual activities, (2) partner activities, (3) activities with scoops, and (4) bowling.

Individual Activities

Each child has a ball and practices by himself. In the first group of individual activities the child remains in the same spot. Next, he utilizes a wall to rebound the ball to himself. In the third group of activities he is performing alone while on the move.

In-Place Activities

1. Controlled Rolling. The child assumes a wide straddle position, places the ball on the floor, and rolls it with constant hand guidance between and around the legs. Other positions are: seated with legs outstretched, cross-legged sitting, and push-up position.

2. Bounce and Catch. Beginning with two hands, bounce and catch. Bounce a given number of times. Bounce at different levels. Bounce one-handed in a variety of fashions. Bounce under the legs. Close eyes, bounce and catch.

3. Toss and Catch. Toss and catch, increasing height gradually. Toss from side to side. Toss underneath the legs, around the body, from behind. Add challenges while tossing and catching: clap hands one or more times, make body turns (quarter, half, or full), touch the floor, click heels, sit down, lie down, etc.

Toss upward and let bounce. Add various challenges as above.

Toss upward and catch the descending ball at as high a level as possible; at a low level. Work out other levels and put into combinations.

From a seated position, toss ball to self from various directions. Lie down and do the same.

4. Bat the Ball (As In Volleyball) to Self. Bat the ball, using the fist, open hand, or side of hand.

Bat and let ball bounce. Catch in different fashions.

5. Foot Skills. Put toe on top of ball. Roll it in different directions, keeping the other foot in place and retaining control of the ball.

Use two-footed pick-up, front and back.

From a sitting position with the legs extended, toss the ball with the feet to the hands.

6. Dribbling Skills. Dribble the ball first with both hands, then with the right and the left. Emphasize that the dribble is a push with good wrist action. Children should not bat the ball downward. Use various number combinations with the right and left hands. Dribble under the legs in turn, back around the body. Kneel and dribble. Go from standing to lying position, maintaining a dribble. Return to standing position.

Against a Wall

The wall should be reasonably free of projections and irregular surfaces, so the ball may return directly to the student. If the ball is to bounce after contact with the wall, the children can stand back farther than if they are to handle the return on the fly.

1. Throwing Practice, Catching on the First Bounce. Throw the ball against the wall and catch the return after a bounce. Practice various kinds of throws — two-handed, one-handed, overhead, side, baseball, chest-pass, etc.

2. Throwing Practice, Catching on the Fly. Repeat the throws used in #1, but catch the return on the fly. It may be necessary to move closer and have the ball contact the wall higher.

3. Batting and Handball Skills. Drop the ball and bat it after it bounces. Keep the ball going, as in handball. Serve the ball against the wall as in volleyball. Experiment with different means of serving.

4. Kicking and Trapping — Foot-Eye Skills. Practice different ways of controlled kicking against the wall and stopping (trapping) the ball on the return. Try keeping the ball going with the foot on the bounce against the wall.

Activities While Moving

1. Rolling. Roll the ball, guide it with the hands in different directions. Roll the ball forward, run and catch up with it.

2. Toss and Catch. Toss ball upward and forward. Run forward and catch after a bounce. Toss ball upward in various directions — forward, sideward, backward — run under ball and catch on fly. Add various stunts and challenges such as touching the floor, heel clicks, turning around, etc.

3. Batting the Ball. Bat the ball with the hand upward in different directions, catch ball on first bounce or on fly.

4. Foot Skills — Soccer Dribble. Dribble ball forward, backward, and in other directions. Dribble around an imaginary point. Make various patterns while dribbling, such as a circle, square, triangle, figure eight, etc.

5. Dribbling as in Basketball. Dribble forward using one hand and back to place with the other. Change directions on whistle. Dribble in various directions, describing different pathways. Dribble in and around cones, milk cartons, or chairs.

Partner Activities
In-Place Activities
(Both Partners Are Stationary)

1. Rolling. Roll the ball back and forth to partner. Begin with two-handed rolls and proceed to one-handed rolls.

2. Throwing and Catching. Toss ball to partner on first bounce, using various kinds of tosses. Practice various kinds of throws and passes to partner. Throw to specific points — high, low, right, left, knee-high, etc. Try various odd throws such as under leg, around the body, backward tosses, centering as in football. Throw and catch over a volleyball net.

3. Batting and Volleyball Skills. Serve as in volleyball. Serve to partner who catches. Toss to partner and have him make a volleyball return. Keep distances short and the ball under good control. Bat back and forth on first bounce. Bat back and forth over a line or over a bench.

4. Kicking. Practice different ways of controlled kicking between partners and different ways of stopping the ball (trapping). Practice a controlled punt, preceding the kick with a step from the nonkicking foot. Place ball between feet and propel forward or backward to partner. Practice foot pickups. One partner rolls the ball and the other hoists ball to self with extended toe.

5. Throwing from Various Positions. Practice different throws from a kneeling, sitting, or lying position. Allow the children freedom for creativity in selecting positions.

Target Practice

Many targets can be devised for throwing skills. Targets with concentric circles painted on the wall are good. Targets can be mounted on the wall. Rolling hoops are challenging targets.

For large yarn balls, wastebaskets serve for targets. Smaller targets can be empty 3-pound coffee cans. The principle of One-Step (page 232) can be used. With the can upright, stand with the toes touching the can. Take one step backward. Holding the arm out straight, shoulder-high, drop the yarn ball into the can. Back up one step and throw underhanded. Repeat several steps. A second child may need to hold the can to avoid tipping.

Activities with Scoops

Scoops for catching can be made from plastic Clorox containers or something similar. Small balls (sponge or old tennis balls), beanbags, fleece balls, yarn balls, or even paper balls can be caught with scoops.

Activities which can be done with balls and scoops follow in many respects the sequence of activities as outlined with beanbags or playground balls. Activities are first done individually and then with partners. Throwing can be done by hand or with the scoop.

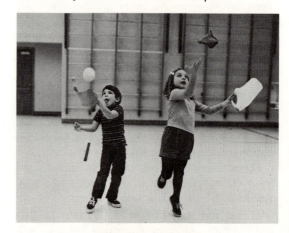

Playing with Scoops

Individual Activities

1. Toss the ball into the air and catch it in the scoop. Let the children experiment with the different forms of tossing and catching.

2. Toss the ball against the wall (if it is the

kind that will rebound) and catch it on the roll, on first bounce, and on the fly.

3. Toss the ball upward with the scoop and catch it with the scoop. Toss against the wall with the scoop and catch.

4. Toss the ball around different parts of the body with the scoop. Practice tossing from a sitting and lying position.

5. Toss at targets, such as waste baskets, hoops, boxes, etc.

Partner Activities

Encourage experimentation and creativity. Begin with one partner having the scoop and then proceed to activities where both partners have scoops.

1. One partner rolls, bounces, or tosses the ball to the other, who catches the missile in the scoop. Stress short distances first and then move back. Vary the type of throw and the type of catch with the scoop.

2. Both partners have scoops. Send the ball back and forth with the scoops. Stress variety in patterns.

3. Bowl with the ball out of the scoop. Use an Indian club for target.

4. Play One-Step.

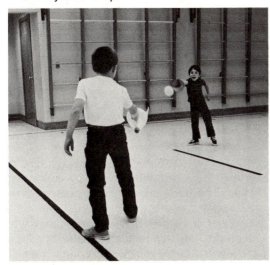

Partner Work Catching a Fleece Ball with Scoops

BOWLING

Children in preschool, kindergarten, and the lower two grades should practice informal rolling. In about the third grade, the emphasis should change from informal rolling to bowling skills, continuing through the sixth grade.

Bowling skills should begin with a two-handed roll and progress to one-handed rolls, using both right and left hands. Various targets can be utilized, including Indian clubs, milk cartons, small cones, blocks, and human targets.

The regular (8½") rubber playground ball is excellent for bowling skills. Volleyballs and soccer balls can also be used. Stress moderate speed in moving the ball.

Bowling activities are organized mostly into partner or group work. When targets are being used, two children on the target end are desirable. One child resets the target, while the other recovers the ball.

The ball should roll off the tips of the fingers with good follow-through.

BOWLING SKILLS — PARTNER ACTIVITY UNLESS OTHERWISE NOTED

1. Begin with two-handed rolls from between the legs, employing a wide straddle stance.

2. Roll the ball right handed and left handed. Receiver can employ the foot pickup, done by hoisting the ball to self (hands) with the extended toe.

3. Practice different kinds of spin (English) on the ball. For a right-handed bowler, a curve to the left is called a "hook ball" and a curve to the right is a "backup ball."

4. Employ human straddle targets. Organize children in groups of four, two on each end. One child on each end becomes the target and the other the ball chaser. Using a stick 2' long, make chalk marks on the floor. The target child straddles the chalk marks so that the marks are on the inside edges of his shoes, making a space of 2' between his feet.

Stress moderate bowling distances (15'-20') at first and adjust as the children become more proficient. Scoring can be based on two points scored for a ball that goes through the legs without touching, and one point scored for a ball that goes through, but touches the leg.

5. Indian clubs, milk cartons, or even regular bowling pins can be used as targets. Begin with one and move up to two, or three. Plastic bowling pins are available for this purpose. Other targets can be made by laying a wastebasket on its side and rolling into it

or using the 3-pound coffee can for the smaller ball.

6. A fine game to round off the activities is Bowling One-Step (page 224).

PADDLE AND BALL ACTIVITIES

Paddle and ball activities are an important part of the program, as they are closely related to paddle and ball sports such as tennis, badminton, squash, and table tennis. The suggested level for regular instruction is from the third grade upward, as younger children have difficulty holding the commercial wooden paddle made for paddle sports. Sponge balls and old tennis balls are excellent, provided they are not too lively.

For those who wish to introduce the activity below the third grade level, a lighter paddle is needed. The regular table tennis paddle can be used for younger children.

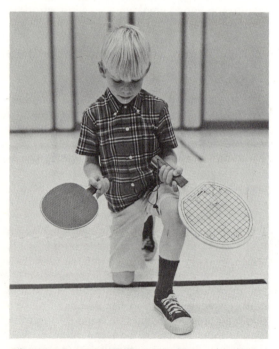

The Smaller Paddle is Better for Younger Children

Instructional Procedures

1. The larger paddles should have leather wrist thongs. The hand should go through the leather loop before grasping the paddle. (See appendix.)

2. Proper grip must be emphasized, and to see that children maintain this is a constant battle. The easiest method of teaching the proper grip is to advise the student to hold his paddle perpendicular to the floor and then shake hands with it. Young people tend to revert to the inefficient "hammer" grip, which is similar to the grip used on a hammer when pounding nails.

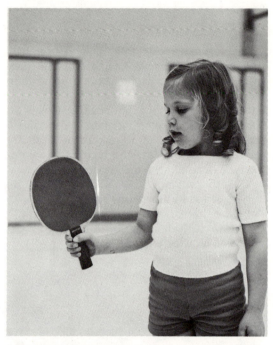

Holding the Paddle Properly — the Handshake Grip

3. Accuracy and control should be goals of this activity, and the children should not be concerned with force or distance.

4. The wrist should be held reasonably stiff and the arm action should be a stroking motion. The body should be turned sideways in stroking.

5. Early activities can be attempted with both right and left hands, but the dominant hand should be developed in critical skills.

6. During a lesson, related information about racquet sports may be quite relevant.

7. Practice in racquet work should move from individual to partner work as quickly as feasible, since this is the basic reality of the racquet sports.

Individual Activities

1. Place ball on paddle and attempt to bal-

lance it to prevent it from falling off. As skill increases, attempt to roll the ball around the edges of the paddle.

2. Bounce the ball in the air using the paddle:

   a. See how many times it can be bounced without touching the floor.

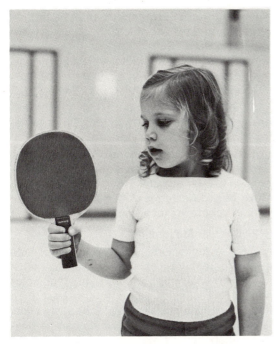

Incorrectly Holding the Paddle — the Hammer Grip

   b. Bounce it off the paddle into the air, and catch it with the other hand.
   c. Increase the height of the bounce.

3. Dribble the ball with the paddle:
   a. From a stationary position.
   b. Moving.

4. Alternate bouncing the ball in the air and on the floor.

5. Bounce the ball off the paddle into the air and "catch" it with the paddle. This requires one to "give" with the paddle and create a soft home for the ball.

6. Bounce the ball off the paddle into the air.

Partner Activities

All partner activity should begin with controlled throwing (feeding) by one partner and the designated stroke return by the other. In this way, the child concentrates on his stroke without worry about the competitive aspects.

1. Forehand
Toss and return stroke.
Stroking back and forth with partner.

2. Backhand
Toss and return stroke.
Stroking back and forth with partner.

3. Continuous Play
Back-and-forth play over a "net." Improvised "nets" can be set up by laying a jumping rope on the floor crosswise to the field of play, also by supporting a wand on blocks or cones, or utilizing a bench for the barrier.

PARACHUTE PLAY

Parachute play can be enjoyed by all children from the first through sixth grades. Activities must be carefully selected for the younger children, however, since some of the skills presented in the recommended list will be difficult for them. One parachute is sufficient for the normal size class of thirty children.

Parachutes come in different sizes, depending upon whether their use was for personnel or cargo. Personnel parachutes are the most suitable for parachute play, as cargo parachutes are usually large and cumbersome.

Each parachute has an opening near the top to allow trapped air to escape and keep the parachute properly shaped. Modern personnel parachutes are generally constructed of nylon.

Values of Parachute Play

Parachutes provide a new and interesting medium of accomplishing physical fitness goals, with good development of strength, agility, coordination, and endurance. Strength development is especially centered on the arms, hands, and shoulder girdle. However, at times strength demands are made on the entire body.

A wide variety of movement possibilities, some of which are rhythmic, can be employed in parachute play. Locomotor skills while manipulating the parachute are much in evidence. Rhythmic beats of the tom-tom or appropriate music can guide locomotor movements.

Parachute play provides many excellent

group learning experiences, as individuality disappears in much of this type of play.

Terminology

As the activities unfold, certain terms peculiar to the activity must be carefully explained. Terms such as inflate, deflate, float, dome, mushroom, and others need to be clarified when introduced.

Grips

The grips used in handling the parachute are comparable to those employed in hanging activities on apparatus. Grips may be with one or two hands, overhand (palms facing away), underhand (palms facing), or mixed, a combination of underhand and overhand grip. They should be varied.

Instructional Procedures

1. For preliminary explanations, the parachute can be stretched out on the ground in its circular pattern with the children seated back just far enough so they cannot touch the parachute during instructions. During explanations when the parachute is held by the children, they should retain their hold lightly, letting the center of the parachute drop to the ground. Children must be taught to exercise control so that they do not manipulate the parachute while explanations are in progress.

2. The teacher explains the forthcoming activity, demonstrating as needed. If there are no questions, he initiates the activity with a command such as: "Ready — BEGIN!" Best success occurs when children start together on signal. At times, the teacher may wish to have the children lay the parachute down, back off a step or two, and sit down for further instructions or for a short rest.

Activities

Activities are presented according to type, with variations and suggestions for supplementary activity included. Unless otherwise specified, activities begin and halt on signal. Pupil suggestions can broaden the scope of activity.

1. Exercise-type Activities

Exercises should be done vigorously and with enough repetitions to challenge the children. In addition to the exercises presented, others can be adapted to parachute play.

a. **Toe Toucher.** Sit with feet extended under the parachute and the chute held taut with a two-hand grip, drawn up to the chin. Bend forward and touch the grip to the toes. Return to stretched parachute.

b. **Curl-Ups.** Extend the body under the parachute in curl-up position so that the stretched parachute comes up to the chin when held taut. Perform Curl-Ups, each time returning to tight parachute.

c. **Backward Pulls.** Backward pulls are made facing the parachute and pulling back, away from its center. Pulls can be made from sitting, kneeling, or standing positions.

d. **Other Pulls.** Side pulls using a flexed-arm position can be structured. Other variations of pulling can be devised.

e. **Hip Walk and Scooter.** Begin with the parachute taut. Move forward with the *Scooter* (page 197) and the *Hip Walk* (page 197). Move back to place with the same movement until the chute is taut again.

2. Circular Movements

Circular movements, where the center hole in the parachute remains above the same spot, offer many opportunities for locomotor movements either free or to the beat of a tom-tom. Rhythmic running, European style, is particularly appropriate. Holds can be one- or two-handed.

Many basic movements can be utilized while children move in a circular fashion, such as walking, running, hopping, skipping, galloping, sliding, draw steps, grapevine steps, and others. The parachute can be held at different levels.

3. Shaking the Rug and Making Waves

Shaking the Rug involves rapid movements, either light or heavy. Making Waves are large movements to send billows of cloth up and down like waves. Waves can be small, medium, or high. Children can alternate turns to see who can make the best waves.

4. Making a Dome

Begin with the parachute on the floor, children holding with two hands and kneeling on one knee. To trap the air under the chute and make a dome shape, each child stands up quickly, thrusting arms above the head and returning to starting position. Vary by having all or part of the children change to

MANIPULATIVE ACTIVITIES   147

Forming a Dome

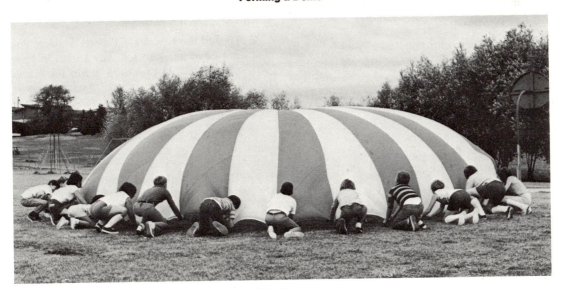

The Dome

the inside of the chute on the down movement, as in a cave. Domes can also be made while moving in a circle.

5. Chute Crawl

One-half the class, either standing or kneeling, stretches the chute out level with the floor. The remaining children crawl under the chute to the opposite side from their starting position.

6. Mushroom Activities

With the chute on the floor and students on one knee holding with two hands, stand up quickly, thrusting arms overhead. Keeping the arms overhead, each walks forward three or four steps toward the center. The arms are held overhead until the chute is deflated.

a. Mushroom Release. All children release at the peak of inflation and either run out from under the chute, or move to the center and sit down, with the chute descending on top of them.

7. Kite Run

One-half the class holds the chute on one

side with one hand. The leader points in the direction they are to run and they do so, holding the chute aloft as a kite.

8. Activities with Beanbags

a. **Popcorn.** Place a number of beanbags (6-10) on the chute. Shake the chute to make them rise like popping corn.

Too few beanbags limits the fun. Too many on the chute makes them bunch up.

WANDS

Wands are made from ¾" doweling and come in two lengths, 36" and 42". If the school purchases one size only, it should be the longer wand. Those with assorted bright colors have a special appeal for children.

Wands are noisy when they hit the floor. Putting rubber crutch tips on each end of the wand alleviates most of this and makes it easier to pick up from the floor. The tips should be put on with mucilage.

The year's supply of wands should include five or six extra beyond the number needed to have one for each child. There will be some breakage.

The recommended level of introduction for wand stunts is the third grade.

Instructional Procedures

1. Since wands are noisy, it is helpful to have the child hold his wand with both hands during instruction or lay it on the floor.

2. Many wand activities require great flexibility, which means that not all children will be able to do them. Girls usually perform flexibility stunts better than boys.

3. An adequate amount of space is needed for each individual, as wand stunts demand room.

4. Wands are not to be used as fencing foils. Stop this nonsense at once.

Individual Stunts

1. Wand Catch. Stand a wand on one end and hold it in place with the fingers on top. Bring the foot quickly over the stick, letting it go and catching the stick with the fingers before it falls. Do this right and left, inward and outward for a complete set. Try to catch it with just the index finger.

2. Thread the Needle — V Seat. Maintaining a V seat position, with the wand held in front of the body with both hands, bend the knees between the arms and pass the wand over them and return, *without touching* the wand to the legs.

3. Thread the Needle — Standing. Holding wand in both hands, step through stick one leg at a time and return without touching stick. Step through again, but this time bring the wand up the back, over the head, and

Popping Popcorn (Beanbags) in the Chute

MANIPULATIVE ACTIVITIES 149

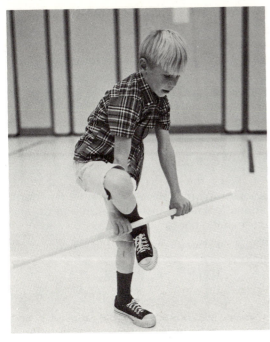

Beginning the Grapevine

around in front. Reverse. Try from side to side with the stick held front and back.

4. Grapevine. Holding wand near the ends, step with right foot *around* right arm and over wand inward towards body. Pass the wand backwards over head and right shoulder until you are standing erect with wand between legs. Reverse back to original position. Try with the left foot leading.

5. Back Scratcher. Hold wand with under grip (palms up), with arms crossed in front of the body. Bend the elbows so that the wand can go over and behind the head. Attempt to pass the wand down the length of the body from the back of the shoulders to the heels. Do not release grip on wand. The wand is worked down behind the back, while the arms stay in front of the body.

6. Wand Whirl. Stand wand upright in front of you. Turn around quickly and grasp wand before it falls. Do it right and left. Try making two full turns and catch the wand.

7. Twist Under. Grasp upright-standing wand with right hand. Twist around under the right arm without letting go of wand, taking it off the floor, or touching knee to floor. Repeat using left arm.

Grapevine — Second Stage. Head ducks under and wand is passed down the back.

Back Scratcher. Wand has been passed overhead and is now being forced down the back.

8. Jump Stick. Holding the wand in front with both hands, jump over the wand. Jump back. The wand passes under the body during the jumps. Hold the wand with the tips of of the fingers. (A rope or towel may be substituted for children having difficulty.)

9. Wand Juggle. Balance wand with one hand or on one finger, keeping it upright. Walk forward and back. Sit down, lie down, or move into other positions keeping the wand balanced.

Partner Stunts

1. Partner Catch. Partners face each other a short distance (5′) apart, each holding his wand in his right hand. On signal each throws his wand to the partner with his right hand and catches the incoming wand with his left.

2. Partner Change. Partners face each other a short distance (5′) apart, each with his wand standing upright, held by the right hand on top. On signal, each runs to the other's wand to catch it before it falls. This can also be done in the same way as the *Wand Whirl,* with each whirling to the other's wand. Proper positioning will need to be determined.

HOOPS

Most American hoops are made from plastic, but Europeans use some made from wood. The plastic variety is less durable, but is more versatile. Extra hoops are needed as there will be breakage. The standard hoop is 36″ in diameter, but it is desirable to have smaller hoops for younger children (30″). The hoop with the lead shot inside is of no advantage.

Instructional Procedures

1. Hoops are a noisy activity. The teacher might find it helpful to have the children lay the hoops on the floor when they are to listen.

2. Hoops can be a medium of creativity for children. Allow them some free time to explore their own ideas.

3. Allow the children an adequate amount of space in which to perform, as hoops require much movement.

4. In activities which require children to jump through hoops, instruct the child holding the hoop to grasp it lightly so that if the performer hits the hoop it will not cause an awkward fall.

5. Hoops can serve as a "home" for various activities. For instance, the children might leave their hoops to gallop in all directions and then quickly return to them upon command.

6. Hoops make good targets. They can be made to stand by placing an individual mat through the hoop and over its base (see appendix).

Hoop Activities

1. Place the hoops on the floor to create various patterns. Have the children perform various locomotor movements in, out of, and between the hoops.

2. **Hula Hoop** using various body parts such as:

   a. Waist   c. Arms
   b. Legs   d. Fingers

While hula hooping on the arms, try and change the hoop from one arm to the other.

3. Jump or hop through a hoop held by a partner. Further challenge can be added by varying the height and angle of the hoop.

4. Roll the hoop and run alongside it. Change directions when a command is given.

5. Use the hoop like a jump rope. Jump forward, backward, and sideward.

6. Roll the hoop with a reverse spin to make it return to the thrower. The key to the reverse spin is to pull down (toward the floor) on the hoop as it is released.

7. Roll the hoop with a reverse spin and jump over the hoop and catch it as it returns.

8. Roll the hoop with a reverse spin and as it returns, kick it up and catch it.

9. Many partner stunts can be performed such as:

   a. Play catch with a partner.
   b. Play catch with two or more hoops.
   c. Hula hoop and attempt to change the hoops from one partner to another.
   d. One partner rolls the hoop with a reverse (comeback) spin, and the other attempts to crawl through the hoop. This is done most easily just after the hoop reverses direction and begins to return to the spinner. Some children can go in and out of the hoop twice.

MANIPULATIVE ACTIVITIES   151

Hoop Floor Patterns for Exploratory Activity

1.

2.

3.

4.

14

Apparatus Activities

- Return Activity
- Multiple Activity Organization
- Apparatus Types
- Rope Climbing
- Horizontal Ladder and Climbing Frames
- Exercise Bar
- Balance Beam
- Activities on Benches
- Activities on Jumping Boxes
- Magic Ropes
- Individual Mats
- Balance Boards
- Bounding Boards
- Gym Scooters
- Combination Sets

Activities on apparatus have an important part in physical education programs. A wider variety of apparatus than ever before is now available from commercial sources or through school construction. Exercising on overhead and climbing apparatus has strong physical effects on the grip, arm, and shoulder girdle. Flexibility and stretching effects have value in the maintenance of posture. The child learns to manage his body free of ground support.

Equipment placed on the floor provides important extensions for basic movement. Exploratory and creative activity, as well as wide experience in body management, should characterize the approach to instructional procedures. Individual response in movement should be stressed, with the emphasis on doing but not on conformity. Variety in apparatus activity can be enhanced by the addition of hand apparatus such as beanbags, balls, wands, hoops, blocks, and other items. Individual or partner manipulative activities as the children perform and move on apparatus add another dimension to the movement possibilities.

Traffic rules should be established, stipulating when the child next in turn starts. His return route to the starting point can be established.

The children, except possibly for preschool age, should set up and store the equipment. Mats should be placed where needed for safety and to cushion dismounts. In addition, children should be instructed in spotting techniques along with the performance items.

Attention to form is relative to the types of activity. Most stunt-type movements involve three sequences in the instructional process: (1) how to mount, or get on the apparatus; (2) doing a skill or meeting a challenge; (3) dismounting. Emphasis should be on "giving it a good try," and "doing things as well as we can." The teacher can think in terms of minimal and maximal performance standards, taking individual differences into consideration. On the lower end of the skill scale, children like to know "did I do it?" On the upper end, they like to know that they achieved marked success.

The Start-and-Expand technique reinforces this kind of an approach by starting at a low point on the progression of skills. Achieving some measure of success is important. Serious enjoyment and fun should keynote the instructional climate in apparatus activities.

Some attention should be given to the dismount as determined by the character of the apparatus. The dismount should be controlled by landing with a bent-knee position and weight balanced over the balls of the feet. The child should land in good control and hold the position momentarily to show control. Many challenges, such as shapes through the air, turns, stunts following the landing, and others, can be structured into dismounts.

Return Activity

The employment of return activity can increase the movement potential of mat work, balance beams, benches, and other selected pieces of apparatus. In this technique, the child performs some kind of movement task on his way back (return) to his place in line. The return activity is usually something different, a change of pace, from the instructional emphasis. The instructional concentration is centered on the lesson activities, so the return movements should demand little supervision. Choice and exploration should characterize return activities.

An illustration of return activity in combination with the balance-beam bench follows. In this, the child performs on the bench, accomplishes his dismount, and does a forward roll on the way back to place. Three children are in place, illustrating the three aspects of the activity. One child is performing, another is dismounting, and the third child is rolling.

Return Activity

MULTIPLE ACTIVITY ORGANIZATION

Multiple activity organization can be effectively employed utilizing apparatus. Groups should be small enough with respect to the amount of available apparatus so that little standing or waiting occurs. The method is effective for squad organization if each squad is provided with enough equipment.

Multiple activity works best if there has been some preliminary instruction or orientation with regard to the apparatus. Children at each station should have specified things to do or challenges to meet, otherwise the activity is merely a type of supervised free play. Rotation is usually by signal, but can be by choice. The latter approach can teach youngsters to share. The teacher circulates around, helping, encouraging, and suggesting.

Group activity leaders can be designated to be responsible for activity at a station. Manipulative activities can be combined with apparatus activities in the multiple activity plan.

APPARATUS TYPES

The following types of apparatus are included in the instructional material which follows:

Climbing and Hanging (Body Support) Types

Climbing ropes, horizontal ladders, climbing frames, the exercise bar.

Apparatus Placed on the Floor

Balance beam, benches, jumping boxes, magic ropes, individual mats, balance boards, bounding boards, gym scooters, combination sets.

ROPE CLIMBING

Rope climbing offers high developmental possibilities for the upper trunk and arms, as well as good training in coordination of the different parts of the body. Adequate grip and arm strength are necessary prerequisites to climbing. Becoming accustomed to the rope and gaining in confidence are important goals in early work on the ropes. Many children need to overcome a natural fear of height.

Instructional Procedures

1. Mats should be under all ropes.

2. The hand-over-hand method should be used for climbing and the hand-under-hand method for descending.

3. Children should be cautioned not to slide, or they may get rope burns on the hands and skinned places on the leg.

4. If a climber becomes tired, he should

154 APPARATUS ACTIVITIES

Rope Climbing on a 10-Rope Set

stop and rest. Proper resting stops should be taught with the climbing.

5. Always leave enough margin to descend safely. No child should go higher than his strength will allow.

6. Spotters should be used where the body is inverted in stunts. Spotters may hold the rope steady while the child climbs.

7. Resin in powdered form and magnesium chalk are aids to better gripping. It is particularly important that they be used when the rope becomes slippery after use.

8. Children swinging on the ropes should make sure the other children are out of the way.

9. Marks to limit the climb can be put on the rope with adhesive tape. A mark 8' to 10' above the floor is the limit for all children until they can demonstrate sufficient proficiency to be allowed to climb higher.

Preliminary Sequences

Progression is important in rope climbing and the basic skill progressions should be followed.

Supported Pull-Ups

In these activities, a part of the body remains in contact with the floor. Pull up hand-over-hand and return hand-under-hand.

1. Kneel directly under the rope. Pull up until on tiptoes.

2. Sitting position. Pull up; legs are supported on the heels.

3. Standing position. Grasp rope, rock back on heels and lower body to floor. Keep a straight body. Return to the standing position.

Hangs

In a hang, the child pulls himself up in one motion and holds the position for a length of time — 5, 10, or 20 seconds. Stress progression.

1. From a seated position, reach up as high as possible and pull the body from the floor except for the heels. Hold.

2. Same as previous stunt, except pull the body completely free of the floor and hold.

3. From a standing position, jump up, grasp, and hang. This should be a bent-arm hang with the hands about even with the mouth. Hold.

4. Repeat previous stunt, but add leg movements:

    One or both knees up
    Bicycling movement of the legs
    Half lever — leg (one or both) comes up parallel to the floor
    Full lever — bring feet up to face

Pull-Ups

In the pull-up, the child raises and lowers his body repeatedly.

Repeat all activities under *Hangs,* except substitute the pull-up for the hang. Pull up each time till the chin touches the hands.

Inverted Hang

Reach up high with both hands. Keep the rope to one side. Jump to a bent-arm position and at the same time bring the knees to the nose, inverting the body, which is in a curled position. In a continuation of the motion, bring the feet higher than the hands and lock the legs around the rope. Body should now be straight and upside down. In learning phases, the teacher should spot.

Swinging and Jumping

Use a bench, box, or stool for a take-off point. To take off, the child should reach high and jump to a bent-arm position while swinging. Landing should be done in a bent-knee drop.

1. Swing and jump. Add half and full turns.

2. Swing and return to perch. Add single and double knee bends.

3. Jump for distance, over a high jump bar, or through a hoop.

4. Carry articles — beanbags, balls, deck tennis rings. Partner stands on side away from take-off bench and puts articles between knees or feet to be carried back to perch.

5. Not using take-off devices, children can run toward a swinging rope, grasp it high up and secure momentum for swinging.

Climbing the Rope

1. Scissors Grip. Approach the rope and reach as high as possible, standing with the right leg forward of the left. Raise the back leg, bend at the knee, and place the rope *inside* of the knee and *outside* the foot. Cross the forward leg over the back leg and straighten the legs out with the toes pointed down. This should give a secure hold. The teacher should check the position.

the process until the following goals are reached:
 a. Climb halfway.
 b. Climb three-fourths of the way.
 c. Climb to the top mark.

A top mark should be established beyond which the children should not be permitted to climb.

2. Leg-Around Rest. Using the left leg and keeping the rope between the thighs, wrap the left leg completely around the rope. The bottom of the rope now crosses over the instep of the left foot *from the outside.* The right foot stands on the rope as it crosses over the instep, providing pressure to prevent slippage. To provide additional pressure, release the hands and wrap the arms around the rope, leaning from the rope at the same time. If the right leg is used, the above instructions should be reversed.

The Scissors Grip

Climbing Using the Scissors Grip. From the scissors grip position, raise the knees up close to the chest with the rope sliding between them while supporting the body with the hand grip. Now lock the rope between the legs and climb up with the hand-over-hand method as high as the hands can reach. Bring the knees up to the chest and repeat

The Leg-Around Rest

Climbing Using the Leg-Around Rest. Climbing with the leg-around rest is similar to climbing with the scissors grip, except that the leg-around rest grip needs to be loosened each time and re-formed higher up on the rope.

Descending

There are four methods of descending the rope. The only differences are in the use of the leg locks, as the hand-under-hand is used for all descents.

1. Reverse of the Scissors Climb. From an extended position, lock the legs and lower the body with hands until the knees are against the chest. Hold with the hands and lower the legs to a new position.

2. Using the Leg-Around Rest. From the leg-around rest, lower hand-under-hand until the knees are against the chest. Lift the top foot and let the rope slide loosely to a lower position. Again secure with the top foot. Repeat until down.

3. Instep Squeeze. The rope is squeezed between the insteps by keeping the heels together. The hand-under-hand movement lowers the body while the rope slides between the insteps.

4. Stirrup Descent. The rope is on the outside of the right foot and is carried under the instep of the foot and over the toe of the left foot. Pressure from the left foot holds the position. To get into position, let the rope trail along the right leg, reach under, and hook it with the left toe. When the force of the left leg is varied, the rope can slide smoothly while the descent is made with the hands.

Stunts Using Two Ropes

Two ropes, hanging close together, are needed for these activities.

1. Straight Arm Hang. Jump up, grasp one rope with each hand, and hang with the arms straight.

2. Bent Arm Hang. Same as above except that the arms are bent at the elbows.

3. Arm Hangs With Different Leg Positions.
  a. Single and double knee lifts.
  b. Half Lever — bring feet up parallel to floor, toes pointed.
  c. Full Lever — bring feet up to face and keep knees straight.
  d. Bicycle — pedal like a bicycle.

4. Pull-Ups. Same as a pull-up on a single rope.

5. Inverted Hangs.
  a. With the feet wrapped around the rope

Spotting for Inverted Hangs on Double Ropes. Holding the performer's hands on the rope gives confidence in learning stages.

  b. With the feet against the inside of the ropes
  c. With the toes pointed and the feet not touching the ropes

6. Skin the Cat. From a bent-arm position, kick feet overhead and continue the roll until the feet touch the mat. Return to the starting position. A more difficult stunt is to start from a higher position so the feet do not touch the mat. Reverse to original position.

HORIZONTAL LADDER AND CLIMBING FRAMES

Horizontal ladders and climbing frames are manufactured in a variety of models. The most usable ladder is one that can be stored against the wall out of the way. If the ladder can be adjusted so it is inclined, the movement possibilities are extended.

The climbing frame pictured below is from Holland, where it is called the *Klimraam*. It stores out of the way against the wall and can be moved into place by children. The frame has two positions, vertical and inclined. In the author's program, three *Klimraams* are combined with climbing ropes for instructional purposes, with half the class on each type of apparatus.

Another effective wall-attached climbing frame is the Hampton Frame, made in Eng-

APPARATUS ACTIVITIES 157

Exploring on Climbing Frames

land but available now in the United States. It offers a wider choice of activity than the *Klimraam*, but does not lend itself as easily to group instruction (page 36).

Instructional Procedures

1. The opposed-thumb grip, in which the thumb goes around the bar, is important. In most activities, the back of the hands should face the child. Vary the grip, however, using other holds. Use other grips, such as the lower grip (palms toward the face) and the mixed grip (one hand facing one way and one the other) for variety.

Upper   Lower   Mixed
(Monkey)

2. Whenever the child is doing an inverted hang, spotters should be present.

3. Speed is not the goal of this activity. In fact, the longer the child is hanging from the ladder, the more beneficial the activity will be. There is value in just hanging.

4. In activities involving movement across the ladder, all children should travel in the same direction.

5. Mats should always be placed under climbing apparatus when they are in use.

6. When dismounting from ladders, the child should be instructed to land in a bent-leg position, on the balls of the feet.

7. Don't force children to climb the wall-attached climbing frames. Many children have a natural fear of height and need much reassurance before they will climb. If necessary, climb the frame with the child until he is confident of his ability.

8. Bars placed out-of-doors should not be used when wet, as they become slippery.

Horizontal Ladder Activities

Hangs. The hangs should be performed with the opposed-thumb grip and with straight arms. Encourage the children to hang in a bent-arm position, however, to involve more muscles in the upper arms. The following hang variations are suggested:

1. Straight leg. Keep legs straight and point toes toward ground.

2. Knees up. Lift the knees as high as possible toward the chest.

3. Bicycle. Lift the knees and pedal the bicycle.

4. Half Lever. Bring the legs up parallel to the ground with the knees straight and the toes pointed.

5. Inverted. Hang with the hands on a rung. Bring the feet up and over the next rung and hook the toes under a second rung. Release the hand grip, and hang in an inverted position.

Note: A spotter should be present during the child's first few attempts at inverted stunts.

6. Flexed Arm. Stand on a box if necessary to get in position. Hang as long as possible with the chin even with the hands.

7. Swinging. Hang from a rung with both hands and swing the body back and forth.

8. Swing back and forth and jump as far as possible. Vary with turns.

Moving Activities on the Horizontal Ladder

1. Travel the length of the ladder using the rungs. Start by traveling one rung at a time and then skip one or more rungs to add challenge.

2. Travel the length of the ladder using both side rails; also use just one rail to travel the ladder.

Wall-Attached Climbing Frame Activities

Hangs. All the hangs possible on the horizontal ladder may be used with the wall-attached climbing frames.

Moving Activities on the Wall-Attached Climbing Frame

1. Climb to the top of the frame on the back side using the hands and the feet. Descend in the same manner.

2. Climb the back side of the frame to the top and descend using only the arms and hands.

3. Climb the front side of the frame, transfer to the back side and descend to the bottom using only the hands.

4. Climb the back side of the frame to the top using only the hands.

5. Climb the frame, transfer *through* the frame from one side to the other.

6. Follow-the-leader activity is excellent for climbing frames.

EXERCISE BAR (LOW HORIZONTAL BAR)

Horizontal bars should be installed on the playground in series of at least three at different heights. The primary program should be limited to simple hangs and climbs. To perform many of the more complicated stunts on the bar, it is necessary to have sufficient arm strength to pull the body up and over the bar. Some of the youngsters in the third grade will begin to have this capacity, but the emphasis in the primary grades should be on a more limited program.

A low turning bar constructed of four-inch pipe, twelve or more feet in length, has value in providing bar experiences for young children. The bar should be about thirty inches above the ground.

Instructional Procedures

1. Only one child should be on a bar at a time.

2. Do not use the bar when it is wet.

3. The basic grip is the opposed-thumb grip, upper style (see page 157 for grip description). The lower and mixed grips should also be used.

Sequence of Activities

1. **Hangs.** Feet pointed, one or both knees up, half or full lever.

2. **Swings.** Swing back and forth, propelling the body forward to a stand.

3. **Moving Along the Bar.** Begin at one side and move hand against hand to the other end of the bar. Move with crossed hands.

4. **Sloth Travel.** Face end of bar, standing underneath. Grasp bar with both hands and hook the legs over the bar at the knees. In this position, move along the bar to the other end. Return by reversing the movement.

5. **Arm and Leg Hang.** Grasp bar with upper grip. Bring one of the legs between the arms and hook the knee over the bar.

6. **Double Leg Hang.** Same as #5, but bring both legs between the hands and hook the knees over the bar. Release the hands and hang in the inverted position. If the hands touch or are near the ground, a dismount can be made by releasing the legs and dropping to a crouched position on the ground.

7. **Skin the Cat.** Bring both knees up between the arms as in the previous stunt, but continue the direction of the knees until the body is turned over backward. Release grip and drop to ground.

BALANCE BEAM

Balance beam activities are valuable in contributing to the control of balance in both static (stationary) and dynamic (moving) balance situations. The balance-beam side of a balance-beam bench is ideal for this activity, with its 2" wide and about 12' long beam. However, balance beams come in many sizes and can be constructed from common lumber materials (see appendix). Some teachers prefer a wider beam for kindergarten and first grade children and, in particular, special education children. Children should graduate to the narrower beam as soon as the activities on the wider beam no longer seem to challenge them.

Learning good control of balance demands a considerable amount of practice and concentration. The teacher should not be discouraged by apparent slow progress. Proper practice will in time greatly increase the children's proficiency.

APPARATUS ACTIVITIES

The Balance-Beam Bench

Instructional Procedures

1. Children should move with controlled, deliberate movements. Speedy movement is not a goal. Advise the performer to recover his balance before taking another step or making another movement.

2. In keeping with the principle of control, children should step slowly on the beam, pause momentarily in good balance at the end of the activity, and dismount with a small, controlled jump from the end of the beam when the routine is completed.

3. Mats can be placed at the end of the bench to cushion the dismount and allow for selected rolls and stunts after the dismount.

4. Visual fixation is important. Children should look ahead at eye level, rather than down at the feet. Eye targets can be marked or attached to walls to assist them in visual fixation. Visual fixation allows balance controls other than vision to function more effectively. From time to time, movements can be done with the eyes closed, entirely eliminating visual control of balance.

5. Children should step off the beam if they lose balance, rather than teeter and fall off awkwardly. Allow the performer to step back on the beam and continue his routine.

6. Success early in a balance-beam activity can be based on two levels. The lower level allows the performer to step off the beam once during his routine. The higher level demands that he remain on the beam throughout. In both levels, he must pause at the end of the beam *in good balance* before dismounting.

7. Both laterality and directionality are important. Corresponding parts of the body (right and left feet) should be given reasonably equal treatment. For example, if the performer does follow steps leading with the right foot, the next effort should be made leading with the left foot. Directions right and left should be given equal weight. A child will naturally use his dominant side and direction with which he feels more skillful and confident, but must be encouraged to perform otherwise.

8. The child next in turn begins when the performer ahead is about three-quarters distance across the beam.

9. Return activities should be a consideration to enhance the breadth of activity. (See page 153 for explanation of return activity.)

Balance Beam Activities

Activities are presented in categories. Generally, each category should be fully exploited and exhausted before proceeding to the next.

Moving Across the Full Length of the Beam

Walk, follow steps, heel and toe, side (draw) steps, tiptoes, step behind, grapevine (step behind, step across), etc.

Different directions — forward, backward, sideward.

Different arm positions — on hips, on head, behind back, out to the sides, pointing to the ceiling, folded across chest, etc.

Balance objects (beanbags or erasers) on various parts of the body — one, two or three on the head, back of hands, shoulders.

Half-and-Half Movements

These repeat the movements, arm positions, and balance objects as previously described, except that the performer goes halfway across the beam using a selected movement, then changes to another type of movement at the center, and does this on the second half of the beam.

Challenge Tasks or Stunts

The performer moves along the beam to the center with a selected movement, performs a particular challenge or stunt at the center, and finishes out his movements on the second half of the beam. Examples of challenges or stunts which can be performed at the center of the beam are:

Balances — Front Balance, Back Layout, Stork Stand.

Challenges — Full Turn, pick up beanbag at center, pick up paper at center with teeth, do a push-up.

Using Wands and Hoops

Carry wand or hoop. Step over wand or through hoop — various fashions.

Step over or go under wands held by partner. Same with hoop.

Use the hula hoop, twirling on arms or around the body while moving across the beam.

Manipulative Activities to Self

Using one or two beanbags, toss to self in various fashions — around the body, under the legs, etc.

Using a ball, toss to self. Circle ball around body, under the legs.

Bounce ball on the floor and on the beam. Dribble on floor.

Roll ball along the beam.

ACTIVITIES ON BENCHES

The balance-beam bench is an effective piece of apparatus of dual use. Bench activities are interesting and challenging to children, and offer a variety of movement possibilities.

Instructional Procedures

1. All activities on the benches should contain three distinct parts: the approach and lead up to the bench, the actual activity on the bench, and, lastly, the dismount off the bench.

2. Mats should be placed at the end of the benches to facilitate the dismount and allow for various rolls and stunts after the dismount.

3. Benches may be positioned horizontally, inclined, or in combination with other equipment for variation and greater challenge.

4. Four to five children assigned to a bench for activity should be the maximum number assigned to one bench.

5. The child next in turn begins when the performer ahead has reached about the three-quarters distance on the bench.

6. Return activities for the child to perform as he returns to his place in line add to the activity potential.

7. Speed is *not* a goal in bench activities. Movements should be done deliberately and carefully with attention given to good body control and management.

8. Attention should be given to use of corresponding parts of the body and directional movements. For example, if a child hops on the right foot, the next effort should be made on the left foot. In jump turns, both right and left movements should be utilized. A child naturally uses the stronger or preferred part of his body. See that he has a balance in the demands.

Bench Activities

1. Animal Walks on the Bench. Perform various animal walks on the bench, such as:

a. Seal Crawl (page 185).

b. Cat Walk (page 181).

c. Lame Dog Walk (page 183).

d. Rabbit Jump (page 181).

2. Locomotor Movements. Perform various locomotor movements on the bench, such as:

a. Step on and off.

b. Skip on the bench.

c. Gallop on the bench.

d. Jump on and off.

3. Pulls. Pull the body along the bench in the various following combinations:

a. Prone Position — head first and feet first.

b. Supine Position — head first and feet first.

c. Side Position — head first and feet first.

Note: Various leg positions such as legs up in a half lever position, knees bent, etc., should be used while performing pulls and pushes.

4. Pushes. Push the body along the bench using the following positions.

a. Prone Position — head first and feet first.

b. Supine Position — head first and feet first.

c. Side Position — head first and feet first.

APPARATUS ACTIVITIES 161

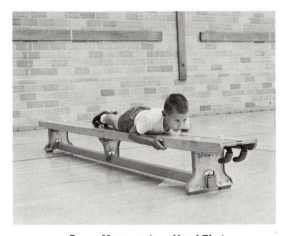
Prone Movements — Head First

Supine Movements — Feet First

Crouch Jumps

A Forward Roll

A Balancing Stunt

Dismounting from an Inclined Bench

5. Movements Along the Side of the Bench. Proceed alongside the bench in the following positions. (Keep the limbs on the floor as far from the bench as possible.)

a. Prone Position — hands on bench.

b. Supine Position — hands on bench.

c. Turnover — proceed along the bench changing from prone to supine positions, hands on bench.

d. All of the above positions performed with the feet on the bench.

6. Scooter Movements. Sit on the bench and proceed along the bench without using hands.

a. Seat Walk — proceed forward by walking on the buttocks. Use the legs as little as possible.

b. Regular Scooter — proceed with the feet leading the body. Try to pull the body along with the feet.

7. Crouch Jumps. Place both hands on the bench and jump back and forth over the bench. Progress the length of the bench by moving the hands forward a few inches after each jump.

a. Straddle Jump—a variation of the crouch jump. Straddle the bench with the legs. Take the weight on the hands and jump the legs as high as possible.

b. Regular — use both hands and both feet. Jump as high as possible.

Dismounts

As stated earlier, all bench activities in which one moves from one end of the bench to the other should end with a dismount. The following are suggested dismounts that may be used:

1. Jump Dismounts

a. Single Jump — forward or backward.

b. Jump with Turns — half, three-quarters or full turn.

2. Jump Dismounts followed by a Stunt on the Mat

a. Jump to a Forward Roll

b. Backward Jump to a Back Roll

c. Side Jump to a Side Roll

Other stunts can be utilized.

Additional Experiences for Expanding Bench Activities

1. The range of activities can be extended with the addition of balls, beanbags, hoops, and wands. Wands and hoops can be used as obstacles to go over, under, around or through. Basic balance and manipulative skills can be incorporated into the activity with balls and beanbags.

2. Different balance positions on the benches can be done. Two children should perform at a time, each near one end of the bench.

3. Children love to go over and under a series of benches in a row, in a kind of obstacle course. Some of the benches can be supported on jumping boxes, making them excellent for vaulting activities.

ACTIVITIES ON JUMPING BOXES

Jumping boxes can be constructed or purchased. They provide opportunities for the children to do the natural activities of running, jumping, and propelling the body through the air. Boxes should be made in two heights; 12" and 24" are suggested. They are usually square in shape, about 18" by 18" for the larger height. The smaller box should be about 16" by 16", so as to fit inside the larger box for storage. The top should be padded and covered with durable leather or plastic cloth. A rubber floor pad can be placed under the box to offer good floor protection. Commercially constructed boxes have sloped sides for better stability. (See appendix.)

Instructional Procedures

1. Attention should be given to "meeting the ground" in proper form, stressing lightness, bent-knee action, balance, and body control.

2. Mats should be used to cushion the landing.

3. The exploratory and creative approach is important as there are few "standard" stunts in jumping box activities.

4. A group of not more than four or five children should be assigned to each series of boxes.

5. Additional challenge can be incorporated into the activity by the use of hoops, wands,

balls, etc. In addition, rolling stunts after the dismount extend the possibilities of movement.

6. Return activities work well with boxes.

7. Children should strive for height and learn to relax as they go through space.

8. The suggested activities which follow can be augmented with a little imagination. Let the children help expand the breadth of the activity.

Jumping Box Activities

1. Mounting the Box. Use combinations of the following locomotor movements to get on the box:
   a. Step
   b. Jump
   c. Leap
   d. Hop

An example of the above activity might be to step on the box and jump off or to hop on the box and leap off.

2. Dismounting. The following dismounts can be used to develop body control:
   a. Jump off with a quarter, half, or full turn.
   b. Jump off with different body shapes such as stretch, curl up into a ball, jackknife, etc.
   c. Jump over, under, or through various objects.
   d. Jump off followed by a forward or backward roll.
   e. Change the above dismounts by substituting a hop or leap in place of the jump.

3. Various Approaches to the Boxes. The approach to the box can be varied by performing various movements, such as:
   a. Run
   b. Gallop
   c. Skip
   d. Hop
   e. Many animal walks, such as bear walk, crab walk, etc.

4. Addition of Equipment. Use various pieces of equipment to enhance the box activities. The following are some suggestions:
   a. Beanbags — throw them up while dismounting, or try to keep them on your head while mounting or dismounting the box.
   b. Balls — try to dribble a playground ball while performing the box routine.
   c. Hoops — jump through a stationary hoop (held by a partner) while dismounting, or use the hoop as a jump rope and see how many times you can jump it while dismounting.
   d. Wands — jump over or under the wand.

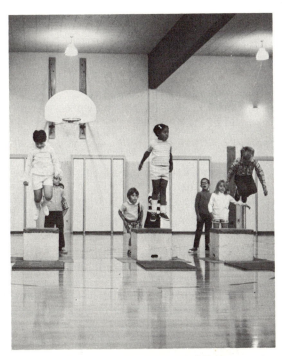

Jump Dismounts from a 16" Box

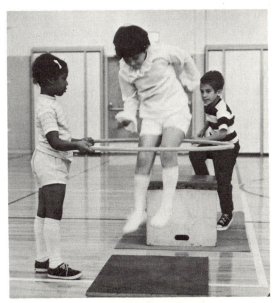

Through the Hoop!

5. Box Combinations. Boxes can be arranged in a straight line or other pattern. The child does a different movement over each box as though running an obstacle course.

MAGIC ROPES

Magic ropes come from Germany. Each rope is similar to a long rubber band. Ropes can be made by knitting wide rubber bands together or can be constructed from ordinary ¾" white elastic tape, available in most clothing stores. Loops on each end enable the child to thrust his hand through and grasp the rope. Ropes should be long enough to stretch to between 30' and 40' (see appendix).

A major advantage of the magic rope is its flexibility; children have no fear of hitting or tripping on it while they are performing. Ropes should be stretched tight enough so there is little sag.

Instructional Procedures

1. Two or more children need to be rope holders while the others are jumping. Develop some type of rotation plan so that all children participate.

2. Many variations can be achieved with the magic ropes by varying their height and by raising and lowering opposite ends of the rope.

3. The jumping activities are strenuous, therefore alternate between jumping activities and those activities that involve crawling under the ropes, etc.

4. Emphasize to the class that they should concentrate on *not* touching the rope. The magic ropes can help develop the child's perception of his body in space if he regards the rope as an obstacle to be avoided.

5. Better use can be made of the ropes using an oblique approach, which involves starting at one end of the rope and progressing to the other end using jumping and hopping activities, etc. By comparison, the straight-on approach allows the child to jump the rope only once.

6. A total of eight ropes is needed for a class, two to each squad. Squads make excellent groups for this activity, as the leader can control the rotation of the rope holders.

7. The child next in turn should begin his movements when the child ahead is almost to the end of the rope.

Magic Rope Activities

Single Rope Activities. Start the ropes at a 6" height and progressively raise them to add challenge.

1. Jump the rope.
2. Hop the rope.
3. Jump the rope and perform various body turns while jumping.
4. Change body shapes and sizes while jumping.
5. Crawl or slide under the rope.
6. Alternate going over and under the rope.
7. Crouch-jump over the rope.

Over a Single Magic Rope

Double Ropes. Vary the height and spread of the ropes.

1. *Ropes parallel to each other*
   a. Jump in one side and out the other.
   b. Hop in one side and out the other.
   c. Crouch-jump in and out.
   d. Perform various animal walks in and out of the ropes.

2. *Ropes crossed at right angles to each other*
   a. Perform various movements from one area to the next.
   b. Jump into one area and crawl out of that area into another.

3. *One rope above the other to create a "barbed wire fence" effect*
   a. Step through the ropes without touching.
   b. Crouch-jump through.
   c. Vary the height and the distance apart at which the ropes are placed. This will add much excitement to the activity as children are challenged not to touch the ropes.

APPARATUS ACTIVITIES

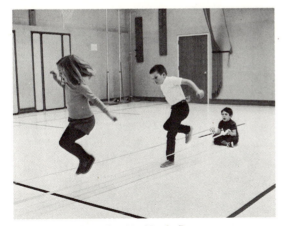

Over Double Magic Ropes

4. *Miscellaneous*
   a. Perform the various activities with a beanbag balanced on the head or bouncing a ball.
   b. Use four or more ropes to create various floor patterns.
   c. Use a "follow the leader" plan to add variety to the activity.
   d. Create an obstacle course with many ropes for a relay.

INDIVIDUAL MATS

Individual mats are English in origin and are the basis for many exploratory and creative movements. Essentially, the mat serves the child as a home base of operation and as an obstacle which he goes over or around.

Mats can vary in size, but 18" by 36" or 20" by 40" seem to be the most popular. In thickness, the ¾" type is standard, but this can also vary. The mat should have a rubber backing, which prevents mat slippage on the floor. Foam-backed indoor-outdoor carpeting of good quality makes an excellent mat.

Instructional Procedures

1. Basic movement techniques are most important in mat work.
2. Much emphasis should be centered on body management and basic skills of locomotor and nonlocomotor movement.
3. Mats should be far enough apart to allow for free movement around them.
4. Each child should have a mat.

Sequence of Activities

Rigid adherence to the sequence presented below is not necessary, as the activities are quite flexible and demand only basic skills.

1. Command Movements. In this the child changes movements on command. Commands used are:

"Stretch": Stretch your body out in all directions as wide as possible.

"Curl": Curl into a little tight ball.

"Balance": Form some kind of a balance.

"Bridge": Make a bridge over the mat.

"Reach": Keeping one toe on the mat, reach out as far as possible along the floor in a chosen direction.

"Rock": Rock on any part of the body.

"Roll": Do some kind of a roll on the mat.

"Twist": Make a shape with a part of the body twisted.

Each of the above can be developed individually by commanding "change," with which the child makes another kind of movement or shape. Balance can be developed by changing for balance on different parts of the body or a different number of parts — one, two, three, four, or five.

2. Movements on and off the Mat. The children do different locomotor movements on

Balance Activities on Individual Mats

166 APPARATUS ACTIVITIES

and off the mat in different directions. Turns and shapes can be added. Levels are another good challenge. Take the weight on the hands going across the mat.

3. Movements over the Mat. This is similar to No. 2 except that the child goes completely over the mat each time.

4. Movements around the Mat. Locomotor movements around the mat are done both clockwise and counterclockwise. Do movements around the mat keeping hands on the mat. Do the same but keep the feet on the mat.

5. Using Mats as a Base. Stretch and reach in different directions to show how big the space is. Do combination movements away from and back to the mat, such as, for example, two jumps and two hops, or six steps and two jumps.

6. Mat Games or Fun Activity. Each child is seated on his mat. On signal, each child arises and jumps over as many different mats as he can. On the next signal, each child takes a seat on the nearest mat. The last child to get seated can be designated or pay a penalty. The game can also be played by eliminating one or two mats and thus having one or two children left without a home base. This is done by the teacher standing on a mat or by turning over mats and putting them out of the game. To control roughness, make a rule that the first child to touch a mat gets to sit on it.

BALANCE BOARDS

Balance boards are small devices on which the child tries to stand and keep the board in balance. Generally, they have either a circular or square platform about 15″ wide and a rounded bottom to provide the challenge for balance. A rubber pad should protect the floor. The activities are somewhat limited, consisting of maintaining balance with a variety of challenges.

Sequence of Activities

1. Secure a balanced position on the board. Change position of arms.

2. Secure balance and gradually lower the body to touch the board.

3. Change from a two-foot to a one-foot balance. Change from one foot to the other.

4. Add manipulative items such as wands

Balancing on Different Balance Boards

to balance, hoops for hooping, beanbags and balls for tossing. Toss to self or toss to partner.

BOUNDING BOARDS

Bounding boards provide a unique type of movement similar to that of a child bouncing on a trampoline. They can be constructed easily from a piece of ¾″ plywood, size 2′ by 6′. The board is supported on pieces of 4″ x 4″ lumber, which are padded with carpet to protect the floor. The plywood must be a quality

Bounding on Bounding Boards

APPARATUS ACTIVITIES

product with few knots. Marine plywood, though expensive, is the best (see appendix).

Two children can work on one board, with the performer moving forward to leave the board and return back to place. Emphasis should be on lightness, height, and relaxation during the bounding. Bounding for the most part should be done in the center of the board. The activity is for younger children only.

Sequence of Activities

1. Bound in the center; two feet, one foot.

2. Bound in the center, using turns and different arm positions. Add hand clapping.

3. Move across the board, using jumping and hopping. Return. Add turns and hand clapping.

4. Bound with numbered foot combinations, alternating two, three, or four hops on one foot and then changing to the other. These are called twoseys, threeseys, and fourseys.

5. To the previous skills, add forward and backward leg extensions, and leg changes sideward.

6. Use different numbers of hops when alternating, such as hopping once on the right foot and twice on the left. Use other combinations as 2-3, 2-4, etc.

7. Add rope jumping with slow time and fast time. Use hoops.

GYM SCOOTERS

Gym scooters make excellent devices for developmental activity if properly used. The minimum number for a class should be one scooter for each two children. However, if the scooters are used only for relays, four to six will suffice.

Two rules are important in the use of scooters. The first is that the children are not to stand on them as they would on skate boards. The second rule is that scooters, with or without passengers, are not to be used as missiles.

Scooters can be used by children individually or with partners. When used individually, many variations are possible by combining the method of propulsion and the method of supporting the body. The child may propel the scooter with his feet, hands, or both. His body position may be kneeling, sitting, prone, supine, or even sideways. His weight may be

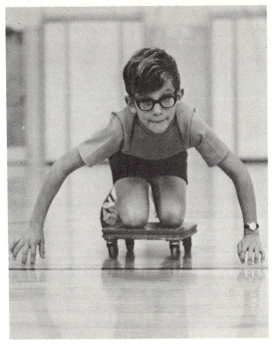

On a Gym Scooter

wholly or partially supported on the scooter. Variation in space factors, particularly direction, add to the interest.

When working with a partner, one child rides and the other pushes. The rider's weight may be wholly or partially supported on the scooter. If only partially on the scooter, the remainder of the weight is supported by the partner.

Basic movement methodology is applicable to scooter work, but care should be exercised so that it is a developmental period and not just a fun session.

COMBINATION SETS

Combination sets come in a variety of shapes, sizes, and units. They include A-frame stands of various heights, connected together with ladders, planks, rails, and other items which can be the basis for movement experiences. The balance-beam bench with a special hook-type device can be used with climbing frames or ladders.

Basically the sets can be used for balancing-type activities, sliding, climbing, moving in and out of openings, vaulting, hanging, stretching, and supporting movement experiences.

168   APPARATUS ACTIVITIES

Floor Portable Combination Set

15

Stunts and Tumbling

The Stunts and Tumbling Program
Progression and Grade Level Placement
Presenting Activities
Instructional Procedures
Additional Considerations in Methodology
Preschool and Nursery School Emphasis
Kindergarten Program
First Grade Program
Second Grade Program
Third Grade Program

THE STUNTS AND TUMBLING PROGRAM

The stunts and tumbling program is an important inclusion in the child's overall physical education experiences and can make significant contribution toward the achievement of physical education goals. Such personal characteristics as dedication and perseverance toward a goal can be furthered, since stunts are seldom mastered quickly or in a few attempts. Since much of the work is individual, the child faces his own challenge and has the opportunity to develop resourcefulness, self-confidence, and courage. On the other hand, foolhardiness and disregard for safety must be avoided.

When a child masters a challenging stunt, his satisfaction, pride of achievement, and sense of accomplishment contribute to a gain in self-respect and improvement in his self-image.

Physical Values

Important physical values can emerge from an instructionally sound program of stunts and tumbling. Exercise in good body management can be provided, fulfilling the objective of offering opportunities for a child to manage his body effectively in a variety of situations. Coordination, flexibility, and agility can be enhanced.

The opportunity to practice control of balance is present in many stunt activities and particularly featured in some. The suggested program includes challenges for all three aspects of balance — static, dynamic, and rotational. In addition, visual control of balance can be eliminated occasionally by having the children close their eyes during balance stunts, thus centering demands on other balance controls.

The raw physical demands of held positions and stunt execution contribute to the development of strength and power of many diverse parts of the body. The many stunts which demand support by the arms, wholly or in part, provide needed development for the often weak musculature of the arm-shoulder girdle region. Basically, stunts and tumbling activities contribute to all areas of physical fitness.

Educational Values

Educationally, stunts and tumbling can provide many sound learning situations. Creative and exploratory activity should be a part of the learning experiences. Basic movement principles with appropriate problem-solving techniques give breadth to the children's responses. Variety of response should be emphasized by applying time, flow, space, quality, and body factors. The teacher needs to wring the maximum variety of response out of each activity.

Stunts and tumbling activities offer a wonderful opportunity for children to acquire fundamental concepts, such as those of right and left, near and far, wide and narrow, up

STUNTS AND TUMBLING

and down, forward and backward, as well as introducing new terminology into their daily lives.

Quality in Movement

Attention must be given to developing quality in movement, which should be relative to the children's abilities, the character of the activity, and the objectives of the lesson. Emphasis should be placed on "doing things as well as we can," and "giving it a good try." Controlled movement rather than speed is essential. Such movement qualities as lightness and sureness, coordination, rhythmic movement, and other body management factors should be relevant teaching points. Principles of good body mechanics should be incorporated where applicable.

Children should develop a sense of achievement and give some attention to form, but concentration on form should not be an overriding consideration. The stunt should first be taught in its simple, basic, mechanical form. Later the tips and points which dress it up can be introduced. Too much emphasis on technical details and refinements at the beginning can destroy the satisfaction of self-achievement. The lower the grade level, the less emphasis there should be on technical details. Much of the emphasis at the primary level should be centered on just doing the basic stunt.

Coaching hints such as "Head up"; "Point your toes"; "Keep your knees straight"; "Arch your back"; "Legs together," etc., will emphasize the important technical points in the stunt being practiced at the time.

PROGRESSION AND GRADE LEVEL PLACEMENT

Progression is the soul of learning experiences in the stunts and tumbling program, and in this manual the activities in this program are allocated in progression within grades. It is essential that the order of those stunts which lead from one grade to another be reasonably maintained. Adherence to grade level placement is secondary to this principle. Teachers may wish to include activities from a higher grade level to provide more challenge. This appears to be more likely true in the case of the physical education specialist, who has more depth in this area than the classroom teacher. If, on the other hand, children come with little or no experience in these activities, the teacher should start them off with activities specified for a lower grade level.

Standard Tumbling Stunts

The essentials of a stunts and tumbling program consist in the standard tumbling activities, such as rolls, stands, springs, and related stunts commonly accepted as basic to such a program. The suggested progression of these *basic* gymnastic type activities is presented in the following chart. Descriptions of the stunts are found in the programs at the indicated grade levels.

Sequence and Grade Level Chart

Preschool-Nursery School
No particular stunts

Kindergarten
Side Roll
Forward Roll
Back Roller

First Grade
Forward Roll
Backward Roll (Hand Clasp Position)

Second Grade
Forward Roll Practice
Climb Up
Three Point Tip-Up
Backward Curl
Backward Roll (Regular)

Third Grade
Forward Roll Variations
Frog Handstand
Headstand

Preschool-Nursery School Program

A stunts and tumbling program *per se* is not really appropriate for preschool children. Simple stunt and tumbling type movements should be included as a part of exploratory and creative experienced. Simple balances, imitative movements, and expressive movements can be important learning experiences for children.

Kindergarten and Primary Level Program

The kindergarten and primary program relies on simple stunts with good developmental possibilities, with a gradual introduction to those tumbling stunts which are classed as lead-up or preliminary to more advanced stunts. Stunts requiring exceptional body control, critical balancing, or the need for substantial strength should be left for higher grades. The program of stunts and tumbling in the lower grades should include the following:

1. A variety of simple stunts involving gross body movements, opportunity for creative expression, control of balance, and directional concepts.

2. A progressive introduction to the basic tumbling stunts such as the forward and backward rolls and basic stands.

3. Introductory work with a partner in couple stunts.

PRESENTING ACTIVITIES

Steps in presenting activities in the daily lesson plan for stunts and tumbling should include the following considerations:

1. Provide warm-up activity as needed.

2. Consider appropriate physical fitness development activity.

3. Arrange children in suitable formation for teaching.

4. Review previously learned materials and practice lead-up activities to the stunts to be presented.

5. Present the new activity with appropriate description and demonstration.

6. Establish basis for variety through appropriate movement methodology.

7. Provide opportunity for practice and improvement of performance.

8. Evaluate progress and, as needed, repeat directions. Bring in stress points, and work toward refining and perfecting performance.

Warm-up Activity

The need for warm-up activity would depend upon the nature of the day's program. Generally, this should include stretching and loosening type movements.

A simple, previously-learned stunt sometimes provides a satisfactory warm-up activity.

Forward and **Backward Rolls,** singly or in combination, prepare children for the activity which is to follow.

Developmental Activity

For the stunts and tumbling program, some teachers prefer to omit a formal fitness developmental period, holding to the premise that the program of activities will make sufficient fitness demands on the children and therefore fitness routines are not needed for this unit.

Approaches for Teaching Stunts and Tumbling

A number of different approaches are available for organizing a class in stunts and tumbling. The arrangement of the children will depend upon the stunts selected and whether or not mats are required. Priorities should be established in this order.

1. All children working and performing at the same time. This can be done readily for stunts which do not require mats by having the children scatter and perform. Where mats are needed, this becomes a problem, as few schools have sufficient mats to allow all children to perform at the same time. With all children active at the same time, some instructional problems are created for the teacher, as he must make a total assessment of class quickly and is limited in the amount of help and coaching he can give to individual children.

2. Children working across the mats sideways. This plan increases the number of children who can work at one time on a mat. On 6' mats, two children can work at a time. On 8' mats, three can work crosswise. Two children can also perform on opposite ends of the mat when engaged in various kinds of stands, with the safety consideration of avoiding falls into each other.

3. Modified squad method. When working lengthwise on mat stunts, children should be divided into at least six groups and preferably eight. If the normal class organization is based on four squads, an alternate grouping of children needs to be established when using six groups. If eight mats are present, each squad can be assigned to two mats. No group should contain more than four to six children.

Formations for Teaching

Formations which have value in organizing a class for conducting stunts and tumbling instruction follow.

Squad Line Formation. Mats are placed in a line with the squads lined up behind the mats. Each child takes a turn and goes to the end of his line with the others moving up. An alternative method is for the child to perform and then return to his position. The children can be seated.

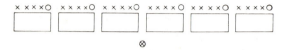

Squad File Formation. By positioning the mats so the children will approach the mats from the ends, a file formation can be arranged. The teacher is in front, and the children perform toward him. As soon as a child has completed his turn, he goes to the end of his line.

A weakness of this formation is that at times some children may be hidden from the teacher by other children, posing problems of control.

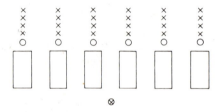

Semicircular Formation. The squad file formation can be changed readily to a semicircular arrangement. This focuses attention on the teacher, who is in the center. Groups are separated more than in the squad file formation.

(Note use for each mat the same as the previous illustration.)

U-Shaped Formation. The mats are formed in the shape of a U. The formation has good visual control possibilities for the teacher, and the children are able to see what their classmates are doing.

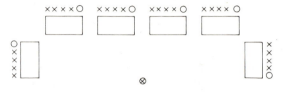

Double Row Formation. In this formation three groups form a row on one side and three on the other. The teacher is never far from any group. Children can view each other.

Demonstration Mat. If sufficient mats are available, one mat may be placed in an appropriate central position, so that little movement of the children is necessary to view the demonstration. The mat should be exclusively for demonstration.

Multiple Activity Organization

The teacher may sometimes wish to utilize groups or squads, each working on a different activity. Careful planning is necessary to ensure that the procedure is a learning experience and not just free play. Since it is not practical to stop the entire class for direction, the teacher must circulate from one group to another offering encouragement, comments, help, and suggestions as the activity unfolds. The problem becomes further complicated if the teacher feels his presence is needed at a station where critical supervision is indicated due to the complexity of the stunt or for safety purposes.

Multiple activity has value where a particular type of equipment is in short supply. It has further value in a problem-solving approach with less emphasis on conforming to a particular pattern. If children can be stimulated to explore and solve problems, educational value is high. Group leadership is important. A work format must be specified at each station, which can then be supervised by the group leader.

The time factor is sometimes a problem. Generally, groups rotate on signal. However, some stations absorb the children's attention longer than others. Some groups may have already completed their chores and be ready to move on while others are not yet finished. The work format at each station must be sufficient to engage the children for the time period.

Return Activities

Return activities are discussed on page 153. They have a place in the stunts and tumbling program and work best in the lesson activities where children perform lengthwise down the mat. Each child should turn in a designated direction (right or left) at the end of the mat and use that pathway for his return task. A popular return activity is to make use of a "magic number." Instructions for the return are given in this way: "Today, our magic number for return activity is five." For example, children may solve this problem by doing three jumps and two hops on the way back, or they may do four push-ups and one frog jump.

Review

Review of the learning experiences from the previous lesson or lessons is important in maintaining good continuity. Points of difficulty from previous lessons should be brought out and solved. Variety beyond that which was previously secured should be developed. Quality of performance should be given consideration. "What was good?" and "How can we make our performance better?" should be key questions. It is possible that much of the new lesson could be devoted to the review and improvement of previously presented experiences.

Attention should be given to extending the variety and limits of movement, encouraging exploratory and creative responses beyond what appeared during the previous lesson. Some attention should be given to the more critical stunts, but quality of movement should be subordinated to the mere task of doing the stunt.

Instructional Procedures

The teacher may describe and provide such demonstration and suggestions simultaneously as needed. Demonstration should be kept to a minimum, particularly by the teacher. Children should have in most cases a chance to experiment and try out movement patterns on their own before being exposed to a standard pattern or response. In presenting a stunt, the following steps can be followed:

1. *The Significance of the Name*

Most of the stunts have a characteristic name and this should be a consideration in teaching. Labels for movement experiences are important to children and whatever is to be represented should be described and discussed.

2. *The Stunt Description*

Stunts can be analyzed from the following steps, which can form the basis for presentation.

The Starting Position

The child needs to know what position or movement is involved in starting the stunt. This may be verbalized or accomplished through minimal demonstration.

The Execution

Next, the child needs to know what he is to do. Just how is he to move and in what manner. For primary children little demonstration in this phase should be done until the child has had an opportunity to try out his idea of meeting the basic challenge as presented. Selected children should be asked to demonstrate unique or different movement patterns which would provide suggestions to the children for movement variations. Early emphasis should be on increasing the variety of movement, with later attention centered on quality of movement.

The Finishing Position

A few stunts, particularly balance stunts, require a definite finish position. In balancing stunts, for example, it is important that the child return to his starting position without losing balance or moving the feet. In other stunts, the requirement may be a particular finishing movement, which should be introduced as the movements are "polished up." Generally, the children should have undergone experimentation and practice before the finishing act is added to the stunt routine. In some cases, the finishing act is a part of the routine description and should be introduced when the stunt is explained.

3. *Demonstration*

If the stunt is one similar to or based on a previously learned movement, there is little need to demonstrate the pattern of movement. If the stunts are such that a wide variety of movement patterns are acceptable as appropriate responses, demonstration is of little value.

The more critical the stunt, the more value demonstration holds in the learning process. A second purpose of demonstration is to show variety of movement. Probably a third need is to show something done well.

Care should be used in selecting children to demonstrate. Be sure the child is capable of the task. Generally, the task can be described, and children can be asked to volunteer. Favoritism should be avoided, but it is difficult to escape using the more capable class members.

Demonstrations also have a place later in the sequence of instruction. Demonstrations partway through the instruction can show successful execution of something that others do not understand or with which they are having difficulty. Demonstrations at the end of a unit can show what has been achieved. Each squad or group can demonstrate its achievements in turn.

Providing Opportunity for Practice and Improvement

The character of each stunt will determine the amount of practice needed and the number of times it should be performed. The teacher should analyze a stunt to the point where he can verbalize the various small points necessary for good performance. Such directions as "Point your toes forward," "Tuck your chin down," and "Fingers spread wide" are examples of cues for successful performance.

A reasonable standard of performance should be a part of the teaching. The teacher must answer the child's question, "Did I do it?" Some stunts are on a pass-fail basis, while others can be evaluated in quality terms.

A child needs standards that are both a challenge and attainable. The instruction must make clear to the child what is involved in the performance criterion of the stunt so that he knows whether or not he is within these bounds.

Quality in movement should be a consideration, but early emphasis should be on *doing the stunt*. Caution should be exercised in giving the child too many directions and details at the beginning which will only tend to confuse him. Directions added a few at a time stimulate the child to continued practice and improvement.

Many of the stunts require a position to be held for a short time. At first, have the child merely do the stunt. Later, have him hold for three and then five seconds. Extend this to a longer period, if indicated.

Practice and repetition are essential in establishing effective movement patterns. Often a teacher will leave an activity too soon to allow for needed progress. The following system is suggested where children take turns.

Whenever explanations and demonstrations are completed and the children begin practice, each child in a group should go through the stunt at least twice. When each child in the group has had two turns at an activity, the group remains in formation awaiting the next instructions. If this system is to function properly, groups need to be of relatively the same size and move at about the same speed. A teacher can ascertain in a glance if the children are ready for the next instructions. This avoids the necessity of whistle blowing to clear the mats.

How closely should children follow one another on the mat? A child should start his routine when the child ahead is just leaving the mat.

Securing Variety of Response

Variety of movement can be secured in two general ways. The first is to make use of the suggestions for variety incorporated in the stunt descriptions. The second is to use basic movement principles to establish problems, limitations, and suggestions which will stimulate the children to extended experiences.

The utilization of movement factors described in basic movement methodology (page 104) is of high importance. The activity potential of any one stunt can be extended by use of time factors, body factors, space factors, flow, and expressive factors.

Since most stunts have a starting position, an execution routine, and a finishing position, one or more of these could be varied to stimulate variety of movement and provide exploratory activity. For example, to secure variety in the forward roll, a child could begin with a rabbit jump, execute the forward roll with arms folded across the chest, and finish with a jump and half-turn.

Laterality is a factor that must be emphasized. The motor portion of the body is bilateral and should be so regarded. In practice, the children's attention will need to be called to using the other side or member of the body. Where appropriate, a directive is included in stunt descriptions. The concept of directionality should be established in children so that they approach performance of stunts with the principle of right and left usage without waiting to be so instructed. If a balancing stunt is done on one foot, then the next time it should be tried on the other. If a roll is made to the right, a comparable roll should be made to the left. A teacher may wish to develop the stunt thoroughly on one side before making the changes to the other side, but the change should be made.

Safety Considerations

Few stunts on the primary level involve safety hazards. However, where needed, the child is entitled to know the inherent dangers of the activity, the safety considerations to be followed, and the duties of the helper or spotter. In addition, the following should be observed.

1. Emphasis should be placed on how to fall. Children should be taught to roll out of a stunt when balance is lost. In the headstand children should try to return to the floor in the direction from which they started. The return is facilitated by bending both at the waist and at the knees.

2. Pockets should be emptied and lockets, glasses, watches, and other articles of this nature removed. A special depository for these articles should be provided, or, better yet, they should be left in the classroom.

3. No practice periods should be conducted without the presence of a teacher or proper supervisor.

4. Fatigue and overstrain in young children should be guarded against.

5. Children should be encouraged but not forced to try stunts. Care should be taken not to use peer pressure to stimulate participation.

6. Control is a basic element of the stunts and tumbling program. Children should learn to use controlled movements. Speed is secondary, and in some cases even undesirable.

Spotting

Spotting as a safety consideration merits special discussion. In the few stunts where spotting is needed with the children spotting each other, sufficient time must be allotted for teaching correct techniques. Children should ask others to spot when such action is indicated. They should be willing to spot and assist as needed.

In stunts where the body is inverted, spotting is an important consideration. In the case of such stunts as the headstand, it is important to control the child's movement so he returns to the floor in the same direction from which he got into position for the stunt.

ADDITIONAL CONSIDERATIONS IN METHODOLOGY

Instructional Emphasis

1. While some stunts do not require mats, it is well to include stunts requiring mats in every lesson. Children like to perform on mats, and rolling stunts using mats are vital.

2. In selecting students for demonstration, be sure the student understands and can perform reasonably correctly.

3. If a class embarks on a program of stunts and tumbling without previous experience, go back a grade or two in suggested activities and work up to the present grade level slowly.

4. Many couple stunts work well only if partners are of about the same size.

5. When a characteristic name is attached to a stunt, this designation should be exploited in the instruction. Time taken out briefly to stress the characteristics and movements associated with the name will bear dividends in more effective and imaginative movements.

6. The instruction should include, in addition to safety considerations, the points to be stressed which are critical to performance. Be sure the performer understands the stress points before proceeding.

7. No two children will perform or do stunts alike. Respect individual differences and allow for different levels of success.

8. While some emphasis on form and control should be established, this, however, should be within the capacity of the children.

9. It is important to relate new activities to those learned previously. A good practice is to review the lead-up stunt for an activity.

10. Horseplay and ridicule have no place in a program of stunts and tumbling. See that the children have fun, but also that they respect the efforts of their classmates.

11. Proper gym shoes are a help in the program. However, children can tumble in bare feet.

12. When a stunt calls for a position to be held for a number of counts, use a standard counting system like "one thousand and one, one thousand and two," or "monkey one, monkey two," etc.

13. Where children are asked to reach out or place objects a distance along the floor, distances can be specified by having the children count boards on the floor away from a line or base position. Generally, the start should be made at a modest distance so all can achieve success, with appropriate increases to follow. In *Balance Touch* (page 185), for example, the teacher can specify that the beanbag should be placed a certain number of board widths away from a line. Distances can then be varied by increasing the number of boards between the line and the object.

14. At times, the teacher can have children work in pairs with one child performing and the second providing a critique.

15. In using small hand apparatus (wands, hoops, etc.) with stunts, it is best to have one item for each child. If this is not possible, a minimum of two pieces is needed for each group so that the child next in line does not have to wait for the return of the needed object. One person, generally the leader of the group, should be designated to secure and return hand apparatus.

16. There should be little shifting of mats during the course of instruction. In arranging a sequence of stunts for a day's lesson, it is well to put the mat stunts together.

17. Occasional soft background music contributes to a pleasant atmosphere, but it should be low enough in volume so as not to interfere with the instruction. Long play records or tapes are excellent, as little attention is needed for the music sources.

18. The beat of a drum or tom-tom can be utilized to direct controlled movements. Children change position in small increments as guided by a beat. In *Lowering the Boom* (page 186), for example, children can lower themselves a little each time the drum sounds.

Start and Expand Technique

The Start-and-Expand technique should be utilized in the conduct of stunt movements. The start is made so simple and basic that all children can experience some measure of success. The instructional sequences then expand to other elements of the stunt, adding variations and movement factors, and refining as indicated.

An example of the Start-and-Expand technique is found in teaching the simple *Heel Click* (page 185). The instructor can begin by saying, "Let's see all of you jump high into the air and land in the same place where you started." (The Start.) "Now, this time jump again and try to click your heels together before you land." (Expansion.) "This time, jump again, click your heels together, and land with your feet apart with a nice bent-knee action to absorb the landing force." (Further expansion.) Additional expansion can be implemented by asking the children to add quarter or half turns before landing, clapping hands overhead simultaneously while clicking heels, and clicking the heels twice before landing. Expansion can also be promoted by allowing the children to experiment with variations or combinations of their own choice.

Social Factors

1. For mixed groups proper attire is essential to eliminate a modesty problem. On days when stunts are scheduled, girls can change to pedalpushers, slacks, or play suits. The best solution, however, is to have all children change to a gymnasium-type uniform.

2. Children should have fun *with* their friends in these types of activities, but they should not be allowed to laugh *at* an inept child.

3. Social goals that should be stressed for the children are cooperating with a partner, a small group, the entire class, and the teacher. Showing consideration in taking turns is important.

4. Children should be taught to have respect for equipment and to care for it. Mats should be lifted clear of the ground and not dragged when being moved.

Basic Mechanical Principles

Certain simple mechanical and kinesiological principles should be established as the foundation of an effective program. If children can build upon these basic principles, instruction is facilitated.

1. Momentum needs to be developed and applied, particularly for rolls. Tucking, starting from a higher point, preliminary raising of the arms, are examples of devices to increase momentum.

2. The center of weight must be positioned over the center of support in balance stunts, particularly the inverted stands.

3. In stunts where the body is wholly or partially supported by the hands, proper positioning of the hands is essential for better performance. Fingers should be spread and pointed forward. The pads of the fingers apply pressure for a good basis of support. This hand position should generally be employed unless there is a specific reason to depart from it.

PRESCHOOL AND NURSERY SCHOOL STUNT EMPHASIS

Stuntlike movement experiences should be included in overall movement experiences for this age group. No program division of stunts as a separate entity is needed or desirable. Within the movement experiences, children should have opportunity in the following:

1. Simple Balance Activities

Using problem solving and exploratory approaches, have the children balance on one foot. Add different hand and arm positions. Balance beanbags on the head or other parts of the body. Balancing on different parts of the body and a different number of parts broadens the movement opportunities and brings in some learning concepts.

2. Imitative Movements

Role playing is important for the small child. To lose himself in a familiar characterization is both satisfying and an important factor in self-discovery of his movement patterns. Satisfaction lies in the opportunity for creative expression and the attainment (for him) of success in a movement pattern.

3. Simple Rolling Experiences

Children love to roll and simple challenges which lead the children to roll broaden their movement patterns. The fact that the child can go "head over heels" is a more important goal than learning the forward roll.

The teacher should examine the recommended stunt experiences in the kindergarten and first grade inclusions to secure ideas for directions, modified of course for younger children. The emphasis should be on what the child can do rather than learning specific activities.

KINDERGARTEN PROGRAM

The kindergarten program makes good use of simple stunts which can be subject to many interpretations. The scope of the movements should include bilateral, unilateral, and crosslateral experiences. Laterality should also be stressed with attention to corresponding parts of the body. Balance is an important quality to be developed with stunt activities. Establishing good directional concepts is an important inclusion in the instruction. The child should be able to distinguish readily and easily such concepts as right and left, near and far, up and down, forward and backward, and wide and narrow.

Most of the stunts listed under the first grade program are quite appropriate for kindergarten children and should be utilized. In particular, the various kinds of walks and imitative movements provide important movement challenges for kindergarten children. Little emphasis should be placed on the so-called standard tumbling events.

It is also important that the movement factors from basic movement methodology (page 104) be given thorough development. The teacher should be able to select a basic movement or stunt and secure good depth and variety of response by judicious use of time, space, force, body, and expressive elements of movement. In addition, opportunity for creative exploratory responses should be included.

ACTIVITIES FOR THE KINDERGARTEN

Simple Balance Stunts
Side Roll
Head Touch
Forward Roll
Back Roller
Directional Walk
Line Walking
Alligator
Fluttering Leaf
Elevator
Cross-Legged Stand
Walking in Place
Kangaroo
Seesaw (Partner Stunt)

SIMPLE BALANCE STUNTS

The child should begin to learn the concept of balance stunts, i.e., that the position should be held for a specified length of time without undue movement or loss of balance *and* a recovery must be made to the original position. Hold for 3 and 5 seconds. Also perform with the eyes closed.

One-Leg Balance

Begin with lifting one leg from the floor. Later, bring the knee up. Arms should be free at first; then proceed to specified positions such as folded across the chest, on hips, on the head, or behind the back.

Double Knee Balance

Kneel on both knees, with the feet pointed to the rear. Lift the feet from the ground and balance on the knees. Vary the position of the arms.

Allow the children to experiment with different positions for balance.

SIDE ROLL

Start on hands and knees with the side selected for the roll toward the direction of the roll. By dropping the shoulder and tucking both the elbow and knee under, roll over completely on the shoulders and hips, coming again to the hands and knees position. Momentum is needed to return to the original position. Children should practice rolling back and forth from one hand-and-knee position to another.

HEAD TOUCH

Kneel on a mat with both knees, with the feet pointed backwards. Arms are outstretched backwards for balance. Lean forward slowly and touch the forehead to the mat. Recover to position. Vary the arm position.

FORWARD ROLL

Introduce the forward roll here as described on page 184 of first grade stunts.

BACK ROLLER

Practice in backward rolling should begin in kindergarten. Start in a crouched position on toes, knees together, with hands resting lightly on the floor. Roll backward and attempt to keep up a rhythmic backward-forward rolling motion.

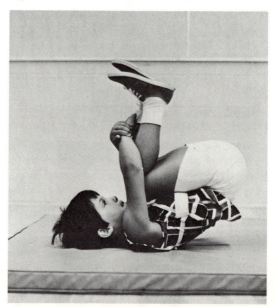

Back Roller

STUNTS AND TUMBLING

DIRECTIONAL WALK

Stand with side toward the desired direction, arms at sides. Take a sidestep in the desired direction (right or left), simultaneously lifting the arm and pointing in the direction of movement. At the same time, turn head in the direction of movement and sound off the direction. Complete the sidestep by closing with the other foot, dropping the arm to the side, and turning the head back to normal position. The movements should be definite and forceful; the directional command should be called out crisply. After a number of sidesteps in one direction, reverse.

The walk serves to reinforce the concept of right and left.

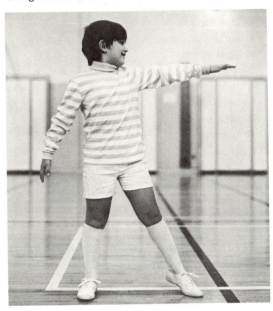

Directional Walk

LINE WALKING

Use a line on the floor, a chalked line, or a board. Children walk forward and backward on the line, as follows:

1. Regular steps.
2. Follow steps. The front foot moves forward and the back foot moves up. One foot always leads.
3. Heel and toe. Take regular steps, but on each step bring the heel against the toe.
4. Hopping on the line. Change to the other foot.

ALLIGATOR

Lie face down on the floor with the elbows bent. Move along the floor alligator fashion keeping the hands close to the body and the feet pointed out.

First, stress unilateral movements, i.e., right arm and leg moving together. Then, change to cross-lateral movements, with the right arm moving with the left leg and vice versa.

Alligator

FLUTTERING LEAF

Keeping the feet in place and the body relaxed, flutter to the ground slowly just as a falling leaf would do in the fall. The arms can swing back and forth loosely to accentuate the fluttering movements.

ELEVATOR

With the arms out level to the sides, pretend to be an elevator going down. Lower the body a little at a time, by bending the knees, keeping the upper body erect and eyes forward. Go into a deep-knee bend. Return to position. Add a body twist to the downward movement.

CROSS-LEGGED STAND

Sit with the legs crossed and the body partially bent forward. Six commands are now given:

1. "Touch the right foot with the right hand."
2. "Touch the left foot with the right hand."
3. "Touch the right foot with the left hand."
4. "Touch the left foot with the left hand."
5. "Touch both feet with the hands."
6. "Touch the feet with crossed hands."

The commands should be given in varied

sequences. The child must interpret that his right foot is on the left side and vice versa.

If this seems too difficult, have the child start with the feet in normal position (uncrossed).

Variation: The stunt can be done as partner activity. One child gives the commands and the other responds as directed.

WALKING IN PLACE

Pretend to walk vigorously by using the same movements as in walking, but not making any progress. This is done by shifting the feet back and forth. Exaggerated arm movement should be made. Children can gain or lose a little ground. Two children can "walk" alongside each other with the first one going ahead and then the other.

KANGAROO

The arms are carried close to the chest with the palms facing forward. A beanbag is placed between the knees. Move in different directions employing small jumps without losing the beanbag.

SEESAW (PARTNER STUNT)

Two children face each other and join hands. One child stoops down. The seesaw moves up and down now, with one child stooping while the other rises. The children can recite the words to this version of "Seesaw, Margery Daw" as they move:

> Seesaw, Margery Daw,
> Maw and Paw, like a saw,
> Seesaw, Margery Daw

Variation: Have the rising child jump into the air at the end of the rise.

Additional Activities

The teacher should make good use of first grade activities. The most appropriate first grade activities are the various locomotor and balance stunts.

FIRST GRADE PROGRAM

The first grade program consists primarily of simple, imitative walks and movements plus selected balance stunts and rolls. Balance stunts use the erect position. The *Forward Roll* is practiced, but its refinement is left to later grades. The *Back Roller* and backward roll from a hand-clasped position show the children some of the possibilities in these kinds of movements.

The teacher should be concerned with the creative aspects of the activities as well as performance standards. Children in this grade level tend to do stunts in different ways because of different interpretations.

The establishment of good directional concepts and the basic understanding of common movement terminology should have a prominent place in the instruction. The "why" of activity should be answered for the children.

ACTIVITIES FOR THE FIRST GRADE

Puppy Dog Run
Bear Walk
Rabbit Jump
Jump Turns
Elephant Walk
Head Balance
Tightrope Walk
Bouncing Ball
One-Legged Balance Stands
Lame Dog Walk
Gorilla Walk
Cricket Walk
Forward Roll
Rising Sun
Balance Touch
Heel Click
Seal Crawl
Crab Walk
Back Roller
Rolling Log
Lowering the Boom
Turn Over
Thread the Needle
Backward Roll — Hand-Clasped Position
Wring the Dishrag

PUPPY DOG RUN

Place hands on the floor, bending the arms and legs slightly. Walk and run like a happy puppy. The teacher should see that the youngsters look ahead. By keeping the head up in good position, the neck muscles are strengthened.

STUNTS AND TUMBLING

Puppy Dog Run

Variations:

1. Children may also use the same position to imitate a cat. Walk softly, stretch at times like a cat. Be smooth and deliberate.

2. **Monkey Run.** Turn the hands so the fingers point in (toward each other).

3. Go sidewards, backwards, etc. Turn around in place.

BEAR WALK

Bend forward and touch the ground with both hands. Travel forward slowly by moving the hand and foot on the *same side together,* i.e., the right hand and foot are moved together, and then the left hand and foot. Make deliberate movements. This movement is classified as unilateral, as the arm and leg on the same side move together.

Variation: Lift the free foot and arm high while the support is on the other side.

RABBIT JUMP

Crouch to the floor with the knees apart. The arms are between the knees with the hands placed on the floor ahead of the feet. Move forward by reaching out first with both hands and then bringing both feet up to the hands. Eyes should look ahead.

Emphasize to the children that this is called a jump rather than a hop because both feet move at once. Note that the jump is a bilateral movement.

Variations: Try with the knees kept together and the arms on the outside. Try alternating the knees together and apart on successive jumps. Go over a low hurdle or through a hoop.

Experiment with taking considerable weight on the hands before the feet move forward. This can be aided by raising the seat higher in the air when the hands move forward.

JUMP TURNS

Jump turns reinforce directional concepts. Use quarter and half turns, right and left. Arms should be kept along the sides of the body. Stress landing lightly without a second movement.

Number concepts can be utilized. The teacher calls out the number as a preparatory command and then says, "Move." Number signals are: one — left quarter turn, two — right quarter turn, three — left half turn, and four — right half turn. Give the children a moment after the number is called before moving.

Variation: Have the arms outstretched to the sides.

ELEPHANT WALK

"The elephant's walk is steady and slow.
  His trunk like a pendulum swings to
    and fro."

Bend well forward, clasping the hands together to form a trunk. The end of the trunk should swing close to the ground. Walk in a slow, deliberate, dignified manner, keeping the legs straight and swinging the trunk from side to side. Stop and throw water over the back with the trunk.

"But when there are children with
  peanuts around
He swings it up and he swings it down."

Follow with appropriate movements.

Elephant Walk

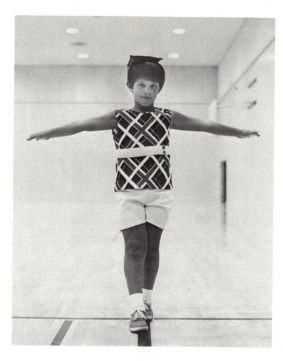

Head Balance

Variation: Arrange children in pairs, one as the mahout (elephant keeper) and the other as the elephant. The mahout walks to the side and a little to the front of the elephant, with one hand touching the elephant's shoulder. The mahout leads the elephant around during the first two lines of the poem, then during the last two lines he releases his touch, walks to a spot in front of the elephant, and "tosses" him a peanut when the trunk is swept up. He returns to the elephant's side and the action is repeated.

HEAD BALANCE

Place a beanbag, block, or book on the child's head. Have him walk, stoop, turn around, sit down, get up, etc.

The object should be balanced so that the upper body is in good posture. Use hands out to the side for balance. Later, vary the position of the arms — folded across the chest, placed behind the back, or down at the sides.

Structure problems by having the children link together a series of movements.

TIGHTROPE WALK

In the Tightrope Walk, children should give good play to the imagination. Set the stage by discussing what a circus performer on the wire might do. Have the children select a line, board, or chalked line on the floor for the "wire." They can pretend to be on the high wire, doing various tasks with exaggerated loss and control of balance. Add such tasks as jumping rope, juggling balls, or riding a bicycle on the wire. Some may "hold" a parasol or a balancing pole while performing.

BOUNCING BALL

Toss a *lively* utility ball into the air and let the children watch how it bounces, lower and lower, until it finally comes to rest on the floor. From a bent-knee position, with the upper body erect, each child imitates a ball by beginning with a high "bounce" and gradually lowering the height of the jump to simulate a ball coming to rest.

Variations: Have the children do this as a partner stunt with one partner serving as the bouncer and the other as the ball. Reverse

STUNTS AND TUMBLING 183

Bouncing Ball

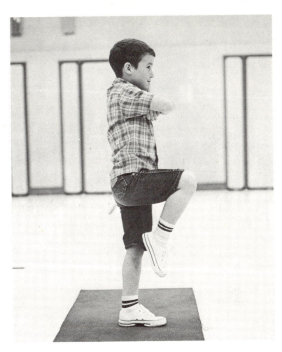

Knee Lift Balance

positions. Try having one partner dribble the "ball" in various positions.

Toss the ball into the air and have the children move with the ball as it bounces lower and lower.

ONE-LEGGED BALANCE STANDS

Each balance stunt should be done with different arm positions. Begin first with the arms out to the side and then have them folded across the chest. Have the children devise other arm positions.

Each stunt can be held first for 3 seconds and then for 5 seconds. Later, eyes should be closed during the count. The child should recover to original position without loss of balance or excessive movement. Stunts should be repeated using the other leg.

Kimbo Stand. With the left foot kept flat on the ground, cross the right leg over the left to a position where the foot is pointed partially down and the toe is touching the ground. Hold this position for a specified count and return to standing position.

Knee Lift Balance. From a standing position, lift one knee up so the thigh is parallel to the ground with toe pointed down. Hold. Return to starting position.

Stork Stand. From a standing position, shift all the weight to one foot. The other foot is placed so that the sole of the foot is against the calf of the standing leg. Hold. Recover to standing position.

LAME DOG WALK

Walk on both hands and one foot. The other foot is held in the air as if injured. Walk a distance and change feet. Eyes should be forward. Also move backwards, in other combinations. See if the children can move with an "injured" front leg.

GORILLA WALK

Bend knees and carry the torso forward. Arms hang at the side. As the child walks forward, he should touch his fingers to the ground.

Variation: Let the children stop and beat on their chests like a gorilla. Also, bounce up and down on all fours with hands and feet touching the floor simultaneously.

184   STUNTS AND TUMBLING

Gorilla Walk

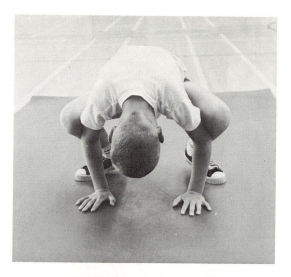

Forward Roll Position. Note the position of the elbows on the insides of the thighs.

CRICKET WALK

Squat. Spread the knees. Put the arms between the knees and grasp the outside of the ankles with the hands. In this position, walk forward or backward. Chirp like a cricket. Turn around right and left.

See what happens if both feet are moved at once!

FORWARD ROLL

Stand facing forward with the feet apart. Squat and place the hands on the mat, shoulder width apart with the elbows against the inside of the thighs. Tuck the chin to the chest and make a rounded back. A push-off with the hands and feet provides the force for the roll. The child should carry the weight on his hands, with the elbows bearing the weight of the thighs. By keeping the elbows against the thighs and assuming weight there, the force of the roll is easily transferred to the rounded back. The child should try to roll forward to his feet. Later, try with the knees together and no weight on the elbows.

Kneeling alongside the child, the instructor can help by placing one hand on the back of the child's head and the other under the thigh for a push, finishing the assist with an upward lift on the back of the neck.

Spotting the Forward Roll. One hand is on the back of the head and one is under the thigh.

STUNTS AND TUMBLING

RISING SUN

Lie on back. Using the arms only for balance, rise to a standing position.

Variation: Have the children fold arms over the chest. Experiment with different positions of the feet. Feet can be crossed, spread wide, both to one side, etc.

BALANCE TOUCH

An object (eraser, block, or beanbag) is placed a yard away from a line. Balancing on one foot, the child reaches out with the other foot, touches the object, and recovers to the starting position. He does not place weight on the object but merely touches it. Reach sidewards, backwards.

Balance Touch

Variation: Try at various distances. On a gymnasium floor, count the number of boards to establish the distance for the touch.

HEEL CLICK

Stand with feet slightly apart. Jump up and click heels, coming down with feet apart. Try with a quarter turn right and left.

Variations:

1. Have the child clap hands overhead as he clicks his heels.

2. Another variation is to have the child join hands with one or more children. A signal is needed. The children can count, "One, Two, THREE," jumping on the third count.

3. Some may be able to click the heels twice before landing. Landing should be with the feet apart.

4. Begin with a cross step to the side, and then click heels. Try both right and left.

SEAL CRAWL

The child is in a front-leaning (push-up) position, the weight supported on straightened arms and toes. Keeping the body straight, he walks forward using his hands for propelling force and dragging his feet.

Watch to see the body is straight and the head is up.

Seal Crawl

Variation: Let the child crawl forward a short distance and then roll over on his back clapping his hands like a seal, with appropriate seal grunts.

CRAB WALK

Squat down and reach back putting both hands on the floor without sitting down. With head, neck, and body level and in a straight line, walk forward, backward, and sideward.

Children have a tendency to lower the hips. See that the body is kept in a straight line.

Crab Walk

Variations:

1. As each step is taken with a hand, the other hand can slap the chest or seat.

2. Move the hand and foot on the same side simultaneously (unilateral movement).

3. Try balancing on one leg and opposite hand. Hold for 5 seconds.

BACK ROLLER

This stunt is a lead-up to the regular *Backward Roll*. Begin in a crouched position, knees together, and hands resting lightly on the floor. Roll backwards, securing momentum by bringing the knees to the chest and clasping them with the arms. Roll back and forth rhyth-

mically. On the backward movement, the roll should go well back on the neck and head. Try to roll forward to original position. Where children have difficulty in rolling back to original position, have them cross the legs and roll to a crossed-leg standing position.

ROLLING LOG

Lie on back with arms stretched overhead. Roll sideways the length of the mat. The next time roll with the hands pointed toward the other side of the mat. To roll in a straight line, keep the feet slightly apart.

Rolling Log

Variation: Alternately curl and stretch while rolling.

LOWERING THE BOOM

Start in push-up position (front-leaning rest position). Lower the body slowly to the floor. The movement should be controlled so that the body remains rigid.

Variations:

1. Have the children pause halfway down.

2. Have them come down in stages inch by inch. Be sure they understand the concept of an inch as a measure of distance.

3. Call this a "flat tire." Children let themselves down slowly to the accompaniment of noise simulating air escaping from a punctured tire. See how they react to a "blowout," initiated by an appropriate noise.

TURN OVER

From a front-leaning rest position (as in *Lowering the Boom*), turn over so that the back is to the floor. The body should not touch the floor. Continue the turn until the original position is assumed. Reverse the direction. Turn back and forth several times.

The body should be kept straight and rigid throughout the turn.

THREAD THE NEEDLE

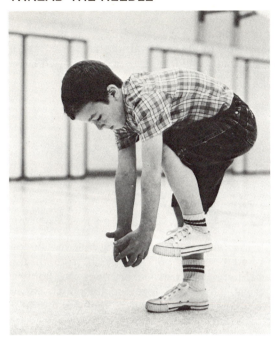

Thread the Needle

Touch the fingertips together in front of the body. Step through with one foot at a time without the tips losing contact. Step back to original position. Now lock the fingers in front of the body and repeat the stunt. Finally, see if children can step through the clasped hands without touching the hands.

BACKWARD ROLL — HAND-CLASPED POSITION

Teachers can have good success teaching the backward roll by beginning with this approach. The child clasps his fingers behind the neck, with the elbows held out to the sides. From a crouched position, he sits down rapidly, bringing his knees to his chest for a tuck to secure momentum. He rolls completely over backwards, taking much of the weight on his elbows. In this method, the neck is protected and the pressure is taken by the elbows.

STUNTS AND TUMBLING 187

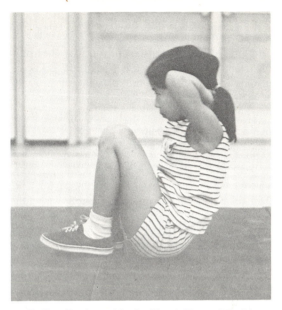

Rolling Backward in the Hand-Clasped Position

Remind the children to keep their elbows back and out to the sides to gain maximum support and assure minimal neck strain.

WRING THE DISHRAG (COUPLE STUNT)

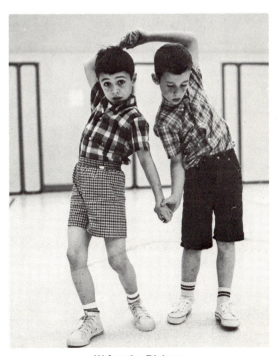

Wring the Dishrag

Two children face each other and join hands. Raise one pair of arms (right for one and left for the other) and turn under that pair of arms, continuing a full turn until back to original position. Care must be taken to avoid bumping heads.

Variation: Try the stunt at a lower level using a crouched position.

SECOND GRADE PROGRAM

Begin with a review of the kindergarten and first grade stunts. Continued practice should be held in the *Forward Roll*. The *Backward Curl* and the regular *Backward Roll* are significant inclusions in this grade level. Additional balance stunts expand the practice opportunities for this quality.

Children of this age group are more amenable to coaching as compared to previous levels and some attention to performance factors can be stressed. However, their span of interest is short, and performance factors should be introduced as opportunities arise.

ACTIVITIES FOR THE SECOND GRADE

    Forward Roll Review and Practice
    Frog Jump
    Seal Crawl Variations
    Heel Slap
    Pogo Stick
    Wicket Walk
    Top
    Measuring Worm
    Leg Balances
    Turk Stand
    Climb Up
    Three Point Tip-Up
    Crazy Walk
    Push-Up
    Backward Curl
    Backward Roll — Regular
    Seat Circle
    Hand and Knee Balance
    Single Knee Balance

FORWARD ROLL REVIEW AND PRACTICE

Review the *Forward Roll* (first grade). Spot and assist as necessary. Work on getting the children to come out of the roll to their feet. Grasping knees at the end of the roll is of help.

Variations:
1. Roll to the feet with the ankles crossed.
2. Some children can try to roll with the knees together.

FROG JUMP

From a squatting position, with the hands placed on the floor slightly in front of the feet, jump forward a short distance, lighting on the hands and feet simultaneously. Note the difference between this stunt and the *Rabbit Jump* (first grade).

Emphasis eventually should be on both height and distance. The hands and arms should absorb part of the landing impact.

SEAL CRAWL VARIATIONS

Review the *Seal Crawl* (first grade). Include the following variations:

1. Crawl with the fingers pointed in different directions — out and in.
2. **Reverse Seal Crawl.** Turn over and attempt the crawl dragging the heels.
3. **Elbow Crawl.** Assume the original position but with the weight on the elbows. Crawl forward on the elbows.

Elbow Crawl

The *Seal Crawl* can also be made more challenging by using the crossed-arm position.

HEEL SLAP

From an erect position with hands at the sides, jump into the air and slap both heels with the hands.

Variations: Use a one, two, three rhythm with small preliminary jumps on *one* and *two*. Make quarter or half turns in the air. During a jump, slap the heels twice before landing.

POGO STICK

Pretend to be a pogo stick by keeping a stiff body and jumping on the toes. Hold the hands in front as if grasping the stick. Progress in various directions.

Stress upward propelling action by the ankles and toes with the body kept stiff, particularly at the knee joint.

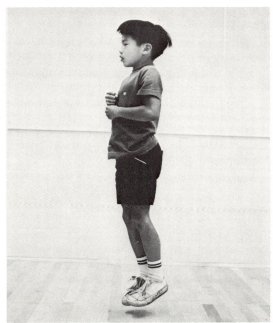

Pogo Stick

WICKET WALK

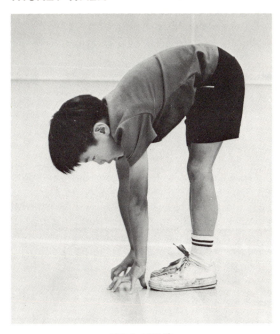

Wicket Walk

Children bend over and touch the floor with their weight *evenly* distributed on hands and feet. By keeping the knees straight, a wicket can be formed. Walk the wicket forward, backward, and sideward. Keep arms and legs as near vertical as possible.

Be sure the knees are kept reasonably straight, as the stunt loses much of its flexibility values if the knees are bent too much.

The stunt gets its name because the child's position resembles a wicket in a croquet game.

A common error in the execution of this stunt is to keep the hands positioned too far forward of the feet.

TOP

From a standing position with arms at the sides, have children try jumping, turning to face the opposite direction, turning three-quarters of the way around, and making a full turn facing the original direction. Number concepts can be stressed in having the children do half, three-quarter, and full turns.

Successful execution of the stunt should call for the child to land in good balance with hands near the sides. No movement of the feet should occur after landing.

Children should turn right and left.

Variation: Fold arms across chest.

MEASURING WORM

From a front-leaning rest position, keeping the knees stiff, bring up the feet as close as possible to the hands by inching forward with the feet. Regain position by inching forward with the hands. Emphasize keeping the knees straight, with necessary bending occurring at the hips.

LEG BALANCES

Backward. With the knee straight, extend one leg forward with the toe pointed so that it is level to the floor. Balance on the other leg for 5 seconds. Use arms out to the side for balance. Lean back as far as possible. The bend should be far enough back so the eyes are looking at the ceiling.

Forward. Extend the leg backward until it is parallel to the floor. Keeping eyes forward and arms out to the side, bend forward, balancing on the other leg. Hold for 5 seconds without moving.

Side. Stand on the left foot with enough side bend to the left so the right (top) side of the

Forward Leg Balance

body is parallel to the floor. Put the right arm alongside the head in a line with the rest of the body. Reverse, using the right leg for support. (Support may be needed momentarily to get into position.)

TURK STAND

Stand with feet apart and arms folded in front. Pivot on the balls of *both* feet and face the opposite direction. The legs are now crossed. Sit down in this position. Reverse the process. Get up without using the hands for aid, and uncross the legs with a pivot to face original direction.

Very little change should occur in the position of the feet.

CLIMB UP

Get down on a mat on hands and knees, with the hands placed about shoulder width apart and the fingers spread and pointed forward. Place the head forward of the hands so the head and the hands form a triangle on the mat. Walk the body weight forward so most of it rests on the hands and head. Climb the knees to the top of the elbows. This stunt is lead-up to the *Headstand* (third grade).

Variation: Raise the knees off the elbows.

THREE POINT TIP-UP

The Three Point Tip-Up ends up in the same general position as the *Climb-Up,* but with the elbows on the inside of the thighs. Squat down on the mat, placing the hands flat, fingers pointing forward, with the elbows inside and pressed against the inner part of the lower thighs. Lean forward, slowly transferring the weight of the body to the bent elbows and hands until the forehead touches the mat. Return to starting position.

This stunt also provides a background for the headstand and for the handstand given at later grades.

Some children may have better success by turning the fingers in slightly, causing the elbows to point out more, offering better support to the thigh contact.

CRAZY WALK

The child makes progress forward in an erect position by bringing one foot behind *and* around the other to gain a little ground each time. Set up a specified distance and see which children can cover this with the least number of steps.

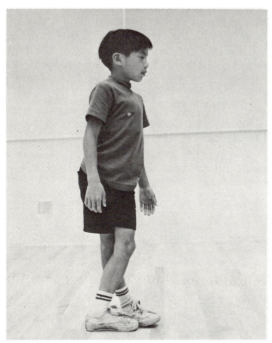

Crazy Walk

Variation: Reverse the movements and go backwards. This means bringing the foot in front and around to gain distance in back.

PUSH-UP

From a front-leaning rest position, lower the body and push-up back to original position. Be sure that the only movement is in the arms, with the body kept rigid and straight.

Variation: Stop halfway down and halfway up. Go up and down by inches.

Note: Since the *Push-Up* is used in many exercises and testing programs, it is important that the children learn proper execution early.

BACKWARD CURL

This stunt has three stages.

1. Begin in a sitting position with the knees drawn up to the chest and the chin tucked down. The arms are placed out to the sides as the shoulders make contact with the mat. Roll backwards until the weight is on the shoulders and the feet and legs come back over the head so that the toes touch the mat. Roll back to starting position.

2. Same action except the hands are placed alongside the head on the mat as the child rolls back. The fingers are pointed in the direction of the roll with the palms down on the mat. A good direction to the children is "Point your thumbs toward your ears and keep your elbows reasonably close to the body."

3. The third stage is similar to #2 except that the child starts in a crouched position on his feet. He is in a deep-knee bend position with his back toward the direction of the roll. He secures momentum by sitting down quickly, bringing his knees to his chest.

The teacher has to recognize that this, like the *Back Roller,* is a lead-up to the backward roll. The hand pressure is an important item to be stressed. Teach the children to push hard against the floor to take the pressure from the back of the neck.

Variations:

1. Touch the knees behind the head instead of the toes.

2. Another interesting challenge can be made using a beanbag. Have the child keep a beanbag between his feet and deposit it behind his head, returning to position. Next, curl back and pick up the beanbag, returning it to original position.

3. A more difficult backward curl, which some children may be able to do, starts with the child sitting with legs crossed and the hands grasping the feet. Roll backwards, touching the floor overhead with the feet. Return to position.

BACKWARD ROLL — REGULAR

Start with the back to the direction of the roll in the same squat position as in the forward roll. Push off with the hands quickly, sit down, and start rolling over on the back.

The knees should be brought to the chest, so the body is tucked and momentum is increased. Quickly bring the hands up over the shoulders, palms up, fingers pointed backward. Continue rolling backward with the knees close to the chest. The hands will now touch the mat at about the same time as the head. It is vitally important at this point to push hard with the hands. Continue to roll over the top of the head and push off the mat until ready to stand.

Proper hand position can be emphasized by telling the children to point their thumbs toward their ears, and to spread their fingers for better push-off control.

Spotting

Care must be taken never to push a child from the hip, forcing him to roll over. This puts undue pressure on the back of the neck.

The proper method of aiding the child who has difficulty with the stunt is as follows. The spotter stands in a straddle position with his near foot alongside at about the spot where the performer's hands and head will make contact with the mat. His other foot is one

Spotting the Backward Roll. The lift is at the hips of the roller. Lift, but do not force the child over.

stride in the direction of the roll. The critical point is for the spotter to lift the hips just as the head and hands of the performer make contact with the mat. This is accomplished by taking the back hand and reaching across to the far hip of the performer, getting under the near hip with the near hand. The lift is applied on the front of the hips just below the beltline. The object is to relieve the pressure on the neck.

SEAT CIRCLE

Sit on the floor, knees bent and hands braced behind. Lift the feet off the floor and push with the hands so the body spins in a circle on the seat as a pivot. Spin right and left.

Seat Circle

HAND AND KNEE BALANCE

Get down on all fours, with support on the hands and knees, supporting also on the feet with the toes pointed backward. Lift one hand and the opposite leg from the floor and balance on the other hand and knee. Keep the foot from touching during the hold. Reverse hand and knee positions.

Hand and Knee Balance

SINGLE KNEE BALANCE

Single Knee Balance

Similar to the previous stunt, except that the balance is made on one knee (and leg), with the arms outstretched to sides. Reverse positions.

THIRD GRADE PROGRAM

In the third grade, in comparison to the K-2 program, more emphasis on form and quality of performance is centered in stunt execution. More couple and group stunts make their appearance in the third grade program.

Among individual stunts, the *Headstand* is an important addition to the tumbling area. Stunts such as the *Frog Handstand* and the *Mule Kick* give the children experience in taking the weight totally on the hands.

ACTIVITIES FOR THE THIRD GRADE

Forward Roll
Forward Roll Variations
Backward Roll Practice
Frog Handstand (Tip-Up)
Heel Stand
Russian Dance
Squat Thrust
Walrus Walk
The Reach Under
Stiff Man Bend
Coffee Grinder
Mule Kick
One Leg Balance Reverse
Curl-up
Tummy Balance
Hip Walk
Scooter
Double Lame Dog
The Turtle
Long Bridge
Headstand
Partner Hopping (Couple Stunt)
Twister (Couple Stunt)
Partner Pull-up (Couple Stunt)
Chinese Get-up (Couple or Group Stunt)
Double Top (Couple Stunt)

FORWARD ROLL

Hands are on the mat, shoulder width apart, with the fingers pointed forward. The knees are *between* the arms. From this position, push off with the feet and rock forward on the hands. Just as you feel yourself falling off balance, tuck the head down between the arms with chin on chest. The back of the head touches the mat and the weight is then borne by the rounded back. Grasp the shins and pull yourself onto your feet. Those who have trouble should put the hands between the knees and the elbows against the thighs.

FORWARD ROLL VARIATIONS

During the roll the performer can cross his legs and come to his feet in this position. The legs can be uncrossed with a pivot which will face him in the direction from which he came. He can then roll back to position.

BACKWARD ROLL PRACTICE

Continue practice with the backward roll. Spot as needed. Practice the backward roll both with the hands clasped behind the neck (first grade) and in the regular manner.

FROG HANDSTAND (Tip-up)

The stunt follows the same directions as the *Three-point Tip-up* (second grade). Squat down on the mat, placing the hands flat, fingers pointing forward, with the elbows inside and pressed against the inner part of the knees. Lean forward using the leverage of the elbows against the knees and balance on the hands. Hold for five seconds. Return to position.

The head does not touch the mat at any time. Hands may be turned in slightly if this makes better contact between the elbows and the insides of the thigh.

Frog Handstand

HEEL STAND

Begin in a full squat position with the arms dangling at the sides. Jump upward to full leg extension with the weight on both heels, flinging the arms out diagonally. Hold momentarily and return to position. Several movements can be done rhythmically in succession.

RUSSIAN DANCE

Squat down on one heel with the other foot extended forward with the weight on its heel. With the back straight and the arms extended forward, rapidly change the position of the feet.

Russian Dance

Variations:

1. Try with the arms folded high in front.
2. Try with one foot out to the side and change to the side each time.

SQUAT THRUST

While the squat thrust later is used as an exercise, the act of completing the cycle successfully is classified as a stunt. The stunt is done in four definite movements. Starting from the position of attention, on count *one* the child squats down on the floor placing the hands flat (shoulder width) on the floor with the elbows inside the knees. On count

STUNTS AND TUMBLING 195

two, the feet and legs are thrust back so that the body is perfectly straight from head to toe in push-up position. On count *three,* the child returns to squat position, and on the *last* count returns to the position of attention.

Girls should do three in 10 seconds and boys four in the same amount of time.

First teach proper positioning during each of the four phases. Then stress the rhythmic nature of the movements. Music may be added.

WALRUS WALK

Similar to the *Seal Crawl* (first grade). Begin with a front-leaning rest position with fingers pointed outward. Make progress by moving both hands forward at the same time. Some children may be able to clap hands as they take each step.

Before giving this stunt, review the *Seal Crawl* and variations.

Variation: Move sideways so the upper part of the body describes an arc while the feet hold position.

THE REACH UNDER

Take a position with the feet pointed ahead and spaced about 2' apart, toes against a line or board of the floor. Place a beanbag two boards in front of and midway between the feet. Without changing the position of the feet, reach one hand behind and between the legs and pick up the beanbag. Pick up with the other hand. Move the beanbag a board out at a time and repeat.

Variation: Allow the heels to be lifted from the floor.

STIFF MAN BEND

Take a standing position with the feet about shoulder width apart and pointed forward. Place a beanbag 6" behind the left heel. Grasp the right toe with the right hand, thumb on top. Without bending the knees, reach the left hand outside the left leg and pick up the beanbag without releasing the toe hold of the right hand. Increase the distance slowly. Reverse positions.

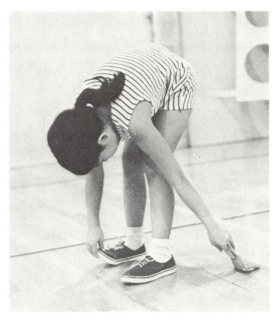

Stiff Man Bend

COFFEE GRINDER

Put one hand on the floor and extend the body with that side to the floor in a side leaning position. The child walks around his hand making a complete circle while keeping his body straight.

The stunt should be done slowly with con-

STUNTS AND TUMBLING

Coffee Grinder

trolled movements. The straight body alignment should remain constant throughout the complete circle movement.

MULE KICK

Stoop down and place the hands on the floor in front of the feet. The arms are the front legs of the mule. Kick out with the hind legs while the weight is momentarily supported by the front legs. Taking the weight on the hands is important.

The stunt can be taught in two stages. First, practice taking the weight momentarily on the hands. Next, add the kick.

Variation: Make two kicks before the feet return to the ground.

ONE LEG BALANCE REVERSE

Assume a forward balance position. In this, the body leans forward, the arms are out to the sides, the weight is on one leg with the other leg extended behind. In a quick movement, swing the free leg down to give momentum to change to the same forward balance position facing in the *opposite* direction (180 degree turn). No unnecessary move-

ment of the supporting foot should be made after the turn is complete. The swinging foot should not touch the floor.

CURL-UP

Two children work together with one child holding the other's feet. The performer lies on his back with the legs extended and feet 1' apart. The knees are up so an angle of 90 degrees is formed at the knee joint. The feet are flat (soles down) on the floor. The hands, with the fingers interlaced, are behind the lower part of the head.

The child curls up, alternating touching the right and left elbows to the opposite knees. One touch is made on each curl-up.

Boys should be able to complete 15 curl-ups while girls should be able to do at least 10.

Be sure the child returns the head completely to the floor each time. No rest should be allowed, as the curl-ups must be continuous. The child may move at his own pace, however.

See page 61 for description of the *Curl-Up*.

TUMMY BALANCE

Tummy Balance

The child lies prone on the floor with arms outstretched to the sides, palms down. He raises arms, head, chest, and legs from the floor, balancing on his tummy. Knees should be kept straight.

HIP WALK

The child sits in the same position as in the *Scooter,* but the arms are in thrust position, with the hand making a partial fist. The child makes forward progress by alternate leg movements. The arm-leg coordination should be cross-lateral.

THE SCOOTER

The *Scooter* is an excellent movement for abdominal development. The child is on the floor in extended sitting position with arms folded in front of the chest but held chin high. To scoot, he pulls his seat toward his heels, using heel pressure and lifting the seat slightly. He then extends his legs forward again, and repeats the process.

DOUBLE LAME DOG

Support the body on a hand and leg (same side). Move forward in this position, maintaining balance. The distance should be short (5'-10') as this is strenuous.

Four leg-arm combinations should be employed. Cross-lateral movements of right arm-left leg and left arm-right leg should be varied with unilateral movements of right arm-right leg and left arm-left leg.

Variation: Keep the free arm on the hip.

THE TURTLE

Turtle

With the feet apart and the hands widely spread, the body is in a wide push-up position about halfway up from the floor (elbows somewhat bent). From this position, move in various directions, keeping the plane of the body always about the same distance from the floor. Movements of the hands and feet should occur only in small increments.

LONG BRIDGE

Begin in a crouched position with the hands on the floor, knees between the arms. Push the hands forward a little at a time until you are in an extended push-up position. Return to position.

Challenge children to extend out as far forward as they can and still retain the support.

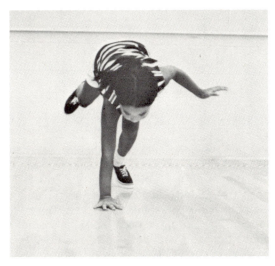

Double Lame Dog

Variations: Begin with a forward movement and then change to sideward movement, establishing as wide a spread as possible. Another variation is to work from a crossed hands position.

THE HEADSTAND

Two approaches are suggested for the *Headstand*. The first is to relate the *Headstand* to the *Climb-Up* and the second is to go directly into a *Headstand* using a kick-up to achieve the inverted position. With either method it is essential that the triangle position of the hands and head be maintained as diagrammed.

In this position, the hands are placed about shoulder width apart, with the fingers pointed forward, spread, and slightly cupped. The head is positioned on the mat about 10″ to 12″ forward of the hands, with the weight taken on the forward part of the head, near the hairline.

In the final inverted position, the feet should be together with the legs straight and toes pointed. The back is arched, with the weight evenly distributed among the hands and forward part of the head.

The safest way to come down from the inverted position is to return to the mat in the direction which was used in going up. Recovery is helped by bending at both the waist and at the knees. If the child overbalances and falls forward, he should tuck the head under and go into a forward roll.

Both methods of recovery from the inverted position should be included in the instructional sequences early in the presentation.

BASING THE HEADSTAND ON THE CLIMB-UP

A spotter is stationed directly in front of the performer and steadies him as needed. However, if the spotter cannot control the performer, he must be alert to move out of the way if the latter goes into a forward roll coming out of the inverted position.

The child takes the inverted position of the *Climb-Up* (page 190) and slowly moves his feet upward to the *Headstand* position, stead-

ied by the spotter only as needed. The spotter can first apply support to the hips and then transfer to the ankles as the *Climb-Up* position is lengthened into a *Headstand*.

HEADSTAND — KICK-UP METHOD

The goal of the kick-up method is to establish a pattern which can be related to other inverted stunts, as well as serving for the *Headstand*. Keeping the weight on the forward part of the head and maintaining the triangle base, walk the feet forward until the hips are high over the body, somewhat similar to the *Climb-Up* position. Keep one foot on the mat with the knee of that leg bent and the other leg somewhat extended backward. Kick the back leg up to the inverted position, following quickly with a push by the other leg, thus bringing the two legs together in the inverted position. The timing is a quick one-two movement.

When learning, children should work in units of three students. One child attempts the stunt with a spotter on either side. Positions are rotated. Each spotter kneels, placing his near hand under the shoulder of the performer. The performer now "walks" his weight above his head and kicks up to position. The spotter on each side supports by grasping the leg.

Spotting

Teaching Points:

The triangle formed by the hands and the head is important, as well as the weight centered on the forward part of the head. The majority of the troubles which occur while doing the headstand come from incorrect head-hand relationship. The correct placement can be ensured by making sure the head is placed the length of the performer's forearm from knees, and the hands placed at the knees.

Do not let children stay too long in the inverted position or hold contests to see who can stand on his head the longest.

Most of the responsibility for getting into the inverted position should rest on the performer. Spotters may help some, but should avoid "wrestling up" the performer.

PARTNER HOPPING (Couple Stunt)

Children coordinate hopping movements for short distances and in different directions. Three combinations are suggested:

1. Stand facing each other. Extend the left leg forward to be grasped at the ankle by the partner. Each then hops on his right leg.

2. Stand back to back. Lift the leg backward (bend knee) and have the partner grasp the ankle. Hop as before.

3. Stand side by side with inside arms around each other's waist. Lift the inside foot from the floor and make progress by hopping on the outside foot.

If either partner begins to fall, the other

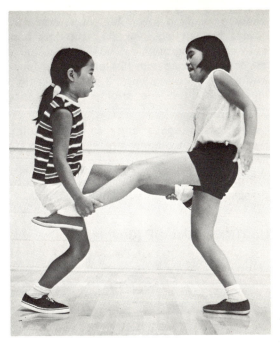

Partner Hopping

should release the leg immediately. Vary by moving in different directions and patterns. Reverse feet positions.

TWISTER (Couple Stunt)

Partners face and grasp right hands as if shaking hands. #1 swings his right leg over the head of #2 and turns around, taking a straddle position over his own arm. #2 swings his left *leg* over #1, who has bent over, and the partners are now back to back. #1 now continues with his left leg and faces in the original direction. #2 swings his right leg over back to the original face to face position.

Partners need to duck to avoid being kicked by each other's feet as the legs are swung over.

Variation: The stunt can be introduced by grasping a wand instead of holding hands.

PARTNER PULL-UP (Couple Stunt)

Partners sit down facing each other in a bent-knee position with the heels on the floor and the toes touching. Pulling cooperatively, both come to a standing position. Return to the floor.

CHINESE GET-UP
(Couple or Group Stunt)

Two children sit back to back and lock arms. From this position both try to stand by pushing against each other's back. Sit down again. If the feet are sliding, do the stunt on a mat.

Variations:

1. Try the stunt with three or four children.

2. From a halfway down position, move like a spider.

DOUBLE TOP (Couple Stunt)

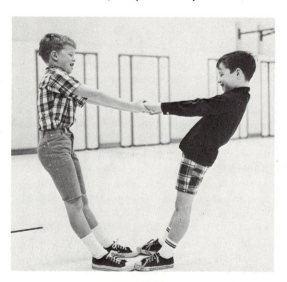

Double Top

Face partner and join hands. Experiment to see which type of grip works best. With straight arms, lean away from each other and at the same time move toes close to partner's. Spin around slowly in either direction, taking tiny steps. Increase speed.

Variation: Use a stooped position.

16

Relays

Instructional Procedures
Selected Relays
Kindergarten and First Grade Approach
Second Grade Relays
Third Grade Relays

Relays have a place in the program of physical education. Not only do they offer fun and enjoyment, but when properly conducted they provide good values in fitness, skills, and social objectives. Children learn to cooperate with others in the interest of winning, to conform to rules and regulations, and to use skills in situations of stress and competition. However, if rules are not enforced and the child finds that he can get by without obeying them, he is learning that he can win by cheating.

Relays can be combined with the teaching of skills. After skills have been taught and practiced sufficiently, they can be incorporated into relays. Children need to have mastered skills sufficiently before they enter relay competitions; otherwise they forget to perform the skills correctly in the haste to win.

In this presentation relays begin in the second grade, as the individualistic characteristics of the younger children do not lend themselves well to organized team efforts. However, some preliminary work can be done in the kindergarten and first grade.

INSTRUCTIONAL PROCEDURES

1. Place from four to eight players on a team. Too many on a team drags out the race and the children lose interest.

2. If the teams have uneven numbers, either some players on the smaller teams should run twice, or a rotation system should be set up by which the extra players wait out in turn.

3. Be definite regarding the starting point, the turning point, and the finishing act. In some races, crossing the line may be the finishing act. In others the captain may be required to hold up the ball while the rest of the players are in a specified formation. A definite finishing act prevents arguments with regard to the determination of the winner.

4. In many relays, particularly of the revolving type, it helps to keep things straight if the last player or runner has some kind of identification. Armbands of crepe paper, hats, pinnies, or colored shirts provide good identification. This keeps the teacher informed of the progress of the race and allows him to anticipate the finish. The teacher can line himself with the finish line so he can make a judgment of the winner.

5. Appoint a captain for each team. Let him arrange the order, be responsible for the application of the rules, and help keep things under control.

6. Be careful of putting too much emphasis on winning. Too much pressure makes the skilled resent being on teams with those who are less able to perform.

7. Demonstrate a relay just enough so that each team understands the procedures. This can entail a simple demonstration by one individual or having the entire team practice

the routine. If the new relay does not seem to be started properly, stop the group and review the instructions.

8. Any dropped or mishandled ball must be retrieved by the person dropping it. It must be started by him in the proper sequence at the point where it was dropped.

9. Distances need to be modified when restricted movements are used, such as the *Puppy Dog Run,* the *Crab Walk,* and others where the physical demands are heavy. When hopping is used, a change to the other foot should be made halfway through the race.

10. Make some rules about the handling of supplies. Have a central source, and appoint one person from each team to secure and return equipment.

11. A block, beanbag, traffic cone, Indian club, chair, standard, or other definite marker should be used for a turning point. A definite turning point is better than just having the children run to a line and back.

12. Infractions should be penalized. It is good social learning for the children to experience the situation where they must conform to rules or be assessed with a penalty. A team could be disqualified, points deducted, or other penalties imposed. Impartiality should be the rule. All teams and players should be on an equal basis.

SELECTED RELAYS

Relays should be selected in keeping with the children's previous experience in stunts and skills. Relays have a universal appeal to children, and this makes it difficult to pinpoint various relays to different grades. However, allocation is desirable so that the children, having followed the progression of relays in this guide, will have experienced a varied and interesting program and secured good fitness values.

KINDERGARTEN AND FIRST GRADE APPROACH

While relays, as such, are a little beyond the capacity of most kindergarten and first grade children, some experiences of handling beanbags and yarn balls in relay sequence are of value. Place the children in a line (side by side) formation and have them pass the articles down to the end, or arrange them in a circle formation and have them pass the beanbag around the circle. The object of the activity is to pass well and not drop the article. Some attention can be given to seeing which group can do it first, but this should not be the goal. The objective should be learning to participate in this kind of activity and to cooperate with others.

Another way to develop relay concepts is to place the squads or teams in a squad file formation and then proceed as follows:

1. The first child (head of the file) in each team moves toward and around a given turning point a short distance away and is asked to return to his place and stand quietly. The first child to complete this action successfully wins a point for his team.

2. The child is asked to go to the rear of the line and the next child has his turn.

3. The next step would be for the child to move directly without delay to the rear of the line after he has completed his turn and stand quietly. Learning to go around the designated side of the turning point and returning up the correct aisle for safety purposes can be conceptualized.

SECOND GRADE RELAYS

LANE RELAYS

With one player at a time running around a turning point and back, many different relays using the basic locomotor skills can be scheduled. Running, walking (forward and backward), hopping, skipping, galloping, sliding, and jumping are movements that can be used in relays.

BEANBAG PASS OR BALL PASS RELAY

Supplies: Beanbag or ball for each team.

Formation: Lane with players facing to the side.

The player on the right starts the beanbag or ball, which is passed from one player to the next down the line. When it gets to the end of the line, the race is over. Be sure each player handles the bag or ball. Rotate.

CIRCLE PASS RELAY

Supplies: Ball for each team.

Formation: Each team forms a separate circle of the same size. At first the circle should be small enough so that the players can hand the ball to each other. Later, as skill increases, the circles can be enlarged.

The leader of each group starts the ball around the circle by handing. As soon as the ball gets back to the leader, the entire team sits down. The first team to be seated in good formation wins.

BOUNCE BALL RELAY

Supplies: Ball that will bounce for each team.

Formation: Lane.

A circle is drawn 10' to 15' in front of each team. The first player runs to the circle, bounces the ball once, runs back to his team, and *gives* the ball to the second player, who repeats the same routine. Each player has a turn, and the team having the last man carry his ball back over the finish line wins. To vary, have the players bounce the ball more than once.

BOWL RELAY

Supplies: Ball for each team.

Formation: Lane.

The player at the head of each team has a ball. A line is drawn 15' to 20' in front of each team. The first player runs to the line, turns, and rolls the ball back to the second player. The second player must wait behind the starting line to catch the ball and then repeats the pattern of the first player. The race is over when the last player has received the ball and carried it over the forward line.

THIRD GRADE RELAYS

LANE RELAYS

Using lane formation and a turning point, lane relays should employ running, walking, and other locomotor movements. In addition, relays can use the animal imitations explained in the stunts and tumbling program. The following are excellent for lane relays:

Puppy Dog Run	Crab Walk
Bear Walk	Seal Crawl
Rabbit Jump	Pogo Stick
Lame Dog Walk	Measuring Worm

PARTNER RELAYS

Supplies: None.

Formation: Lane formation of partners.

Children run with partners (inside hands joined) just like a single runner. Use running, walking, skipping, hopping, and galloping. Sliding can be used to make an interesting relay. Children face each other with both hands joined (as partners) and slide one way to a turning point, sliding back to starting point leading with the other side.

CROSS OVER RELAY

Supplies: Ball for each team.

Formation: Lane.

Review *Bowl Relay* from the second grade. This relay is similar. Two lines are drawn about 15' apart. The teams are in lane formation behind one of the lines. The player in front has a ball. On signal, each player with a ball runs to the next line and tosses the ball back to the one at the head of the line, who runs forward and repeats the throw. The race is over when the last player in line catches the ball and runs forward across the forward line.

SNOWBALL RELAY

Supplies: None.

Formation: Lane.

Teams are in lane formation, but the lanes must be from 10' to 15' apart. The first player runs forward, around the turning point, and back to his team, where he takes the next player by the hand. He repeats the trip with the second player in tow. When the two reach the team again, the second player takes the hand of the third one in line. The trip is repeated and so on until, on the last trip, the entire team will run around the turning point and finish over the starting line.

Variation: There is a variation of this race called *Locomotive*. The second player hooks on the engine (first player), and in turn each of the players hooks on until the entire team forms a train.

PASS THE BUCK RELAY

Supplies: None.

Formation: Lane with teams facing sideways.

Players are facing sideways with lanes about 5' apart. All players of a team are linked by joining hands. The leader is on the right of each team. On signal, the leader "passes the buck" to the next player (by squeezing his hand), who in turn passes the squeeze to the next and so on down the line. The end player, when he receives the "buck," runs across the front of his team and becomes the new leader. He starts the squeeze, which is passed down the line. Each player, in turn, comes around to the end of the line with the original leader finally returning to his original position.

Variation: Instead of "passing the buck," teams could pass a beanbag, Indian club, or ball.

STOOP AND STRETCH RELAY

Supplies: Beanbag for each team.

Formation: Lane.

The players stand in lane formation about 2' apart. The player in front has a beanbag which he reaches over his head and drops. Using *both* hands, the second player picks the bag up, reaches over his head, and drops it behind him. The bag continues down the line until the last player picks it up. He comes to the front of the line and starts the bag back down the line. Each player in turn comes to the front, and the relay is over when the team has returned to its original position.

BENCH RELAYS

Formation: Lane. A balance beam bench or ordinary bench is in front of each two teams.

Procedure: Several interesting races can be run using benches. The following are suggested:

1. Run forward, jump over the bench, jump back again, return, and tag off.

2. Each team has a beanbag. Run to the bench, pass the beanbag underneath, and return to the team, giving the beanbag to the next player, who repeats the run.

3. Each team has a beanbag which is placed about 3' in front of the bench. The first player runs forward, picks up the beanbag, and jumps over the bench carrying the bag with him. He drops it on the far side of the bench. He then jumps back over the bench and tags off. The next runner jumps over the bench, picks up the bag, jumps back over the bench with the bag, and places the bag on the floor near original position. The players alternate carrying the bag over and bringing it to the near side.

17

Game-Type Activities

Introducing Variations
Safety Suggestions for Games
Maintaining Balance in Games
Instructional Procedures for Conducting Games
Exploration with Games
The Games Program for Kindergarten
The Games Program for First Grade
The Games Program for Second Grade
The Games Program for Third Grade

Every boy and girl in the public schools should have a chance to engage in a variety of games which are the collective heritage of centuries of children. The games have good recreational values, provide fitness values, and provide a necessary outlet for natural exuberance.

Some important objectives of a good games program for children are:

1. To provide a vigorous large-muscle activity with developmental potential, resulting in good muscular development and control.

2. To develop ability to run, maneuver, dodge, start, and stop.

3. To learn to manage and control one's body under stress.

4. To foster mental alertness in reacting strategically to the game situation.

5. To be able to understand and follow rules and directions.

6. To learn to play with others in a socially sound manner without bickering, quarreling, and fighting.

7. To encourage fair play and sportsmanship.

8. To understand self and others better.

The greatest values for development in the games program are inherent in those activities in which many children are active at once and must strain and "put out" good physical effort. Some games are useful, however, in providing a period of lesser activity following a more strenuous activity. Games which make lesser demands on children are those in which there is a runner and a chaser while the remainder of the children have little part in the play.

Each game should be analyzed from the standpoint of whether or not it requires a skill which the children should practice before playing the game. If practice is indicated, the teacher selects the appropriate drills and brings the children up to the point of necessary skill to play the game pleasurably. Drills and the acquisition of necessary skills become more meaningful when the children see their purpose.

The games for preschool through second grade do not require a high degree of skill, and the lesser skilled children have an opportunity to excel. The third grade presents a different picture. While many of the games are of the so-called low-organized type, a number are introduced which represent the first lead-up activities in the program. A lead-up game is defined as one which introduces a skill, strategy or part of a sport. *Circle Kick Ball* is a good example of the principle of a lead-up activity. The children form a circle, and the ball is kicked back and forth until it goes between or through one of the players. The players learn to kick, trap, and defend. The concentration is on these skills.

INTRODUCING VARIATIONS

The introduction of variations is an important instructional device which the games leader can use effectively. You can see the children's faces light up when the instructor says, "Let's try playing the game *this* way," and introduces an interesting variation. Variations can revive interest when it lags and can help the teacher to extract more "mileage" from an activity.

The following are effective devices which can be used to vary activities:

1. Change the distance to be run by shortening or lengthening it.
2. Vary the runner's route. This is particularly helpful in circle games.
3. Change the method of locomotion. Use hopping, walking, skipping, galloping, etc., instead of running.
4. Play the game with partners. Have two children join inside hands and act as a single person.
5. Change the method of tagging. Limit where on the body a player may be tagged or with which hand he may be tagged.
6. Change the formation.
7. Vary the boundaries. Make the formation larger or smaller.
8. Include penalties. A person who is caught a number of times (say, three) has to undergo a penalty.
9. Increase the number of key men, taggers, or runners. This gets the game moving a little faster.
10. Use other helps or hindrances. In *Cat and Rat,* players may raise or lower arms, depending on whether the cat or the rat is coming through.
11. In tag or chase games, call out "Reverse." This means that the chaser now becomes the runner and the runner the chaser. Also, this can be used to change the direction of a ball around a circle.
12. Change the method or means of scoring. Make goals larger or smaller.

SAFETY SUGGESTIONS FOR GAMES

Because of the competitive spirit aroused, games have some built-in hazards which must be anticipated and for which safety considerations need to be established.

Slipping and Falling. Emphasis should be placed on the importance of running properly and practice in turning and changing direction properly. The playing area should be kept free of dangerous objects. The teacher should make certain that all players are aware of hazardous conditions of the playing area, such as slickness, holes, or loose pebbles.

Collisions and Tripping. Stress the need for all players to be alert. Goal games, where the children are divided and begin to run through each other from opposite goals, are collision-prone. If there is more than one chaser or catcher the danger is multiplied. The group should be scattered to avoid collisions. If players are running in opposite directions, they should pass each other to the right. Children should be taught to tag by touching, not shoving, and the teacher should insist that tagging be done properly.

Hitting Each Other with Wands, Beanbags, or Balls. Proper use of supplies should be taught.

Playing Dodgeball Games Safely. Dodgeball games for children provide much enjoyment and competition. Some controls are necessary, however. Glasses should be removed whenever possible. A soft, slightly deflated volleyball or rubber playground ball should be used. Avoid a basketball or heavy ball which may punish the players. Hits should be made below the waist or at least below the shoulders. A penalty should be imposed on any throw that hits a player on the head. Restraining lines, if carefully marked and observed, will prevent the thrower from getting too close to the targets. Good direction will prevent vicious throwing and ganging up on certain individuals. A better game results when teams are balanced and one or two players do not monopolize the throwing.

Maintaining Control. Participants should be coached to stop immediately when the whistle blows. A child may be down or some other safety hazard may need attention. The whistle should be used mainly for stopping the action. Start action with a verbal command.

Spatial Factors. Sufficient room for the games should be established. Colliding with fences and walls during running and chase games is an ever-present danger. Establish boundaries far enough from these and other obstacles to preserve safety. If separate groups of children are playing games, keep them far enough apart so they will not overrun each other.

MAINTAINING BALANCE IN GAMES

Balance between offense and defense or success and failure in games is important. In the tag or capture type game, there should be good opportunity to remain "safe" and still provide a strong challenge of being caught. This means that the teacher should look carefully at the basic rules concerning boundaries and other restraints. The distance to be run to a base, or between goal lines, can be lengthened or shortened as indicated.

Balance in games involving teams is important. The sides should be reasonably equated so that one side does not annihilate the other. If there is no chance of winning, children can hardly be expected to give it a good try. Rotate positions so that one or two very skilled children will not dominate the game. On the other hand, take measures to see that the team does not lose continually because of the presence of a low-skilled or inept child, creating resentment against that child.

INSTRUCTIONAL PROCEDURES FOR CONDUCTING GAMES

1. The principal ingredient of successful games leadership is a vigorous, snappy approach. A hustling attitude combined with a spirit of enthusiasm will do much toward producing the desired results.

2. Know the game well before attempting to teach it. This means identifying the safety hazards, anticipating the difficulties, and adapting the game to the group and the situation.

3. Carry on much of the explanation in the classroom, so the youngsters have maximum activity on the playground.

4. Complete all preparations before starting to introduce the game. Draw lines and boundaries, and have supplies ready for distribution.

5. Put the group in formation with all possible speed. Be careful of too formal methods of organization. Use a modified "close" formation for explanations and then allow the children to fall back to game positions to start the activity.

6. Every unit or group should have a leader or someone in charge. Use these people to secure needed equipment for the game.

7. Where mingling of teams can cause confusion, identify a team with pinnies, crepe armbands, colored shoulder loops, or similar devices.

8. For maximum participation, divide the class into a number of groups as determined by the character of the activity. Many games play best with ten to fifteen players.

9. When explaining the game, talk briefly and to the point. Tell what is to be done and what is to be avoided. Demonstrate or diagram as needed. Students should be comfortable during explanations.

10. To clear up hazy points, ask for questions and then reply so all can hear. If desirable, repeat the question before supplying the answer.

11. Do not attempt to cover all rule infractions prior to participation. Cover enough to get the game underway and fill in with additional rules as needed. Minor faults can be corrected during the course of the game.

12. Sometimes it is well to have a trial period so children can understand the game before playing "for real." Children resent losing a point or getting caught if they feel this is due to their lack of understanding of the game.

13. Enforce the rules impartially once they have been established. Discuss the reasons for the rules with the children.

14. Where lines and limits are important, establish them definitely so that there is no question when a child is out of bounds or beyond the limits. Make clear and enforce the penalty for an infraction.

15. Suggestions for better performance and coaching hints should be a part of the instructional procedures in games. "Lean forward a little for a faster start," or "Give with your knees when you want to stop," are examples of appropriate comments by the teacher.

16. Play with the class occasionally. They like to have the teacher play with them. Do not dominate the play, however.

17. Watch the game carefully for a decrease of interest. Kill or change the game before it dies a natural death. Sometimes the teacher can stop a game even at the height of interest, and children will look forward with anticipation to the activity at a later time.

18. Stress social learning in game experiences. Allow children to call infractions or hits on themselves. Insist on respect for decisions by officials, particularly in judgment calls.

19. Be sure everyone has had a turn whenever this is practicable. Have children identify themselves by raising their hands or by the use of some other device to show that they have not had a turn.

20. Avoid overemphasis on competition. Centering too much attention on winning makes the skilled resent being on the same team with the less skilled.

21. Arrange for full participation. Rotate with a planned system or use the "sideline" players as officials or equipment monitors.

22. Most games can be modified to meet the equipment and supplies available. Some games, however, are best played with the equipment and supplies designed for them.

23. Help and encourage the losing side, but avoid biased officiating to aid the losing side. We want our children to be good losers but not "easy" losers.

24. Watch for fatigue, especially in a chaser who is unable to catch a runner. Make a change with another child as chaser.

25. Be careful of the poor citizenship situation where some child is made the "goat" or butt of jokes. Psychological hurt or trauma may be deep and permanent. The possibility of physical hurt or punishment must not be ruled out. The slow, heavy child, who cannot move readily, is at a disadvantage in dodgeball games and other activities demanding mobility.

26. While games which eliminate children in the course of play have a place in the program, these should be used with caution. Elimination should not be carried down to the "bitter end." It is better to play the game so a minor portion of the children are eliminated and then declare the remainder the winners.

EXPLORATION WITH GAMES

Children should have opportunity to make up or design games of their own origin. The teacher should set the problem by specifying what is available to them in the nature of space, equipment, and number of participants. For example, the space could be designated as a 20' square or two parallel lines 30' apart. The game could be created without any equipment, or the children could be given a ball (any size) with which to work.

The teacher should divide the class into small enough groups so each child is able to make a contribution. If a group is large, there is difficulty in resolving differences of opinion. Unless there is a specific reason, not more than three or four children should be assigned to a group. The groups can also be given different game problems to solve with respect to size of space, the equipment, and other details.

After a period of time, the groups should present the games they have originated. Discussion can be held with regard to value and possible changes that might make the game better. This is an excellent learning experience and prepares children for their own free time play.

THE GAMES PROGRAM FOR PRESCHOOL AND KINDERGARTEN

The games program for the preschool and kindergarten levels features mostly individual and creative play. There is some emphasis on games with cognitive learning goals. Little emphasis is centered on team play or on games which demand a scoring system. The games are simple, easily taught, and not demanding on particular skills. Beanbags are used in some of the activities, but ball games are not particularly appropriate for this level.

Dramatic elements are present in many of the games, while others help establish number concepts and recognition of shapes. Games based on stories and poems are popular with children of this age.

In addition to the games presented in this section, the teacher should make use of first grade games and also those presented in Chapter 12, featuring story games and dramatic play.

Preschool and Kindergarten Games

Blind Man's Buff
Colors
Fireman
Guess the Leader
I'm Very, Very Tall
Kneeling Tag
Magic Fountain
Marching Ponies
Mother, May I?
Popcorn
Scarecrow and the Crows
Shapes
Statues
Tommy Tucker's Land
Who Am I?

BLIND MAN'S BUFF

Playing Area: Playground, gymnasium, classroom.

Players: 8-10.

Supplies: 1 blindfold for each game.

Blind Man's Buff is one of the old, traditional games. One child is blindfolded and stands in the center of a small circle formed by the other children. Another child is chosen to be inside the circle, and the Blind Man tries to catch him. As his quarry dodges him the Blind Man calls out "Where are you?" whereupon the other must respond immediately by making a sound like that of a baby chick, "Cheep, cheep!"

When the Blind Man has caught the other player, he tries to identify him by feeling his face, arms, and clothes. Identification does not affect the outcome of the game, but simply adds to the fun. Two other children are chosen to replace the first two players.

Circles should be kept small, otherwise catching is difficult and protracted. The blindfold should be adequate, as the game is spoiled if the child can see under it.

Variation: The circle children can make a buzzing sound (Z-z-z-z-z-z), which becomes louder as the Blind Man nears his quarry.

COLORS

Playing Area: Playground, gymnasium, classroom.

Players: Entire class.

Supplies: Colored paper or colored construction paper cut into circles, squares, or triangles as markers.

Five or six different colored markers should be used, with a number of children having the same color. The children are seated in a circle. Each places his marker in front of him.

The teacher calls out one of the colors, upon which all having that color run counterclockwise around the circle and back to place. The first one seated upright and motionless is declared the winner. Different kinds of locomotor movements can be specified, such as skipping, galloping, walking, etc.

After a period of play, leave the markers on the floor and have the children move one place to the left.

Variations:

1. Use shapes instead of colors. Use a circle, triangle, square, rectangle, star, diamond.

2. Use numbers.

Note: Many other articles or categories such as animals, birds, fishes, etc., can be used. The game has value in teaching elements of identification and recognition.

FIREMAN

Playing Area: Playground, gymnasium, classroom.

Players: Entire class.

Supplies: None.

A "Fire Chief" is appointed. He runs around the outside of a circle of children and taps a number of them on the back, saying "Fireman" each time. After making his round of the circle the Chief goes to the center. When he says, "Fire," the "Firemen" run counterclockwise around the circle and back to place. The one who returns first and is able to stand in place motionless is declared the winner and the new Chief.

The Chief can use other words in an attempt to fool the Firemen, but they run only on the word, "Fire." This merely provides a fun aspect, as there is no penalty for a false start. To add to the gaiety, the circle children can sound the siren as the Firemen run.

GUESS THE LEADER

Playing Area: Indoors or outdoors.
Players: Entire class.
Supplies: None.

One or two children are designated as guessers and hide their eyes. The remaining children are scattered in the area. The teacher points to one child who is the leader. The object of the game is for the guessers to guess who the leader is.

While the guessers have their eyes hidden, the leader strikes a pose (statue), which is imitated by the children. Now, the guessers turn and try to guess who the leader is. The leader changes the pose, which is again held by all the children. The guessers try to tell who the leader is. The children should attempt not to give away the leader.

The guessers can consult with each other and point to one of the children who they think is the leader. If this is a correct guess, other children are selected to replace the guessers and the leader. If not, two more guesses are allowed, at which time the game is stopped and new children are chosen even if no correct guess appeared.

I'M VERY, VERY TALL

Playing Area: Classroom or gymnasium.
Players: Entire class.
Supplies: None.

One child is in the center and hides his eyes. The remainder of the children form a circle, with one of them designated as leader. The leader directs the action. The action follows the verse which is recited by the children. The leader indicates "tall" or "small" by his actions as the last line is repeated. The child in the center then guesses whether the children are "tall" or "small."

> Sometimes I'm very, very tall,
> Sometimes I'm very, very small,
> Sometimes tall, sometimes small,
> Guess what I am now.

KNEELING TAG

Playing Area: Playground, gymnasium.
Players: Entire class.
Supplies: None.

Two or more children are "It." They attempt to tag the other children, who can be safe by kneeling on one knee. The child tagged changes places with "It."

The teacher should specify which knee is to be used. This should be changed partway through the game. The game can be played progressively with the children tagged joining the taggers, but it cannot be played until all children are tagged because of its safe position feature. Play until about one-half the children are tagged and then reorganize.

Children need to be encouraged to dare a little, as no one will be caught if he kneels all the time. Players kneeling on the wrong knee are not safe.

Variation: Color concepts can be stressed by selecting a color for safety. This is more appropriate for a gymnasium where lines of different colors are already on the floor, but construction paper in different colors can be taped to the floor as safe bases. Markers of this type are not likely to survive long, however.

THE MAGIC FOUNTAIN

Playing Area: Playground, gymnasium, classroom.
Players: Entire class.
Supplies: Pictures of animals, a box, and a stool or table.

A supply of animal pictures (10-15) is placed in a box on a stool or table to one side. This is the magic fountain. The children are seated in a circle on the floor. Four to five children are selected by the teacher; one of them is designated to draw out a picture from the magic fountain. He shows the picture to the rest of his group, but keeps it hidden from the remainder of the children in the circle.

As soon as all the chosen children have seen the picture, they return to the circle area and imitate the animal they saw in the picture. When the circle players guess the animal, the animal imitators return to the circle formation and another group of players is chosen.

Children who wish to guess what animal is being imitated should raise hands for recognition.

MARCHING PONIES

Playing Area: Playground, gymnasium, classroom.

Players: Entire class.

Supplies: None.

One child is the "Ringmaster" and crouches in the center of a circle of "Ponies" formed by the other children. Two goal lines on opposite sides of the circle are established as safe areas. The Ponies march around the circle in step, counting consecutively as they step. At a predetermined number (which has been whispered to the Ringmaster by the teacher) the Ringmaster jumps from his crouched position and attempts to tag the others before they can reach the safety lines. Anyone tagged must join the Ringmaster in the center, helping him catch the next time.

The game should be reorganized after six to eight children have been caught. Those left in the circle are declared the winners.

Variation: Ponies must gallop to the safe area.

MOTHER, MAY I?

Playing Area: Playground, gymnasium.

Players: 8-10.

Supplies: None.

A starting and finishing line are established about 40' apart. In a gymnasium, the game can proceed sideways across the floor. One child is "It" and stands between the two lines. The remainder of the children stand on the starting line. The object of the game is to reach the finish line first.

"It" tells one of the players how many steps he can take and what kind. The player must ask, "Mother, may I?" and await the answer before he moves. If he fails to ask the question, he goes back to the starting line. Even if the question is asked, "It" may say, "No."

The steps should be varied to provide different kinds of movements. Steps such as baby steps, scissors steps, giant steps, hopping steps, bunny steps (jumps), and others are appropriate for the game. The first to the finish line is "It" for the next game.

POPCORN

Playing Area: Playground, gymnasium, classroom.

Players: Entire class, divided into two groups.

Supplies: None.

The children should be given a short preliminary explanation of how popcorn pops in response to the heat applied. One-half the children are designated as "popcorn" and crouch down in the center of the circle formed by the rest of the children. The circle children are indicators of the heat cycle. One of them should be designated the leader, whose actions will serve as a guide to the other children. The circle children, who are also crouched down, gradually rise to a standing position, extend their arms overhead and shake them vigorously to indicate high heat. In the meantime the "popcorn" in the center begins to pop. This should begin at a slow pace and increase in speed and height as the heat is applied. In the final stages the children are popping up rapidly.

Change groups and repeat.

THE SCARECROW AND THE CROWS

Playing Area: Playground, gymnasium, classroom.

Players: Entire class.

Supplies: None.

The children form a large circle to represent the garden, which the Scarecrow is guarding. Six Crows scatter on the outside of the circle. The Scarecrow assumes a characteristic pose inside the circle. The circle children raise their joined hands and let the Crows run through into the garden, where they pretend to eat. The Scarecrow tries to tag one of the Crows, and the circle children help the Crows by raising their joined hands, allowing them to leave the circle, but try to hinder the Scarecrow. If the Scarecrow runs out of the circle, all the Crows immediately run into the garden and start to nibble at the vegetables, while the circle children hinder the Scarecrow's reentry.

When the Scarecrow has caught one or two Crows (the teacher can decide), a new group of children are selected to be Scarecrow and Crows. If after a reasonable period of time the Scarecrow has failed to catch any Crows, a change should be made.

SHAPES

Playing Area: Indoors or outdoors.

Players: Entire class.

Supplies: Two sets of cardboard shapes are needed, one of each shape in the large size (say 18 to 24 inches) and enough of the smaller size (about 12 inches) to supply at least one for each child. The shapes can be triangles, squares, rectangles, ovals, full circles, half circles, diamonds, pentagons, and hexagons. The shapes can be made as a class project.

The large shapes are placed around the outer borders of the playing area and are used only to provide a shape for identification. The smaller shapes are scattered around the playing area. There can be extra small shapes.

On signal, the children hop, jump, run, or leap over as many shapes as they can. On a second signal each child selects a shape near him and stands on it. After each child is standing on a shape, a third signal is given, upon which each child picks up his shape and places it in front of the larger matching shape. The matching is then checked for accuracy.

A second approach is to have the children signal according to the shape on which they are standing. The teacher can say, for example, "Triangles, raise your hands." Or, "All standing on circles, hold up your hands."

STATUES

Playing Area: Playground, gymnasium.

Players: Entire class, organized by pairs.

Supplies: None.

Children are paired off around the area. One child is the swinger and the other the statue. The swinger takes the statue by one or two hands and swings it around in a small circle. The teacher voices a directive such as "pretty," "funny," "happy," "animal" or some other descriptive term. The swingers immediately release the statues and sit down on the floor. The statues take a pose in keeping with the directive. The teacher or a committee of children can determine which children are making the best statues. The object is to hold the position without moving.

After the winners have been determined, the partners reverse positions. Children should be cautioned that the swinging helps to position the statues, but must be controlled.

TOMMY TUCKER'S LAND

Playing Area: Playground, gymnasium, classroom.

Players: 8-10.

Supplies: About 10 beanbags for each game.

One child is "Tommy Tucker" and stands in the center of a 15' square, within which the beanbags are scattered. Tommy is guarding his land and the treasure. The other children chant:

I'm on Tommy Tucker's land
Picking up gold and silver.

The children attempt to pick up as much of the treasure as they can while avoiding being tagged by Tommy. Any child who is tagged must bring back his treasure and retire from the game. The game is over when there is only one child left or all the beanbags have been successfully filched. The teacher may wish to call a halt to the game earlier if it reaches a stalemate. In this case, the child with the most treasure becomes the new Tommy.

Variation: This game can be played with a restraining line, but there must be boundaries to limit movement.

WHO AM I?

Playing Area: Indoors or outdoors. Sufficient room to maneuver.

Players: Entire class.

Supplies: Place markers which can be hoops, individual mats, beanbags, or large pieces of cardboard.

The game stresses important knowledge which the children should have at their fingertips. Markers, which serve as home bases, are scattered around the area — one less than the number of players. The children are challenged to use different locomotor movements to move around the room. At the signal (hand clap or drum beat) each attempts to find a home base. The child left out (without a base) must give his full name. Later, home addresses and telephone numbers can be added. If the class is large, then two "empty" spots should be used. If a child is caught a second time, he exchanges with a child who has not been caught and has not stated his name.

The teacher should have a list of the names, addresses, and telephone numbers to check for accuracy of the answers.

THE GAMES PROGRAM FOR THE FIRST GRADE

The games for the first grade can be divided into two categories: running and tag games, and ball games. Few team activities are included, as at this level children are quite individualistic, and team play is beyond their capacities. The ball games should require only the simple skills of throwing and catching.

First Grade Games

Review Kindergarten Games
Animal Tag
Back-to-Back
Cat and Rat
Charlie Over the Water
Circus Master
Gallop Tag
Midnight
Old Man (Old Lady)
One, Two, Button My Shoe
Squirrel in the Trees
Tag Games — Simple
Where's My Partner?
Ball Passing
Ball Toss
Call Ball
Teacher Ball (Leader Ball)

ANIMAL TAG

Playing Area: Playground, gymnasium. Two parallel lines are drawn about 40' apart.
Players: Entire class.
Supplies: None.

The children are divided into two groups, each of which takes position on one of the lines. The children of Group 1 get together with their leader and decide what animal they wish to imitate. Having selected the animal, they move over to within 5' or so of the other line. Here they imitate the animal and Group 2 tries to guess the animal correctly. If they guess correctly, they chase Group 1 back to its line, trying to tag as many as possible. Those caught must go over to the other team.

Group 2 now selects an animal and the roles are reversed. However, if the guessing team cannot guess the animal, the performing team gets another try.

To avoid confusion, have the children raise hands to take turns naming the animal. Otherwise, there will be many false chases.

If the children have trouble guessing, then have the leader of the performing team give the initial of the animal.

BACK-TO-BACK

Playing Area: Playground, gymnasium, classroom.
Players: Entire class.
Supplies: None.

The number of children should be uneven. If the number is even, the teacher can play. On signal, each child stands back-to-back with another child. One child will be without a partner. This child can clap his hands for the next signal, and all children change partners with the extra player seeking a partner.

Variation: Considerably more activity can be secured by putting in an extra command. After the children are in partner formation back-to-back, the teacher can say, "'Everybody — run!" (or skip, hop, jump, slide, etc.). Other commands can be given, such as, "Walk like an elephant." The children move around the room in the prescribed manner. When the whistle is blown, they immediately find a partner and stand back-to-back.

CAT AND RAT

Playing Area: Gymnasium, playground.
Players: 10 to 20.
Supplies: None.

All children except two form a circle with hands joined. One of the extra players is the "Cat" and the other is the "Rat." The Rat is on the inside of the circle, and the Cat is outside. The following dialogue takes place:

"I am the Cat."
"I am the Rat."
"I can catch the Rat."
"Oh no, you can't."

Whereupon the Cat chases the Rat in and out of the circle. The circle players raise their arms to help the Rat, and lower them again to hinder the Cat. When the Cat catches the Rat or after a period of time if the Rat is not caught, the two children can select two others to take their places.

Variation: Instead of having the children raise and lower their hands to aid or hinder the runners, the teacher can call out, "High windows," or "Low windows." The circle players raise and lower their hands only on these signals.

CHARLIE OVER THE WATER

Playing Area: Playground, gymnasium, classroom.

Players: 15 to 20.

Supplies: None.

The children are in circle formation with hands joined. One or more extra children are in the center, depending on the number of children in the circle. The one in the center is "Charlie." The circle children skip around the circle to the following chant:

Charlie over the water, Charlie over the sea,
Charlie caught a bluebird, but can't catch *me!*

On the word "me" all circle children drop hands, stoop, and touch the ground with both hands. The center players try to tag the circle players before they stoop. Any player tagged changes places with the center player. The game then continues.

Children should be held to retaining their balance while stooping. If they fall, they can be tagged.

The following chant can be used if a girl is in the center:

Sally over the river, Sally over the sea, etc.

Other positions can be stipulated instead of stooping. Balancing on one foot, crab position, push-up position, and others can be used.

CIRCUS MASTER

Playing Area: Playground, gymnasium, classroom.

Players: 10 to 40.

Supplies: None.

One child, the "Circus Master," is in the center of the circle formed by the other children. He stands in the center, pretends he has a whip, and gets ready to have the animals perform. He gives a direction like the following: "We are going to walk as elephants do, like this!" He then demonstrates in a small circle how he wishes the children to perform. He commands, "Elephants ready — WALK." The children imitate an elephant walking around the large circle while the Circus Master performs in a small circle in the center. When ready, the Circus Master calls "Halt." He takes a place in the circle, and another child comes forward to the center.

A prearranged order for Circus Masters can be established; this is excellent for young children, as they can be prepared with a particular animal imitation. However, interest would die long before all the children could be in the center. Make arrangements for other children to be in the center when the game is played at a later date.

GALLOP TAG

Playing Area: Playground, gymnasium.

Players: 12 to 20.

Supplies: None.

Children are in circle formation, facing in. One child walks around the outside and tags another child on the back. Immediately, he gallops around the circle in either direction with the child who was tagged chasing him, also at a gallop. If the player in the lead gets around to the vacated spot before being tagged, he joins the circle. If he is tagged, he must try again with another child.

Variations:

1. The children can run or skip.

2. *Slap Jack.* Have the child tagged run in the *opposite* direction. The child who gets back to the vacant place first gets to keep the place. The other child tags again for another run.

3. *Run for Your Supper.* The children stand with clasped hands. The runner goes in either direction, tags a pair of clasped hands, and says, "Run for your supper." The two children whose hands have been tagged run in opposite directions, with the one getting back first keeping the place. The original runner after tagging the clasped hands merely steps into the circle, leaving only one space for which the two runners compete. Having the two runners, when they meet on the opposite side of the circle, bow to each other or shake hands before continuing the run back to place makes the game more enjoyable.

4. *Duck, Duck, Goose.* All children are seated cross-legged. The runner goes in either direction around the circle, tapping each child *lightly* on the head. As he does this he says, "Duck." When he wishes, he changes the word to "Goose," and that child then arises quickly and chases him around the circle back to the vacant place. If the runner gets back safely, the chaser is the new runner. If the runner is tagged, then he must take another try as runner.

Cautions: These types of games should be played as resting activities and as such have a place in the curriculum. They are fun, but are low in developmental values. Also, there must be rapid action to keep things moving. Make a rule that the runners may travel only partway around a circle before choosing a chaser.

MIDNIGHT

Playing Area: Playground.

Players: 6 to 15.

Supplies: None.

A safety line is established about 40' from a den in which one player is standing as the "Fox." The others stand behind the safety line and move forward slowly, asking, "Mr. Fox, what time is it?" The Fox answers in various fashions such as "Bed time," "Pretty late," "Three-thirty," and so on. He continues to draw the players toward him. At some point, he answers the question of time with "Midnight," and chases the others back to the safety line. Any player caught joins the Fox in his den and helps him catch others. However, no player in the den can leave until the Fox calls out "Midnight."

OLD MAN (OLD LADY)

Playing Area: Playground, gymnasium, classroom.

Players: Entire class.

Supplies: None.

A line is drawn through the middle of the area. Any convenient line can be used. Half the children are on one side and half on the other. The children hold hands with a partner across the center line. There must be an odd person, the teacher or another child. The teacher gives a signal for the children to move as directed on their side of the line. They can be directed to run, hop, skip, etc. At a whistle, the children run to the center line, and each reaches across to join hands with a child from the opposite group. The one left out is the "Old Man" (if a boy) or the "Old Lady" (if a girl). Children may reach over, but not cross the line. The odd person should alternate sides so that the Old Man can be on the other side at times.

The game can also be done to music with the players rushing to the center line to find partners when the rhythm stops.

ONE, TWO, BUTTON MY SHOE

Playground Area: Playground, gymnasium. Two parallel lines are drawn about 50' apart.

Players: Entire class.

Supplies: None.

One child is the leader and stands to one side. The remainder of the children are behind one of the lines. The leader says "Ready." The following dialogue takes place between the leader and the children:

Children	**Leader's Response**
One, two	Button my shoe
Three, four	Close the door
Five, six	Pick up sticks
Seven, eight	Run, or you'll be *late!*

The children carry on the above conversation with the leader and are toeing the line ready to run. When the word "late" is given by the leader, the children run to the other line and return. The first child across the original line is the winner and becomes the new leader.

The leader can give the last response in

any timing he wishes by pausing or dragging out the words. No child is to leave before the "late."

A variation is to have the children pantomime the leader's directions.

SQUIRREL IN THE TREES

Playing Area: Playground, gymnasium.
Players: 15 to 35.
Supplies: None.

A tree is formed by two players facing each other with hands held or on each other's shoulders. A "Squirrel" is in the center of each tree, and one or two extra Squirrels are outside. A signal to change is given. All Squirrels move out of their trees to another, and the extra players try to find trees. Only one Squirrel is allowed in a tree.

To form a system of rotation, as each Squirrel moves into a tree, he changes places with one of the two players forming the tree.

TAG GAMES — Simple

Playing Area: Playground with established boundaries, gymnasium.
Players: Any number.
Supplies: None.

Tag is played in many different ways. Children are scattered about the area. One child is "It" and chases others to tag one of them. When he does, he says, "You're IT." The new "It" chases other children. Different tag games are listed:

1. Being safe through touching a specified object or color. Touching wood, iron, the floor, or a specified color can make a runner safe.

2. Seeking safety by a particular action or pose. Some actions used to become safe are:
   Stoop — touch both hands to the ground.
   Stork — stand on one foot (the other cannot touch).
   Turtle — be on one's back, feet pointed toward the ceiling.
   Hindoo — make an obeisance with forehead to the ground.
   Nose and toe — nose must be touched by the toe.
   Back to back — stand back-to-back with any other child.

3. *Locomotor Tag* — "It" specifies how the children shall move. "It" also must use the same kind of movement, i.e., skip, hop, jump, etc.

4. *Frozen Tag* — two children are "It." The rest are scattered over the area. When caught they are "frozen" and must keep both feet in place. Any free player can tag a "frozen" player and release him. The object of the taggers is to freeze all the players.

WHERE'S MY PARTNER?

Playing Area: Playground, gymnasium, classroom.
Players: Entire class.
Supplies: None.

Children are arranged in a double circle by couples, with partners facing. The inside circle has one more player than the outside. When the signal is given, the circles skip to the right. This means that they are skipping in opposite directions. When the command "Halt" is given, the circles face each other to find partners. The player left without a partner is in the "Mush Pot."

Children can gallop, walk, run, or hop instead of skipping. Reverse circles.

Variation: The game can also be played with music. When the music stops, the players seek partners.

BALL PASSING

Playing Area: Playground, gymnasium, classroom.
Players: Entire class, divided into two or more circles.
Supplies: 5 to 6 different kinds of balls for each circle.

The basis of this game is the child's love of handling objects. Not over 15 children should be in any one circle. Two or more teams combine to form a circle. The children need not be in any particular order.

The teacher starts a ball around the circle; the ball is passed from player to player in the same direction. The teacher introduces more balls until five or six are moving around in the circle at the same time in the same direction. If a child drops a ball, he must retrieve it, and a point is scored against his team. After a period of time, a whistle is blown, and the points against each team are totaled. The team with the lowest score wins.

In the absence of sufficient balls for passing, bean bags, large blocks, or softballs can be substituted.

BALL TOSS

Playing Area: Playground, gymnasium, classroom.

Players: Groups of 6 to 8.

Supplies: A ball or beanbag for each group.

The children form a circle with one in the center. The center player throws the ball to each child in turn around the circle. The ball is returned to the center player each time. The object of the game is to make good throws and catches completely around the circle. After each child has had a turn in the center, the teacher can ask each circle to total the number of center players that were able to complete their throws without any errors.

Good form should be stressed.

CALL BALL

Playing Area: Playground, gymnasium, classroom.

Players: 6 to 8 in each circle.

Supplies: A large playground ball or volleyball.

The children form a circle with one in the center. The center child has a ball. He throws the ball into the air, at the same time calling out the name of one of the circle children. This child runs forward and tries to catch the ball *before* it bounces. If successful, he becomes the center player. If not, the center player throws again. If there are many in the circle, the game moves quite slowly for the children. Other versions are:

1. Give the children numbers with more than one child having the same number. This makes the catching competitive.

2. Use colors or animals with more than one child assigned to the same color or animal.

3. Move the children back and have them catch the ball on first bounce.

4. *Catch the Cane.* Instead of tossing a ball into the air, balance a wand on one end of the floor. The child whose number is called tries to catch the cane before it hits the ground. A little experimentation will determine how far back the circle should be from the cane.

TEACHER BALL (Leader Ball)

Playing Area: Playground, gymnasium.

Players: 6 to 8.

Supplies: Volleyball or rubber playground ball.

One child is the "Teacher" or leader and stands about 10' in front of the others who are lined up facing him. The object of the game is to move up to the Teacher's spot by not making any bad throws or missing catches.

The Teacher throws to each child in turn, beginning with the child on his left, who must catch and return the ball to him. Any child making a throwing or catching error goes to the foot of the line, on the Teacher's right. Those in the line move up, filling the vacated space.

If the Teacher makes a mistake, he goes to the foot of the line, and the child at the head of the line becomes the new Teacher.

The Teacher scores a point for himself if he remains in position for three rounds (3 throws to each child). He takes his position at the foot of the line, and another child becomes the Teacher.

This game should be used only after the children have practiced throwing and catching skills. It can be worked in as a part of the skill teaching program.

Variation: Provide specific methods of throwing and catching like, "Catch with the right hand only" or "Catch with one hand; don't let the ball touch your body."

THE GAMES PROGRAM FOR THE SECOND GRADE

The games program is quite similar to that of the first grade. The second grade teacher should make use of all games presented in the first grade. Particularly, the simple ball games of the first grade have good values and should be included as a regular part of the second grade program.

Second Grade Games
Review First Grade Games
Animal Chase
Automobiles

Caged Lion
Cat and Mice
Charlie Over the Water — Ball Version
Flowers and Wind
Forest Ranger
Hill Dill
Hot Potatoes
Hound and Rabbit
Hunter
I Can Do What You Can!
In the Creek
Last Couple Out
Leap the Brook
May I Chase You?
Mouse Trap
Red Light
Stop and Start
Two Deep
Circle Straddle Ball
Exchange Dodgeball
Roll Dodgeball
Straddle Bowling

ANIMAL CHASE

Playing Area: Playground. Two goals are marked out 50′ apart. Halfway between the lines and off to one side, a square represents the zoo.

Players: Entire class.

Supplies: None.

One child is the animal hunter and stands in the center of the area. All children are stationed on one of the two goal lines. Each player is secretly given the name of an animal, several players having the same animal designation.

The hunter calls out the name of an animal. If no one has this name, he continues different names until he hits upon one that a player has. The players run to the opposite goal line and return. As soon as the runners start, the hunter must return to his zoo (to get his gun), return to the center area, and try to tag a runner. Generally, the runners can get to the other goal line without difficulty. On the return trip, they must dodge the hunter to return to the other animals.

Any animals caught are taken to the zoo and sit until all have run. If there are quite a number of children playing the game, the number of times the hunter can chase before getting a replacement may be limited.

AUTOMOBILES

Playing Area: Playground, gymnasium.

Players: Entire class.

Supplies: Each child has a "steering wheel."

Each child is to be a driver of an automobile and needs a "steering wheel." This can be a hoop, deck tennis ring, or something the child has made out of cardboard. The teacher has three flash cards, colored red, green, and yellow respectively. These are the traffic control colors.

The children drive around the area, steering various paths, responding as the teacher raises the cards aloft one at a time. The children follow the traffic directions: red — stop, green — go, and yellow — caution.

An ambulance station and a fire station can be established with appropriate "cars." When one of these comes forward with the characteristic siren noise (made by the driver), all other "cars" pull over to the side of the road and wait until the ambulance or fire engine has gone by.

Teaching Suggestion: Have the children use the proper hand signals for making turns, slowing down, and stopping.

CAGED LION

Playing Area: Classroom or gymnasium. A ten-foot square is drawn.

Players: 10 to 20.

Supplies: None.

One child is selected to be the "Lion" and takes a position on his hands and knees inside the ten-foot square. Other players tantalize the Lion by standing in the cage area or running through it. The Lion tries to tag any of the children. Any child who is tagged by the Lion trades places with him.

Variation: *The King's Land.* The forbidden area, consisting of a twenty-foot square, is known as the King's Land. A warden is appointed who tries to catch (tag) anyone who is on the King's Land. If successful, he is released, and the tagged player becomes the new warden.

CAT AND MICE

Playing Area: Playground, gymnasium, classroom.

Players: 10 to 30.

Supplies: None.

The children form a large circle. One child is chosen to be the Cat and three others are the Mice. The Mice cannot leave the circle. On signal, the Cat chases the Mice inside the circle. As they are caught, they join the circle. The last Mouse caught becomes the Cat for the next round. The teacher should start at one point in the circle and go round the circle selecting Mice so that each child gets a chance to be in the center.

CHARLIE OVER THE WATER
— Ball Version

Playing Area: Playground, gymnasium.

Players: 8 to 12.

Supplies: 1 volleyball or playground ball.

The children are in circle formation with hands joined. One child, "Charlie," is in the center of the circle holding a ball in his hands. The children skip around the circle to the following chant:

  Charlie over the water,
    Charlie over the sea,
  Charlie caught a bluebird,
    but can't catch ME!

On the word "me" the children drop hands and scatter. On the same signal, Charlie tosses the ball into the air. He then catches it and shouts, "Stop!" All children stop immediately and must not move their feet. Charlie rolls the ball in an attempt to hit one of the children. If he hits a child, that child becomes "Charlie," and if Charlie misses, he must remain as "Charlie," and the game is repeated. However, if he misses twice, he should pick another child.

If a girl is in the center, the chant should go: Sally over the water, Sally over the sea, etc.

FLOWERS AND WIND

Playing Area: Two parallel lines are drawn long enough to accommodate the children. The lines are about 30' apart.

Players: 10 to 30.

Supplies: None.

The children are divided into two equal groups, one is the "Wind" and the other the "Flowers." Each of the teams takes a position on one of the lines facing the other. The Flowers secretly select the name of a common flower. When ready, they walk over to the other line and stand about 3' away from the Wind. The players on the Wind begin to call out, trying to guess the flower chosen. When the chosen flower has been guessed, the Flowers take off and run to their goal line, chased by the players of the other team.

Any player caught must join the other side. The roles are reversed, and the other team chooses a flower.

If one side has trouble guessing, then give the first letter, the color, or the size of the flower.

FOREST RANGER

Playing Area: Playground, gymnasium, classroom.

Players: Entire class.

Supplies: None.

One-half of the children form a circle facing in. These are the trees. The other half of the children are the "Forest Rangers" and stand behind the trees. An extra child, the "Forest Lookout," is in the center. The Forest Lookout starts the game with the command, "Fire in the forest, *Run, run, run!*" Immediately, the Forest Rangers run around the outside of the circle to the right (counterclockwise). After a few moments, the Lookout steps in *front* of one of the trees. This is the signal for each of the Rangers to step in *front* of a tree. One player is left out, and he now becomes the new Forest Lookout. The trees become Rangers and vice versa. Each time the game is played, the circle must be moved out somewhat, as the formation narrows when the Rangers step in front of the trees.

HILL DILL

Playing Area: Playground. Two parallel lines are drawn about 50' apart.

Players: 10 to 50.

Supplies: None.

One player is chosen to be "It" and stands

in the center. The other children stand on one of the parallel lines. The center player calls, "Hill Dill! Come over the hill!" The children run across the open space to the other line while the one in the center tries to tag them. Anyone caught helps "It" in the center. The last man caught is in the center for the next game.

Once the children cross over to the other line they must await the next call.

HOT POTATOES

Playing Area: Gymnasium, playground, or classroom.

Players: 8-12 in each group.

Supplies: 6 balls, 6 beanbags.

Children are seated in a small circle close enough together so that objects can be handed from one to another around the circle. Balls and/or beanbags are passed around the circle, a few being introduced at a time. The object of the game is to pass the balls or beanbags rapidly so no one gets "stuck" with more than one object at a time. If he does, the game is stopped, and he moves back and waits. After three are out of the circle, the game starts over.

Start the game with two or three objects and gradually add objects until someone has more than one at a time.

Variation: Reverse the direction of passing on signal.

HOUND AND RABBIT

Playing Area: Playground, gymnasium.

Players: 15 to 30.

Supplies: None.

Players are scattered around the area in groups of three. Two of the three make a tree by facing each other and putting hands on each other's shoulders. The third child, who takes the part of a rabbit, stands between them. An extra "Rabbit" is outside and is chased by a "Hound." The Hound chases the odd Rabbit, who takes refuge in any tree. No tree may hold more than one rabbit, so the other child must leave and look for another tree. When the Hound catches the Rabbit, they exchange places and the game continues.

A rotation system should be used whenever a Rabbit enters a tree. The three in any one group should rotate so that the entering Rabbit becomes a part of the tree, and one of the children making up the tree becomes the Rabbit.

THE HUNTER

Playing Area: Playground, gymnasium, classroom.

Players: Entire class.

Supplies: Individual markers are needed for the children. In the classroom, the seats can be used for home.

A leader, the "Hunter," walks around the room in any manner he wishes. He begins the game with the question, "Who wants to hunt ducks (bears, lions, rabbits)?" The players volunteering fall in line behind him and start on the hunt. The Hunter can go through various creeping and hunting motions. When he is ready, he shouts, "Bang!" All run for a marker or a seat, including the Hunter. The first one back to a marker or seat is chosen as leader for the next game.

To make the game interesting, the leader should take quite a few children on the hunt. Be sure that all get a chance to hunt.

Variation: A novel method of making leader changes is to have one place (seat or marker) designated as the leader for the next time. This is chosen only after the Hunter takes the occupant out. The teacher can make this selection, the location of which is unknown to the runners.

I CAN DO WHAT YOU CAN!

Playing Area: Playground, gymnasium, classroom.

Players: Not more than 6 or 7 in a group. Any number of groups can play.

Supplies: Usually none. The game can be played with each child using the same piece of equipment, such as a ball, wand, beanbag, etc.

This is primarily a "follow-the-leader" type of game. Each group works independently of the others. Each group forms a semicircle with the leader in front. The leader starts any type of activity he wishes, and the other children attempt to make the same moves along with him. After a brief period, the teacher blows the whistle, and another leader takes his place in front of the group.

This works well with selected pieces of hand apparatus, provided each child in the group has the same type of equipment. Tossing, throwing, catching, bouncing, wand stunts, and beanbag tricks are some activities which are easily adapted to the game. Caution children not to demand outlandish or silly performances from the group.

IN THE CREEK

Playing Area: Playground, gymnasium, classroom.

Players: Entire class.

Supplies: None.

A creek is formed by drawing two parallel lines 2′ to 3′ apart, depending upon the ability of the children. The lines should be long enough to accommodate the children comfortably with enough room for each to jump. If necessary, two or three sets of lines can be drawn.

The children line up on one of the banks, all facing the creek and facing the same direction. The object of the game is to make the children commit an error in the jumping.

The teacher or leader gives one of two directions:

"In the creek."
"On the bank."

Children now on the bank jump into the creek or over to the other bank depending upon the command. When they jump on the bank, they immediately turn around and get ready for the next command.

If children are in the creek and the command "In the creek" is repeated, they must not move.

Errors are committed when a child steps on a line, makes a wrong jump, or moves when he should remain still.

Children who make a mistake can be sent down to another game or eliminated. The first is the better suggestion, as this keeps them in activity.

After a period of time, the original directions may not challenge the children. Different combinations can be set up. "In the creek" means to jump and land with both feet. "On the bank" one way would be a leap. "On the bank" the other way would be a hop. Also, false commands can be given, such as "In the ocean," or "In the lake." No one is to move on these commands under penalty of elimination.

It is a good plan to keep things moving fast with crisp commands. Children should be charged with judging their own errors.

LAST COUPLE OUT

Playing Area: Playground, gymnasium.

Players: 10 to 15.

Supplies: None.

Players are lined up by couples in a column formation with an "It" standing at the head of the column. He has his back to the column. He calls, "Last couple out!" The object of the game is to have the last couple separate and rejoin beyond the place where "It" is standing without being tagged by him. If "It" tags either of the two, that person becomes "It." The old "It" joins the remaining player as his partner, and the pair go to the head of the line.

If the couple is able to join hands without being tagged, they take places at the head of the column, and "It" takes a try at the next couple.

"It" is not permitted to look back and cannot start his chase until the separated couple comes up even with him on both sides.

Variation: The game can be played by partners who have inside hands joined.

LEAP THE BROOK

Playing Area: Gymnasium or other flat surface.

Players: Entire class.

Supplies: None.

A brook is marked off on the floor for a distance of about 30′. For the first 10′ it is 3′ wide, for the second 10′ 4′ wide, and for the last 10′ the width becomes 5′.

The children form a single file and jump over the narrowest part of the brook. They should be encouraged to do this several times, using different styles of jumping and leaping.

Stress landing as lightly as possible on the balls of the feet in a bent-knee position.

After they have satisfactorily negotiated the narrow part, the children move up to the next width, and so on.

Teachers should remember that fitness values are only in repeated effort. Good form should be stressed throughout the game.

The selection of the distances is arbitrary, and they may be changed if they seem unsuitable for any particular group of children.

Variation: Use different means of crossing the brook — leaping, jumping, hopping. Also, specify the kinds of turns to be made — right or left; quarter, half, three-quarter or full turns. Have the children use different body shapes, arm positions, etc.

MAY I CHASE YOU?

Playing Area: Playground.
Players: 10 to 30.
Supplies: None.

The class stands behind a line long enough to accommodate all. The runner stands about 5' in front of the line. One child in the line asks, "May I chase you?" The runner replies, "Yes, if you are wearing - - -." He can name a color, an article of clothing, or a combination of the two. All who qualify immediately chase the runner until one tags him. This person becomes "It."

The children will think of other ways to identify those who may run.

MOUSE TRAP

Playing Area: Playground, gymnasium, classroom.
Players: 20 to 40.
Supplies: None.

Half of the children form a circle with hands joined, facing the center. The other children are on the outside of the circle. Three signals are given for the game. These can be given by word cues, or whistle.

The circle players represent the mouse trap, and the outer players are the mice.

Signal 1. The "Mice" skip around the circle, playing happily.

Signal 2. The trap is opened, that is, the circle players raise their joined hands to form arches. The Mice run in and out of the trap.

Signal 3. The trap snaps shut (the arms come down). All Mice caught join the circle.

The game is repeated until all or most of the Mice are caught. The players exchange places, and the game begins anew. Do not allow the children to run in and out using adjacent openings.

RED LIGHT

Playing Area: An area 60' to 100' across with goal toward which the players move.
Players: Entire class.
Supplies: None.

The object of the game is to be able to move across the area successfully without getting caught. One player is the leader and stands on the goal line. He counts very rapidly from one to ten while he has his back to the players. He quickly adds the words "Red Light" to the counting and turns around. In the meantime, the players have been moving across the area during the counting and must freeze on the words "Red Light." Any player caught moving after "Red Light" must return to the starting position. The first player across the area wins and is the leader for the next game.

After the leader has sent back all who were caught, he turns his back again to begin his count. The players may move when his back is turned. However, he may turn around quickly and catch any movement. Once he starts his counting he cannot turn around until he has called "Red Light."

Variations:

1. Instead of counting, the leader (with his back turned) can clap his hands five times, turning around to catch movement on the fifth clap.

2. Another excellent variation of the game is to have the leader face the oncoming players. He calls out "Green Light" for them to move and "Red Light" for them to stop. He can call other colors and the players should not move.

3. Different types of locomotion can be worked in. The leader names the type of movement (i.e., hop, crawl, etc.) before turning his back to the group.

STOP AND START

Playing Area: Playground.
Players: Any number can play.
Supplies: None.

The children are in the center of the playground, scattered enough so each has room to maneuver. The teacher or leader stands a little to one side and gives directions. He points in a direction and calls "Gallop." Any other locomotor movement can be used. Suddenly, he calls "Stop." All children must stop immediately without further movement. Anyone moving can be sent over to the side to another group.

TWO DEEP

Playing Area: Playground, gymnasium.
Players: 15 to 20.
Supplies: None.

All children except two form a circle standing about fingertip distance apart and facing the center. A runner and chaser stand on the outside. The chaser tries to catch the runner, who can save himself by stopping in front of any player. This player now becomes the runner and must avoid being caught. When the chaser tags the runner, the positions change immediately, and the runner becomes the chaser.

Encourage the children to make changes often. If there seems to be too much running, make a rule that a child may travel only halfway around the circle before he must make a change.

Since this game is a lead-up to *Three Deep*, it should be learned reasonably well.

CIRCLE STRADDLE BALL

Playing Area: Playground, gymnasium, classroom.
Players: 10 to 15.
Supplies: 2 volleyballs or rubber playground balls.

Children are in circle formation, facing in. Each stands in wide straddle step with the side of his foot against the neighbor's. The hands are on the knees.

Two balls are used. The object of the game is to throw one of the balls between the legs of any player before he can get his hands down and stop it. Each time the ball goes between the legs of an individual, a point is scored against him. The players having the least points against them are the winners.

Be sure the children catch and roll the ball rather than bat it. Children must keep their hands on their knees until a ball is thrown at them.

After practice, the following variations should be played.

Variation: One child is in the center with a ball and is "It." The other children are in the same formation as above. One ball is used. The center player tries to roll the ball through the legs of any child he chooses. He should mask his intent, using feints and changes of direction. Any child allowing the ball to go through his legs becomes "It." All players start with hands on knees until the ball is thrown.

EXCHANGE DODGEBALL

Playing Area: Playground, gymnasium.
Players: 12 to 20.
Supplies: Volleyball or rubber playground ball.

Children form a circle with one child, "It," in the center. The children are numbered off by fours or fives in such a way that there are three or four children who have the same number. The center player also has a number which he uses when he is not "It."

The center player has a ball which he places at his feet. He calls a number, picks up the ball, and tries to hit one of the children who are exchanging places. When a number is called, all children with that number exchange places. The center player remains "It" until he can hit one of the children below the waist.

Variation: Use animal names instead of numbers.

ROLL DODGEBALL

Playing Area: Playground, gymnasium.
Players: 20 to 30, divided into two teams.
Supplies: 2 volleyballs or rubber playground balls.

Half of the children form a circle and the other half are in the center. Two balls are given to the circle players. The circle players roll the balls at the feet and shoes of the center players, trying to hit them. The center players move around to dodge the balls. When a center player is hit, he leaves the circle.

After a period of time or when all the children have been hit, the teams trade places. If a specified time limit is used, the team having the fewest hits wins. Or, the team which puts out all the opponents in the shortest space of time wins.

Variation: Center players are down on hands and feet. Only one ball is used, otherwise the game is the same. Do not play too long in this position as this is quite strenuous.

Teaching Suggestion: Be sure to have practice in rolling a ball first. Balls which stop in the center are "dead" and must be taken back to the circle before being put into play. It is best to have the player who recovers a ball roll it to one of his teammates rather than to have him return to his place with the ball.

STRADDLE BOWLING

Playing Area: Playground, gymnasium.
Players: 4 to 6.
Supplies: Volleyball or rubber playground ball.

Children may compete within a group, or teams can compete against each other. One child is the bowling target and stands in straddle position with his feet wide enough apart so the ball can pass through easily. Another child is the ball chaser and stands behind him.

A foul line is drawn 15′ to 25′ away from the target, depending upon the ability of the children. The bowlers line up behind this line for turns.

Children can be given one chance or a number of tries. To score a point, the ball must go between the legs of the target. When the children on the throwing line have bowled, two of them relieve the target and chaser.

Variations:

1. Scoring can be changed to allow 2 points if the ball goes through the legs and 1 point if it hits a leg.

2. Other targets can be used. A box lying on its side with the opening pointed toward the bowler forms a good target. Two or three Indian clubs at each station make excellent targets. Scoring could be varied to suit the target.

3. *Bowling One Step.* For groups of squad size or smaller, each of the players in turn gets a chance to roll at an Indian club or bowling pin. A minimum distance is set up, short enough so most bowlers can hit the pin (10′ to 15′). The player keeps rolling until he misses. The object is to take a step backward each time the pin is knocked down. The winner is the one who has moved the farthest back.

Children should be cautioned that accuracy, not speed, is the goal. Also, the players should experiment with different spin effects to curve the ball.

THE GAMES PROGRAM FOR THE THIRD GRADE

Compared with the first two grades, the games program undergoes a definite change in the third grade. The chase and tag games become more complex and demand more maneuvering. Introductory lead-up games make an appearance. The interests of the children are turning toward games which have a sports slant. Kicking, throwing, catching, batting, and other sports skills are beginning to mature. Outside sports influences like the Little League program add force to the sports interests.

Third Grade Games
Review Second Grade Games
Bronco Tag
Busy Bee
Couple Tag
Cross Over
Crows and Cranes
Eagle and the Sparrows
Flying Dutchman
Fly Trap
Follow Me
Frog in the Sea
Galloping Lizzie
Jump the Shot
Poison Circle
Right Face, Left Face (Maze Tag)
Steal the Treasure

Three Deep
Through the Tunnel Race
Triple Change
Weathervane
Balance Dodgeball
Bat Ball
Beanbag Target Toss
Bounce Ball
Circle Team Dodgeball
Club Guard
Competitive Circle Contests
Newcomb
One Step
Toss Target Ball
Circle Kick Ball* (page 298)
End Ball* (page 296)

*These are lead-up games and descriptions are found on the pages indicated, among the sports outlines.

BRONCO TAG

Playing Area: Playground, gymnasium.

Players: 15 to 30.

Supplies: None.

One child is a runner and another the chaser. The remainder of the children are divided into groups of three. Each group of three forms a bronco by standing one behind the other with the last two grasping the waist of the player in front. The front player is the head, and the player on the end is the tail. The runner tries to hook on to the tail of any bronco. The head of that bronco now becomes the runner.

The chaser pursues the runner who tries to avoid being caught by hooking to a bronco. The chaser now has to pursue the new runner. If tagged, the roles are reversed, and the runner becomes the chaser.

The game is more interesting if the children change places rapidly.

BUSY BEE

Playing Area: Playground, gymnasium, classroom.

Players: Entire class.

Supplies: None.

Half the children form a large circle facing in and are designated as the stationary players. The other children seek partners from this group, and each stands in front of one of the stationary players. An extra child is in the center and is the "Busy Bee."

The Busy Bee calls out directions which are followed by the children:
"Back to back."
"Face to face."
"Shake hands."
"Kneel on one knee," (or both).
"Hop on one foot."

The center child then calls out "Busy Bee." Stationary players stand still, and all inner circle players seek another partner while the center player also tries to get a partner. The child without a partner becomes the Busy Bee.

Children should be thinking of the different movements they might have the class do if they should become the Busy Bee. In changing partners, children should be required to select a partner other than the stationary player next to them.

After a period of time, rotate the active and stationary players. Also, vary by using different methods of locomotion.

Variations:

1. Select a definite number of changes — ten for example. All children who have not repeated any partner during the ten exchanges and who have not been "caught" as the Busy Bee are declared the winners.

2. Instead of having the children stand back-to-back, have them lock elbows and sit down as in the *Chinese Get-up.* After they sit down and are declared "safe," they can get up and the game proceeds as described above.

COUPLE TAG

Playing Area: Playground, gymnasium. Two goal lines are established about 50' apart.

Players: Any number.

Supplies: None.

Children run by pairs with inside hands joined. All pairs, except one, line up on one of the goal lines. A pair is in the center and is "It."

The pair in the center calls, "Come," and the children run to the other goal line, keeping hands joined. The pair in the center tries to tag any pair using *only* the joined hands.

As soon as a couple is caught, it helps the center couple. The game continues until all are caught. The last couple caught is "It" for the next game.

CROSS OVER

Playing Area: Playground with two parallel goal lines about 40' apart.

Players: 15 to 20.

Supplies: None.

Divide the players in two groups; each group stands on one of the goal lines. A catcher is in the center between the two lines. He faces one of the lines and calls out the name of one of the players. This player immediately calls out the name of a player in the other line. These two players try to change goal lines while the catcher tries to tag one of them. Any player tagged becomes the catcher for the next call.

If there are more than twenty children, it is best to divide the group into two games. Since only two children run at a time, the game can drag with a large group as chances to run will not occur frequently. Watch out for favoritism among the children.

Variation: With a larger group, this game can be played by partners. In calling out names, it would be necessary to call only one of the partners. Tagging would be done by the free hands with the inside hands kept joined. No tagging would count if the catchers separated, and a pair running across the area would be counted as caught if they were unable to keep together.

CROWS AND CRANES

Playing Area: Playground, gymnasium. Two goals are drawn about 50' apart.

Players: Any number.

Supplies: None.

Children are divided into two groups, the "Crows" and the "Cranes." The groups face each other at the center of the area about 5' apart. The leader calls out either "Crows" or "Cranes" using a "Kr-r-r-r-r" sound at the start of either word to mask the result.

If "Crows" is the call, the Crows chase the Cranes to the goal. If "Cranes" is given, then the Cranes chase. Any child caught goes over to the other side. The team which has the most players when the game ends is the winner.

Variations:

1. Have the children stand back-to-back in the center about a foot apart.

2. The game can be played with the two sides designated as "Black" and "White." A piece of plywood painted black on one side and white on the other can be thrown into the air between the teams instead of having anyone give calls. If black comes up, the black team choses, and vice versa.

3. The game can also be played as "Blue, Black, and Baloney." On the commands "Blue" and "Black," the game proceeds as described above. On the command "Baloney" no one is to move. The caller should be sure to sound the "Bl-l-l-l" before ending with one of the three commands.

4. Another variation of the game is to have a leader tell a story using as many words beginning with "cr" as possible. The players run only when the words "Crows" or "Cranes" are spoken. Words which can be incorporated into a story are crazy, crunch, crust, crown, crude, crowd, crouch, cross, croak, critter, etc. Each time one of these words is spoken the beginning of the word is lengthened with the cr-r-r-r sound. No one may move on any of the words except Crows or Cranes.

EAGLE AND THE SPARROWS

Playing Area: Playground with two parallel lines drawn about 50' apart. A circle representing the eagle's nest is drawn in the center.

Players: Entire class.

Supplies: None.

One player is the "Eagle" and is down on one knee in his nest. The other players circle around him flying like sparrows, until the Eagle suddenly gets up and chases the "Sparrows" to either line. Any Sparrow caught joins the Eagle and helps him catch others. However, no center player can chase until the Eagle starts first.

If the group is large, begin with two or three Eagles in the center.

Variation: All Sparrows must take three hops before they can start running.

FLYING DUTCHMAN

Playing Area: Playground or gymnasium.
Players: 20 to 30.
Supplies: None.

The children are in a circle with hands joined. Two children with hands joined are the runners. The runners go around the outside of the circle and tag a pair of joined hands. Immediately, the runners continue around the circle while the tagged pair runs around in the other direction. The first pair back to the vacated spot gets to keep the spot, and the other pair becomes the runners. Be sure to establish rules for passing when the couples go by each other on the way around. Couples should keep to the right in passing.

Variations:

1. The runners reverse their direction immediately when tagging.

2. The game can be played by groups of threes instead of couples. The tag is made on the back of any one person, who with the persons on each side of him makes it a group of three. Groups should keep hands clasped or be disqualified.

FLY TRAP

Playing Area: Playground, gymnasium.
Players: Entire class.
Supplies: None.

One-half the class is scattered around the playing area sitting on the floor in tailor (cross-legged) fashion. These children form the trap. The other children are the "Flies" and buzz in and around the seated children. When a whistle is blown, the Flies must freeze at the spot. If any of the trappers can reach the Flies, that fly is seated at his location and becomes a trapper.

The game continues until all the Flies have been caught. Some realism is given to the game if the Flies make buzzing sounds and move with their arms out as wings.

A little experience with the game will enable the teacher to determine how far apart to place the seated children. In tagging, the children must keep their seats on the ground.

After all the Flies have been caught, the children trade places.

Change the method of locomotion occasionally.

FOLLOW ME

Playing Area: Playground, gymnasium.
Players: 8 to 30.
Supplies: A marker for each child. Squares of cardboard or plywood can be used.

Children are arranged roughly in a circle, each standing or sitting with one foot on his marker. An extra player is the "Guide." He moves about the circle pointing at different players and asking them to "follow me." Each player as chosen falls in behind the Guide. The Guide now takes his group on a tour with the members of the group performing just as the Guide does. The Guide may hop, skip, do stunts, or perform other movements and the children following him must do likewise. At the signal "Home" all run for places at the markers. One child will be without a marker. This child chooses another Guide.

It is not a good idea to make the last child the new leader, as this will cause some children to lag and try to be last. In our version, he gets to choose a new leader. One way to overcome the tendency to lag would be to make the first one back the leader or have a special leader marker. The first one to this marker becomes the new leader.

A penalty can be imposed on the one who doesn't find a marker.

FROG IN THE SEA

Playing Area: Any small area indoors or outdoors.
Players: 6 to 8 in each game.
Supplies: None.

One player is the "Frog" and sits down tailor fashion (crossed legs). The others mill about him trying to touch him, but at the same time, keeping out of his reach. They can call, "Frog in the sea, can't catch me." The Frog must stay in his sitting position and try to tag those tantalizing him. Anyone tagged exchanges places with the Frog.

Care should be taken so that the children do not punish the Frog unnecessarily.

GAME-TYPE ACTIVITIES

Variations:

1. The Frog may not tag anyone until the teacher says, "Jump Frog."

2. The game proceeds as originally described. When the teacher says, "Jump Frog," the Frog can project himself in any direction with a jump. He is permitted to tag both during the original part of the game and at the jump.

GALLOPING LIZZIE

Playing Area: Playground.
Players: 10 to 15.
Supplies: Beanbag.

This is a version of the game of *Tag.* One player is "It" and has a beanbag. The other players are scattered on the playground. The player with the beanbag runs after the others and attempts to hit one with the beanbag below the shoulders. This person becomes "It" and the game continues. Be sure that "It" must throw the bag and not merely touch another person with it.

Variation: The game can be played by children in pairs. In this case, a pair of children become "It" with one of the players handling the beanbag. A specific kind of a toss can be specified — overhand, underhand, left hand.

JUMP THE SHOT

Playing Area: Playground, gymnasium.
Players: 10 to 20.
Supplies: A jump-the-shot rope.

The players stand in circle formation. One player with a long rope stands in the center. A soft object is tied to the free end of the rope to give it some weight. An old, deflated ball makes a good weight.

The center player turns the rope under the feet of the circle players, who must jump over it. Anyone who touches the rope with his feet is eliminated and must stand back from the circle. Re-form the circle after three or four children are eliminated.

The center player should be cautioned to keep the rope along the ground. The speed can be varied. A good way to turn the rope is to sit cross-legged and turn the rope over the head.

POISON CIRCLE

Playing Area: Playground, gymnasium.
Players: 8 to 12 in each circle.
Supplies: Volleyball or rubber playground ball.

Players form a circle with hands joined with good solid grips. Inside the circle of players, another circle is drawn on the floor with chalk. This should be a foot or two smaller than the circle of children. The ball is placed in the center of this area.

At a signal, the circle pulls and pushes trying to force a child to step into the inner circle. When this occurs, everyone yells, "Poison," and the children scatter. The one who stepped in the circle quickly picks up the ball and tries to hit one of the other children below the waist. He must throw from within the circle. If he hits a child, it is a "dud" against the child. If he misses, it is a "dud" against the thrower. Anyone with three "duds" pays a penalty.

RIGHT FACE, LEFT FACE (Maze Tag)

Playing Area: Playground, gymnasium.
Players: 25 to 35.
Supplies: None.

Children stand in straight rows both from front to rear and side to side. A runner and a chaser are picked. The children all face the same way and join hands with the players on each side. The chaser tries to tag the runner going up and down the rows, but not breaking through or under the arms. The teacher can help the runner by calling "right face" or "left face" at the proper time. At this command, the children drop hands, face the new direction, and again grasp hands with those who are now on each side. New passages are now available to the runner and chaser. When the runner is caught or the children become tired, a new runner and chaser are chosen.

Variations:

1. Directions can be used instead of the facing commands. The teacher can call out, "North, South, East, or West."

2. The original game from which the game above was taken is called "Streets and Alleys." In this version, the teacher calls out,

"Streets," and the children face in one direction. The call "Alleys" causes them to face at right angles.

3. The command "Air Raid" can be given, which means that the children drop to their knees and make themselves into a small ball, tucking their heads and seats down.

STEAL THE TREASURE

Playing Area: Playground, gymnasium, classroom.
Players: 8 to 12.
Supplies: 1 Indian club.

A playing area twenty feet square is outlined with a small circle in the center. An Indian club is the treasure and is placed in the circle. A "Guard" is set to protect the treasure. Players now enter the square and try to steal the treasure without getting caught. The Guard tries to tag them. Anyone tagged must retire from the circle and wait for the next game. The player who gets the treasure is the next Guard. If getting the treasure seems too easy, make a rule requiring the child to carry the treasure to the boundaries of the square.

Bear and Keeper. This game is similar in action. Instead of a treasure a "Bear" is seated cross-legged on the ground and is protected by his "Keeper." Anyone who touches the Bear without being tagged becomes the new Keeper, with the present Keeper becoming the Bear. A rougher version of this game played by boys is that the Bear stands crouched over and the boys try to swat him on the seat without getting tagged.

THREE DEEP

Playing Area: Playground, gymnasium.
Players: 20 to 30.
Supplies: None.

A runner and chaser are chosen. One-half of the remaining children form a circle, facing in. Each of the other children stands behind one of the circle players, forming a double circle formation with all facing in.

The chaser tries to tag the runner, who can escape by taking a position in front of any pair of players. This forms a three-deep combination, from which the game gets its name. The outer player of the three now is the runner. When the chaser tags the runner, the positions are reversed.

The game becomes more interesting if frequent changes are made. It may be well to limit running to halfway round the circle. In no case should the runner leave the immediate circle area.

Variation: The teacher may call out, "Reverse," which means that the positions of the runner and chaser are reversed.

THROUGH THE TUNNEL RACE

Playing Area: Playground, gymnasium, classroom.
Players: 6 to 8 on each team. Many teams can compete.
Supplies: None.

Teams compete against each other and are lined up in relay (lane) formation. The players spread their legs in straddle position, and the last man of each line crawls through the legs. The other players follow in turn until the team is back in original order. As soon as a player has crawled through the tunnel, he stands up so the player coming through next can go through his legs. The team that gets back in original order first wins.

TRIPLE CHANGE

Playing Area: Playground, gymnasium.
Players: 15 to 30.
Supplies: None.

Players form a large circle, facing in. Three children stand in the center. Those forming the circle and those in the center are numbered off by threes. The players in the center take turns, each calling out his own number. When a number is called, all those with that number change places. The one in the center *with this number* tries to find a place. The child without a place goes to the center and waits until the other center players have had their turns.

Variation: The teacher could call out the numbers, not necessarily in order, to add an element of suspense to the game.

WEATHERVANE

Playing Area: Playground, gymnasium, classroom.
Players: Entire class.
Supplies: None.

Children stand alongside their desks or are scattered throughout the area. A leader stands at the front of the class and gives the directions. He calls out the four main compass directions — North, South, East, and West. The children jump in place making the necessary turn in the air to face the called direction. This could involve a quarter, half, or three-quarter turn. If the direction is called which the children are facing, then each child jumps in the air with no turn. All turns should be in the same direction for a period of time to avoid confusion.

A child can sit down after a stipulated number of errors. An alternate method would be for each child to keep track of the number of errors he made.

Variations: After the children become skillful in turning, a number of variations could be used.

1. A full turn could be required when a direction is repeated.
2. Right and left turning could be alternated.

BALANCE DODGEBALL

Playing Area: Playground or gymnasium.
Players: Entire class.
Supplies: A ball for each child who is "It."

Children are scattered over the area. One or more children have a ball and are "It." Children are safe from being hit if they are balanced on one foot. This means that one foot must be off the ground, and the other foot which supports the weight must not be moved on penalty of being hit. Hits should be made below the shoulders. Anyone legally hit becomes "It."

Teaching Suggestion: To avoid having "It" stand by a child waiting for him to lose his balance or touch a foot to the ground, have the child count rapidly up to ten. "It" must then leave him and seek another child.

Variation: Footsie Dodgeball. To be safe from being hit, the child must have both feet off the ground at the time of being hit.

BAT BALL

Playing Area: A serving line is drawn across one end of a field which is approximately 70′ by 70′. A 3′ by 3′ base is drawn in the center of the playing field about 50′ from the serving line.
Players: Two teams, 8 to 15 on each team.
Supplies: Volley or similar ball.

One team is scattered out in the playing area. The other team is behind the serving line with one player up at bat. The batter puts the ball in play by batting it with his hand into the playing area. The ball must land in the playing area or be touched by a member of the fielding team to be counted as a fair ball. As soon as the ball is hit, the batter runs to the base and back across the serving line. In the meantime, the fielding team fields the ball and attempts to hit the runner below the shoulders.

Scoring: The batter scores a run each time a fair ball is hit and he touches the base and gets across the serving line before being hit by the ball. He also scores a run if the fielding team commits a foul.

Out: The batter is out if the ball is caught on a fly. Two consecutive foul balls also put the batter out. The batter is out if hit by a thrown ball in the field of play.

Fouls: Fielders, in recovering the ball and attempting to hit the batter, may not run with the ball. The ball must be passed from fielder to fielder until thrown at the batter. A pass may not be returned to the fielder from whom it was received.

BEANBAG TARGET TOSS

Playing Area: Classroom, gymnasium. Three concentric circles are drawn on the floor with radii of 10″, 20″, and 30″.
Players: 2 to 6 for each target.
Supplies: 5 beanbags, blocks of wood, or round, smooth stones.

Players, in turn, toss the five beanbags in sequence toward the target. A throwing line should be established 10′ to 15′ from the target; the distance depends upon the children's skill.

Scoring:
- Center area — 15 points
- Middle area — 10 points
- Outer area — 5 points
- Any bag touching a line — 3 points

To score in an area the bag must be completely in the area and not touching a line. If the bag touches a line, it scores 3 points.

Each child is given 5 throws and the score is determined from the final position of the 5 bags.

Variations:

1. Two children can compete against each other alternating single throws until each has taken the allotted five. The score of each is noted. For a second turn, the child scoring the highest from the previous effort throws first.

2. Outside, players can use flat stones on a hard surface.

BOUNCE BALL

Playing Area: A rectangular court 40' by 60' divided into two halves by a center line. Each half is 30' by 40'.

Players: Two teams, 8 to 15 players on each.

Supplies: 2 volleyballs or rubber playground balls of about the same size.

Each team occupies one of the halves and is given a volleyball. One or two players from each team should be assigned as ball chasers to retrieve balls behind their own end lines.

The object of the game is to bounce or roll the ball over the opponent's end line. A ball thrown across the line on a fly does not count.

Two scorers are needed, one at each end line. Players can move wherever they wish in their own areas but cannot cross the center line. After the starting signal, the balls are thrown back and forth at will.

Variation: Use a row of benches across the center line. Throws must go over the benches and bounce in the area to score.

CIRCLE TEAM DODGEBALL

Playing Area: Playground, gymnasium.
Players: 20 to 40.
Supplies: Volleyball or rubber playground ball.

The children are divided into two teams, one of which forms a large circle. The other team grouped together is in the center of the circle. One of the circle players has the ball.

When the starting signal is given, the circle players try to hit the center players with the ball. Any center player hit below the shoulders is eliminated and leaves the circle. Scoring can be done in several ways.

1. Establish a throwing time of one minute. Count the number of center players remaining.

2. Play until all center players have been eliminated. Score is determined by the number of seconds it takes to eliminate the players.

3. Allow a throwing time of one minute. Do not eliminate any center players but give one point to the circle players for each successful hit.

4. Limit the number of throws a team can take. After the specified number of throws, count the remaining center players.

The teams trade places and the scores are compared to determine the winner.

CLUB GUARD

Playing Area: Gymnasium, outdoor smooth surface.
Players: 8 to 10 in each game.
Supplies: Indian club, volleyball.

A circle about 15' in diameter is drawn. Inside this circle at the center, an 18" circle is drawn. The Indian club is put in the center of the small circle. One child guards the club. The other children are back of the larger circle which is the restraining line for them. This circle should be definite.

The circle players throw the ball at the club and try to knock it down. The guard tries to block the throws with his legs or body. He must, however, stay out of the smaller inner circle.

The outer circle players pass the ball around rapidly so one of the players can get an opening to throw, as the guard needs to maneuver to protect the club. Whoever knocks down the club becomes the new guard.

If the guard steps in the inner circle, he loses his place to whoever has the ball at that time.

A small circle cut from plywood or similar material makes a definite circle so that it is known when the guard steps inside. A hoop can be used.

Variation: Set up more than one club to be guarded.

COMPETITIVE CIRCLE CONTESTS

Playing Area: Playground, gymnasium.

Players: Two teams, 10 to 15 on each.

Supplies: 2 volleyballs or rubber playground balls, 2 Indian clubs.

Two teams can compete against each other in the form of independent circles. The circles should be of the same size, and lines can be drawn on the floor to assure this. The players of each team are numbered consecutively so that there is a player in each circle with a corresponding number.

These numbered players go to the center of the opponent's circle in turn and compete for their teams against the circle of opponents.

To begin, the #1 players go to the opponent's circle. Three different contests are suggested, using the above arrangement as the basis.

Individual Dodgeball. The circle players throw at the center players, who represent the other team. The circle which hits the center player first wins a point.

Club Guard. In this contest, the center player guards an Indian club as in *Club Guard*. Whichever circle knocks down the club first wins a point.

Touch Ball. The circle players pass the ball from one to another while the center players try to touch it. Whichever center player touches the ball first wins a point for his team.

After the #1 players have competed, they return to their own team circle and the #2s go to the opponent's circles. This is continued until all players have competed. The team with the most points wins.

NEWCOMB

Playing Area: Volleyball Court.

Players: Two teams, 8 to 10 on each.

Supplies: Volleyball.

Each team occupies one side of the court. The children may be positioned in two or three lines of players, depending upon the number of children and the size of the court. There is no rotation system, and service is informal.

The object of the game is for one team to throw the ball underhanded over the net in such a way that it will not be caught. The game starts with a member of one team throwing the ball into the opposite court. The ball is thrown back and forth until an error is committed. Each time a team commits an error, a point is scored for the opposite team. Errors are: (1) failure to catch a ball, (2) not throwing the ball across the net successfully, and (3) throwing the ball so it falls out-of-bounds on the other side of the net. The first team reaching a score of 15 is the winner.

There is no formal rotation, but the teacher can change the lines from front to back at times. The child nearest to the ball which touched the floor or went out-of-bounds starts the play with a throw. The ball may be passed from one player to another before it is thrown across the net.

Variation: Use more than one ball.

ONE STEP

Playing Area: Playground.

Players: 2. Any number of pairs can compete against each other depending upon the space available.

Supplies: Ball or beanbag.

The game is excellent for practicing throwing and catching skills. Two children stand facing each other about 3' apart. One has a ball or beanbag. The object of the game is to throw or toss the ball in the stipulated manner so that the partner can catch it *without moving his feet* from their position on the floor. When the throw is completed successfully, the thrower takes one step backward. He awaits the throw from his partner. Limits can be established back to which the partners step, or the two children who can move to the greatest distance apart as compared to other couples are the winners. Variables to provide interest and challenge are (1) the type of throw, (2) the type of catching, and (3) the kind of a step. Throwing can be underhand, overhand, two-handed, under one leg, around the back, etc. Catching can be two-handed, left hand, right hand, to the side, etc. The step can be a giant step, a tiny step, a hop, a jump, or some similar designation.

When either child misses, moves his feet, or fails to follow directions, the partners move forward and start over. A line of children facing each other makes a satisfactory formation for having a number of pairs compete at the same time.

TOSS TARGET BALL

Playing Area: Playground with sufficient clear space.

Players: 10 to 15.

Supplies: A ball for each child plus a basketball for the center player.

Each child stands in a circle and has a small ball (tennis or sponge) suitable for throwing. One child stands in the center with a basketball. The center player tosses the basketball straight up about 15′ to 20′. Children throw at the basketball and try to hit it while it is up in the air. Children should be cautioned to throw at the target when it is at its zenith. A child that hits the ball scores a point for himself.

Variation: Divide the group into teams, each designated by a number or color (if various colored balls are available). The teacher calls a number or color, and only that team throws, scoring a point for each hit. The teacher can call the numbers in order or at random to provide the element of suspense. All should have an equal number of turns.

18

Rhythmic Activities

Rhythmic Accompaniment
Characteristics of Rhythmic Background
The Program of Rhythmic Activities
Fundamental Rhythms
Creative Rhythms — Identification
Creative Rhythms — Dramatization
Singing Games
Folk Dance
Preschool Singing Games
Kindergarten, First Grade, Second Grade, Third Grade Rhythms
Rope Jumping to Music
Games Using Rhythmic Background

Rhythmic movement should be a part of each child's school experience. Children have a natural love for rhythmic movement and for using the body in expressive movement. Such movement is both a need and a delight. Not only are dance activities a tool for self-expression, but inherent in rhythmics are excellent possibilities for physical development. Progress toward the perfection of simple skills is enhanced by the accompaniment of rhythm.

Through gross body movements and locomotor patterns, children gain better appreciation and understanding of the use of their bodies. Several other important objectives grow out of the program of rhythmics. Certainly, it is an important goal for each child to be able to keep time — to be able to move in keeping with the rhythm. An appreciation of the place that rhythmic activity has in our lives is another important immediate goal. This probably will be gained in proportion to the pleasure and satisfaction which children derive from dance activities.

Important attitudes and social learnings can be promoted through a well-conducted program of dance activities. To be at ease with the opposite sex, to learn social graces, and to make common elements of courtesy a practice are important goals of a rhythmic program.

Developmental possibilities for fitness are high in a well-conducted rhythmic program, particularly in the types of activities stressed on the primary level. Vigorous movements and gross body activities make up many of the rhythms for children. Rhythmic activities offer a maximum of participation for children, as an entire class or a good portion of it can be active at one time. Once the children have been stimulated by the desire for imitation and self-expression, their movement experience can produce good fitness values.

Movement expression through rhythm offers good opportunities for incidental and direct teaching in body mechanics and posture. The proper carriage of the body and the most efficient ways of moving should be included in the teaching of rhythmics. With the encouragement of an appropriate rhythm, children acccept postural coaching and correction naturally as a part of the teaching procedure.

RHYTHMIC ACCOMPANIMENT

The rhythmic accompaniment should be of good quality, since it must stimulate the child to movement. The following are some of the sources which can supply suitable rhythmic background for movement.

The first is the tom-tom or dance drum. Good commercial varieties of both instruments are available at nominal cost. A resonant drumbeat seems to have a stimulating effect on the children. Reasonably satisfactory substitutes can be made from simple materials. For example, a sheet of rubber, plastic, or parchment can be stretched tightly enough over both ends of a #10 tin can with top and bottom removed to produce an acceptable beat.

A second source of accompaniment is the record player, for which specialized record sets are on the market for a variety of activities. Basic and other rhythmic sets are available from many sources.* The record sets are excellent, containing a number of short selections on regular and long-play discs. Each selection for basic skills is identified with the type of movement for which it was designed. In addition, many standard records for specific dance steps, marches, folk dances, fox trots, and modern combo selections serve a variety of purposes. In fact, any record with good accent and rhythm can be utilized somewhere in the rhythmic program.

The teacher should build up a personal collection of records so that eventually he will be familiar with them and able to derive maximum benefit from his own record assortment. Nursery school, kindergarten, and primary teachers should possess personal record sets for basic skills and creative expression. Odd-lot used records can sometimes be secured inexpensively at rummage sales.

The record player should be of good quality with a variable speed control. It should be adaptable to a range of record types (33, 45, or 78 rpm). Some protection against needle bounce is needed. Either it must have built-in protection or it should be cushioned on foam rubber pads. The volume must be sufficient to carry the music over the competition of the activity's noise. It should also have an input for a microphone.

A third source of rhythmic accompaniment, the tape recorder, adds another important tool, as music can be recorded on tape in an infinite number of ways, the simplest of which is the straightforward recording of music. With a little practice, directions can be recorded along with the music as desired. The tape recorder is particularly valuable in specialized routines where a number of abrupt changes of music are required. No delay of action, as in changing records on a record player, is encountered. The tape recorder has the disadvantage that the tempo cannot be adjusted, as with most recorders little or no variation in tempo is possible once the music has been recorded on the tape.

The piano is the fourth source of accompaniment. It offers excellent possibilities but does demand a reasonable degree of skill, or the program will suffer. It has the further drawback that if the teacher plays and follows the printed music, it is difficult for him to observe the children's progress. It is also difficult to provide demonstration and offer individual coaching help when one is playing the piano.

A fifth source is the use of songs, poems, spoken phrases, and other vocal forms. The children can express themselves to a poem recited in a rhythmic manner. With singing games, the children can learn the music and the words, and the activity can proceed using only the children's voices.

Several other instruments or devices for providing rhythmic accompaniment merit mention. The tambourine plays a useful role in the rhythmic program, as it can be used to provide two different types of percussion accompaniment. Shaking it gives a metallic, ringing type of noise, while striking it with the knuckles or on the elbow produces a drumlike sound. The metallic sound can stimulate the children to one kind of movement, and the drumlike beat to a contrasting movement.

Another simple percussion device can be made by using two 12" sticks about the thickness of a broom handle. Blocks, coconut shells, and tin can rattles are examples of other useful sound makers.

Because the wealth of fine recordings of well-selected rhythms and music presently available can provide a good basis for a broad program of rhythmics, some teachers rely on recordings entirely. The use of percussion instruments provides the teacher with a measure of variety and class control not possible with a recording. It should be remembered that there will be times when the record player or tape recorder is not operating or is not available, and so other means of providing the rhythmic background will need to be supplied.

At times, it is desirable to have the children operate or provide the rhythmic background. While it is of value for children to have this

---

*See appendix for list of record sources.

experience, a poor rhythmic accompaniment can nullify much of the effectiveness of a good rhythmic lesson. Providing proper accompaniment with a drum or other percussion instrument demands a reasonable degree of skill which comes from practice and perhaps some innate skill.

CHARACTERISTICS OF RHYTHMIC BACKGROUND

Music has essential characteristics which the children should recognize, understand, and appreciate. These characteristics are also present in varying degrees in other types of rhythmic accompaniment.

The teacher should make use of proper terminology when discussing characteristics of a piece of music. The following terms should be employed.

Tempo. Generally, tempo is the speed of the music. Tempo can be constant, show a gradual increase (acceleration), or show a decrease (deceleration).

Beat. This is underlying rhythmic quality of the music. The beat can be even or uneven. Music with a pronounced beat is easier for the children to follow.

Meter. Meter refers to the manner in which beats are put together to form a measure of music. Common meters used in rhythmics are 2/4, 3/4, 4/4, and 6/8.

Accent. The notes or beats which carry the heavier emphasis define accent, usually given to the first underlying beat of each measure. Accent is generally expressed by a heavier movement.

Intensity. The force of the music can be loud, soft, light, or heavy.

Mood. Mood is related somewhat to intensity, but carries the concept deeper into human feelings. Music can interpret many human moods, such as feeling cheerful, sad, happy, gay, warlike, fearful, stately, and others.

Phrase. A phrase is a natural grouping of measures. In most cases, the group of measures will total eight underlying beats or counts.

Patterns. Phrases of music are put together into rhythmic patterns. Children should recognize when the music pattern repeats or changes to another pattern.

THE PROGRAM OF RHYTHMIC ACTIVITIES

The various types of rhythmic activities should be balanced in the program. The chart which follows shows a broad rhythmic program in which the activities are allocated according to grade level.

An examination of the chart reveals that the program for grades P-2 emphasizes fundamental rhythms, creative rhythms, and singing games, with lesser attention to folk dances in the lower two grades. As the program moves into the third grade, singing games fade, and rope jumping and musical games enter the picture, as well as simple folk dances. Mixers appear to a limited extent in the third grade.

Rhythmic Activity Types — Grade Level Placement

Activity Type	P	K	1	2	3
Fundamental Rhythms	X	X	X	X	X*
Creative Rhythms — Identification	X	X	X	X	X
Creative Rhythms — Dramatization	X	X	X	X	X
Singing Games	X	X	X	X	
Folk Dances		S	S	X	X
Mixers					S
Rope Jumping to Music				S	S
Musical Games				S	S

*Key: X means the activity is an integral part of that grade level.
S means the activity is given only minor emphasis.

FUNDAMENTAL RHYTHMS

The fundamental rhythm program sets the basis for rhythmic movement in all forms of dance activities. Essentially, it is Basic Movement using the medium of rhythm. It centers on basic skills — locomotor, nonlocomotor, and manipulative, with the most attention given to locomotor skills.

The general purpose of a program of fundamental rhythms is to provide a variety of basic movement experiences so that the child can move effectively and efficiently and develop a sense of rhythm in connection with these movements. While the creative aspects of fundamental rhythms are important, it is necessary first to establish a vocabulary of movement competencies for each child so that he has a basis on which to create.

Since rhythm in movement means essentially moving in time to a beat or rhythm, having children concentrate on beat patterns early is an effective way to introduce and reinforce the sense of rhythm. Not only can this lead to a sense of rhythm, but it can serve to introduce the various meters with their related accents. Some movement is involved, but the chief emphasis is on conformance to the rhythmic pattern.

RHYTHMIC BEAT REPETITION AND REPRODUCTION

Based on the theories of Kodaly and others, the introduction of practice in rhythmic beat repetition and reproduction has provided an extension of movement experiences to rhythm. The experiences are valuable for all levels, including preschool through third grade. The approach begins with the provision of a beat pattern of some nature, generally by a drum, which the children repeat or reproduce either singly or in sequence.

Several different approaches are possible. The enterprising teacher should be able to devise others.

1. Children clap in unison as directed by a drum. This should include the four basic meters — 2/4, 3/4, 4/4, and 6/8. In this the children are clapping with the drum. The patterns by the drum can be varied to include accents and different combinations of beats.

2. Children reproduce the beat pattern. A pattern generally covers two or three measures. Some ways this can be expanded are:

a. Substitute some gesture on the accented beat.

b. While reproducing, step forward on the beginning of a pattern and backward on the next beginning.

c. Reproduce first with clapping, then with a beat by the foot.

d. Add two patterns together. The first pattern is given and the children follow. The second pattern is provided, and the children reproduce the first pattern followed by the second. A third pattern can be added. More than three, however, is usually too much challenge for young children.

e. Combine any of the above with locomotor movements.

Suggested Beat Patterns

Of the beat patterns to be presented, 2/4 and 4/4 patterns are quite similar. Most of our illustrations of patterns for these two meters will be in 4/4 time, but a few 2/4 examples are also included. In the illustrations, a bar under a note will indicate that this is an accented note.

Each of the meters is presented in a separate section, with the basic beat structure illustrated first followed by an accented basic structure second. Accents are not provided for all the patterns, allowing the teacher flexibility in selecting accented patterns as desired. The teacher should regard the beat patterns only as a starting point, as many others can be devised.

2/4 Meter

4/4 Meter

3/4 Meter

6/8 Meter

FUNDAMENTAL MOVEMENT PATTERNS TO RHYTHM

The previous discussion centered on developing a sense of rhythm and acquiring basic concepts relevant to the rhythmic patterns. Fundamental movement patterns of an elementary nature can be added to the rhythmic beat. This can be somewhat structured or can emphasize creative aspects.

The skills in a fundamental rhythm program are important not only in providing background in creative dance, but also in setting the basis for the more precise dance skills of folk, social, and square dances, which follow later in school programs. The basic skills are also related to effective movement in all forms of living and, in particular, to the activities in the physical education program.

Instructional Procedures

In practice, the program depends much upon the teacher to initiate and guide the simple patterns. It is important that the rhythms be conducted in an atmosphere of fun and enjoyment. Furthermore, the accompaniment should be suitable and proper for the movements to be experienced.

The element of creativity must not be stifled in a program of fundamental movements. The instruction can be directed toward a specific movement (like walking), and a reasonable range of acceptability can be established. In other words, we are practicing walking, but we can walk in many different ways.

Teachers who may feel awkward and insecure in developing rhythmic programs with a strong creative approach will find the fundamental rhythms a good starting point. Combining the child's love of rhythmic movement with the basic movements which he enjoys can be the beginning of a refreshing and stimulating experience.

The approach to fundamental rhythms should be a mixture of direct and indirect teaching. For many of the movements there is a "standard" or "preferred" technique. For example, there is a correct way to walk, and children should recognize and learn the correct fundamentals. Within the framework of good technique, a variety of movement experiences should be elicited.

The following pattern represents an effective approach the teacher may take in teaching a basic movement skill.

1. With the children comfortable, let them listen to the music. Discuss with them the elements of tempo, beat, meter, accent, and other characteristics of music. As the children listen for phrasing, they become aware of any special changes or effects which are present in the music. Active listening is important as differentiated from merely hearing. Good listening techniques are developed only with practice.

2. To gain a sense of the beat, the children may clap hands to the rhythm. Other simple rhythmic movements done with the hands, arms, legs, or feet help get the feel of the rhythm.

3. Discuss the important qualities and key factors of the movement. What are the important considerations in doing the movement? What are the things which must be observed?

4. The children now move about the room, using the selected basic movement or combination of movements. Movement patterns in the early stages of teaching may need to be somewhat controlled, but as soon as possible, movement should be free, informal, and in every direction instead of around the room in a circular direction.

5. Increasing variety and combinations should be encouraged to reinforce the learning potential. Children should be encouraged to experiment with directional changes and other combinations. Often the teacher can call a halt and have one of the children demonstrate a novel and interesting movement variation which he has employed.

6. During and after the lesson, discussions can be held with the children with regard to "What are we doing that is good, and how can we improve on our movement?" "What different kinds of things can be done to the rhythm?"

It is well to have a child handle the record player. For this the child needs some training. A system of signals for good control is also needed. This frees the teacher for other instruction.

Creative Approach to Fundamental Rhythms

In a lesson emphasizing the creative aspects of fundamental rhythmics, the approach differs from one emphasizing specialized patterns. The purpose of the creative approach to fundamental learning is to have the child gain an interpretation or impression from the selected rhythm and then move creatively as he chooses, using basic skills.

As in the previous approach, the child listens to the music and also gains a sense of the beat by clapping or other simple movements.

After discussing with the children the characteristics of the music, the children are encouraged to select the kinds of movements that the music suggests to them. Movement then is free and unstructured. Extension of movement experiences with variety and different combinations is now possible.

Ideas to Utilize Different Movement Fundamentals

In exploring the range of ideas using movement, the following suggestions should be of value. The resourceful and imaginative teacher, with the aid of the children, can make use of these ideas and others to make up interesting lessons in movement.

An effective and interesting method of stimulating variation is to have the children change movement patterns or combinations with the completion of a phrase of music (8 counts or beats). The music provides the cue for changes, and the children must think ahead to plan the new patterns.

The concept of laterality must be stressed. Movements performed with one side of the body should be done with the other. Directions should be reversed to include the opposite way of moving.

Rhythm Variations

The factors discussed previously (page 104) for securing a variety of response in basic movement can be utilized in the program of fundamental rhythms.

The rhythm can be varied with different tempos. In most instances, early instruction or experience is presented to a slower tempo, which is increased after the movement patterns are learned. The music selected can be changed to provide a variety of tempo, mood, and quality.

In working with fundamental rhythmic patterns, a good rhythmic beat pattern is basic. The tom-tom is especially valuable in working with children in basic rhythm teaching, providing an easy way to vary the tempo, accents, and other characteristics of the basic beat. Stops and starts, changes to different rhythms, and many other innovations are possible with skillful handling of the tom-tom. Combinations of different rhythms can be put together easily and effectively with a tom-tom or drum.

Intensity or force of the music can be changed, giving rise to different modes of response, resulting in movements which can be light or heavy, strong or weak.

Space factors such as direction, level, and different floor patterns add variation. Floor patterns can reinforce learning concepts as children recognize and employ circles, squares, figure eights, etc.

The use of different parts of the body singly or in various combinations is important in establishing variety. The different positions of the arms and legs provide many ways of moving. One can perform high on the toes, with toes in or out, on the heels, with stiff knees, kicking high in front or to the rear, with knees brought up high, in a crouched position, and in many other positions.

Arms can swing at the sides or be held stiff, be held out in front or overhead. Arms can move in circles or in different patterns, and in other poses. The body can be bent forward, backward, sideward, and it can be twisted, or turned. By combining different positions of the arms, legs, and body, the children can assume many interesting variations of position.

Working with a Partner or a Group

A child may work with a partner or as a member of a group. Be sure that the tasks or directions are appropriate and that sufficient practice and mastery has been accomplished before partner or group work is instituted.

Fundamental Movement Patterns

Movement patterns in fundamental rhythms divide themselves into three categories:
1. Locomotor Movements
2. Nonlocomotor Patterns
3. Manipulative Activities

In the discussions which follow, the movements are analyzed and suggested movement patterns are presented.

Locomotor Movements

Even Types. Walking, running, hopping, leaping, jumping, draw steps, and such variations as marching, trotting, stamping, and twirling.

Uneven Types. Skipping, galloping, sliding.

Walking. In walking, one is always in contact with the ground or floor, and the feet move alternately. This means that the stepping foot must be placed on the ground before the other foot is lifted for its step. Marching is a more military, precise type of walk, accompanied with lifted knees and swinging arms.

The weight of the body is transferred from the heel to the ball of the foot and then to the toes for the push-off for the next step. The toes are pointing straight ahead with the arms swinging freely from the shoulder in opposition to the feet. The body is erect and the eyes are focused straight ahead at eye level. Legs are swung from the hips with the knees bent only enough to clear the foot from the ground.

Some ways that walking can be used as an activity are:

1. Walk forward one phrase (8 counts) and change directions. Continue to change at the end of each phrase.

2. Use high steps during one phrase and low steps during the next.

3. Walk forward for one phrase and sidewards during the next. The side step can be a draw step or it can be of the grapevine type. To do a grapevine step to the left, lead with the left foot with a step directly to the side. The right foot crosses *behind* the left

and then in front on the next step with that foot. The pattern is a step left, cross right (behind), step left, cross right (in front), and so on.

4. Find a partner, face each other and join hands. Pull your partner by walking backwards as he resists somewhat (8 counts). Reverse roles. Try using pushing action by walking forward (8 counts) as partner resists when he moves backward. Reverse roles.

5. Walk slowly and gradually increase the tempo. Begin fast and decrease.

6. Walk in various directions while clapping hands alternately in front and behind. Try clapping hands under the thighs at each step or clap hands above the head.

7. Walk forward four steps, turn completely around in four steps. Repeat.

8. While walking, bring up the knees and slap with the hands on each step.

9. On any one phrase take four fast steps (one count to each step) and two slow steps (two counts to each step).

10. Walk on heels, toes, or with a heavy tramp.

11. Walk with a smooth gliding step or walk silently.

12. Gradually lower the body while walking (going downstairs) and raise yourself again (going upstairs).

13. Use a waltz with good beat and walk to it accenting the first beat of each measure. Add a sway of the body to the first beat of the measure.

14. Walk high on tiptoes, rocking back and forth.

Running. Running, as contrasted to walking, is to move more rapidly in such a manner that for a brief moment both feet are off the ground. Running varies from trotting, a slow run, to sprinting, a fast run for speed.

Running should be done lightly on the toes, with lifted knees. It should be a controlled run and not a dash for speed. Children may cover some ground on the run or they can run in place.

Running should be done with a slight body lean. The knees are bent and lifted. The arms swing back and forth from the shoulders with a bend at the elbows.

Many of the suggested movements for walking are equally applicable to running patterns. Some additional suggestions are listed:

1. Walk during a phrase of music and then run for an equal length of time.

2. Run in different directions, turning at times.

3. Left the knees as high as possible while running.

4. Run and touch different spots on the floor or on the wall.

Hopping. In hopping, the body is sent up and down by one foot. The body lean, the other foot, and the arms serve to balance the movement. Hopping on one foot should not be sustained too long. Children should change to the other foot after a short period

Some variations and combinations for hopping include:

1. Hop like a bouncing ball. Hop very high, gradually reducing the height. The procedure can be reversed.

2. Hop along a line, crossing back and forth over the line each time.

3. Draw a small circle (about 18" across) on the floor. Hop across, in and out of the circle.

4. Hop in different figures like a circle, triangle, square, etc.

5. Trace out numbers by hopping. Try writing short words by hopping.

6. Alternate big and little hops. Form other combinations.

7. Hop on one foot a specific number of times and change to the other foot.

8. Turn around hopping in place.

Leaping. Leaping is an elongated step designed to cover distance or to go over a low obstacle. Leaping is usually combined with running, as a series of leaps is difficult to maintain. It can be included in a running sequence, using the music phrase as the cue. An excellent piece to use for leaping is "Pop Goes the Weasel." The youngsters can take a leap on the "Pop" part of the piece.

Jumping. Jumping, as the term is used in fundamental movements, means to take off with both feet and land on *both* feet. The arms aid in the jump with an upswing, and the movement of the body helps lift the weight along with the force of the feet. A jumper lands lightly on the balls of his feet with his knees bent.

The suggestions listed for hopping can be applied to jumping. In addition, the teacher can devise other movement patterns such as these:

1. Jump with the body stiff and arms held at the sides.

2. Jump and turn in the air. Quarter, half, and even full turns can be done to rhythm. Work gradually into full turns.

3. Combine jumping with hopping, walking, running, and skipping.

4. Increase and decrease the speed of jumping.

5. Land with feet apart or crossed. Alternate feet forward and back.

Draw Step. The draw step is a two-count movement to either side. A step is made directly to the side and on the second count the other foot is drawn up to it. The cue is made by "left (or right), close; left, close; left close"; etc.

Skipping. Skipping is actually a series of step-hops done with alternate feet. To teach a child to skip, ask him to take a step with one foot and then take a small hop on the same foot. He now takes a step with the other foot and a hop on that foot. Skipping should be done on the balls of the feet with the arms swinging to shoulder height in opposition to the feet.

Almost all of the combinations suggested for walking and running are useful for skipping movements. Combinations of skipping, walking, and running can be devised in many different fashions.

Galloping. Galloping is similar to sliding, but the progress of the individual is in a forward direction. One foot leads, and the other is brought up rapidly to it. The hands can be in a position as if holding a horse's reins. Since later in the rhythmic program the gallop is used to teach the polka, it is important that the children learn to change the leading foot. The leading foot can be changed after a series of eight gallops with the same foot leading. Later, the changes can be reduced to four gallops and finally to two gallops. These changes have value in perceptual-motor training.

Sliding. Sliding is done usually to the side. It is a one-count movement with the leading foot stepping out to the side and the other foot following quickly. A novel way to use sliding is to head in a direction with a definite number of slides and then do a half-turn in the air and continue the slide leading with the other foot but retaining the original direction.

Nonlocomotor Patterns

Simple Movements. Bending, swaying, twisting, swinging, raising, lowering, circling, and rotating various parts of the body.

Mimetics. Striking, lifting, throwing, pushing, pulling, hammering, and other common tasks.

Nonlocomotor movements include those movements that the body is able to execute while the feet remain in place. They provide for dramatic and expressive movement and involve movements by the arms, legs, head, or torso, singly or in combination. Specific movements used in this portion of the rhythmic program include swinging, circling, rotating, twisting, lowering, raising, bending, extension, flexion, and combinations of the movements. These can be used strictly as nonlocomotor movements or in combination with locomotor movement. Large, free, unhampered movements to the full range of flexibility are a goal. Instruction can range from specific movements to creative opportunity of free choice.

Manipulative Activities

A fruitful area for primary children is found in the application of rhythm to ball skills. Hoops, wands, and chairs are occasionally used in movement to rhythm. To get full value from such activities, each child should have an object of his own with which to work.

While the school normally has volleyballs, soccer balls, and rubber playground balls, these can be supplemented by small balls of various types, provided that they have a lively bounce.

Ball Skills. The following ball skills lend themselves well to rhythm:

1. Bounce and catch. Bounce a number of times and then catch. Various combinations. Combine with various locomotor movements.

2. Throw against a wall and catch. Volley against a wall.

3. Bounce continuously (dribble).
   Dribble in place.
   Dribble under the legs. Also, dribble behind the individual.
   Dribble and move. Form circles, triangles, and other patterns. Dribble forward, backward, sideward, stop and go.
   Dribble using different locomotor movements — hopping, jumping, sliding, and skipping.

4. Volley continuously in rhythm, using the hands, elbows, head, knees, etc. Add locomotor movements.

5. Work with a partner or in groups passing a ball or balls from one to another in rhythm. Vary with bounce passes.

For bounce and catch skills, a little experimentation by the teacher with various selections will uncover suitable music. A number of firms now produce music especially made for various bouncing, dribbling, and catching skills. The sets of records for fundamental rhythms usually have numbers adaptable for various skills using balls.

Dribbling skills with rhythm are particularly appropriate for sports-minded children. The tie-up of a basketball skill with rhythm tends to make the rhythmic program more attractive to boys.

A selected polka with a definite beat makes a suitable selection for dribbling. If the record player has a variable speed control, a finer adjustment can be made coordinating the tempo of the record with the dribbling skills.

The record, "Pop Goes the Weasel," provides a fine rhythmic background for partner work. One child can dribble and work creatively in any manner he wishes until the music comes to the "Pop" part of the chorus, which is the signal for passing the ball to his partner, who repeats the performance. The children should be encouraged to move in different directions with a variety of locomotor movements while dribbling and to move back toward the partner when the music is approaching the signal for the ball exchange.

Rope jumping skills are manipulative activities, but are given special attention (page 274) because of their uniqueness to the rhythmic program.

Hoops and wands are sometimes included in rhythmic routines, generally in nonlocomotor activities. Swinging, lifting, and other movements of a graceful type can be combined into sequence routines. Some type of waltz music provides a suitable background for the movements.

CREATIVE RHYTHMS — IDENTIFICATION

In an identification rhythm, the child expresses himself by trying to "be something." The child in his own mind takes on the identity, for example, of a soldier, giant, horse, elephant, train, or other familiar character, creature, or object. He proceeds to interpret this identity with expressive movements to the accompaniment of a suitable rhythm.

There are many sources of subjects for interpretations through these rhythms. Some of the following will be found useful:

1. Animals — elephants, ducks, seals, chickens, dogs, rabbits, lions, and other animals.
2. People — soldiers, Indians, firemen, sailors, various kinds of workers, forest rangers, cowboys, etc.
3. Play Objects — seesaws, swings, rowboats, balls, various toys, and many common articles with which the children play.
4. Make-Believe World — giants, dwarfs midgets, gnomes, witches, trolls, dragons, pixies, and fairies, among others.
5. Machines — trains, planes, jets, rockets, automobiles, bicycles, motorcycles, tractors, elevators, etc.
6. The Circus — clowns, various trained animals, trapeze artists, tight and slack wire performers, jugglers, acrobats, and bands.
7. Nature — fluttering leaves, grain, flowers, rain, snow, clouds, wind, tornado, hurricane, and others.

Instructional Procedures

An atmosphere of creative freedom must be a part of each lesson. Encourage children to explore, interpret, and express themselves in varied and original movement as they react to the rhythm. They need to "lose themselves" in the interpretation by assuming the identity of what they are imitating.

While there are variations, three general approaches can be used:

1. The first is to begin with a rhythm and let each child decide what he would like to be, based on the character of the rhythm. The approach is, "What does this rhythm make you think of?" The children may be many things and move in many different ways.

2. A second approach is to select a piece of music and have the children listen and choose what they are to imitate. All children would be imitating the same character, object, or thing. Within the selection each child would have the privilege of creating as he wished. If the choice were a giant, the child would interpret his concept of the giant.

3. The third approach to creative identification is to have the children choose a character or object with which they wish to be identified and then look for a suitable rhythm in keeping with the choice. From sets of records where bands are labeled for various imitations, an appropriate band could be selected. Or, the children could listen and experiment with several choices before making a final selection.

Some questions which can be posed to the children are:

"What does the music make us think of?"
"What does the music tell us to do?"
"How can we move with the music and our selected interpretation?"

Listening is important, as the children must get the mood of the music. To be effective the music must be appropriate for the identity to be assumed; otherwise movement becomes artificial. In pantomiming the selected identity, the child should keep his movements in time with the rhythm.

There are many specialized recordings which provide excellent musical background for identification rhythms. Although designated for a particular identity, the selections can be adapted for other characterizations.

CREATIVE RHYTHMS — DRAMATIZATION

Both identification and dramatization rhythms have in common the basic purpose that the child should react creatively and rhythmically to the selected rhythm. However, the approach differs. In an identification rhythm, the child should listen to the music, determine its quality and characteristics, and then act creatively in assuming the identity of his selection.

In a dramatic rhythm, the children act out an idea, a familiar event, or an ordinary procedure. This could be based on a story, an idea, a poem, an emotion, or a song. It could take almost any form. A variety of rhythmic background can accompany the unfolding of the story. Recordings, a piano selection, percussion rhythms, or even a rhythm band can be used. A teacher or a student reader can provide the verbal background and directions for the drama, but the story can unfold without this.

A second method would be to begin with a piece of music, generally a recording, and develop an idea to fit the music. The piece of music selected should have sufficient changes of tempo and pattern to provide different kinds and quality of background. A general idea or plan of action can be selected and fitted to the music. An idea like "Going to the Fair" may be selected. A recording is chosen which is adaptable. The children can devise a script in keeping with the idea and following the music.

A third opportunity in a dramatic rhythm is for children to express moods or feelings. A piece of music is played, generally a recording, and the children discuss its qualities and how it makes them feel. Children can and will interpret the music differently, however. Moods which can be expressed are being happy, gay, sad, brave, fearful, cheerful, angry, solemn, silly, stately, sleepy, funny, cautious, bold, and nonchalant.

The teacher aids in setting the stage, and the children carry the activity to its point of fulfillment in the event or story selected. The teacher should avoid setting preconceived standards for the children and attempting to hold to these. An idea may be expanded in many directions, and success in the activity can be judged by the degree to which the children have been able to interpret freely and creatively.

An example of how an idea can be exploited for a rhythmic lesson of creativity is "The Wind and the Leaves." One or more children are chosen to be the "Wind," and the remainder of the children are the "Leaves." Two kinds of rhythm are needed. The first indicates the blowing of the Wind. The second rhythm is quieter and stimulates the Leaves to flutter to the ground after the wind has stopped. Thus, the story divides itself into two parts, each of which offers many possibilities of creativity.

Rhythm 1. Fast, high, shrill — indicating the blowing of the Wind. The intensity and the tempo would illustrate the speed and force of the Wind.

Rhythm 2. Slow, measured, light beat to match the Leaves fluttering in the still air and finally coming to rest at various positions on the ground.

During the first rhythm, the children representing the Wind can show how they would represent a heavy blow. While this is going on, the Leaves show what they feel it means to be blown about.

During the second rhythm, the Wind is still and the Leaves are fluttering to the ground.

Other characterizations could be added. "Street Sweepers" could come along and sweep the Leaves up.

Other ideas useful for dramatic rhythms are:

1. Building a house, garage, or other project.
2. Making a snowman. Throwing snowballs. Going skiing.
3. Flying a kite. Going hunting or fishing. Going camping.
4. Acting out stories which include Indians, cowboys, firemen, engineers.
5. Interpreting familiar stories like Sleeping Beauty, The Three Bears, Little Red Riding Hood, and others.
6. Building from household task ideas like chopping wood, picking fruit, mowing the lawn, cleaning the yard.
7. Celebrating holidays like Halloween, Fourth of July, Thanksgiving, Christmas.
8. Ideas using the seasons — spring, summer, fall, winter.
9. Sports activities. Playing football, basketball, baseball, track and field, swimming, tennis, golf, and others.

Two other ideas may be of help. One teacher had success with her class by devising a game called "Guess What." The class was divided into groups, and each was given the task to act out an idea using percussion accompaniment. Each group put on its performance before the others, and at the completion the other groups guessed what the interpretation was. Be sure that the interpretations are not too long.

Another idea of value in dramatic rhythms is to use a tape recorder. In this way, bits of music and other accompaniment can be put together as desired. This procedure allows for the story or idea to be structured with its own individually designed rhythmic background.

SINGING GAMES

A singing game is described as a dance where the children sing verses, and the verses give direction to the movement. Usually there is considerable latitude in the resultant movement patterns as the children follow and interpret the action picture of the words. A singing game is usually an interpretation of an old story, fable, or some kind of a task.

Instructional Procedures

In presenting a singing game, the following steps provide a logical sequence of progression. Seat the children on the floor.

Background. Tell something about the singing game, discussing its nature and meaning. Set the stage so the children can make an appropriate interpretation.

Analyzing the Music. Have the children listen critically to the music and analyze with respect to tempo, mood, rhythmic qualities, and major parts. They can clap to the beat.

Learning the Verses. Writing the verses on a blackboard or on a poster card speeds learning and saves time. It is generally better to learn one verse at a time and put this into action before proceeding with the others, but if the verses are learned in the classroom before the activity period, then all should be learned. Sometimes the music teacher and the physical education teacher can cooperate. The children can learn the music and the verses during the music period and add the action during the activity period.

Adding the Action. Arrange the children in formation quickly and proceed with the action. Encourage creative interpretation as determined by the framework of the singing game. Begin with the largest workable part of the activity which the children can handle at one time. After this is learned, add other increments.

In most cases there will be little need to practice a step pattern to be used in the activity, as most singing games involve only simple basic steps, which are subject to individual interpretation.

Including Variations. The teacher should be alert to possible variations, which may be suggested by the children.

Other Suggestions. The source of music must be loud enough for the children to hear as they sing, otherwise the singing will be out of time with the music. After the children learn the verses and can sing reasonably well, the music source may not be necessary, as the children's singing can carry the activity.

In singing games where a key figure is the center of attention, several children may assume the part, spreading the attention and involving more children. In activities where children select partners during the course of the action, boys should select girls and vice versa.

FOLK DANCE AND OTHER DANCE ACTIVITIES

A folk dance is defined as a traditional dance of a given people. In this form, a definite pattern of dance routine is usually specified and followed. In the original form little variation from the traditional dance pattern was permitted, but in physical education practice the elementary school program utilizes many variations and departures.

Few, if any, of the folk dances for kindergarten and primary children involve special dance steps. Rather, the simple fundamental locomotor movements are the basis for the dances. The more specialized steps such as the two-step, polka, schottische, waltz, and others are a part of the intermediate level program.

Usually, there is little need to practice specific steps involved in a dance, as the majority of the dances for children demand only simple movements, which can usually be mastered during the conduct of the dance.

Introducing a New Dance

Most dances are taught by the whole-part-whole method, wherein the largest whole part of the dance which the children can grasp at one time is taught.

1. With the children sitting informally or in the formation for the dance, tell them about the dance and its characteristics.

2. Have the children listen to and analyze music for accents, phrases, or changes.

3. Singly or with partners (as indicated), have the children walk through as much of the dance as they can absorb. Practice without and then with the music, using a slowed tempo until enough has been learned to proceed to the next part. Provide at this point only the basics needed for the dance, as too many details and refinements tend to cause confusion.

4. A technique of value in the whole-part-whole method of presentation is to have the children learn one-half of a two-part dance or one-third of a three-part dance and put this to music. When the music comes to the part the children do not know, have them stand and listen, awaiting the repetition of the portion they have learned. Listening to the music during the unknown part of the piece emphasizes the changes, and fixes the relationship of the parts to the whole in the children's minds.

5. Teach the remaining portions of the dance and put the whole together, beginning at a slow tempo, then gradually increasing this to the normal tempo of the dance.

6. Add such refinements as partner changes (if a mixer), needed points of technique, and other details.

7. Change partners and repeat the dance.

Instructional Procedures for Dance Activities

1. Progression is important in teaching rhythmic activities. It is sound instructional procedure to progress from the simple to the more complex, from a slowed to a normal tempo, from solo to partner activity, from the familiar to the unfamiliar, and from a simple to the stipulated partner position.

2. In the lower grades, the teacher need not be too concerned with strict mechanics. Children should be held to reasonable standards

for their age. Too high standards breed frustration and kill some of the enjoyment in the activity.

3. Time is saved if a monitor can be sent into the dance room or area to warm up the record player before the other children come in. Third graders are quite capable of handling this chore. When the class comes in, the activity can proceed without undue delay. Newer record players with transistors need little warm-up, but should be made ready.

4. The teacher can be freed for better instructional duty if someone handles the record player. Have definite signals for starting and stopping the music. Normally music should be stopped at the completion of a full pattern.

5. The teacher should have definite starting and stopping signals for the dancers, such as "Ready and begin," "Ready — Now" and "Stop." The signal for the dancers to begin should be given on the musical phrase just prior to the beginning of a full pattern. The phrase is usually 8 beats in length, and the starting signals can be given on the fifth and seventh beats of the phrase in the following manner:

```
BEATS            ↓       ↓
 1    2    3    4    5    6    7    8
              "Ready and begin"
              "Ready  —  Now!"
```

6. The proportion of activity to rest periods should be well-balanced. The children can be seated on the floor to analyze and discuss the dance, the music, or the movements.

7. The dance should be repeated often enough so that the movements and the dance are reasonably learned. Too much repetition or emphasis on mastery may cause the children to react negatively.

8. Get the group in formation as quickly as possible. Children are able to grasp an understanding of the dance or step more easily if they are in the formation used for the activity.

9. Individual help is to be given as needed, but do not hold the class to the pace of the slow learner.

10. Stress the enjoyment which comes from knowing a dance and being able to do it well. As an instructor, know the dance, have the instructional sequences thought out beforehand, and have appropriate music ready.

11. Conduct activities as informally as possible, but retain control of the group.

12. Stress a good social environment. Folk dance instruction offers good opportunity for healthful boy-girl relationships and implementation of good standards of courtesy.

13. Change partners often and make frequent use of mixers. This makes for better sociability, adds interest, and gives all an equal opportunity to have good dancing partners.

14. Stress postural points for proper carriage and efficient movement.

Arranging for Partners

Some teachers believe in having the boys choose girl partners, but this should be used with caution if it will cause embarrassment or distress to those chosen last. Other methods can be used which will avoid the problem of some children being looked over and overlooked.

1. Down the center by twos. The boys are on the right side of the room and girls on the left, both facing the same direction towards one end of the room. All march forward to the end of the room, turn toward each other, march down the center by twos, and then into a circle formation.

2. Boys join hands in a circle formation and each girl steps behind a boy.

3. Boys stand in a circle facing counterclockwise while the girls form a circle around them facing clockwise. Both circles move in the direction they are facing and stop on signal. The boy takes the girl nearest him as his partner.

4. Squad exchange. Two squads can be assigned to establish partners. The boys in one squad are paired off with the girls in the other. The squad leaders can supervise this chore.

Partners should be changed with regularity. Changing can be done formally by having the boys move forward one or more places in a circle formation to take a new partner. Mixers are an important activity for this purpose in the program.

Both boys and girls should accept partners with grace and courtesy. Allow them to discuss and help set their own standards in this area. It is important to help them to be at ease with the opposite sex.

If the class is unbalanced and several members of one sex are left over after partners are chosen, find some way to include them in the activity by rotation. In some cases girls can dance with girls, but it is better not to have boys dancing with each other.

Formations for Singing Games and Folk Dances

The formations illustrated below cover almost all of the singing games and dances. The teacher should be able to verbalize the formation, and the children should be able to take their places in formations without confusion. The formations are listed under single circle, double circle, or other categories.

Single Circle
1. All facing center, no partners.
2. All facing counterclockwise.
3. By partners, all facing center.
4. By partners, with partners facing.

Double Circle
5. Partners facing each other.
6. Partners side by side, facing counterclockwise.

Other Formations
7. Longways Set.

Dance Positions

In most dance positions, where the girl clasps the boy's hand, the boy holds his hands palms up and the girl joins the grip with a palms down position. The following dance positions for partners are common to many dances.

Partners Facing Position. Partners are facing. The boy extends his hands forward with palms up and the elbows slightly bent. The girl places her hands in the boy's hands.

Side-by-Side Position. Partners stand side by side, boys usually to the left of the girl. The boy offers his partner his right hand, held above waist level, palms up. The girl places her left hand in the upraised hand.

PRESCHOOL SINGING GAMES

A vast fund of rhythmic materials exists for the preschool children. Not only are there the old favorites which have been handed down for centuries, but another whole area of simple songs and music written especially for children. The presentation in this section will concentrate on the old, familiar favorites, which will acquaint children with some of the songs which they can cherish.

These singing games will not only help children discover rhythms, but will also allow them to express themselves with their own movements based on the selected songs. In addition, each child should have the opportunity to sing easily and with expression in

RHYTHMIC ACTIVITIES   249

Partners Facing Position

Side-by-Side Position

reasonable tune to the music. He learns to sing with others and to match his singing with the accompaniment. Ultimately, it is hoped that he will like and enjoy music, building a foundation for future participation and appreciation of this important aspect of our culture.

The following represent some of the types of music which are suitable for preschool children:

Around We Go
Baa, Baa, Black Sheep
Bow-wow-wow
Brother John
The Cuckoo Clock
Diddle, Diddle Dumpling
The Donkey
Eency Weency Spider
Good Morning
Jack Be Nimble
Little Boy Blue
Mary Had A Little Lamb
Oh Where, Oh Where Has My Little Dog Gone?
Ring Around the Rosie
Rock-a-bye, Baby
Trot, My Pony, Trot
Who's That Knocking on My Door?
Yankee Doodle

AROUND WE GO
Music:

Formation: Single circle facing center with hands joined.

Verse and **Directions:**

1. Around we go, around we go, one big circle marching so.
   (All circle clockwise.)

2. Down we go, down we go, one big circle sinking so.

250 RHYTHMIC ACTIVITIES

(All stop and slowly go down, bending knees.)

3. Up we go, up we go, one big circle rising so.
  (All slowly rise.)
4. Repeat 1.
5. In we go, in we go, one big circle shrinking so. (Players go towards center.)
6. Out we go, out we go, one big circle stretching so.
  (Players walk backward to place and stretch.)

BAA, BAA, BLACK SHEEP
Music:

Formation: Scattered. Can be seated.

Verse:
Baa, baa, black sheep, have you any wool?
Yes sir, yes sir, three bags full.
One for my master, one for my dame,
And one for the little boy who lives in the lane.

Directions:
Line 1. Pretend to be sheep with horns.
Line 2. Nod head twice, hold up three fingers.
Line 3. Hold up finger to emphasize the "one," and repeat the action.
Line 4. Again hold up one finger.

BOW-WOW-WOW
Music:

Formation: Children are seated in a circle. One child occupies a chair in the center.

Verse:
Bow, wow, wow; whose dog art thou?
Little (Freddie Jones's) dog; bow, wow, wow.

Directions: One child is in the center and becomes the owner of the dog. During the first line, children clap three times and look in all directions as they ask the question. For the second line, they point four times at the center person, reciting his name, and then clap three times. Change the person in the center as the game is repeated.

Other animals could be named such as:
"Woof, woof, woof; whose bear art thou?"
"Meow, meow, meow; whose cat art thou?"
"Roar, roar, roar; whose lion art thou?"

RHYTHMIC ACTIVITIES 251

BROTHER JOHN

Music:

Formation: Children are scattered.

Verse:
  Are you sleeping, are you sleeping?
  Brother John, Brother John.
  Morning bells are ringing, morning bells are ringing,
  Ding, ding, dong; ding, ding, dong.

Directions:
  Line 1. Children walk around, asking the question of each other.
  Line 2. Continue to walk and talk to each other.
  Line 3. Hold their heads and sway back and forth.
  Line 4. Pretend to ring bells.

THE CUCKOO CLOCK

Music:

Formation: Scattered, seated.

Verse:
  Cuckoo, cuckoo, calls from the clock
  Let us be singing, when hours are ringing
  Fun time, fun time, soon will be here.

Directions: This is an adaptation of an old German folk song. The children can pretend to be cuckoo clocks and react accordingly.

DIDDLE, DIDDLE DUMPLING

Music:

Formation: Scattered.
Verse:
   Diddle, diddle, dumpling, my son John
   Went to bed with his stockings on;
   One shoe off, and one shoe on
   Diddle, diddle, dumpling, my son John.

Directions:
   Line 1. Do a jig in place, turning around.
   Line 2. Pretend to sleep with hands alongside face and then point to stockings.
   Line 3. Bounce on one foot, thrusting the other foot forward, reverse feet.
   Line 4. Repeat action for line 1.

THE DONKEY
Music:

Formation: In a circle, seated.
Verse:
   Sweetly sings the donkey as he looks for hay.
   If you do not feed him, this is what he'll say,
   Hee-haw, hee-haw; hee-haw, hee-haw, hee-haw.

Directions: Children sit and sing the first two lines. On the third line, they arise, place both thumbs in the ears, and flap the "ears" on each "hee-haw."

EENCY WEENCY SPIDER
Music:

Formation: Scattered. Children can be seated.
Verse:
   Eency weency spider went up the water spout.
   Down came the rain and washed the spider out.
   Out came the sun and dried up all the rain,
   And the eency weency spider went up the spout again.

Directions: This can be done as a finger play or with gross movements reacting to the words. Discuss with the children the kinds of things they should do with each line, stressing the concepts of up and down.

GOOD MORNING
Music:

Formation: One child is designated as king (or queen) for the day. The others are scattered around the room.

Verse:
Good morning to you, good morning to you.
Good morning, dear (use child's name), good morning to you.

Directions: During the first line children walk about bowing to each other. During the second line they face the king, bowing to him while repeating his name. They bow to the king again on the last "good morning." This can be used to teach the bow for boys and the curtsey for girls.

JACK BE NIMBLE
Music:

Formation: Scattered.

Supplies: Each child can make his own candlestick.

Verse:
1. Jack be nimble, Jack be quick
   Jack jump over the candlestick.
2. Jack be nimble, Jack be quick
   Jump back over the candlestick.

Directions: Each child has a candlestick (real or imaginary). He skips around to the words but places himself in position to "jump over the candlestick." At the completion of the second verse, he jumps back over from the opposite direction.

LITTLE BOY BLUE
Music:

Formation: Scattered.

Verse:
Little Boy Blue, come blow your horn.
The sheep's in the meadow, the cow's in the corn.
Where is the boy who looks after the sheep?
He's under the haystack fast a-sleep.

Directions: Children pantomime as desired while singing the words.

MARY HAD A LITTLE LAMB
Music:

Formation: Children organized by pairs, one of which is "Mary" and the other the "lamb."

Verses:

1. Mary had a little lamb, little lamb, little lamb,
   Mary had a little lamb, its fleece was white as snow.
2. And ev'rywhere that Mary went, Mary went, Mary went,
   Ev'rywhere that Mary went, the lamb was sure to go.
3. It followed her to school one day, school one day, school one day,
   It followed her to school one day, which teacher did not like.

Directions:

Verse 1. Mary pets her lamb and pretends to like it very much. Lamb crouches down.

Verse 2. Lamb follows Mary around wherever she goes.

Verse 3. Mary brings her lamb to school and teacher shakes her head.

OH WHERE, OH WHERE HAS MY LITTLE DOG GONE?
Music:

Formation: Scattered.

Verse:

Oh where, oh where has my little dog gone,
Oh where, oh where can he be?
With his ears cut short and his tail cut long,
Oh where, oh where can he be.

Directions: This is another flexible type of response song wherein the teacher and the children can work out the responses.

RING AROUND THE ROSIE   *Record:* Folkraft 1199
Music:

Formation: Single circle, all facing the center, hands joined.

Verse:

Ring around the rosie, a pocketful of posies

RHYTHMIC ACTIVITIES 255

One, two, three, and we'll all fall DOWN!

Directions: Children circle to the left as they sing. At the word "DOWN," children jump upward and land in a squat position in control. The game is repeated by circling in the opposite direction.

Children who fail to assume the squat position in control step back out of the circle for one game repetition. This is to counteract the tendency of some children to take the words "fall DOWN" too literally.

ROCK-A-BYE, BABY
Music:

Formation: Scattered. Can be seated.
Verse:
Rock-a-bye, baby, in the tree top
When the wind blows, the cradle will rock
When the bough breaks, the cradle will fall,
And down will come baby, cradle and all.

Directions: The children pantomime the action.

TROT, MY PONY, TROT
Music:

Formation: Scattered.
Verse:
Trot, trot, trot; trot my pony, trot,
Over fields and over gravel,
Oh what fun it is to travel,
Trot, trot, trot; trot, my pony, trot.

Directions: Children gallop informally around the area.

Variation: The first and last lines can be changed to, "Gallop, gallop, gallop; gallop, pony, gallop."

WHO'S THAT KNOCKING ON MY DOOR?
Music:

Formation: Scattered.
Verse:
Who's that knocking on my door?
Who's that knocking on my door?
Who's that knocking on my door?
It is (Susie Johnson).

RHYTHMIC ACTIVITIES

Directions: This is an action song with the children pantomiming the action. All sing and act out the first three lines. Either by prior arrangement or by selection (pointing) at the time, one child answers the last line, giving his name.

Other verses can be created such as:
"Who's that jumping up and down?"
"Who's that skipping to and fro?"
"Who's that turning round and round?"
Actions follow the word directions. The children can come up with many more suggestions.

YANKEE DOODLE
Music:

Formation: With partners. One partner is the pony and the other Yankee Doodle. Reins should be made so Yankee Doodle can drive the pony.

Verse:
Yankee Doodle went to town, a-riding on a pony
Stuck a feather in his cap and called it macaroni.
Yankee Doodle doodle doo, Yankee Doodle dandy,
All the lassies are so smart, And sweet as sugar candy.

Directions: Pretend to be a high-stepping ponies during the first two lines. During the second line, Yankee Doodle "sticks a feather in his cap." All gallop around during the last two lines.

KINDERGARTEN

The kindergarten list is made up primarily of singing games. The list of suggested activities is not extensive, as the kindergarten program should make good use of the activities listed under both the preschool and first grade programs. Some of the dances are individual, and some require partners. The movements demand only the simplest kind of locomotor steps. The following are suggested rhythms for kindergarten, for which the required skill is specified:

Dances	Skills
Farmer in the Dell	Walking
Baa Baa Blacksheep	Stamping, Walking
Twinkle, Twinkle, Little Star	Tiptoe Steps
Mulberry Bush	Walking or Skipping
Bluebird	Walking
Let Your Feet Go Tap, Tap, Tap	Skipping
Ten Little Indians	Indian Dancing
Pease Porridge Hot	Turning in a Circle
Snowball	Walking
Touch your Shoulders	Body Identification

FARMER IN THE DELL

Records: Victor 21618 and 45-5066 (Album E 87)
Folkraft 1182

Formation: Children are in single circle with hands joined and facing the center. One child is chosen to be the farmer and stands inside the circle.

Verses:
1. The farmer in the dell
   The farmer in the dell
   Heigh-ho! the dairy-O!
   The farmer in the dell
2. The farmer takes a wife
3. The wife takes a child
4. The child takes a nurse
5. The nurse takes a dog
6. The dog takes a cat
7. The cat takes a rat
8. The rat takes the cheese
9. The cheese stands alone

Directions:

Verse 1. The circle players walk to the left with hands joined while the Farmer is deciding on a child to be selected for his "wife."

Verse 2. The Farmer chooses another child who is led to the center and becomes his wife. The child selected joins hands with him, and they walk around the inside of the circle in the opposite direction from that of the big circle.

Verses 3 to 8. Each child selected in turn joins the center group.

Verse 9. All children in the center with the exception of the child who is the "cheese" return to the outside circle. The circle stops and the children face the center clapping hands during this verse.

Suggestions: The game should be repeated until all children have had an opportunity to be in the center.

Variations:

1. Several farmers may be chosen to start. When the outer circle gets smaller, the children can no longer join hands.

2. Verse 8 can be: "The cat chases the rat." During this, the Cat does chase the Rat in and out of the circle with the children raising and lowering their joined hands to help the Rat and hinder the Cat. If the Cat catches the Rat, he gets to be the Farmer for the next game. If not, the Rat becomes the Farmer. The Rat must be caught during the singing of the verse.

BAA BAA BLACKSHEEP

Records: Folkraft 1191
Russell 700A
Victor E-83

Formation: Single circle, all facing center.

Verse:
Baa Baa Blacksheep, have you any wool?
Yes sir, yes sir, three bags full.
One for my master and one for my dame,
And one for the little boy who lives down the lane.

Directions:

Line 1. Stamp three times, shake forefinger three times.

Line 2. Nod head twice and hold up three fingers.

Line 3. Bow to the person on the right and then to the left.

Line 4. Hold one finger up high and walk around in a tiny circle, again facing the center.

TWINKLE, TWINKLE, LITTLE STAR

Record: Childcraft EP-C4

Formation: Children are in a single circle, facing in.

Verse:
Twinkle, twinkle, little star.
How I wonder what you are.
Up above the world so high
Like a diamond in the sky.
Twinkle, twinkle, little star.
How I wonder what you are.

Directions: Children are in a large enough circle so that they can come forward seven short steps without crowding.

Line 1. Children have arms extended overhead and fingers extended and moving. Each child takes seven tiptoe steps toward the center of the circle.

Line 2. Continue with seven tiptoe steps in place, making a full turn around.

Line 3. Each child makes a circle with his arms and hands, rocking back and forth.

Line 4. All form a diamond with the fingers in front of the face.

Line 5. With the arms overhead and the fingers extended, move backward to original place with seven tiptoe steps.

Line 6. Turn in place with seven tiptoe steps.

MULBERRY BUSH

Records: Victor 20806, 45-5065;
Columbia 90037-V;
Folkraft 1183

Formation: Single circle, facing center, hands joined.

Chorus:
Here we go round the mulberry bush,
The mulberry bush, the mulberry bush,
Here we go round the mulberry bush,
So early in the morning.

Verses:

1. This is the way we wash our clothes,
   Wash our clothes, wash our clothes,
   This is the way we wash our clothes,
   So early Monday morning
2. This is the way we iron our clothes,
   (Tuesday morning)
3. This is the way we mend our clothes,
   (Wednesday morning)
4. This is the way we sweep our floor,
   (Thursday morning)
5. This is the way we scrub our floor,
   (Friday morning)
6. This is the way we make a cake,
   (Saturday morning)
7. This is the way we go to church,
   (Sunday morning).

Directions: The singing game begins with the chorus, which is also sung after each verse. As each chorus is sung, the children skip (or walk) to the right. On the words "so early in the morning," each child drops hands and makes a complete turn in place.

During the verses, the children pantomime the actions suggested by the words. Encourage the children to use large and vigorous movements.

BLUEBIRD

Record: Folkraft 1180.

Formation: Single circle, hands joined and facing the center. One child stands outside the circle and is the "Bluebird."

Verse:
Bluebird, bluebird, through my window,
Bluebird, bluebird, through my window,
Bluebird, bluebird, through my window,
Hi diddle dum dum dee.

Chorus:
Take a little boy (girl) and tap him (her) on the shoulder
(repeat twice more)
Hi diddle dum dum dee.

Directions: During the verse all circle children lift joined hands high, forming arches, under which the "Bluebird" weaves in and out. At the completion of the verse the Bluebird should stand directly behind one of the circle players. During the chorus, the Bluebird taps the child in front of him lightly on the shoulders with both hands. This child then becomes the new Bluebird, with the old Bluebird keeping his hands on his shoulders, forming a train. As the chorus is sung, the Bluebird train moves around the various directions in the center area of the circle. When the verse is sung again, the train moves in and out of the arches. Continue the action until seven or eight children form the train. Return the train children to the circle formation and begin anew with a new Bluebird.

LET YOUR FEET GO TAP, TAP, TAP

Record: Folkraft 1184.

Formation: Double circle, partners facing.

Verse:
Let your feet go tap, tap, tap,
Let your hands go clap, clap, clap,
Let your finger beckon me,
Come, dear partner, dance with me.

Chorus
Tra, la, la, la, la, la, la, etc.

Directions:

Line 1. Tap foot three times.
Line 2. Clap hands three times.
Line 3. Beckon and bow to partner.
Line 4. Join inside hands and face counterclockwise.

Chorus. All sing and skip counterclockwise.

Note: This can be sung to "Merrily We Roll Along," with a little adjustment for line 2.

TEN LITTLE INDIANS

Record: Folkraft 1197.

Formation: Children are in a circle. Ten children are selected and numbered consecutively from 1 to 10, but remain in the circle.

Sequence: The piece is played four times to allow a complete sequence of the dance.

1. One little, two little, three little Indians,
   Four little, five little, six little Indians,
   Seven little, eight little, nine little Indians,
   Ten little Indian Braves (Squaws).

   During this verse, the Indians as numbered go from the circle to the center when their number is mentioned in the singing, while the remainder of the circle children clap lightly.

2. During the second repetition of the music, the Indians in the center do an Indian dance, each in his own way.

3. The verse under #1 is again sung, but this time the Indians in the center return to the circle when their numbers are sung.

4. During the last rendition of the piece, all children dance as Indians, moving in any direction they wish, not retaining the circle formation.

   The dance is repeated with another set of Indians.

PEASE PORRIDGE HOT

Record: Folkraft 1190.

Formation: Double circle, partners facing.

Verse:
Pease porridge hot,
Pease porridge cold,
Pease porridge in a pot,
Nine days old!
Some like it hot,
Some like it cold,
Some like it in a pot,
Nine days old!

Directions: The dance is in two parts. The first is a patty-cake rhythm, done while the children sing the above verse. During the second part, the children dance with a circular movement.

Part I

Line 1. Clap own hands to thighs, clap own hands together, clap own hands to partner's hands.

Line 2. Repeat action of line 1.

Line 3. Clap hands to thighs, clap own hands together, clap right hand against partner's right, clap own hands together.

Line 4. Clap left hand to partner's left, clap own hands together, clap both hands against partner's hands.

Lines 5-8. Repeat lines 1-4.

Part II

Join both hands with partner and skip around in a small, turning circle counterclockwise for the first four lines, ending with the word "old!" Reverse direction and skip clockwise for the remainder of the verse. Move one step to the left for a new partner.

SNOWBALL

Playing Area: Indoors or outdoors.

Players: Entire class.

Supplies: None.

Tell the children that this activity is like a snowball. We roll a small snowball and as we roll (keep going) the snowball gets larger and larger. Two children are chosen to start, with the remainder seated in a circle. Appropriate music is needed.

The active children walk around the interior of the circle to music. When the music stops, each child goes to a circle player, bows (girls curtsy), and says, "Will you follow me?" The music is started again and the two active players turn around and lead out, followed by the chosen partner. They can weave out in different directions, using turns and various patterns, each followed by his partner. At this point, we have four children moving in the circle area.

The music stops and all four active players move to the circle players, each choosing a partner. The actions and dialogue are repeated. When the music starts anew, we now have four couples moving. The sequence is repeated until all the children have been chosen.

Variation: Different locomotor movements can be done as determined by the music.

TOUCH YOUR SHOULDERS

Music: Verses are sung to the tune of "Mary Had a Little Lamb."

Formation: None needed, but children can be in any arrangement.

Verses:

1. Touch your shoulders and your knees.
   Touch your shoulders and your knees.

Touch your shoulders and your knees.
Make your feet go stamp, stamp, stamp.
2. Touch your elbows and your toes, etc.
Make your hands go clap, clap, clap.
3. Touch your ankles, reach up high, etc.
Shake yourself up in the sky.
4. Touch your hips and touch your heels, etc.
Jump up high; one, two, three.

Directions: The verses are self-explanatory in describing the action. Children use both hands in touching. Additional verses can be devised by the children using body parts not previously mentioned and a different finishing line.

FIRST GRADE

The first grade singing games and folk dances are introductory in nature and involve simple formations and uncomplicated changes. The movements are primarily walking, skipping, and running. Only a few of the dances are done with partners, so the problem of getting the boys and girls paired off as partners is not important. Most of the activities are quite flexible in nature, and the children can interpret the words and music in various ways.

The rhythmic activities listed under the kindergarten program should be added to the list of suggested activities.

Dances	**Skills**
The Farmer in the Wheat	Skipping
London Bridge	Walking
The Muffin Man	Skipping
Oats, Peas, Beans, and Barley Grow	Walking, skipping
Looby Loo	Skipping
Pussy Cat	Walking, draw step, jumping
The Thread Follows the Needle	Walking
I See You	Skipping, two-handed swing
Sing a Song of Sixpence	Walking
Dance of Greeting	Running, bowing
Hickory Dickory Dock	Running
Chimes of Dunkirk	Sliding

THE FARMER IN THE WHEAT

Records: Victor 21618 and 45-5066. Folkraft 1182.

Formation: Single circle, facing center. Three children — the Farmer, the Sun, and the Rain — stand in the center.

Verses:

1. The farmer in the wheat.
   The farmer in the wheat.
   Heigh-ho the dairy-o,
   The farmer in the wheat.
2. The farmer sows his wheat, etc.
3. He covers them with dirt, etc.
4. The sun begins to shine, etc.
5. The rain begins to fall, etc.
6. The wheat begins to grow, etc.
7. The farmer cuts his grain, etc.
8. The farmer stacks his grain, etc.
9. They all begin to dance, etc.

Directions:

Verse 1. Children in the circle walk to the left with hands joined.

Verse 2. The Farmer skips around the inside of the circle counterclockwise and sows his wheat, while the children continue to walk.

Verse 3. The children stop, drop hands, and face the center. The Farmer skips around the circle, tapping each child on the head; as he is touched, the child sinks down to the ground, becoming a wheat stalk.

Verse 4. The Sun skips around spreading sunshine.

Verse 5. The Rain skips around showering the wheat.

Verse 6. Children rise slowly and jerkily to a standing position with arms overhead to simulate the heads of wheat.

Verse 7. The Farmer skips around the inside of the circle and cuts the grain. Each child falls to the ground.

Verse 8. The Farmer skips around the group, arranging children by pairs to lean against each other to form stacks. (May be repeated.)

Verse 9. Paired children, inside hands joined, skip counterclockwise around the circle. The Farmer, Sun, and Rain form a small circle and skip clockwise.

LONDON BRIDGE

Records: Victor 20806.

Formation: Single circle moving either clockwise or counterclockwise. Two children are chosen to form the bridge. They face and join hands, holding them high in the air representing a bridge ready to fall.

Verses:

1. London Bridge is falling down,
   Falling down, falling down.
   London Bridge is falling down,
   My fair lady.
2. Build it up with iron bars, etc.
3. Iron bars will rust away, etc.
4. Build it up with gold and silver, etc.
5. Gold and silver I have not, etc.
6. Build it up with pins and needles, etc.
7. Pins and needles rust and bend, etc.
8. Build it up with penny loaves, etc.
9. Penny loaves will tumble down, etc.
10. Here's a prisoner I have got, etc.
11. What's the prisoner done to you? etc.
12. Stole my watch and bracelet too, etc.
13. What'll you take to set him free? etc.
14. One hundred pounds will set him free, etc.
15. One hundred pounds we don't have, etc.
16. Then off to prison he (or she) must go, etc.

Directions: All children pass under the bridge in a single line. When the words "My fair lady" are sung, the bridge falls and the child caught is a prisoner. He or she must choose either gold or silver and must stand behind the side of the bridge which represents his choice. No one must know which side is gold or silver until after he has made his choice as a prisoner. When all have been caught, the game ends with a tug-of-war.

Variation: Using more bridges will speed up the game.

THE MUFFIN MAN

Record: Folkraft 1188.

Formation: Children are in a single circle, facing the center with hands joined. One child, the Muffin Man, is in the center.

Verses:

1. Oh, do you know the muffin man,
   The muffin man, the muffin man?
   Oh, do you know the muffin man,
   Who lives in Drury Lane?
2. Oh, yes we know the muffin man, etc.
3. Four of us know the muffin man, etc.
4. Eight of us know the muffin man, etc.
5. Sixteen of us know the muffin man, etc.
6. All of us know the muffin man, etc.

Directions:

Verse 1. The children in the circle stand still and sing, while the Muffin Man skips around the circle. He chooses a partner by skipping in place in front of him. On the last line of the verse, "Who lives in Drury Lane," the Muffin Man and his partner go to the center.

Verse 2. The action is the same except two children now skip around in the circle and choose two partners.

Verse 3. The action is repeated with four skipping and four partners being chosen.

The verses continue until all children have been chosen. When all have been chosen, the last verse is sung while the children skip around the room.

OATS, PEAS, BEANS, AND BARLEY GROW

Records: Victor 20214. Folkraft 1182.

Formation: Single circle with a "farmer" in the center.

Verses:

1. Oats, peas, beans, and barley grow,
   Oats, peas, beans, and barley grow.
   Do you and I, or anyone know, how
   Oats, peas, beans, and barley grow?
2. First, the farmer sows the seed,
   Then he stands and takes his ease,
   He stamps his foot and claps his hands
   And turns around to view his lands.
3. Waiting for a partner,
   Waiting for a partner,
   Open the ring and choose one in
   While we all gaily dance and sing.
4. Now you're married, you must obey
   You must be kind in all you say
   You must be kind, you must be good,
   And keep your wife in kindling wood.

Directions:

Verse 1. The children walk clockwise around the Farmer.

Verse 2. All stand in place and follow the actions suggested by the words of the verse.

Verse 3. Circle players again move clockwise while the Farmer chooses a partner, which should be done before the end of the verse.

Verse 4. Everyone skips during this verse. The circle continues in the same direction it has been, while the Farmer and his partner (wife) skip in the opposite direction.

LOOBY LOO

Records: Victor 20214. Russell 702. Folkraft 1102, 1184. Columbia 10008D.

Formation: Single circle, all facing center with hands joined.

Chorus: A chorus is repeated before each verse. During the chorus all children skip around the circle to the left.

  Here we dance looby loo
  Here we dance looby light
  Here we dance looby loo
  All on a Saturday night.

Verses:
1. I put my right hand in
   I take my right hand out
   I give my right hand a shake, shake, shake,
   And turn myself about.
2. I put my left hand in, etc.
3. I put my right foot in, etc.
4. I put my left foot in, etc.
5. I put my head way in, etc.
6. I put my whole self in, etc.

Directions: On the verse part of the dance, the children stand still facing the center and follow the directions of the words. On the words "And turn myself about," they make a complete turn in place and get ready to skip around the circle.

The movements should be definite and vigorous. On the last verse, the child jumps forward and then backward, shakes himself vigorously, and then turns about.

PUSSY CAT

Record: Russell 700B.

Formation: Single circle, all facing center with hands joined. One player, the "Pussy Cat," is in the center. If desired, more than one Pussy Cat can be in the center.

Verse:
  Pussy Cat, Pussy Cat, where have you been?
  I've been to London to visit the Queen!
  Pussy Cat, Pussy Cat, what did you there?
  I frightened a mouse from under her chair!

Chorus: The chorus is a repeat of the same music, but the children sing tra la, la, la, etc., instead of the words.

Directions:
Line 1. Sung by the circle children as they walk counterclockwise around the circle.

Line 2. Sung by the Cat as the children reverse the direction and walk around the other way.

Line 3. Sung by the children as they drop hands, walk toward the center, and shake a finger at the Cat.

Line 4. Sung by the Cat who on the last word "chair" jumps high into the air, and the others pretend fright and run back to the circle.

Chorus:
Line 1. Children take two draw steps (one to each measure) to the right, followed by four stamps.

Line 2. Repeat to the left.

Line 3. Four steps (one to each measure) to the center.

Line 4. Three steps backward in the same tempo as line 3, followed by a jump.

A draw step is made by stepping directly to the side and bringing the other foot in a closing movement. It is a step with one foot and a close with the other.

Variation: Have more than one Pussy Cat in the circle or have a number of smaller circles, each with a Pussy Cat.

THE THREAD FOLLOWS THE NEEDLE

Records: RCA Victor 22760 (Album E87). Pioneer 3015.

Formation: A single line of about eight children is formed. Hands are joined and each child is numbered consecutively.

Verse:
  The thread follows the needle
  The thread follows the needle
  In and out the needle goes
  As mother mends the children's clothes.

Directions: The first child (#1) is the needle and leads the children, forming stitches until the entire line has been sewn. When the music starts, the needle leads the line under the raised arms of the last two children (#7 and 8). When the line has passed under their arms, they turn and face the opposite direction, letting their arms cross in front of them. This forms the stitch.

The leader now repeats the movement and passes under the next pair of raised arms (#6 and 7). Number 6 is now added to the stitch when he reverses his direction. This is repeated until the entire line has been stitched, with the leader turning under his own arm to complete the last stitch.

To "rip" the stitch, children raise their arms overhead and turn back to original positions.

The game can be repeated with a new leader.

I SEE YOU

Records: Victor 20432. Russell 726. Folkraft 1197.

Formation: The boys and girls stand in two longways sets as follows.

```
(1)   x x x x x x x   boys
(2)   o o o o o o o   girls
(3)   x x x x x x x   boys
(4)   o o o o o o o   girls
```

Lines 1 and 2 are facing lines 3 and 4. The space between the two middle lines (2 and 3) should be from 10' to 12'.

Lines 1 and 4 are the active players. Each active player's partner is directly in front of him and stands with hands on hips.

Verse:

I see you, I see you
Tra, la, la, la, la, la.
I see you, I see you
Tra, la, la, la, la, la.

Chorus:

Tra, la, la, etc.
Tra, la, la, etc.

Directions:

Verse:

Line 1. On the first "I see you" each active player looks over partner's left shoulder in peekaboo fashion. On the second "I see you" active player looks over partner's right shoulder in same peekaboo fashion.

Line 2. Tempo is doubled and active players make three fast peekaboo movements, left, right, left.

Line 3. Repeat the action of line 1, except the first peekaboo is made to the right.

Line 4. Repeat the action of line 2, except the movements are right, left, right.

Chorus:

Line 1. All children clap on the first note ("tra") and the active players, passing to the left of their partners, meet in the center with a two-handed swing, skipping around once in a circle, clockwise.

Line 2. All children clap again ("tra") and each active player now faces his own partner, skipping around with him once in a circle, clockwise.

Partners have now changed places with the active players, and the entire pattern is repeated with a new set of players in the active roles.

SING A SONG OF SIXPENCE

Records: Folkraft 1180. Victor 22760. Russell 700.

Formation: Players are in circle formation facing the center. Six to eight players are crouched in the center as blackbirds.

Verses:

1. Sing a song of sixpence, a pocket full of rye,
   Four and twenty blackbirds, baked in a pie,
   When the pie was opened the birds began to sing,
   Wasn't that a dainty dish to set before the king?
2. The king was in his counting house, counting out his money,
   The queen was in the pantry, eating bread and honey,
   The maid was in the garden, hanging out the clothes,
   And down came a blackbird and snipped off her nose!

Directions:

Verse 1:

Line 1. Players walk around in a circle.

Line 2. Circle players walk with shortened steps toward the center of the circle with arms outstretched forward.

Line 3. Players walk backward with arms now up. The blackbirds in the center fly around.

Line 4. Circle players kneel as if presenting a dish (blackbirds continue to fly around).

Verse 2:

Lines 1, 2, and 3. Pantomime action of words, counting out money, eating, and hanging up clothes.

Line 4. Each blackbird snips off the nose of a circle player who now becomes a blackbird for the next game.

DANCE OF GREETING

Records: Victor 45-6183, 20432. Folkraft 1187. Russell 726.

Formation: Single circle, all facing center. Each boy stands to the left of his partner.

Measures:

1	All clap, clap, and bow to partner (girl curtsies).
2	Repeat but turn back to partner and bow to neighbor.
3	Stamp right, stamp left.
4	Each player turns around in four running steps.
5–8	Repeat action of measures 1–4.
9–12	All join hands and run to the left for four measures (16 counts).
13–16	Repeat action of measures 9–12 with light running steps in the opposite direction.

Variation: Instead of using a light running step, use a light slide.

HICKORY DICKORY DOCK

Record: Victor 22760.

Formation: Children are in a double circle, partners facing.

Verse:

Hickory Dickory Dock, tick tock,
The mouse ran up the clock, tick tock.
The clock struck one, the mouse ran down.
Hickory, Dickory, Dock, tick tock.

Directions:

Line 1. Stretch arms overhead and bend the body from side to side like a pendulum, and finish with two stamps on "tick, tock."

Line 2. Repeat action of line 1.

Line 3. Clap hands on "one." Join hands with partner and run to the right in a little circle.

Line 4. Repeat the pendulum swing with the two stamps.

CHIMES OF DUNKIRK

Records: Victor 45-6176, 17327. Folkraft 1188. Columbia A-3016.

Formation: A single circle with boys and girls alternating. Partners face each other. Hands are on own hips.

Measures:

1–2	All stamp lightly left, right, left.
3–4	Clap hands overhead, swaying back and forth.
5–8	Join hands with partner and make one complete turn in place clockwise.
9–16	All join hands in a single circle facing the center and slide to the left (16 slides).

SECOND GRADE

The second grade includes many activities similar to those taught in the first grade. In addition, there is more emphasis on partner-type dances and change of partners. The dance patterns tend to become more definite, and more folk dances are included. The movements are still confined primarily to the simple locomotor types, with additional and varied emphasis in more complicated formations.

Dances	Skills
Down the Mississippi	Bending, scooter movements
Did You Ever See a Lassie	Walking
Go Round and Round the Village	Walking
Shoemaker's Dance	Skipping
Jolly Is the Miller	Marching
Shoo Fly	Walking, skipping
Ach Ja	Walking, sliding
A Hunting We Will Go	Sliding, skipping
How D'ye Do, My Partner	Bowing, skipping

Rig-a-jig-jig — Walking, skipping
Broom Dance — Marching, skipping
The Popcorn Man — Jumping, skipping

DOWN THE MISSISSIPPI

Records: To the tune "Here We Go Round the Mulberry Bush." Victor 20806, 45-5065; Columbia 90037-V; Folkraft 1183.

Formation: None. Children can be scattered or in a circle as desired. Each child is seated on the floor with his legs together and extended forward.

Verses:
1. This is the way we row our boat, row our boat, row our boat,
  This is the way we row our boat,
  Down the Mississippi!
2. This is the way we glide along, etc.
3. This is the way we rock the boat, etc.
4. This is the way we turn around, etc.
5. This is the way we float for home, etc.
6. This is the way we spell Mississippi, spell Mississippi, spell Mississippi.
  This is the way we spell Mississippi,
  M-I-S-S-I-S-S-I-P-P-I WOW!

Directions:

Verse 1. Each child rows his boat in time to the music.

Verse 2. Each child folds his arms across his chest and bends forward and backward.

Verse 3. Each child, with arms outstretched to the side, bends from side to side.

Verse 4. Each child by rowing with one "paddle" only, turns on his side completely around in stages.

Verse 5. Each child folds his arms across his chest and moves in any direction he wishes using scooter movements. Reach out with the heels and pull the seat up to the heels.

Verse 6. Children sing the first three lines (no action) and then sound out (spell) Mississippi in staccato fashion.

(May they never misspell Mississippi!)

DID YOU EVER SEE A LASSIE

Records: Victor 45-5066, 21618; Folkraft 1183; Columbia 10008D.

Formation: Children are in a single circle, facing half left with hands joined. One child is in the center.

Verse:
  Did you ever see a lassie, a lassie, a lassie?
  Did you ever see a lassie do this way and that?
  Do this way and that way, and this way and that way.
  Did you ever see a lassie do this way and that?

Directions:

Measures:
1–8 Children with hands joined walk to the left in a circle. Since this is fast waltz time, there should be one step to each measure. The child in the center gets ready to demonstrate some type of movement.

9–16 All stop and follow the movement suggested by the child in the center.

As the verse starts over, the center child selects another to do some action in the center and changes places with him.

The word "laddie" should be substituted if the center person is a boy.

GO ROUND AND ROUND THE VILLAGE

Record: Folkraft 1191.

Formation: Single circle, hands joined. Several extra players stand outside, scattered around the circle.

Verses:
1. Go round and round the village,
  Go round and round the village,
  Go round and round the village,
  As we have done before.
2. Go in and out the windows, etc.
3. Now stand and face your partner, etc.
4. Now follow me to London, etc.

Directions:

Verse 1: Circle players move to the right and the extra players on the outside go the other way. All skip.

Verse 2: Circle players stop and lift joined hands, forming the windows. Extra players go in and out the windows, finishing inside the circle.

Verse 3: Extra players select partners by standing in front of them. Should select opposite sex.

Verse 4: The extra players and partners now skip around the inside of the circle while the outside circle skips the opposite way.

Variations:

1. All chosen players can continue and repeat the game until the entire circle has been chosen.

2. An excellent way is to have the boys in the circle and the girls as extra players. In this way, everyone will select and be selected as a partner. Reverse and put the girls in the circle and leave the boys as the extras.

SHOEMAKER'S DANCE

Records: Victor 20450, 45-6171; Russell 750; Folkraft 1187; Columbia A-3038.

Formation: Double circle, partners facing, boys on the inside.

Verse:
See the cobbler wind his thread,
Snip, snap, tap, tap, tap.
That's the way he earns his bread,
Snip, snap, tap, tap, tap.

Chorus:
So the cobbler blithe and gay,
Works from morn to close of day,
At his shoes he pegs away,
Whistling cheerily his lay.

Directions:

Measures:

1–2 Clenched fists are held in front about chest high. On "see the cobbler" one fist is rolled forward over the other three times. On "wind his thread" roll the fists over each other backwards three times.

3 Fingers of the right hand form a scissors and make two cuts on "snip, snap."

4 Double up fists and hammer one on top the other three times.

5–8 Same action, except finish up with three slaps instead of hammering fists.

Chorus: Partners join inside hands, outside hands on hips. All skip to the left around the room. Near the end of the chorus, all slow down and face each other. All children take one step to the left to secure a new partner.

JOLLY IS THE MILLER

Records: Victor 45-5067 or 20214, E-87; Folkraft 1192; American Play Party 1185.

Formation: Double circle, partners with joined inside hands facing counterclockwise. Boys are on the inside. A "Miller" is in the center of the circle.

Verse:
Jolly is the Miller who lives by the mill;
The wheel goes round with a right good will.
One hand on the hopper and the other on the sack;
The right steps forward and the left steps back.

Chorus: The children march counterclockwise with inside hands joined. During the second line when the "wheel goes round" the dancers should make their outside arms go in a circle to form a wheel. Children change partners at the words "the right steps forward and the left steps back." The Miller then has a chance to get a partner. The child left without a partner becomes the Miller.

SHOO FLY

Records: Folkraft 1102, 1185; Decca 18222.

Formation: All are in a circle with hands joined facing in. Boy stands with his girl on right.

Verse:
Shoo fly, don't bother me,
Shoo fly, don't bother me,
Shoo fly, don't bother me,
I belong to Company G.
I feel, I feel, I feel like a morning star,
I feel, I feel, I feel like a morning star.

Directions: The dance is in two parts and finishes with a change of partners.

Measures:

1–2 Walk forward four steps toward the center of the circle swinging arms back and forth.

3–4 Walk four steps backward to place with arms swinging.

5–8 Repeat all of above.

9–16 Each boy turns to the girl on his right, takes hold of both hands and skips around in a small circle, finishing so this girl will be on his left when the circle is re-formed. His new partner is on his right.

The dance is repeated with new partners.

Variation: For the second part of the dance the following is an interesting substitute for the two-handed swing.

Designate one couple to form an arch by lifting joined hands. This couple now moves forward toward the center of the circle. The couple on the opposite side moves forward, under the arch, drawing the circle after it. When all have passed through the arch, the couple forming the arch turn under their own joined hands. The dancers now move forward to form a circle with everyone facing out. The dance is repeated with all facing out.

To return the circle to face in again, the same couple again makes an arch and the lead couple backs through the arch, drawing the circle after them. The arch couple turn under their own arms.

In this version, there is no change of partners.

ACH JA

Record: Evans, Child Rhythms, VII.

Formation: Double circle, partners facing counterclockwise, boys on the inside.

Verse:

When my father and my mother take the children to the fair,
Ach Ja! Ach Ja!
Oh, they have but little money, but it's little that they care,
Ach Ja! Ach Ja!
Tra la la, tra la la, tra la la la la la la
Tra la la, tra la la, tra la la la la la la
Ach Ja! Ach Ja!

Directions:

Measures:

1–2	Partners walk eight steps in line of direction.
3	Partners drop hands and bow to each other.
4	Each boy now bows to the girl on his left, who returns the bow.
5–8	Measures 1–4 are repeated.
9–10	Partners face each other, join hands and take four slides in line of direction (counterclockwise).
11–12	Four slides are taken clockwise.
13	Partners bow to each other.
14	Boy bows to girl on his left, who returns the bow. To start the next dance, the boy moves quickly toward this girl, who is his next partner.

A HUNTING WE WILL GO

Records: Folkraft 1191; Victor 45-5064, 22759.

Formation: Longways set with the children in two lines facing each other, boys in one line and girls in the other.

Verse:

Oh, a-hunting we will go,
A-hunting we will go,
We'll catch a fox and put him in a box
And then we'll let him go!

Chorus:

Tra, la, la, la, la, la, la, etc.

Directions: Everyone sings.

Lines 1 and 2. Head couple with hands joined slides between the two lines to the foot of the set (8 counts).

Lines 3 and 4. Head couple slides to original position (8 counts).

Chorus. Couples join hands and skip in a circle to the left following the head couple. When the head couple reaches the place formerly occupied by the last couple in the line (foot couple), they form an arch under which the other couples skip. A new couple is now the head couple and the dance is repeated until each couple has had a chance to be at the head.

Variation:

1. On the chorus, the head couple separates, and each leads his own line down the outside to the foot of the set. The head couple meets at the foot and forms an arch for the other couples. The other dancers meet two by two and skip under the arch back to place.

2. The first two couples slide down the center and back on lines 1, 2, 3, and 4. Otherwise the dance is the same.

HOW D'YE DO, MY PARTNER

Records: Victor 21685; Folkraft 1190.

Formation: **Double circle, partners facing, boys on the inside.**

Verse:

How d'ye do, my partner?
How d'ye do today?
Will you dance in the circle?
I will show you the way.

Directions:

Measures:

1–2 Boys bow to their partners.

3–4 Girls curtsy.

5–6 Boys offer right hand to girl, who takes it with her right hand. Both turn to face counterclockwise.

7–8 Couples join left hands and are now in a skater's position. They get ready to skip when the music changes.

9–16 Partners skip counterclockwise in the circle slowing down on measure 15. On measure 16 the girls stop and the boys move ahead to secure a new partner.

RIG-A-JIG-JIG

Record: Ruth Evans, Childhood Rhythms, Series VI, Folkraft 1199.

Formation: Single circle, all facing center, boys and girls alternating. One child is in the center.

Verse:
As I was walking down the street,
Heigh-ho, heigh-ho, heigh-ho, heigh-ho,
A pretty girl I chanced to meet,
Heigh-ho, heigh-ho, heigh-ho.

Chorus:
Rig-a-jig-jig, and away we go,
   away we go, away we go.
Rig-a-jig-jig, and away we go,
Heigh-ho, heigh-ho, heigh-ho.

Directions: While all sing, the center player walks around the inside of the circle until the words "a pretty girl" and then stands in front of a partner. Girls choose boys and vice versa. He then bows to her on the last line of the verse.

He takes her hands in skater's position and on the chorus they skip around the inside of the circle while the circle players clap hands in time.

The dance is repeated with the partners separating and choosing new partners until all have been chosen.

On the second time the verse is sung, the words "a nice young man" or "a handsome man" can be substituted for "a pretty girl."

Variation: The dance can be done by alternating boys and girls and using the appropriate verses. Select four or five boys to begin in the center. They choose partners and after the skip return to the circle. The girls continue the dance choosing five more boys, and so on.

BROOM DANCE

Record: Victor 20448.

Formation: Double circle, partners facing counterclockwise with boys on the inside. An extra boy with a broom is in the center.

Verse:
One, two, three, four, five, six, seven,
Where's my partner, nine, ten, eleven?
In Berlin, in Stettin,
There's the place to find him (her) in.

Chorus:
Tra la la, etc.
(repeats the music)

Directions: The record has three changes of music and then a pause. The verse is sung during the first change and repeated during the second change. The chorus is the third change. During the verse, which is repeated, all march counterclockwise. The boy in the center hands the broom to another boy and takes his place in the inner line. The boy with the broom in turn hands the broom to another inner line member and takes his place, and so on. The one who has the broom after the two verses are sung (on the word "in") takes the broom to the center. He then pretends to sweep while the others skip with inside hands joined. If there are extra girls, the dance can be done with the girls exchanging the broom by making the direction of the march clockwise.

Variation I: The first verse is sung during the first music change and the children march as in the original dance. During the second music change, the following routine is done. Note that in this routine the broom may be exchanged only when the boys move to a new partner.

Routine for the second music change.
Measures:

1–2 Beginning with the outside foot, take seven steps forward and pause on the eighth.

3–4 Beginning with the inside foot, take seven steps backward and pause as before.

5   Beginning on the outside foot, take three steps away and pause.

6   Beginning with the inside foot, take three steps in and pause.

7–8   Swing once around in place with a right elbow swing. As the boy comes back to place, he moves forward to the next girl. During the exchange of partners, the broom man gives the broom to another boy and takes his place.

Variation II: This routine is used during the first change of the music.

Boys and girls form separate lines facing each other about 20′ apart. The broom man is in the center. The teacher holds the broom to one side.

Measures:

1–2   Lines advance toward each other with seven steps.

3–4   Lines retreat with seven steps.

5–6   Lines again advance seven steps.

7–8   Lines retreat seven steps until the word "in"! All, including the broom man, rush for a partner and get ready to march around the room. The player left goes to the center to become the new broom man. The new broom man now takes the broom from the teacher, and the dance proceeds in the second and third changes of the music as in the original dance. Note that the broom should not be given to the broom man until after the first music change.

THE POPCORN MAN

Record: Folkraft 1180 (The Muffin Man).

Formation: Children are in a single circle, facing the center with hands at sides. One child, the Popcorn Man, stands in front of another child of opposite sex.

Verses:

1. Oh, have you seen the Popcorn Man,
   The Popcorn Man, the Popcorn Man?
   Oh, have you seen the Popcorn Man,
   Who lives on - - - Street?

2. Oh, yes, we've seen the Popcorn Man,
   The Popcorn Man, the Popcorn Man.
   Oh, yes, we've seen the Popcorn Man,
   Who lives on - - - Street?

Directions:

Verse 1. The children stand still and clap hands lightly, with the exception of the Popcorn Man and his partner. These two join hands and jump lightly in place keeping time to the music.

Verse 2. The Popcorn Man and his partner now skip around the inside of the circle individually, and near the end of the verse each stands in front of a child, thus choosing new partners.

Verse 1 is now repeated with two sets of partners doing the jumping. During the repetition of Verse 2, four children now skip around the inside of the circle and choose partners. This continues until all the children are chosen.

Boys should choose girls, and girls should choose boys for partners. The children should choose the name of a street which they would like to put into the verses.

THIRD GRADE

In the third grade most of the emphasis shifts to the folk dance. Simple locomotor skills are still the basis of the movement patterns. Continued emphasis is on the simple skills, with more attention to sliding and draw steps. The formations tend to be more of the partner type with partner changes included in many of the dances. Some basic formations are introduced which are later used in more advanced dances in the intermediate grades.

Most of the steps used in the dances — draw steps, sliding, and skipping — have been previously described and employed in dances. To these are added the step-hop and the Bleking step. To do the step-hop, the child takes a short step with one foot and then hops on that foot. He then takes a step with the other foot and hops on it. A description of the Bleking step is found in the dance directions for the Bleking dance.

Dances	Skills
Paw Paw Patch	Skipping
Yankee Doodle	Marching, turning
Three Blind Mice	Skipping
Jump Jim Joe	Jumping, running, draw steps

Carrousel	Draw steps, sliding
Children's Polka	Draw steps, running
Bleking	Bleking step, step-hops
Crested Hen	Step-hops, turning under
Hansel and Gretel	Bleking step, skipping
Gustaf's Skoal	Walking, skipping, turning
Csebogar	Skipping, sliding, draw steps, elbow swing

Rope Jumping to Music.

PAW PAW PATCH

Records: Victor 45-5066; Folkraft 1181; Honor Your Partner 103.

Formation: Children are in a longways set of five or six couples; boys are in one line and the girls are in another on the boys' right, all facing forward.

Verse:

1. Where, Oh where is sweet little Nellie,
   Where, Oh where is sweet little Nellie,
   Where, Oh where is sweet little Nellie,
   Way down yonder in the paw paw patch.
2. Come on, boys, let's go find her, etc.
3. Pickin' up paw paws, puttin' in your basket, etc.

Description:

Verse 1. Girl at the head of her line turns to her right and skips around the entire group and back to place. All others remain in place, clap, and sing.

Verse 2. The first girl turns to her right again and follows the same path as in verse 1. This time she is followed by the entire line of boys who beckon to each other.

Verse 3. Partners join inside hands, and skip around in a circle to the right following the head couple. When the head couple is at the foot of the line, they make an arch under which the other couples skip back to original formation, with a new head couple.

The entire dance is repeated until each couple has had a chance to be the head couple.

Instead of using the name "Nellie," the name of the girl at the head of the line can be sung.

Variation: The dance can be arranged to feature the boys instead of the girls. In verse 1, substitute the name of "Freddie" for "Nellie." In verse 2, change to "Come on, girls, let's go find him." The action is changed as follows:

Verse 1. Boy at the head of the line turns to his left and skips around the group.

Verse 2. The boy turns again to the left, followed by the entire line of girls.

Verse 3. Partners turn to the left.

YANKEE DOODLE

Records: Victor 22760; Victor 45-5064.

Formation: Children are in sets of threes. The sets are a line of three with a boy in the center, holding to a girl on either side of him. The sets are facing counterclockwise in a large circle formation.

Verse:

Yankee Doodle came to town
Riding on a pony,
Stuck a feather in his hat
And called it macaroni.

Chorus:

Yankee Doodle keep it up,
Yankee Doodle dandy;
Mind the music and the step,
And with the girls be handy.

Description: On the verse, the dancers march around the circle with knees up high like prancing ponies. Arms are swung back and forth.

On the first two lines of the chorus, the center dancer of each set takes the dancer on his right by the right hand and they walk (or skip) around each other. On the next two lines, he does the same with the left-hand dancer but using the left hand. When the center dancer (boy) comes back to his place in the line of threes, he moves forward to the set ahead of him and the dance repeats.

THREE BLIND MICE

Record: None.

Formation: Children are in a hollow square formation facing the inside of the square with six to eight on each side of the square. Each of the sides performs independently in turn as one part of the four-part round.

Verse (all sing):
   Three blind mice,
   Three blind mice,
   See how they run,
   See how they run,
   They all ran after the farmer's wife
   Who cut off their tails with a carving knife
   Did you ever see such a sight in your life, as
   Three blind mice

Description: Sides of the square are numbered 1, 2, 3, and 4. Each acts as one part of the round and begins in turn. All perform the same movements when their turn comes up as part of the round.

Line 1. Clap hands three times.
Line 2. Stamp the floor three times.
Line 3. Four skips forward.
Line 4. Four skips backwards to place.
Line 5. Turn in place with four light steps.
Line 6. Face the center, raising one hand above the other, and make a cutting motion.
Line 7. Put both hands over the ears with a rocking motion sideways.
Line 8. Clap hands three times.

Sing through twice. Do not overlap the lines at the corners or there will be crowding when the children skip forward.

JUMP JIM JOE
Record: Folkraft 1180.

Formation: Double circle, partners facing. Boys are on the inside. Both hands are joined.

Verse:
   Jump, jump, and jump, Jim Joe,
   Take a little twirl and away we go,
   Slide, slide, and stamp just so — and
   Take another partner and jump, Jim Joe

Description:
Line 1. Two slow and then three fast jumps in place.
Line 2. Partners run around each other clockwise in a small circle in place and return to position.
Line 3. With hands on hips each person moves to his left with two draw steps (step left, close right, step left, close right), followed by three stamps. Each person has a new partner.

Line 4. Join hands with the new partner and run around each other back to place, finishing the turn with three light jumps on the words, "Jump, Jim Joe."

CARROUSEL
Records: Victor 45-6179; Folkraft 1183.

Formation: Children are in a double circle, all facing inward. The inner circle, representing the merry-go-round, joins hands. The outer players, representing the riders, place hands on the hips of the partner in front of them.

Verse:
   Little children, sweet and gay, carrousel is
      running. It will run to evening,
   Little ones a nickel, big ones a dime,
   Hurry up, get a mate, or you'll surely be too
      late.

Chorus:
   Ha, ha, ha, happy are we,
   Anderson and Peterson and Henderson and
      me,
   Ha, ha, ha, happy are we,
   Anderson and Peterson and Henderson and
      me.

Description: During the verse, the children take slow draw steps (step, close) to the left. This is done by taking a step to the side with the left foot and closing with the right on count 2. This gets the merry-go-round underway slowly. Four slow stamps replace the draw steps when the words, "Hurry *up,* get a *mate,* or you'll *surely* be too *late.*" A stamp is made on each of the italicized words. The circle now has come to a halt.

During the chorus, the tempo is increased, and the movement is changed to a fast slide. Be sure to have the children take short, light slides.

All sing during the dance.

CHILDREN'S POLKA (KINDERPOLKA)
Records: Victor 45-6179, 2042; Russell 750; Folkraft 1187.

Formation: Single circle, partners facing. Hands are joined and extended sideways.

Although this dance is called a polka, it does not use the polka step.

Measures:
   1–2   Take two draw steps to the center

RHYTHMIC ACTIVITIES

— step, close, step, close. Finish with three light stamps.

3–4 Repeat, moving away from the center.
5–8 Repeat measures 1–4.
9–10 Clap thighs with the hands and then the hands together in slow tempo. Clap hands to partner's hands in three fast claps.
11–12 Repeat 9–10.
13 Extend the right foot forward on the heel, place the right elbow in left hand, and shake the forefinger three times at partner.
14 Repeat, extending the left foot and using the left forefinger.
15 Turn self around in place using four running steps.
16 Face partner and stamp lightly three times.

BLEKING

Records: Victor 45-6169, 20989; Folkraft 1188.

Formation: Single circle, partners facing with both hands joined. Boys are facing counterclockwise and girls clockwise.

Part I. The Bleking Step

Measures:

1 Hop on the left foot and extend the right heel forward with the right leg straight. At the same time thrust the right hand forward. Hop on the right foot, reversing the arm action and extending the left foot to rest on the heel.
2 Repeat the action with three quick changes — left, right, left.
3–4 Beginning on the right foot, repeat the movements of measures 1 and 2.
5–8 Repeat measures 1–4.

Part II. The Windmills

Partners now extend their joined hands sideways shoulder high.

Measures:

9–16 Partners turn in place with a repeated step-hop. At the same time, the arms move up and down like a windmill. The turning is done clockwise with the boy starting on his right foot and the girl with her left. At the completion of the step-hops (16) the partners should be in the original places ready for Part I again.

Variations: Change original position to double circle, partners facing, the boys with backs to the center.

Part I. As above.

Part II. All face counterclockwise, partners with inside hands joined. Partners do the basic schottische of "step, step, step, hop" throughout Part II.

CRESTED HEN

Records: Victor 45-6176, 21619; Methodist M-108; Folkraft 1159, 1194.

Formation: Children are in sets of three, two girls and one boy. Groups are scattered around the room.

Part I

Measures:

1–8 Dancers in each set form a circle. Starting with a stamp with the left foot, each set circles to the left using step-hops.
1–8 (Repeated). Dancers reverse direction, beginning again with a stamp with the left foot and following with step-hops. The change of direction should be vigorous and definite with the left foot crossing over the right in changing the direction.

Part II

During this part, the dancers use the step-hop continuously in making the pattern figures. The girls release their hands to break the circle and stand on each side of the boy.

Measures:

9–10 The girl on the right with four step-hops dances under the arch formed by the other girl and the boy.
11–12 The boy turns under his own left arm with four step-hops, forming again the line of threes.
13–16 The girl on the left now repeats the pattern, going under the arch formed by the other two. The boy turns under his right arm to unravel the line.

As soon as Part II is completed, dancers again join hands in a small circle. The entire dance is repeated.

HANSEL AND GRETEL

Records: Victor 45-6182, Folkraft 1193.

Formation: Double circle, partners facing with boys on the inside.

Part I

Measures:

1–2 Boys bow and girls curtsy.

3–4 Take partner's hands in crossed arm position, right hand to right hand and left to left.

5–6 Jump and extend the right heel forward. Repeat with the left heel.

7–8 Leaning away from partner, turn around in a small circle with seven light fast steps.

Part II

9–16 Take sixteen skips with partner around the circle with inside hands joined.

Part III

Measures:

17 Face partner, hands on hips.

18 Stamp right, left, right.

19 Stand still facing partner, hands on hips.

20 Clap hands three times.

21–22 Join hands, crossed hands position. Jump and extend the right heel then the left.

23–24 Turn with partner in a small circle using seven light steps.

Part IV

This repeats Part III except that in measure 18 nod head three times instead of stamping. In measure 20, snap fingers three times instead of clapping. Hold hands about shoulder high when snapping.

Variation: The dance can be made a mixer by having the dancers, when they finish turning around in a small circle, move directly to the left to get a new partner. Thus there would be changes of partners at the finish of the partner turn for Part I, III, and IV. The inside circle of boys would be moving counterclockwise on the change while the outer circle would be moving clockwise.

GUSTAF'S SKOAL

Records: Methodist M-108; Victor 45-6170, 20988; Folkraft 1175; Linden 701; RCA Victor EPA-4135.

Formation: Similar to a square dance set of four couples, each facing the center. Boy is to the left of his partner. Couples join inside hands, and outside hands are on the hips. Two of the couples facing each other are designated as the "head couples." The other two couples, also facing each other, are the "side couples."

The dance is in two parts. During Part I, the music is slow and stately. The dancers perform with great dignity. Part II is light and represents fun and dancing.

Part I

Measures:

1–2 Head couples holding inside hands walk forward three steps and bow to the opposite couple.

3–4 Head couples take three steps backward to place and bow to each other. During all of this the side couples hold their places.

5–8 Side couples perform the same movements while head couples hold places.

1–8 Dancers repeat entire figure.

Part II

9–12 Side couples raise joined hands, forming an arch. Head couples skip to the center where they meet opposite partners. Each, after dropping his own partner's hand, takes the hand of the dancer facing him and skips under the nearest arch. After going under the arch, drop hands and head back to home spot to original partner.

13–16 Clap hands smartly on the first note of measure 13 while skipping. Skip toward partner, take both hands and skip once around in place.

9–16 (repeated). Head couples form the arches and the side couples repeat the pattern just finished by the head couples.

Variation: During the first part of Part I where the dancers take three steps and bow, a shout of "Skoal" at the same time raising the right fist about head high as a salute can be substituted for the bow. The word "Skoal" means a toast.

CSEBOGAR

Records: Victor 45-6182, 20992; Kismet 141; Methodist M-101.

Formation: Single circle with partners. Girls are on the right; all are facing center with hands joined.

Part I

Measures:

  1–4   Take seven slides to the left.
  5–8   Seven slides to the right.
  9–12   Take four skips to the center and four backwards to place.
  13–16   Hook elbows with partner and turn around twice in place skipping.

Part II

Partners are now facing each other with hands joined in a single circle.

Measures:

  17–20   Holding both hands of the partner, take four draw steps (step, close) toward the center of the circle.
  21–24   Four draw steps back to place.
  25–26   Toward the center of the circle with two draw steps.
  27–28   Two draw steps back to place.
  29–32   Hook elbows and repeat the elbow swing, finishing up with a shout facing the center of the circle in the original formation.

Variation: Instead of the elbow turn, partners may use the Hungarian Turn. Partners stand side by side and put the right arm around the partner's waist. The left arm is held out to the side, elbow bent with the hand pointing up, and the palm facing the dancer.

ROPE JUMPING TO MUSIC*

Music enhances rope jumping and makes this activity quite attractive to children. While conditions vary, probably the activity should be introduced at the second grade level. Care must be taken to establish basic routines with attention to a few basic steps. Refinement of the activity can be accomplished in the intermediate grades.

Rope jumping is an excellent complete body activity. It increases coordination, rhythm, and timing. It tones up the circulorespiratory system and increases both speed and endurance. It makes a contribution to weight control and total physical condition. It can contribute to good posture habits. It has good carry-over values.

Some people prefer to refer to the activity as rope skipping. In the material which follows, the terms are used interchangeably.

From an educational standpoint, rope jumping has good value in the school program. It allows a maximum amount of student activity within a minimum amount of time and space. The activities are in good progression. The teacher can begin at the student's level and develop from that point. It is inexpensive and easily taught.

It provides a creative activity that has unlimited possibilities for new material. The further the youngsters progress, the more they tend to invent steps and routines of their own. The activity is not seasonal in character.

For the teacher and administrator, it provides excellent program material for PTA meetings and other demonstrations.

Records for Rope Jumping

Any record with a steady tempo of 120 to 150 beats per minute will suffice for beginning instruction. Some records that have been found to work well are:

1. PR980 Ball Bouncing and Rope Skipping, Album #12 — Durlacher.

2. Marches, Album #1 — Durlacher.

3. Waiting for the Robert E. Lee — 45 RPM, Jack Barbour — Accent Sunny Hills AC102-S.

4. Wheels and Orange Blossom Special — 45 RPM, Billy Vaughn, Dot, 45-161774.

5. Yankee Doodle — El Molino — Shoo Fly, all on Windsor School Series Record — Happy Hour Records — A-7S1, Windsor.

---

*The material on rope skipping is used by permission of the Seattle Public Schools, William Haroldson, Director of Physical Education. The Seattle Public School Bulletin on Rope Skipping was based originally on terminology and steps excerpted in part from the pamphlet, *Rope Skipping Fundamentals,* by Paul Smith, Physical Education Supervisor, Shoreline Public Schools, Seattle, Wash.

6. Pop Goes the Weasel is another record which is good for rope jumping. The fact that there is a verse and a chorus arrangement means that one type of jumping (slow time) could be done to the verse and another (fast time) could be done to the chorus. Folk Dancer MH1501 and Victor 45-6180 are good records.

The teacher will discover many other records and albums which will work well as the children progress and become more familiar with the various rope skipping activities.

The Rope

To determine the proper length of rope for a particular individual, stand on the center of the rope. The ends, when drawn up each side of the body, should terminate at approximately armpit height.

Two lengths are recommended for children from preschool and through the third grade: (1) the seven-foot rope for younger children and (2) the eight-foot rope for second and third graders.

Explanation of Terminology

The recommended steps can be done in any of three rhythms: slow-time, fast-time, and double-time. Concentration should first be made on slow-time and fast-time rhythms. Later, double-time rhythm can be added. Before introducing the three rhythms, the concept of rebound must be understooood.

1. Rebound

This is simply a hop in place as the rope passes over the head. Better jumpers will only bend the knees slightly without actually leaving the floor. It is used only in slow-time jumping (explained below), and its object is to carry the rhythm between steps.

2. Slow Time

In slow-time rhythm the performer jumps over the rope, rebounds (jumps in place) as the rope passes over the head, then executes the second step, or repeats the original step a second time, on the second jump.

The performer actually jumps over the rope to every other beat of the music in slow-time rhythm. The odd beat occurs as the rope passes over the head. The rhythm is carried by the rebound.

The rope is rotating slowly (passes under the feet on every other beat), and the feet also move slowly since there is a rebound between each jump.

Slow-time rhythm — slow rope, slow feet, with a rebound.

3. Fast Time

In fast-time rhythm we have the opposite of slow time. The rope rotates in time with the music, which means twice the number of rope turns for the same time as in slow time. The rope will be turning fast (120 to 180 turns per minute, depending upon the tune's tempo), and the performer executes a step only when the rope is passing under the feet.

Fast-time rhythm — fast rope, fast feet.

4. Double Time

In double-time rhythm the rope is turned at the same speed as for slow time, but rather than taking the rebound the performer executes another step while the rope is passing over the head. A slow rope with fast feet.

Double time is the most difficult to master. When the feet are speeded up there is a tendency also to speed the rope up (which is wrong).

Double-time rhythm — slow rope, fast feet.

Progression of Rope Jumping

All explanations are given and should usually be learned first in slow-time rhythm. After the students master all the steps in the various rhythms, routines may be devised combining the different steps and rhythms.

If a student has difficulty with a step, have him go through the foot motions without the rope first.

Placing offset marks on the gym floor with a marking pen helps students keep their stations.

Begin with music almost immediately. The music tells the performer when to do the step and also helps him to keep a steady rhythm.

Basic Steps

Three basic steps are presented and should be reasonably mastered. However, concentration should be on keeping in good rhythm and on efficient handling of the rope. The two foot basic step serves to introduce rope jumping and to emphasize slow-time and fast-time concepts. The step is not particularly suited for double-time rhythm. The alternate foot basic step and the swing step forward can be used with any of the three rhythms, but have particular value in illustrating the change from slow time to double time.

1. Two Foot Basic Step

With feet together, jump over the rope as it passes under the feet and take a preparatory rebound while the rope is over the head.

2. Alternate Foot Basic Step

As the rope passes under the feet, the weight is shifted alternately from one foot to the other, raising the unweighted foot in a running position.

3. Swing Step Forward

Same as alternate foot basic step, except that the free leg swings forward. Keep knee loose and let foot swing naturally.

Crossing Arms Forward

Crossing the arms in jumping adds variety and supplies additional challenge for children. When the rope is above the head starting the downward swing, the hands exchange position, crossing the arms. Jumping can be continued in this position or the arms can be crossed and uncrossed on alternate turns of the rope.

Going from Forward to Backward Jumping Without Stopping the Rope

As the rope starts downward in forward jumping, rather than allowing it to pass under the feet, the performer swings both arms to the left (or right) and makes a half turn of his body in that direction (turn facing the rope). On the next turn spread the arms and start turning in the opposite direction. This method can be used from forward to backward jumping and vice versa.

Rope Jumping Routines

It is in this area that the opportunities for creative activity are many. The teacher can select a basic piece of music with suitable rope jumping rhythm, and the children can devise routines.

The best type of music to use has a definite two-part format, which can be labeled a verse part and a chorus part. The table shows how a number of basic jumping steps can be organized using slow and fast time.

1st verse part	Two foot basic step	Slow time
Chorus	Two foot basic step	Fast time
2nd verse part	Alternate foot basic step	Slow time
Chorus	Alternate foot basic step	Fast time
3rd verse part	Swing step forward	Slow time
Chorus	Swing step forward	Fast time
4th verse part	Swing step sideward	Slow time
Chorus	Swing step sideward	Fast time

The Bleking Record (Third Grade Dance, page 272) offers interesting variety for jumping. The rhythm is slow-slow: fast-fast-fast (repeated four times). The rope should be turned in keeping with the music. The chorus part allows for considerable variety of response.

GAMES USING RHYTHMIC BACKGROUND

A number of interesting games can be played using music as a part of the game. Most of them are simple in principle and are based on the idea of movement changes when the music changes or stops. Some of them are similar to the old, old game of Musical Chairs.

CIRCLE STOOP

Children are in a single circle facing counterclockwise. A march or similar music can be used or the game can be played to the beat of a tom-tom. The children march in good posture until the music is stopped. As soon as the child no longer hears the music or beat of the tom-tom, he stoops and touches both hands to the ground without losing balance. The last child to touch both hands to the ground successfully pays a penalty by going into the mush-pot (center of the circle) or being eliminated. Children should march in good posture and anyone stooping, even partially, before the music is stopped should be penalized. The duration of the music should be varied, and the children should not be able to observe the stopping process if a record player is used.

Variations:

1. Employ different locomotor movements like skipping, hopping, or galloping while using suitable music.

2. Use different positions for stopping instead of stooping. Positions like the push-up, crab, lame dog, balance on one foot, or touch with one hand and one foot add to the interest and fun.

PARTNER STOOP

The game follows the same basic principle of stooping as in Circle Stoop but is done with partners. The group forms a double circle with partners facing counterclockwise, boys on the inside. When the music starts, all march in line of direction. After a short period of marching, a signal (whistle) is given, and the inside circle (boys) turns around and marches the other way — clockwise. Partners are now separated. When the music is stopped, the outer circle (girls) stands still, and the boys *walk* to rejoin their partners. As soon as a boy reaches his partner, they join inside hands and stoop without losing balance. The last couple to stoop goes to the center of the circle and waits out the next round.

Variation: The game can be played with groups of three instead of partners. The game begins with the groups of three marching abreast holding hands and facing counterclockwise. On the signal, the outside players of the threes continue marching in the same direction. The middle players of the threes stop and stand still. The inside players reverse direction and march clockwise. When the music stops, the groups of three attempt to reunite at the spot where the middle player stopped. The last three to join hands and stoop are put into the center for the next round.

FOLLOW ME

The game has its basis in the phrasing of the music. The children are in circle formation facing in with a leader in the center. The leader performs a series of movements of his choice, either locomotor or nonlocomotor, for the duration of one phrase of music (8 beats). The children imitate his movements during the next phrase. The leader takes over for another set of movements, and the children imitate during the next phase following. After a few changes, the leader picks another child to take his place.

Variations:

1. A popular way to play this game is to have the children follow the leader as he performs. This means changing movement as the leader changes and performing as the leader does, with everyone keeping with the rhythm. A change is made as soon as the leader falters or loses his patterns or ideas.

2. The game can be done with partners. One partner performs during one phrase, and the other partner imitates his movements during the next phrase. The teacher can decide which couple is making the most vivid and imaginative movements and is doing the best job of following the partner's movements.

FREEZE

Children are scattered around the room. When the music is started, they move around the room guided by the character of the music. They walk, run, jump, or use other locomotor movements dependent upon the selected music or beat. When the music is stopped, they freeze and do not move. Any child caught moving after the cessation of the rhythm pays a penalty.

A tom-tom or piano provides a fine base for this game, as the rhythmic beat can be varied easily and the rhythm can be stopped at any time. In the absence of a tom-tom or drum, two sticks or Indian clubs can be knocked together to provide the beat.

Variations:

1. Specify the level at which the child must freeze.

2. Have the child fall to the ground or go into one of the different positions like the push-up, crab, lame dog, a balance, or some other defined position.

RIGHT ANGLE

A tom-tom can be used to provide the rhythm for this activity. Some of the basic rhythm records also have suitable music. The children change direction at right angles on each heavy beat or change of music. The object of the game is to make the right angle changes on signal and not bump into other children.

ARCHES

The game is similar to *London Bridge*. Arches are placed around the playing area. To form an arch, two players stand facing one another with hands joined. When the music starts, the players move in a circle, passing under the arch. Suddenly, the music stops and the arches come down by dropping the hands. All players caught in an arch immediately pair off together to form other arches, keeping in a general circle formation. If a "caught" player does not have a partner, he should wait in the center of the circle until one is available. The last players caught (or left) form arches for the next game.

The arches should be warned not to bring down their hands and arms too forcefully, so that the children passing under them will not be pummeled. Also, children with glasses need consideration in the process of catching, as when the arches close, glasses can be knocked to the floor. Glasses should be removed, or children with glasses can begin as part of the arches.

Variation: Different types of music can be used and the children can move according to the pattern of the music.

WHISTLE MARCH

A record with a brisk march is needed. The children are scattered around the room individually walking in various directions, keeping time to the music. A whistle is blown a number of times, at which signal lines are formed of that precise number, no more and no less. The lines are formed by having the children stand side by side with locked elbows. As soon as a line of the proper number is formed, it begins to march to the music counterclockwise around the room. Any children left over go to the center of the room and remain until the next signal. On the next whistle signal (single blast) the lines break up and all walk individually around the room in various directions as before.

Teaching Hint: It may be well to make a rule that children may not lock elbows with the same children with whom they formed the previous line.

19

Individual and Dual Activities for All Grades

Individual Rope Jumping — Without Music
Long Rope Jumping
Other Activities

Included in this section are several types of activities which are difficult to allocate to specific grade levels because allocation would in many cases depend upon previous experience. The section includes individual rope jumping without music, long rope activities, *Tetherball* and several miscellaneous activities.

INDIVIDUAL ROPE JUMPING — WITHOUT MUSIC

Rope jumping as a rhythmic activity has been presented just previously. There is some repetition in the material which follows, but the activity is now presented on an individual basis, without music. With or without music, the carry-over values are excellent, and the children should be given an opportunity to practice and learn both ways.

General Suggestions

The rope should be turned with a quick, easy motion of the hands and wrists in contrast to forceful turning by the arms. The body should be erect and relaxed, and the jumping done in a relaxed, easy motion.

The bounce of the body should be made lightly, usually on the toes, with just enough straightening of the knee joints to propel the body into the air. The clearance from the ground should be minimal and easy, enough to allow the rope to go under the feet. The ends of the rope should be held primarily with the thumb and first two fingers.

The teaching should include postural considerations. Performed properly with the body in good alignment, rope jumping can contribute important values to the maintenance of posture. In particular, the head and upper part of the body should maintain proper positioning.

Working with Children in Rope Jumping Without Music

Children should work with various speeds in rope jumping. However, fast-time jumping is more demanding and has better fitness values than the slower routines, slow-time and double-time jumping. The three routines were discussed just previously in the chapter on rhythmics.

To establish rhythm and practice new routines, the rope first can be turned to the side, using slow-time rhythm. Take both ends of the rope in one hand (usually the right) and turn the rope forward but at the side of the body. Work on the rhythm of the turn, gradually adding the bounce of the toes. The rope should slap the floor lightly on each turn. The bounce of the body is coordinated with the turn of the rope so that the feet are off the ground when the rope hits the floor.

After sufficient practice, the rope can be shifted to normal jumping position and the routine practiced in regular position.

Numerous combinations are possible in rope jumping when the following variations and approaches are considered.

1. Changes in the speed of the turn, utilizing slow-time, fast-time, and double-time routines. Also accelerate and decelerate.
2. The use of the various steps and foot patterns described on page 276.
3. Crossed hand positions, forward and backward.
4. Going from forward to backward and return. Carry the rope to the side when making the change.

LONG ROPE JUMPING

Groups of five make a convenient group for practicing long rope skills. Two of the group are turners and the others jumpers. The children should rotate between turning and jumping. The rope should be 12' to 16' long.

INTRODUCTORY SKILLS

1. Hold the rope 6" from the ground. Children jump over, back and forth. Raise the rope a little each time. Be sure to hold the rope loosely in the hands.
2. The *Ocean Wave* is another stationary jumping activity. The turners make waves in the rope by moving the arms up and down. The children try to time it so as to jump over a low part of the "wave."
3. *Snake in the Grass.* The holders stoop down and wiggle the rope back and forth on the floor. Children try to jump over the rope and not touch it as it moves.
4. Swing the rope in a pendulum fashion. Children jump the rope as it passes under them.
5. Have the child stand in the center between the turners. Carefully turn the rope in a complete arc over the jumper's head. As the rope completes the turn, the jumper jumps over it. He immediately exits in the same direction as the rope is turned.
6. Run through the turning rope without jumping.
7. While the rope is being turned, the jumper runs in and jumps once. He runs out immediately. The rope must be coming toward the jumper (front door).

BASIC LONG ROPE SKILLS

1. Front Door — When the rope is turned forward toward the jumper, it is called the front door.

2. Back Door — The rope is turned away from the jumper.
3. With the line of children at a 45-degree angle, try the following:
   Run in front door, out back door.
   Run in front door, jump once, run out.
   Run in back door, jump once, run out.
   Run in front or back door, increase the number of jumps, run out.
   Run in front or back door, jump any number of times, but do a quarter, half, three-quarter, or full turns in the air.
4. Hot Pepper — Turners turn the rope with increased speed with the jumper trying to keep up with the rope.
5. High Water — The rope is turned so that it is gradually higher and higher off the ground.
6. Two, three, or four children jump at a time. After some skill has been reached, children in combination can run in, jump a specified number of times, and run out keeping hands joined all the time.

RHYMES

As the jumpers become proficient, they can make use of many familiar rhymes which are used for long ropes. For example —

1. Teddy Bear, Teddy Bear, turn around
   Teddy Bear, Teddy Bear, touch the ground
   Teddy Bear, Teddy Bear, show your shoe
   Teddy Bear, Teddy Bear, you better skidoo.

   or

   Teddy Bear, Teddy Bear, say your prayers
   Teddy Bear, Teddy Bear, go upstairs
   Teddy Bear, Teddy Bear, turn out the light
   Teddy Bear, Teddy Bear, say good night.

2. For counting a definite number of turns —
   Bulldog, poodle, bow wow wow
   How many doggies have we now?
   One, two, three, etc.

   or

   Lady, lady, at the gate
   Eating cherries from a plate.
   How many cherries did she eat?
   One, two, three, etc.

The rope is turned a specified number of turns, after which the jumper exits from the jumping.

3. For Red Hot Pepper —
   Mable, Mabel, set the table
   Bring the plates if you are able
   Don't forget the salt and
   Red Hot Pepper!

On the words "Red Hot Pepper" the rope is turned as fast as possible until the jumper misses.

OTHER ACTIVITIES

TETHERBALL

Tetherball is a popular game and is a natural where space is limited. The equipment consists of a pole and a tetherball attached to the pole by a length of rope. Pole assemblies outside are generally put in permanently with a concrete installation.

Two to four players can participate, but the game is generally played by two children.

The first server is picked by lot. One player stands on each side of the pole. Server puts ball in play by tossing it in the air and hitting it in the direction he chooses. The opponent must not strike the ball on the first swing around the pole. On the second time around the pole, he hits the ball back in the opposite direction. As the ball is hit back and forth, each player tries to hit the ball so that the rope winds completely around the pole in the direction in which he has been hitting the ball. The game is won by the player who succeeds in doing this or whose opponent forfeits the game by making any of the following fouls:

1. Hitting ball with any part of the body other than the hands or forearms.

2. Catching or holding the ball during play.

3. Touching the pole.

4. Hitting the rope with the forearm or hands.

5. Throwing the ball.

6. Winding the ball around the pole below the 5' mark.

After the opening game, winner of the previous game serves. Winning four games wins the set.

HOPSCOTCH

Playing Area: Diagram as drawn on a hard surface area.

Players: Not more than 4 or 5 to any one game.

Supplies: A lagger for each player. A stone makes a good lagger.

The first player starts the game by tossing his lagger into the first (#1) box. He then hops *over* the first box into the second box. He then hops into box #3 on the same foot. The general rule is to hop on one foot in the single boxes and both feet (one in each) into the double boxes. When he reaches boxes #7-8, he turns around completely in place with a jump exchange of the feet into the opposite boxes. He hops back with a jump into boxes #4-5. When he reaches box #2, he reaches over and picks up his lagger, hops into box #1 and out. He now tosses his lagger into box #2 and repeats the routine. He continues into the other boxes with his lagger until he has covered all eight. Certain rules are basic.

1. The player may not hop into the box where his lagger is tossed. He picks up the lagger on the way back by stopping in the box immediately in front. After he has picked up the lagger, he can hop into the box.

2. A player loses his turn if his lagger fails to be tossed into the correct box or rests on a line.

3. Stepping on a line, missing a box, falling, or stepping into a box where the lagger rests are fouls and stop the turn at that point.

4. After a player has gone completely through the boxes (through the "eighties"), he may write his name in any box, and no one but that player may step in that box. The player whose name is in the most boxes wins.

There are innumerable forms of hopscotch and each area has its favorites. Hopscotch formations take the forms of simple lines of boxes, crosses, squares, snail, and other varied figures. It is truly an international game, played in almost every country.

KICK SHUFFLE

Playing Area: Diagram as illustrated, on a hard surface.

Players: 2–4.

Supplies: 3 kicking blocks (2" x 4" x 4").

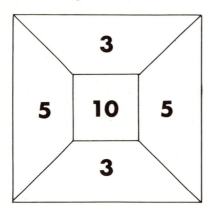

The target can be laid out permanently with paint or temporarily with chalk. The blocks are made from regular 2" x 4" lumber. They should be cut a little short of 4" in order to match the width of the lumber.

The first player stands at a kicking line drawn about 15' from the front of the target. He stands at the line with the forward foot, and with the other slides or kicks the blocks, one at a time, at the court. He scores the points as listed if the block rests in a particular space. If the block is on a line *between* two spaces, he scores the lower figure. If the block stops on an outside line, it scores nothing.

The game can be played by two or three players who take turns at a target. With larger numbers or using partners, it would be better to lay out a court with two targets, one at each end, similar to shuffle board courts.

Other diagrams could be arranged.

O'LEARY

O'Leary is an individual contest played with each child having a small ball or it can be played with a number of children taking turns when a player makes an error. The child chants the following to the tune of "Ten Little Indians": "1-2-3 O'Leary, 4-5-6 O'Leary, 7-8-9 O'Leary, 10 O'Leary, Postman." He bats the ball with the open hand to the ground (as in basketball dribbling), keeping time to the counting. On the word "O'Leary" he gives a harder bounce and performs a stipulated task. This means that the task is repeated four times during the course of one routine. On the word "Postman" the child catches the ball. The tasks can vary, but should have the same established order for each game. The following progression is suggested for the game, with each task being done on the word "O'Leary."

1. Swing the right leg outward over the ball.
2. Swing the left leg outward over the ball.
3. Swing the right leg inward over the ball.
4. Swing the left leg inward over the ball.
5. Grasp hands together forming a circle with the arms. Ball passes through arms from below.
6. Same as 5, ball passes through from above.
7. Form a circle with the forefingers and thumbs. The ball passes upward through the circle.
8. Same as 7, but ball passes downward through the hands.
9. Alternate 1 and 2 on each "O'Leary."
10. Alternate 3 and 4.
11. Alternate 5 and 6.
12. Alternate 7 and 8.
13. Do 1, 2, 3, and 4 in order.
14. Do 5, 6, 7, and 8 in order.
15. Finish with a complete turn around on each "O'Leary."

20

Classroom and Limited Area Activities

Guides for Conducting Classroom and Limited Space Activities
Suggested Classroom Activities

One of the most difficult problems confronting physical education teachers is how to conduct a program when adverse weather forces the activity inside and the gymnasium facilities are not adequate to handle the load. When no appropriate gymnasium facility is available, it may be necessary to use classroom and other limited spaces, such as the hall or cafeteria. The indoor situation can be broken down into four categories:

The Relaxation Period

This is designed to provide a break in the day's routine, and in a sense it is like recess. It is a kind of safety valve which allows the children to let off steam, but it can also be used to enrich their experiences while it offers them relaxation. Since it is in addition to regular physical education experiences, the relaxation period should provide different activities from those of the regular program. This period is usually short, not more than ten minutes or so.

The Occasional Classroom Physical Education Lesson

This is an emergency situation, when the physical education lesson must be taught in the classroom or related facility because the usual facility is not available, and for this reason it is the most difficult type to plan. The program emphasis has to be shifted, as the usual rugged, active program of the gymnasium or playground is not suitable for the classroom conditions.

The Split Gymnasium-Classroom Program

Where facilities are available but not adequate for a daily program, the classes held in regular physical education facilities have to be supplemented by classroom physical education. For example, in a school where twenty classrooms share one gymnasium a particular classroom is scheduled only twice a week for regular physical education. This can be supplemented by lessons in the classroom to meet the weekly time requirement.

Planning must include both aspects, the regular and the classroom programs. The more rugged activities and instructional emphasis on skills are centered in the regular physical education program. To the classroom are allocated those activity areas which are suitable for limited spaces.

Indoor Classroom Physical Education

In this situation, no suitable gymnasium facilities are present at all, and so all physical education which cannot be conducted on the playground must be carried on in the classroom, or no program is possible. Planning for this situation must include two programs, one for the playground and one for the classroom. The classroom program should be in sequential lessons, which means that the lesson order is established and followed consecutively as the indoor program days materialize.

GUIDES FOR CONDUCTING CLASSROOM AND LIMITED SPACE ACTIVITIES

The following considerations are presented which have relevance in degree to one or more of the situations previously described for conducting activities in a classroom situation.

The Noise Problem

The noise problem must be solved. Several suggestions are offered. The children have to recognize that the activity is a privilege and their cooperation is essential. They must keep their exuberance under control to the point that the class activity does not interfere with other classes. Another solution would be for the same section of the school to have physical education periods at the same time. If all classes in the same part of the building are playing at the same time, there is little disturbance with each other. This would also be true if one class were directly above the other. The noise, particularly from shuffling and moving feet, would seriously interfere with a recitation, lecture, or study period.

Equipment and Supplies

If there is to be an appreciable amount of classroom physical education, a separate set of equipment and supplies from that used in the regular physical education program is needed. A supply cart which contains most of the normal items needed is an efficient answer. It can be rolled directly into the classroom and saves sending monitors to a central point to carry in needed items.

Equipment carts containing balance beams (portable), light folding mats, balance boards, individual mats, and other equipment are also timesavers. Tumbling mats should be the light, folded variety, which can be handled by the children with ease.

Each classroom should also have a special collection of games, targets, manipulative objects, and other special items for indoor play. Many of the items can be constructed by the children.

Only supplies that will not damage should be used. Small sacks stuffed with excelsior, fleece balls, beanbags, yarn balls, sewn rolled-up sox, balloons, and articles of this nature can be used with little danger to the facilities.

Preparing the Facilities

If the classroom desks and chairs are moveable, flexibility is present to provide space for a variety of activities. Equipment can be pushed together to permit circle activities and rhythms. Chairs and desks can be pushed to one side to form an open space. If mats, balance beams, or benches are to be used, several wider aisles can be made by pushing adjacent rows together.

Instruction should be given in how to prepare desks for moving. All personal items must be put away; desk tops should be cleared, and books and other things stacked underneath so they will not fall out when the desks are moved. Items and projections which might cause tripping or damage should be placed in safe positions.

Windows should be opened and the temperature lowered, which may involve an adjustment of the thermostat.

If the desks and chairs are fixed, then space is more limited. The aisles as established should be used. As much space as possible should be cleared.

Halls have a low priority for use. The noise permeates the entire building, and the activity interferes with the passage of students.

Program Suggestions

Too many teachers look for special classroom activities when the necessity to use the room for physical education occurs. Some end up with a program of trivial games, which only provide entertainment and relief from tension. Granted, they do play a part in the program, but their importance is minor compared to that of other activities.

The activities of the regular physical education program should be carefully examined to determine which can be utilized and which can be modified for the classroom program. Stunts and tumbling, certain pieces of apparatus (moveable), selected manipulative equipment, rhythmic activities, and movement experiences should be considered.

Six tumbling mats (4' x 7') can be positioned in the available space. Four balance beams fit easily in the regular aisles or can be placed in the spaces available. Benches can be used in the classroom, but present a problem in getting them in and out of the area.

Target activities with beanbags, yarn balls,

and regular rubber playground balls can be used. Targets can be placed at the end of the rows. Balls can be rolled or bounced. Ring toss games also contribute to skills.

Rhythmic activities are excellent for classroom work. The formations depend upon the size of the room and whether or not the desks are moveable. Nonlocomotor creative rhythms and ball bouncing rhythms are valuable.

Relays, particularly the modified (number calling) type, have a place in classroom activities. Many can be modified for the classroom environment. Regular rows can be used with the last child performing first and the leader positioned at the head of the row. Fast walking should be substituted for running.

Movement experiences are also an important inclusion. Traffic patterns are important for locomotor movements. Story plays and poems also have a place in the picture. These should require only limited locomotor movement.

Fitness activities can be adapted to classroom work. Many exercises are quite appropriate for this. Isometric exercises without equipment and with wands are readily done in the classroom. Partner isometrics consume little space. Jumping and hopping in place cause few spatial problems.

Many of the regular physical education games can be adapted for the space available. In addition, other activities, identified as classroom-type games, should be included. These vary from reasonably active games to quiet games.

This source questions a heavy emphasis and reliance on social recreation and intellectual games. Movement is the key to physical education, and the games should induce movement and/or provide an opportunity to practice skills.

Other Considerations

Children should accept responsibility to a considerable degree for their own conduct. They should realize and accept the limitations of classroom physical education.

Small group play has a place in classroom activity. A number of groups scattered around the room may be involved in different activities.

Rules, strategies, and techniques of sports activities can sometimes be covered in indoor sessions. Good visual aids are also invaluable.

As many children as possible should engage in activity at one time, since activity is the key to physical education. Some system of rotation should be established to ensure that all children have a proportionate share of the activity time.

Watch for overheating. Have the children remove excess clothing. Allow them to wear gym shoes, depending on the activity.

Stress safety. Caution players about colliding with chairs and desks. If the aisles are used for activity, tell the children to keep their feet well under their desks to avoid tripping players.

SUGGESTED CLASSROOM ACTIVITIES

ADD AND SUBTRACT

Playing Area: Classroom.

Players: 2–4.

Supplies: 2 rubber heels or blocks of wood for each player. One is marked with a plus sign and one with a minus sign. Different colored beanbags could be used.

Lay out a nine-square diagram with each square 12″ wide. The squares are numbered 1 through 9. Each player tosses two rubber heels (or beanbags) toward the target on the floor, one at a time. He adds the score made by the plus throw and subtracts the score of the minus throw. Scores are determined where the heel rests on the target. If the heel rests on a line between two squares, the higher value is taken. Any throws falling completely outside the target area are scored minus 5.

The game adapts itself well to the classroom, as a target can be drawn at the front of each aisle.

AROUND THE ROW

Formation: Row in a classroom.

Players: Whatever number there is in a row.

Supplies: None.

The game is played by rows with an extra player for each row. The children form a row plus the extra player on the command "March" and walk around the row. At a signal they stop marching and attempt to get a seat. One player is left out. The game continues to the next row using the player left out as the extra.

BALLOON VOLLEYBALL

Formation: A rope is stretched across the middle of the classroom.

Players: Entire class.

Supplies: 2 balloons. Extras should be availabe as there is breakage.

This is an informal game with the children trying to bat the ball back and forth across the rope. Two balloons should be used at once to provide good action. Several variations are possible.

1. All children standing. Rope should be stretched just over their reach.
2. All children sitting on the floor. Rope about 3′ from the floor.
3. Children in seats that cannot be moved. Rope should be about 5′ high.

In each case, a system of rotation should be set up. Scoring is done when a side fails to control a balloon and allows it to touch the floor or a wall. The balloon can be batted as often as possible.

Variation: If a small marble or button is put *inside* the balloon, the balloon will take an erratic path, adding to the interest.

BASKETBALL BOUNCE

Formation: Individual or by team formation.

Players: 2 to 6 for each basket.

Supplies: Basketball, volleyball, or other rubber ball. Wastepaper basket.

Each player on his turn stands behind a line which is 5′ to 10′ from a wastepaper basket. Five chances are allowed to bounce the ball on the floor in such a fashion that it goes in the basket. Score 5 points for each successful "basket."

BEANBAG PITCH

Playing Area: Classroom.

Players: 2 to 6 for each target.

Supplies: Beanbags and a small box for target for each team.

A target box is placed at the head of each row. A pitch line is drawn 10′ to 15′ back of the target. Each player takes a specified number of pitches at the box. Scores are taken for each player, and the team with the highest score wins.

BICYCLE RACE

Playing Area: Classroom.

Players: One-half the class.

Supplies: The desks are needed.

Alternate rows perform at a time. The children stand in the aisle between two rows of desks. Each child places one hand on his own desk and one on the desk next to him. Upon the signal, "Go," each child imitates riding a bicycle with his legs, while supported by his hands. The child who rides the longest without touching the floor with his feet is the winner for his row. Winners can compete later for the champion bicycle rider of the room.

BOILER BURST

Playing Area: Classroom, playground.

Players: Entire class.

Supplies: None.

The seats are arranged so that there will be one less seat than players. The extra player stands at the front of the class and begins a story. At a dramatic moment, he says, "And the boiler burst!" The children exchange seats, and the narrator tries to secure a seat. If he is successful, another child replaces him. The new narrator may develop his own story or continue that begun by his predecessor.

The game can be adapted to an outdoor situation by having markers for each child. To make the game more vigorous, the children could be required to run to a turning point and back. The child who does not secure a marker is the new storyteller.

BOWLING

Formation: File by rows.

Players: 2–6.

Supplies: Bowling pin or pins. Balls for rolling.

Many bowling games are possible in the classroom, using the aisles as the "alleys." Various kinds of balls can be used for rolling. The target can be a single pin or group of pins. Competition can be between individuals in a row or between rows.

CAT AND MICE (Classroom Game)

Playing Area: Classroom, playground.

Players: 5–20.

Supplies: None.

This is an excellent activity in the classroom. One player is designated as the "Cat," sits at the front desk (teacher's), and puts his head down on his hands on the desk so he cannot see. The remainder of the children are the "Mice." One Mouse from each row comes to the front, stealthily approaches the desk, and scratches on the desk. When he is ready, the Cat gets up from his chair and chases the Mice back to their seats. Any child caught joins the Cat at the desk and helps catch the others. The game is over when each of the children has had a chance to approach the desk.

CHAIR QUOITS

Formation: File.

Players: 2–6.

Supplies: Chair for each group; 5 deck tennis rings or rope rings.

A line is established about 10′ from a chair turned upside down so that the legs are pointed toward the thrower. Each throws the 5 rings for the following scores.

Ringer on back legs..........10 points
Ringer on front legs............5 points

Make a score sheet and keep score for several rounds.

Variation: Fruit jar rings can be used with the chair or with other targets.

CHANGE SEATS

Playing Area: Classroom.

Players: Entire class.

Supplies: None.

All seats should be occupied, removed, or books put on them to indicate that they are not to be used. The teacher gives the commands "Change left, Change right, Change front," or "Change back." One or more children are "It" and do not have seats.

At each command, the children move *one seat* in the direction of the call. The children who are "It" try to move into any seat they can. When the command, "Change front," is given, the child in the front seat must turn and move to the rear seat of his row. Similarly, those on the outside rows on "Change left," or "Change right," must move around to the other side of the room to get their proper seats.

It needs to be emphasized that on command each child is to move to the designated seat in keeping with the command. If he is in error, one of the players who is "It" takes his seat.

If the game seems to become too boisterous, the children should be made to walk.

DO THIS, DO THAT

Playing Area: Playground, gymnasium, classroom.

Players: Entire class.

Supplies: None.

One child is the leader and performs various movements, which are accompanied by either "Do this," or "Do that." All players must execute the movements which are accompanied by "Do this." If the directions are "Do that," no one is to move. Those who move at the wrong time are eliminated and sit down in place.

Play until a portion is eliminated and re-form the game with another leader, selected from the children not caught.

FLOOR PING PONG

Formation: Regular table tennis court marked off on the floor.

Players: 2 to 4.

Supplies: Table tennis ball; a paddle for each player.

Play as in regular table tennis. Games should be short (10 points), so many children can be accommodated. A makeshift net can be set up with blocks and a wand.

GERONIMO

Formation: Children seated in regular classroom arrangement.

Players: Entire class.

Supplies: None.

One child is the leader and walks among the children seated in the classroom. He suddenly points to a child and says, "Geronimo." This child must immediately put both hands to his ears. The child directly behind him must put both hands on top of his head. The children on either side must cover the ear next to "Geronimo" with the opposite hand. Play with duds as penalties. Three duds is out.

The game can be made harder with more intricate movement tasks. Change the movement of the child on either side to holding the near ear with the opposite hand and holding the nose with the other hand.

HUNTER, GUN, RABBIT

Playing Area: Classroom.
Players: Entire class.
Supplies: None.

The children are divided into two teams, which line up facing each other. They can be sitting or standing. Each team has a captain.

Each team privately decides on one of the following three imitations:

Hunter — bring hands up to the eyes and pretend to be looking through binoculars.

Gun — bring hands and arms up to a shooting position and pretend to shoot.

Rabbit — put hands in back of head with fingers pointed up. Move hands back and forth like moving rabbit ears.

A signal "Go" is given, and each team pantomimes its choice. To score, the following priorities have been set up.

1. If one side is the hunter and the other the gun, the hunter wins as the hunter shoots the gun.

2. If one team selects the gun and the other imitates a rabbit, the gun wins as the gun overcomes the rabbit.

3. If one side is the rabbit and the other the hunter, the rabbit wins as it can run away from the hunter.

4. If both teams have the same selection, no point is scored.

The first team scoring ten points wins.

IMITATION

Formation: Children scattered around the room. The leader is in front.
Players: Entire class.
Supplies: Record player, records.

The game is based on the music phrase length of 8 counts. The leader performs for 8 counts with any kind of movement he wishes. For the next 8 counts, the children imitate his movements in the same sequence. The leader sets another round of movements and the children imitate.

After a period of imitation, the leader selects another child to be in front as leader.

LOST CHILDREN

Playing Area: Classroom.
Players: Entire class.
Supplies: None.

One child is chosen to be the policeman (or policewoman) and leaves the room. The other children walk around the room. The teacher or leader calls the policeman in and says, "The children are lost. Will you please take them home safely?"

The policeman then takes each child to his seat. The players stay where they are until the policeman seats them. Success for the policeman is determined by the number of children he can seat correctly. He is not permitted to look in the desks or in books for clues to correct seating.

OVERHEAD RELAY

Playing Area: Classroom.
Players: Each row in a classroom forms a team.
Supplies: Beanbag, eraser, or similar object for each team.

The first person in each row has the object to be passed on his desk in front of him. At the signal to pass, he claps his hands, picks up the object, and passes it overhead to the child behind him. This child places the object on the desk, claps his hands, and passes overhead. When the last child in the row receives the object, he runs forward to the head of the row, using the aisle to his right. *After* he has passed by, each child, using the *same* aisle, moves back one seat. The child who has come to the front now sits down in the first seat, places the object on the desk, claps his hands, and passes overhead.

This continues until the children are back in their original seats and the object is on the front desk. The first row done wins.

PUT HANDS

Formation: Students are standing or seated. They can be scattered around the room.
Players: Entire class.
Supplies: None.

One child is the leader and stands in front

of the class. He gives certain directions verbally and tries to confuse the class by doing something else. He can say, "Put your hands on top of your head." He might put his own hands on top of his shoulders. Those who are in error have a point scored against them. Directions he can give, to which he should make other movements, are:

"Put your hands on—shoulders, toes, knees, head, chest, etc."

"Reach out to the — side, front, back, high."

"Put your right hand (or left) on your shoulder, behind your back, etc."

After a short time, the leader should be changed.

SIMON SAYS

Playing Area: Classroom.

Players: Entire class.

Supplies: None.

One player is selected to be "Simon" and stands in front of the class. He gives a variety of commands like, "Stand up," "Clap your hands," "Turn around," and others. He may or may not precede a command by the words, "Simon says." No one is to move unless the command is preceded by these words. Those who move at the wrong time are eliminated and must sit out the game.

The leader gives commands rapidly, changing to different movements. He tries to confuse the class by doing all movements himself.

Variation: *Birds Fly*. In this game, the children hold their hands and arms out as if to fly. The leader calls out commands like "Dogs fly," "Birds fly," and "Horses fly." Each time he makes a flying motion as he calls out. The children should move their arms only when the creature is one that can fly. Otherwise, they are eliminated.

SNAP

Formation: Children seated in a circle.

Players: 10–15.

Supplies: None.

This is a rhythm game involving a three-count rhythm. The children must practice the rhythm well before the game can be successful. The action is as follows:

Count 1	Slap knees
Count 2	Clap hands
Count 3	Snap fingers

Each child in the circle has a number. The leader calls a number on the third count (snap fingers). The player whose number was called then calls another when he snaps his fingers. The object of the game is to keep the precise rhythm and keep the numbers called back and forth across the circle.

Errors:

Breaking the rhythm.

Not calling another number after yours has been called.

Calling when your number has not been called.

Calling a number of a player who has been eliminated.

Players are eliminated after they have made three errors. The number of an eliminated player is dead and cannot be called.

TEN, TEN, DOUBLE TEN

Playing Area: Classroom.

Players: Entire class.

Supplies: Small object.

All the children except one leave the classroom. The child left in the room places the object in some place visible but not too easily found. The children come back into the room. As soon as a child sees the object, he continues searching for another moment so as not to give away the position. He calls out, "Ten, ten, double ten, forty-five, fifteen, buckskin six" and sits down in his seat. The child who found the object first gets to place it for the next game. The child who was last finding it, or any who did not, must remain in their seats for the next turn.

WHERE, OH WHERE

Playing Area: Classroom.

Players: Entire class.

Supplies: Spool or other small object which can be hidden in a closed hand.

The children are seated in regular seats or can be in a circle formation seated on the floor. One child is chosen to be "It" and turns his back to the group while hiding his eyes.

The object is passed among the children from hand to hand until a signal is given. "It" turns around and attempts to guess who has the object. He gets three guesses. All children, including the one who has the object, do various movements and stunts to confuse the guesser. The object must be held in the hand, however. If the guess is correct, the child with the object becomes the new guesser. If not, "It" tries again. If a child misses on three turns in a row, he should choose another child to be "It."

If the number is large, two children can be "It," thus doubling the chances of guessing, as each should be allowed three guesses.

WHO'S LEADING

Formation: Children are in a circle formation either sitting in chairs or on the floor. They can be standing, but this gets fatiguing.

Players: Entire class.

Supplies: None.

One child is "It." He steps away from the circle and covers his eyes. The teacher points to one child who is the "Leader." The leader starts any motion he chooses with his hands, feet, body, etc. All children follow the movements as he does them. The child who is "It" watches the group as they change from one motion to another to try to determine who is leading. Players should cover up for the leader, who also tries to confuse "It" by looking at other players.

"It" gets three guesses. If not successful, he chooses another child to be "It." If he guesses correctly, he gets another turn (limit of 3 turns).

ZOO

Playing Area: Classroom.

Players: Entire class.

Supplies: None.

Seven children are chosen to stand in front of the class and one of them is selected as the leader. The leader directs each of the other six children to choose his favorite animal, and then places them in line, saying the name of the animal as he does so.

On signal 1 the six children, performing in the order in which they were just announced by the leader, imitate the animal they have chosen. Ten to fifteen seconds should be allowed for this.

On signal 2 the rest of the children stand, wave their arms, jump or hop in place, turning round if they wish, and then sit down, close their eyes, cover them with their hands, and put their heads down on the desks.

The leader now arranges the six "animals" in a different order. When this has been done the seated children return to sitting position. Another signal is given, and the animals perform once again for a short period.

Once this has been completed, any seated child can volunteer to place the six children in their original positions, naming the animal in each case. If this child succeeds in placing the animals in their original stand position and calling them by their chosen name, he may become an animal in the zoo and choose a name for himself. He then takes his place among the animals, and the game continues until twelve or some other designated number are in the zoo.

Other categories such as flowers, Mother Goose, play characters, and so on can be used.

OTHER GAMES

The teacher should examine the sections on games, both primary and intermediate, for activities of possible use.

21

Integration with Other Subjects

Art
Geography
Health and Safety
History
Language Arts
Music
Number Concepts — Mathematics
Projects

Many physical education experiences and learning situations provide opportunity for the use of and combination with other subject areas for the purpose of broadening the learning environment. Conversely, other subject areas can be of use in broadening and enriching the physical education program.

Even in the unit-of-work study program, physical education should be considered for its contributions. Take the example of the class which is studying the Oregon Trail as its unit of work. Combining with the geographical, historical, home economics, health, music, and social study approaches, the unit can also study the recreational life of the pioneers. Games and dances used by the Trail youngsters as well as Indian games and dances can be a part of the study.

The opportunities for integrating physical education activities with other subject media are numerous and limited only by the ingenuity of the teacher and the interests of the children. Some suggestions about the ways in which physical education can relate to and complement other subject areas are presented. These introduce the topic and provide some examples. Many other integrations can be devised.

ART

Children like to make things for their own programs. Posters, decorations, and costumes bring together art and physical education areas. Others are:

1. Art work for games — toss games, clown faces, etc.

2. Bulletin boards and displays — offer numerous possibilities.

3. Drawing action figures related to different activities.

4. Making costumes for demonstrations.

5. Making charts of field or game areas with player positions.

6. Making programs for demonstrations.

GEOGRAPHY

Since the origins of physical education materials are diverse and scattered, geographical associations provide the classroom teacher with another outlet for learning experiences. Is it possible to find clues for the play and sports habits of people in their location, terrain, and other geographical factors? Some areas of study are:

1. Climate in different areas — how this affects the play habits of the people.

2. Games of different countries — how others play.

3. Folk Dances — origins, characteristics of the country and of the people.

4. Students from other countries explaining their play habits and games.

HEALTH AND SAFETY

It is difficult to separate health and safety from physical education. Physical education should be carried on in a healthful and safe atmosphere. Many opportunities for incidental teaching of health concepts arise. Safety considerations for each activity are important in the planning. Other examples are:

1. Fitness concepts — knowledge of basic understandings, the development of fitness, and its relationship to the health of the individual.

2. Exercise and health — the part exercise plays in our health.

3. Safety campaigns — playground and gymnasium safety.

4. Recreation and health — the importance of recreation in our living.

5. Learning the why and wherefore of physical examinations.

6. Studying the mechanics of posture.

7. Learning the part nutrition, rest, and body care can play in daily living.

8. Checking and inspecting equipment and facilities for safety standards.

HISTORY

Physical education is rich in historical background. Practically all activities have a historical aspect with regard to origin and background. Many of today's activities have a traditional basis. The historical aspects of physical education offer many possibilities for historical study and should be developed. Appreciations and favorable attitudes can be furthered if children understand the background of an activity. Some suggestions for incorporating history are:

1. The origins of activities — events like the discus throw, shot-put, and the pole vault are performed now only because of the tradition behind them. The origins of such games as baseball, basketball, and American football are equally interesting.

2. Dances — ethnic background, historical period emphasis, meanings.

3. Fitness of other peoples — the ancient Greek, Persian, and Roman civilizations. Modern emphasis on fitness — the U.S.S.R. and other countries.

4. The Ancient and Modern Olympics — the ancient games and how the modern games came into being.

5. Knighthood and the tournaments.

LANGUAGE ARTS

Physical education materials make useful subjects for written and oral expression. The world of sports and games provides many examples of outstanding individuals who can serve as topics for presentations. Additional suggestions follow.

1. Reading — children can read game descriptions, rules, and related materials.

2. Writing — biographies, summaries of game programs.

3. Oral expression — pupil demonstrations, explanations, speaking at evaluation sessions.

4. Spelling — new words in the coming physical education lesson, difficult sports terms.

5. Creative expression — working out story plays for the story periods.

6. Word origins — study of physical education terminology. Terms like gymnasium, calisthenics, and exercise have special origins.

7. Explanation of games or directions for an activity.

8. Announcing at demonstrations.

9. Writing sports stories.

MUSIC

Rhythm is an integral part of physical education, and much of the program features both music and rhythm. Musical training should not be isolated from physical education. The two areas overlap and should blend in the children's experiences. Examples of combining musical and physical education are:

1. Understanding rhythm — learning the characteristics of the music and rhythm while physical education provides the interpretation through movement.

2. Learning singing games — the words and music can be taught by the music teacher, and the movement patterns taught later in the physical education class.

3. Learning about music — learning the

names of different musical selections, becoming familiar with the heritage of music.

4. Working out rope jumping routines to a selected piece of music.

NUMBER CONCEPTS — MATHEMATICS

Concepts of numbers can be strengthened. Practical application of the processes of addition, subtraction, division, multiplication, percentage computation, and measurement can be demonstrated through selected physical education procedures. Ways in which number concepts can be related to physical education are:

1. Measuring performance—distance, time, height.

2. Working out averages — from tests and other measured performances.

3. Working with percentages — batting, team standings, other comparisons.

4. Geometric principles — layout of fields and areas.

5. The metric system — comparison of European records (metric system) and American performances. Measurements taken with metric system.

6. Number perception — in games where numbers are called for signals, different combinations could be used. For example, instead of calling out "8," the teacher could say, "36 divided by 3 minus 4."

PROJECTS

Class projects in physical education or related areas form excellent educational opportunities. The teacher and the children should plan together. Many ideas can be found for these projects. Playdays form an excellent area. A playday could be organized with one or more classes in the same school, with a class in another school, or just among the children of the class itself. Demonstrations and exhibitions for parents are fruitful projects. A convocation program or demonstration in the gymnasium before other children merits consideration.

Other projects could be a study of games of other lands, the Olympic Games, a sport, or other physical education activity. Another suggestion is to have a rhythmic party, inviting another class.

The program can be planned, invitations written, committees formed, and all the necessary details arranged.

The enterprising teacher will think of many other ideas which can be used as projects for the children. The project could be on a yearly basis or could be one for each season.

22

Introductory Sports Units

The Sports Unit
Basketball
Skills in Basketball
Soccer
Soccer Skills
Softball
Softball Skills for the Third Grade

A sports unit is a planned sequence of learning experiences based on a sports area, directed toward certain valid program goals in the form of selected competencies for the students. It involves the concept of time, since a period of time is established during which the unit is to be completed. It should be organized as a meaningful whole, stipulating the body of material which is to be covered.

Sports units should be introduced in the third grade, since this seems to be the level where children become psychologically and physically ready for this approach. Three sports have been selected as appropriate for introductory skills in the third grade which also meet the criteria of seasonal participation. Soccer can be scheduled in the fall, basketball during the winter, and softball in the spring. Flag football, volleyball, and track and field are reserved for introduction during the intermediate years. The three sports selected for the third grade (soccer, basketball, and softball) also undergo continued development in the intermediate grades.

In the third grade introductory emphasis should be on the development of skills. A focal game (lead-up game) should be designated toward which the unit of sports activity is directed. The achievement of the focal game can be used as a basis of evaluation. While the acquisition of relevant skills is a goal in itself, the unit becomes more meaningful if the development of a selected focal game is the ultimate goal.

THE SPORTS UNIT

The sports unit should introduce the child to the elements of the sport, which become the goals of the learning experiences which are to follow. While the instruction should zero in on the acquisition of skills, other elements such as concepts, rules, strategies, and background should be brought in where relevant. An examination of the suggested goals for a primary level sports unit will reveal the nature of this broader approach than merely teaching skills.

An introductory sports unit for the primary grades usually is simpler and not so complex as one for the intermediate grades. There are a number of divisions into which a unit may be divided, depending upon the sport selected. For the primary grades, a sports unit can be comprised of these divisions:

1. General Purposes of the Unit. Included here should be a statement in broad terms of what the unit is attempting to accomplish.

2. Specific Goals

a. *Knowledges and Understandings.* These items should be in terms of the maturity and background of the children, listing cognitive goals for the unit.

b. *Habits and Attitudes.* These include the social and ethical concepts which are to be an outgrowth of the learning experiences of the unit.

c. *Skills to be Acquired.* Skills to be included as part of the learning experiences should be listed in proper progression as they are to be accomplished.

d. *Activity Experiences.* The focal game of the unit should be identified and other activities which are used as steps along the way to the focal game should be designated. These are considered lead-up activities to the focal game.

3. Facilities and Equipment

This generally takes the form of a list of items needed for the unit, and any particular considerations needed for the facilities. The type of field lining is an example of an item under facilities.

4. Procedures

Considered here would be a description of how the unit will be developed, presenting sequential order and approximate time allotments to the segments of the unit. Evaluative criteria and procedures should be established.

5. Weekly Schedule

a. *General Schedule for the First Week.* If the unit is presented for only one week or less, the entire schedule can be planned. If the unit is more than one week in length, the schedule beyond the first week should be withheld until the first week's schedule has been completed. A lesson plan covering the first week's work is based on the suggested schedule. The progress during the first week will largely determine what is to follow.

6. Instructional Procedures

Critical instructional procedures should be listed, centering attention on the important approaches not to be overlooked.

7. Instructional Materials Sources

a. Bibliography.
b. Audio-visual aids.

BASKETBALL

Level of Introduction — Third Grade
Expected Skill Competencies

1. **Passing** — Chest or Push Pass, One-Hand (Baseball) Pass, Bounce Pass.
2. **Catching** — Above the Waist, Below the Waist.
3. **Shooting** — Two-Hand Chest Shot.
4. **Dribbling** — Standing and Moving.

Knowledges

Rules pertaining to the dribble.
Travel violations.

Focal Games

End Ball, Free Throw End Ball, Corner Ball.

Instructional Procedures

1. Many basketball skills, particularly on the third grade level, do not stipulate the use of basketballs. Other balls such as volley, playground, and rubber balls can be used successfully.

2. The junior size basketball should be used for the elementary school program.

3. If practical, the baskets should be lowered to 9' as compared with the high school height of 10'.

4. The program should concentrate on skills with many drills. Basketball offers endless possibilities, and drills should be utilized to give variety and breadth to the instructional program.

5. Each child should have an opportunity to practice all the skills. This is not possible when a considerable portion of the class time is devoted to playing the game.

6. One ball should be available for each child for dribbling practice and one ball for each two children for passing, catching, and shooting.

7. Organization should be informal for practice. There is little need for the more structured drills of the intermediate level.

SKILLS IN BASKETBALL

The basic skills in basketball to be covered in the elementary school class program in physical education can be divided into passing, catching, shooting, dribbling, and game skills.

Passing

Chest or Two-Hand Push Pass. The feet may be in an even position or one may be slightly ahead of the other. The ball is held at chest level with the fingers spread slightly above the center of the ball. The elbows are comfortably bent, and the delivery is made with a snap of the wrists. As the arms are extended, the fingers and wrists release the ball. A step is taken in the direction of the throw, or the weight shifts from rear to front foot.

Baseball or One-Hand Pass. Stand with the side toward the direction of the throw. The ball is brought back with both hands to a point over the shoulder or at the side of the head. The ball is now thrown like a softball, using the hand and wrist of the throwing arm for good follow-through.

Bounce Pass. Either of the previous two passes described can be adapted to make a bounce pass. The object is to throw the ball to a teammate on first bounce so the ball comes up to the outstretched hands. It should rebound waist high by hitting the floor 4' to 5' from the receiver. Do not bounce the ball at the receiver's feet.

Catching

A player should move to meet a basketball when catching it. The fingers should be relaxed and spread. To receive a high pass, the thumbs are together, and the little fingers meet for one caught low. For passes received at waist level, the hands are in a parallel position. A little "give" with the hands and arms to absorb the recoil is important.

Dribbling

The wrist and hand furnish most of the force for the dribble. The dribble is a push with the partially cupped hand. The hand should "feel" the ball coming back up just before pushing for the next dribble. The ball should not be batted.

Shooting

Children should start with the two-hand set shot. Later, they can be introduced to the more popular one-hand variety.

Push Shot. The feet may be together or one foot ahead with the knees slightly bent. The hands are placed behind the ball and a little to the side. The wrist action should start when the ball is at eye level. There should be good follow-through.

END BALL

Players on each team are divided into three groups: forwards, guards, and end men. The object is for a forward to throw successfully to one of his end zone players.

Playing Area: A court 20' by 40' is divided in half by a center line. End zones are marked 3' wide, completely across the court at each end.

Players: 9 to 12 on each team.

Supplies: Basketball or 10" rubber playground ball.

The players from each team are positioned as follows. The end zone players take a position in one of the end zones. Their forwards and guards then occupy the half of the court farthest from this end zone. The forwards are near the center line, and the guards are back near the end zone of that half.

The ball is put in play with a center jump between the two tallest opposite forwards. When a team gets the ball, the forwards try to throw over the heads of the opposing team to an end zone player. To score, the ball must be caught by an end zone player with *both* feet inside the zone. No dribbling or moving with the ball is permitted by any player.

Fouls: Fouls result in loss of the ball to the other team. Fouls are:

1. Holding a ball more than five seconds.
2. Stepping over the end line or stepping over the center line into the opponent's territory.
3. Walking (travel) with the ball.
4. Pushing or holding another player.

Out of Bounds: The ball belongs to the team that did not cause it to go out of bounds. The nearest player retrieves the ball out at the sideline and returns it to the guard of the proper team.

Teaching Suggestions: Encourage fast, accurate passing. Players in the end zones must practice jumping high to catch and still land with both feet inside the end zone area.

A system of rotation is desirable. Each time a score is made, players on that team can rotate one person. (See diagram.)

Variations:

1. A game which carries the progression one step farther is *Free Throw End Ball*. In

keeping with the rules, the end zone player scores one point when he catches the ball. He is allotted one free throw, which gives him the chance to score an additional point.

2. **Corner Ball.** This differs from End Ball only in that the scoring zone is located in the corners. A 3' by 3' square is drawn in each corner which imposes the limitation that only two players from each team are in position to receive the ball, one in each corner on the respective end of the playing area.

A valuable addition to the game is a set of four small boxes about 2" square and 8" or 12" high upon which each of the corner players stand. This puts them above the defenders and makes scoring easier. However, this demands reasonably accurate passing. Otherwise the game is the same as End Ball. Be sure to rotate the corner players.

SOCCER

Level of Introduction — Third Grade
Expected Skill Competencies

1. **Kicking** — Instep Kick, Side of the Foot Kick, Toe Kick.
2. **Trapping** — Toe Trap, Foot Trap.

Knowledges

Rules pertaining to illegal touching.

Focal Game

Circle Kick Ball.

Instructional Procedures

1. Much concentration should be centered on just kicking and trapping. This provides the basis for future play. American children usually have little prior experience with handling the ball with the feet and foot-eye coordination must be developed.

2. Sufficient number of balls should be present for the soccer practice period. As a minimum, one ball should be available for each two students.

3. Insist early on keeping the hands from handling balls. This impresses the children with the importance of the "no touch" rule regarding the hands and forearms.

4. Early kicking should stress control over short distances.

5. Kicking and trapping should be taught in the same drill.

SOCCER SKILLS

Soccer is a game based on kicking, so it is important that the students learn to control the ball with the feet. Practice must be intense enough to develop foot-eye coordination.

The basic kick for soccer is the instep kick, used for distance and for scoring.

Two other kicks are introduced in the third grade. The first is the side of the foot kick, primarily for ball control and passing. The second is the toe kick.

Control of the ball demands the ability to stop the ball, which is called trapping. The toe trap and the foot trap are selected as basic third grade skills.

Basic Soccer Kicks

Instep Kick. The kicker approaches the ball from a 45° angle from the left, if he is a right-footed kicker. In the kick, the top of the instep meets the ball as in punting a football. It is necessary to approach from the side and kick with a moderate sideswing, or the toe will drive into and make contact with the surface. On the step into the ball, the left foot is placed close beside the ball, taking the weight of the body for the kick. With the body in a somewhat forward lean, the kicking foot makes contact with the ball with the instep. The power comes from the knee by snapping the bent leg forward. The eye is on the ball, which is contacted with the instep. The child must kick through the ball with good follow-through.

Inside Foot Kick. Contact is made with the inside of the foot. The kick is used for passing or goal kicking. The knee is slightly bent, and the leg is swung from the hip. The kick is used for short distances only. The toe should be held down during the kick.

Toe Kick. The toe kick is not considered to be as accurate as other kicks, but has some use in kicking off and driving the ball for distance. The technique is different from the instep kick in that the ball is approached directly from behind. The step made with the nonkicking foot should be to a point slightly back of the ball. The kicking toe is kept up, with the foot at right angles with the leg. The force is from the snap of the knee with good follow-through.

Trapping

Relaxation and "giving" with the ball are important in all traps.

1. *Toe Trap.* This is the simplest of all traps and involves stopping a rolling ball by putting the toe of the foot on the ball and holding it to the ground.

2. *Foot Trap.* Using the inside of the foot and giving with the ball, the motion of the ball is stopped by the inside of the foot.

Soccer Touch Rule

The ball may not be deliberately played with the hands, forearms, or arms. Mere incidental touch should be disregarded. If the arms are in contact with the body and are used only to block or stop the ball from this position, there is no violation.

Focal Game

CIRCLE KICK BALL

Formation: Circle.

Players: 10–20.

Supplies: Soccer or 10" playground ball.

Players kick the ball (with the side of the foot) back and forth inside of the circle. The object is to kick the ball out of the circle *underneath* shoulder level of the circle players. A point is scored against each of the players where the ball left the circle. Any player kicking the ball *over* shoulder level gets a point against him. A variation is to eliminate the offending players instead of scoring points against them.

When players are eliminated, have them stay out only until the next pair has erred, thus moving players back into the action quickly.

SOFTBALL

Level of Introduction — Third Grade
Expected Skill Competencies

1. Throwing — Gripping the Ball, Overhand Throw, Underhand Toss.
2. Catching and Fielding — Catching Thrown Balls, Fly Balls, Grounders.
3. Batting — Simple Skills.
4. Base Running — To First Base.
5. Pitching — Simple Underhand.

Knowledges

Defining the strike zone, when a batter is safe or out, difference between a fair or foul ball.

Focal Games

Throw It and Run.
Two-Pitch Softball.

Instructional Procedures

1. Safety is of utmost importance. The following precautions should be observed.

   a. Throwing the bat is a constant danger. The members of the batting team should stand on the side opposite the batter. For a righthanded batter, the batting team
   b. (1) Have batter touch bat to the ground before dropping it.
      (2) Call the batter "out" if he throws the bat.
      (3) Have the batter carry the bat to first base.
      (4) Have the batter change ends with the bat before dropping it.
      (5) Have the batter place the bat in a 3' circle before running.
   c. Sliding leads to both injury and destruction of clothing. No sliding should be permitted. Runner should be called out.
   d. If a catcher stands close behind the plate while catching, he must wear a mask.
   e. Colliding while running for the ball can be held to a minimum if players are taught to call for the ball and not to trespass on other players' areas.

2. Care of equipment is a responsibility of all. The trademark of the bat should be kept up when contacting the ball in the middle of the swing. The bat should be used to bat softballs only. Hitting rocks and sticks with the bat injures the bat and lessens its effectiveness and life. The bat should be carried, not thrown, from one person to another.

3. Players should rotate positions often. A good rule in physical education classes is that everyone, including the pitcher, should rotate to another position at the start of a new inning.

4. The distance between the bases has a heavy effect on the game. The distance should be lessened or increased according to the game and the capacities of the children.

5. Umpires can be appointed or the team at

bat can umpire. A rule that can be followed is that the person who made the last out of the previous inning is the umpire for the coming inning. There should be instruction for all in umpiring. To expect a child to umpire properly without proper instruction is poor teaching.

6. Encourage good players to recognize and give approval to those who are less skillful. Since there are many differences in ability, an opportunity for a lesson in tolerance is present. It is important not to let an error become a tragedy to a child.

7. Each player should run out his hit, no matter how hopeless it seems.

8. Teach respect for officials and acceptance of the umpire's judgment. The disreputable practice of baiting the umpire should be no part of the child's softball experiences.

BASIC RULES FOR SOFTBALL

For the few lead-up games and as an introduction to softball, it is necessary to establish certain selected rules for use in the third grade. The following provides a minimum.

1. The nine players on a softball team are the catcher, pitcher, first baseman, second baseman, shortstop, third baseman, left fielder, center fielder, and right fielder. The right fielder is the outfielder nearest first base.

2. All pitching is underhand.

3. A pitch to be called a strike must be over the plate and between the knees and shoulders of the batter. A ball is a pitch which does not go through this area.

4. A foul ball is a batted ball that settles outside the foul lines between home and first or home and third. A ball that rolls over a base is a fair ball. Also, any fly ball that lands in foul territory is a foul ball.

5. No lead-off from any base is permitted in softball. The runner must keep his foot on the base until the pitcher releases the ball.

6. The batter is out if a fly ball, either foul or fair, is caught.

7. The batter is safe if he reaches first base before the fielding team can get the ball to the first baseman with the foot on the base.

8. A batter is out if he misses the ball three times. This is called striking out.

9. A run is scored if the baserunner makes the circuit of bases (first, second, third, and home) before the batting team has three outs.

SOFTBALL SKILLS FOR THE THIRD GRADE

Overhand Throwing. The ball is held with two fingers on top, third and fourth fingers on one side, and the thumb on the other. The hand is brought back so the hand is well behind the shoulder at about that height. The left side of the body is turned in the direction of the throw, and the left arm is raised and in front of the body. The weight is on the back (right) foot with the left foot advanced with the toe touching the ground. The arm comes forward, and the ball is thrown with a downward snap of the wrist. The weight of the body is brought forward into the throw, with the weight shifting to the front foot. There should be good follow-through.

Underhand Toss. The hand and arm are brought back with the palms facing forward in a pendulum swing. The elbow is held slightly bent. The weight is mostly on the back foot. The arm comes forward almost like a bowling motion, and the ball is tossed. The weight shifts to the front foot during the toss.

Pitching. Stand with both feet facing the batter, and the ball held in front. As the ball is brought back for the toss the forward step of the left foot begins. When the toss is made, the weight is shifted to the forward (left) foot.

Catching Fly Balls. There are two methods for catching a fly ball.

1. For a low ball, the fielder keeps his little fingers together and forms a basket with his hands.

2. For a higher ball, the thumbs are together, and the ball is caught just in front of the chin.

There should be "give" with the catching hands. Care should be taken with a spinning ball to provide sufficient squeeze of the hands to stop the spinning.

Fielding Grounders. Always play the ball, don't let the ball play you. Advance on the ball. Try to catch it on a high hop or just as it hits the ground. Feet should be well apart and the eyes on the ball.

The little fingers are together and the hands are lower, with a stooping motion rather than being bent over. For right handers, the left foot should be slightly ahead.

Batting (Right Handed). Stand with the left side of the body toward the pitcher with the feet spread and the weight on both feet. The body should be facing the plate. Hold the bat with the trademark up so that the left hand (for right-handed batters) grasps the bat lower than the right. The bat is held over the right shoulder pointing both back and up. The elbows are away from the body for free swinging.

The swing begins with a hip roll and a short step forward in the direction of the pitcher. The bat is now swung level with the ground at the height of the pitch. Eyes are kept on the ball until it is hit. After the hit, there is good follow-through.

Beginning batters should use the choke grip, which is to hold the bat several inches above the small end of the bat.

Base Running. Children should be taught to run directly toward first base and run to a spot past the base. Too often, they run to first base, stop, and put a foot on it.

Focal Games

THROW IT AND RUN SOFTBALL

Playing Area: Softball diamond reduced in size.

Players: Two teams of 7 to 11 each. Usually 9 players are on a side.

Supplies: Softball or similar ball.

The game is played very much like softball with the following exception. With one team in the field at regular positions, the pitcher throws the ball to the "batter" who, instead of batting the ball, catches it, and immediately throws it out into the field. The ball is now treated as a batted ball, and regular softball rules prevail. However, no stealing is permitted, and the runners must hold bases until the batter throws the ball. A foul ball is out.

Variations:

1. **Under-Leg Throw.** Instead of having the batter throw directly, have him turn to the right, lift his left leg, and throw the ball under the leg into the playing field.

2. **Beat-Ball Throw.** The fielders, instead of playing regular softball rules, throw the ball directly home to the catcher. The batter, in the meantime, runs around the bases. He gets one point for each base he touches before the catcher gets the ball and calls out, "Stop." There are no outs, and each batter gets a turn before changing sides to the field. A fly ball caught would mean no score. Similarly, a foul ball would score no points but would count as a turn at bat.

TWO-PITCH SOFTBALL

Playing Area: Softball diamond.

Players: Regular softball teams but the numbers can vary.

Supplies: Softball, bat.

This introductory game is played like regular softball with the following changes:

1. A member of the team at bat is the pitcher. Some system of rotation should be set up so every child takes a turn as pitcher.

2. The batter has only two pitches in which to hit the ball. He must hit a fair ball on either of these pitches or he is out. He can foul the first ball, but if he fouls the second he is out. There is no need to call balls or strikes.

3. The pitcher, because he is a member of the team at bat, does not field the ball. A member of the team at field acts as the fielding pitcher.

4. If the batter hits the ball, regular softball rules are followed. However, no stealing is permitted.

Variation: Three Strikes

In this game, the batter is allowed three pitches (strikes) to hit the ball. Otherwise, the game proceeds as in *Two-Pitch*.

Appendix I
Diagrams for Constructing Physical Education Equipment and Supplies

Diagrams are presented for constructing the following physical education materials:

1. Balls, Yarn
2. Balance Beams
3. Balance Boards
4. Blocks and Cones
5. Bounding Board
6. Hoops
7. Individual Mats
8. Jumping Boxes
9. Jumping Standards
10. Magic Ropes (Stretch Ropes)
11. Paddles
12. Plastic Markers and Ball Scoops
13. Quoits or Deck Tennis Rings
14. Wands
15. Slide-Gym Set

In most cases the diagrams present measurements which can be subject to variation. In some instances several designs are presented to provide choice. The selection of materials is also subject to choice.

BALLS, YARN

To make a yarn ball the following materials are needed:

One skein of yarn per ball
Piece of box cardboard 5" wide and 10" or so long
Strong light cord for binding

Wrap the yarn 20 to 25 times around the 5" width of the cardboard. Slide the yarn off the cardboard and wrap it in the middle with the cord, forming a tied loop of yarn. Continue until all the yarn is used up.

Take two of the tied loops and connect (tie) them together at the centers, using several turns of the cord. This forms a bundle of two tied loops as illustrated.

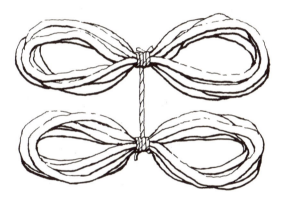

Next, tie bundles together by pairs. Then, form the ball by tying the paired bundles together until all bundles are used.

The final step is to cut and trim the formed ball. Cutting should be carefully done so that the lengths are reasonably even or considerable trimming will be needed.

The ball can be soaked in hot water or steamed to make it shrink and become more firm. Only cotton and wool yarns will shrink. Nylon and similar materials are impervious to water.

BALANCE BEAM

1" X 4" X 8"

2" X 4" STOCK

2" X 4" X 8'

7"

12"

2"X4"

3/4" PLYWOOD

BALANCE BOARDS

1. SINGLE AXIS

2. SQUARE TOP, SQUARE BOTTOM

3. CIRCULAR BOARD

BLOCKS AND CONES
USED TO MAKE HURDLES AND OBSTACLES

BLOCKS   4"X4"X12"   OR   4"X4"X8"

DOWN POSITION

NOTCHES CUT ½"X½" BY TABLE SAW

UP POSITION

CONES

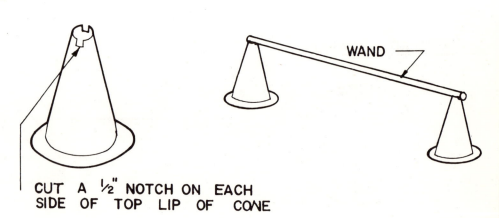

CUT A ½" NOTCH ON EACH SIDE OF TOP LIP OF CONE

BOUNDING BOARD

USE ¾" PLYWOOD TOP
6'
2'
4" X 4"

DETAIL
CARPET
⅜" X 4" CARRIAGE BOLT

HOOPS – CONSTRUCTION, SUPPORT

DOWEL
½" PLASTIC WATER PIPE
DETAIL
TAPE
DOWEL
TACKS
INDIVIDUAL MAT

HOOP SIZE	PIPE LENGTH
30"	95"
36"	113"
42"	132"

INDIVIDUAL MATS

INDOOR – OUTDOOR CARPETING

20" X 40"   OR   24" X 48"

JUMPING BOXES

JUMPING STANDARDS

MAGIC (STRETCH) ROPES

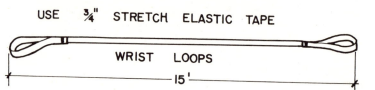

PADDLE DIAGRAM

PADDLE FOR YOUNGER CHILDREN

PLASTIC MARKERS AND BALL SCOOP

APPENDIX I   309

QUOITS OR DECK TENNIS RINGS

½" GARDEN HOSE
PLASTIC ELECTRICIAN'S TAPE
⅝" WOODEN DOWELL 2" LONG

WANDS

⅝" OR ¾" DOWLING

LENGTHS: K-1 = 30",   1-3 = 36",   4-6 = 42"

SLIDE-GYM SET

Appendix II

Sources for Records for the Rhythmic Program in the Elementary School

The following sources, in most cases, handle a variety of records. It is suggested that you write and ask for descriptive literature. The request should include the type of rhythmic program and the grade level for which the records are intended.

Bee Cross Media Inc.
Dept. JH
36 Dogwood Glen
Rochester, N. Y. 14625

Bowmar Records
Dept. J-569
622 Rodier Dr.
Glendale, Calif. 91201

Canadian F. D. S.
Educational Recordings
605 King Street
W. Toronto, 2B, Canada

Cheviot Corporation, Dept. J-33
P. O. Box 34485
Los Angeles, Calif. 90034

Children's Music Center
5373 W. Pico Blvd.
Los Angeles, Calif. 90019

Dance Record Center
1161 Broad Street
Newark, N. J. 07114

David McKay, Inc.
750 Third Ave.
New York, N. Y. 10017

Educational Activities, Inc.
P. O. Box 392
Freeport, N. Y. 11520

Educational Recordings of America, Inc.
P. O. Box 6062
Bridgeport, Conn. 06606

Folkraft Records
1159 Broad Street
Newark, N. J. 07714

Freda Miller Records for Dance
Department J, Box 383
Northport, Long Island, N. Y. 11768

Herbert
1657 Broadway
New York, N. Y. 10019

Hoctor Educational Records, Inc.
Waldwick, N. J. 07463

Instructor Publications, Inc.
Dansville, N. Y. 14437

Kimbo Educational Records
P. O. Box 55
Deal, N. J. 07723

Leo's Advance Theatrical Co.
32 West Randolph Street
Chicago, Ill. 60601

Loshin's
215 East Eighth St.
Cincinnati, Ohio 45202

Master Record Service
708 East Garfield
Phoenix, Ariz. 85000

Merrback Records Service
P. O. Box 7308
Houston, Tex. 77000

RCA Victor Education Dept. J
155 E. 24th Street
New York, N. Y. 10010

Record Center
2581 Piedmont Road N. E.
Atlanta, Ga. 30324

Rhythms Productions Records
Dept. J., Box 34485
Los Angeles, Calif. 90034

Rhythm Record Co.
9203 Nichols Road
Oklahoma City, Okla. 73120

Russell Records
P. O. Box 3318
Ventura, Calif. 93003

Selva and Sons, Inc.
Dept. J, 1607 Broadway
New York, N. Y. 10019

Square Dance Records
P. O. Box 689
Santa Barbara, Calif. 93100

Stanley Bowmar Co., Inc.
4 Broadway
Valhalla, N. Y. 10595

Appendix III

Bibliography and Related Materials Resource

For the user's convenience this bibliography is divided into major subject areas. Addresses of the various publishers can be obtained at most libraries and from the *Publishers' Trade List Annual* and *Books in Print.* A listing of card packets for games, rhythms, and stunts has also been included. It should be noted that in some instances titles include more than one area; however, these were classified under the area of greatest emphasis.

"AAHPER" refers to the American Association for Health, Physical Education and Recreation, 1201 Sixteenth Street, N.W., Washington, D.C. 20036.

The bibliography is organized under the following headings:
1. Curriculum in Elementary School Physical Education
2. Fitness and Exercise
3. Games and Similar Activities
4. Rhythms, Songs, and Dances
5. Stunts, Tumbling, and Apparatus
6. Health, Safety, and Posture
7. Perceptual-Motor Development
8. Card Packets for Games, Rhythms, and Stunts
9. English Books on Movement
10. Growth and Development; Miscellaneous

1. CURRICULUM IN ELEMENTARY SCHOOL PHYSICAL EDUCATION

AAHPER. *Essentials of a Quality Elementary School Physical Education Program.* Washington, D. C., 1970.

———. *Promising Practices in Elementary School Physical Education.* Washington, D. C., 1969.

———. *Trends in Elementary School Physical Education.* Washington, D. C., 1970.

Anderson, Elliot, and laBerge. *Play with a Purpose.* New York: Harper & Row, 1966.

Andrews, Sauborn, and Schneider. *Physical Education for Today's Boys and Girls.* Boston: Allyn & Bacon, 1960.

Arra, Carl. *Physical Education in the Elementary School.* Cranbury, N. J.: A. S. Barnes, 1970.

Association for Childhood Education International. *Physical Education for Children's Healthful Living.* Washington, D. C.: ACEI, 1968.

Boyer, Madeline Haas. *The Teaching of Elementary School Physical Education.* New York: J. Lowell Pratt, 1965.

Brown, Margaret C., and Betty K. Sommer. *Movement Education: Its Evolution and a Modern Approach.* Reading, Mass.: Addison-Wesley, 1969.

Bucher, Charles A., and Evelyn M. Reade. *Physical Education and Health in the Elementary School.* New York: Macmillan, 1971.

Cherry, Clare. *Creative Movement for the Developing Child.* Belmont, Calif.: Fearon Publishers, 1971.

Corbin, C. *Becoming Physically Educated in the Elementary School.* Philadelphia: Lea & Febiger, 1969.

Cratty, Bryant, et al. *Movement Activities, Motor Ability, and the Education of Children.* Springfield, Ill.: C. C. Thomas, 1970.

Demeter, Rose. *Hop-Run-Jump: We Exercise with Our Children.* Edited by M. Wuest and M. Moskin. New York: John Day, 1968.

Department of Education, N. S. W. *Physical Education in Primary Schools.* Sydney, N. S. W., Australia; Minister for Education, N. S. W., n. d.

Detroit Public Schools. *It's All in the Game — About Children in Play.* Detroit: The Board of Education of the City of Detroit, 1961.

Espenschade, Anna S. *Physical Education in the Elementary Schools (#27 of the Series, What Research Says to the Teacher).* Washington, D. C.: National Education Association, 1963.

Fabricius, Helen. *Physical Education for the Classroom Teacher.* Dubuque, Iowa: Wm. C. Brown, 1965.

Fait, Hollis F. *Physical Education for the Elementary School Child.* Philadelphia: Saunders, 1971.

Frostig, Marianne. *Movement Education: Theory and Practice.* Chicago: Follett Educational Corporation, 1970.

Gilliom, Bonnie Cherp. *Basic Movement Education for Children: Rationale and Teaching Units.* Reading, Mass.: Addison-Wesley, 1970.

Glass, Henry "Buzz." *Exploring Movement.* Freeport, N. Y.: Educational Activities, Inc., 1966.

Greene, Arthur S. *Physical Activities for Elementary Schools.* Minneapolis, Minn.: T. S. Denison, 1963.

Hackett, Layne C., and Robert G. Jenson. *A Guide to Movement Exploration.* Palo Alto, Calif.: Peek Publications, 1966.

Halsey, Elizabeth, and Lorena Porter. *Physical Education for Children, A Developmental Program.* New York: Henry Holt (Dryden Press), 1963.

Hatcher, Caro, and Hilda Mullin. *More than Words — Movement Activities for Children.* Pasadena: Parents-for-Movement Publications, 1969.

Humphrey, James H. *Child Learning Through Elementary School Physical Education.* Dubuque, Iowa: Wm. C. Brown, 1965.

Jordan, Diana. *Children and Movement.* New Rochelle, N. Y.: Sportshelf, 1968.

Kirchner, Cunningham, Worrell. *Introduction to Movement Education.* Dubuque, Iowa: Wm. C. Brown, 1970.

Kirchner, Glenn. *Physical Education for Elementary School Children.* 2d ed. Dubuque, Iowa: Wm. C. Brown, 1971.

Latchaw, Marjorie. *A Pocket Guide of Movement Activities for the Elementary School.* Englewood Cliffs, N. J.: Prentice-Hall, 1970.

Latchaw, Marjorie, and G. Egstrom. *Human Movement: With Concepts Applied to Children's Movement Activities.* Englewood Cliffs, N. J.: Prentice-Hall, 1970.

Miller, Arthur G., and Virginia Whitcomb. *Physical Education in the Elementary School Curriculum.* Englewood Cliffs, N. J.: Prentice-Hall, 1969.

Mosston, Muska. *Developmental Movement.* Columbus, Ohio: Charles E. Merrill Books, 1965.

Neilson, Van Hagen, and Comer. *Physical Education for Elementary Schools.* New York: Ronald Press, 1966.

Ontario Department of Education. *Physical Education — Junior Division.* Toronto, Ontario: Canadian Association for Health, Physical Education, and Recreation (515 Jarvis St.), 1960.

Porter, Lorena. *Movement Education for Children.* Washington, D. C.: AAHPER, 1969.

Schurr, Evelyn. *Movement Experiences for Children.* New York: Appleton-Century-Crofts, 1967.

Smalley, Jeannette. *Physical Education Activities for the Elementary School.* Palo Alto, Calif.: National Press Publications, n.d.

Society of State Directors of Health, Physical Education, and Recreation. *A Statement of Basic Beliefs.* Washington, D. C., 1964.

Spath, Martha. *Education in Play.* Kirksville, Mo.: Simpson, 1966.

Stanley, Sheila. *Physical Education: A Movement Orientation.* Scarborough, Ontario: McGraw-Hill Book Co. of Canada, 1969.

Sweeney, Robert T. *Selected Readings in Movement Education.* Reading, Mass.: Addison-Wesley, 1970.

Tillotson, Joan, et al. *A Program of Movement Education for the Plattsburgh Elementary Public Schools.* Plattsburgh, N. Y., 1969.

Vannier, Maryhelen, and Mildred Foster. *Teaching Physical Education in Elementary Schools.* Philadelphia: Saunders, 1963.

Wickstrom, Ralph L. *Fundamental Movement Patterns.* Philadelphia: Lea & Febiger, 1970.

Wiener, Jack, and John Lidstone. *Creative Movement for Children: A Dance Program for the Classroom.* New York: Van Nostrand-Reinhold, 1969.

Young, Helen L. *A Manual-Workbook of Physical Education for Elementary School Teachers.* New York: Macmillan, 1963.

2. FITNESS AND EXERCISE

Available at the AAHPER

Exercise and Fitness (Statement by the American Medical Association and the AAHPER). 1964.

Fitness Test Manual. 1965.

Your Child's Health and Fitness. (Brochure. Available in quantities.)

Your Child's Health and Fitness Filmstrip.

Also available from the AAHPER is a variety of fitness materials, including record forms, certificates, emblems, and bar patches. Write for descriptive literature.

Available from the President's Council on Physical Fitness. Write to Superintendent of Documents, U. S. Government Printing Office, Washington, D. C.

Vim (Fitness program for girls), 1964.

Vigor (Fitness program for boys), 1964.

Youth Physical Fitness. Suggested Elements of a School Centered Program, 1966.

Physical Fitness Elements in Recreation, 1963.

Nelson, Dale O. *Special Exercises for Physical Fitness.* Logan, Utah: Dept. of Health, P. E., and Rec., Utah State University, 1964.

Wallis, Earl L., and Gene A. Logan. *Exercises for Children.* Englewood Cliffs, N. J.: Prentice-Hall, 1966.

3. GAMES AND SIMILAR ACTIVITIES

AAHPER. *How We Do It Game Book.* Washington, D. C., 1964.

―――. *ICHPER Book of Worldwide Games and Dances.* Washington, D. C., 1967.

Bancroft, Jessie H. *Games,* revised edition. New York: Macmillan, n.d.

Bell, R. C. *Board and Table Games from Many Civilizations.* New York: Oxford University Press, 1960.

Bentley, William G. *Indoor and Outdoor Games.* Palo Alto, Calif.: Fearon Publishers, 1966.

Borst, Evelyne. *The Book of Games for Boys and Girls: How to Lead and Play Them.* New York: Ronald Press, 1953.

Cratty, Byron J. *Active Learning — Games to Enhance Academic Abilities.* Englewood Cliffs, N. J.: Prentice-Hall Co., 1971.

Depew, Arthur M. *The Cokesbury Game Book.* Nashville: Abingdon Press, 1960.

Donnelly, Richard J., William G. Helms, and Elmer D. Mitchell. *Active Games and Contests.* New York: Ronald Press, 1958.

Ewing, Neil. *Games, Stunts, and Exercises.* Palo Alto, Calif.: Fearon Publishers, 1964.

Frankel, Lillian and Godrey. *Games for Boys and Girls.* New York: Sterling, n.d.

Gardner, Grace H. *Games We Like to Play.* New York: Williams-Frederick Press, 1959.

Geri, Frank. *Illustrated Games and Rhythms for Children* (Primary Grades). Englewood Cliffs, N. J.: Prentice-Hall, 1955.

Harbin, E. O. *Games of Many Nations.* Nashville: Abingdon Press, 1954.

_____. *Games for Boys and Girls* (Gr. 3-5). Nashville: Abingdon Press, 1951.

Hindman, Darwin A. *Complete Book of Games and Stunts.* Englewood Cliffs, N. J.: Prentice-Hall, 1956.

_____. *Handbook of Indoor Games and Stunts.* Englewood Cliffs, N. J.: Prentice-Hall, 1955.

Hunt, Sarah E. *Games and Sports the World Around.* New York: Ronald Press, 1964.

Kraus, Richard. *The Family Book of Games.* New York: McGraw-Hill, 1960.

_____. *Play Activities for Boys and Girls.* New York: McGraw-Hill, 1957.

Latchaw, Marjorie. *A Pocket Guide of Games and Rhythms for the Elementary School.* Englewood Cliffs, N. J.: Prentice-Hall, 1958.

LeCrone, Harold and Mary Jane. *Let's Play A Learning Game.* Oklahoma City, Okla.: Harold and Mary Jane LeCrone, 819 N.W. 92nd St., 1966.

LeCrone, Mary Jane. *Fun While Learning.* Oklahoma City. Okla.: Harold and Mary Jane LeCrone, 819 N.W. 92nd St., 1964.

Lowenfeld, Margaret. *Play in Childhood.* New York: Wiley, 1967.

Macfarlan, Allan and Paulette. *Fun with Brand-New Games.* New York: Association Press, 1961.

Matterson, E. M. *Play and Playthings for the Preschool Child.* Baltimore: Penguin, 1967.

Nagel, Charles. *Play Activities for Elementary Grades.* St. Louis: Mosby, 1964.

Stuart, Frances R. *Classroom Activities.* Washington, D. C.: AAHPER, 1963.

4. RHYTHMS, SONGS AND DANCES

Andrews, Gladys. *Creative Rhythmic Movement for Children.* Englewood Cliffs, N. J.: Prentice-Hall, 1954.

Ashton, Dudley. *Rhythmic Activities — Grades K-6.* Washington, D. C.: AAHPER, 1964.

Barr, Lillian J. *Motion Song for Tots.* Minneapolis: T. S. Denison, n.d.

Bley, Edgar S. *Best Singing Games for Children of All Ages.* New York: Sterling, 1959.

Boorman, Joyce. *Creative Dance in the First Three Grades.* New York: McKay, 1969.

Carabo-Cone, Madeleine. *Playground as Music Teacher.* New York: Harper & Row, 1959.

Doll, Edna, and Mary Jarman Nelson. *Rhythms Today.* Morristown, N. J.: Silver, 1965.

Driver, Ann. *Music and Movement.* New York: Oxford University Press, 1936.

Evans, Ruth. *40 Basic Rhythms for Children.* Putnam, Conn.: U. S. Textbook Co., 1958.

Fox, Grace and Kathleen G. Merrill. *Folk Dancing.* New York: Ronald Press, 1957.

Harris, Pittman and Waller. *Dance-A-While.* Minneapolis: Burgess, 1964.

Heaton, A. *Fun Dances.* Dubuque, Iowa: Wm. C. Brown, 1959.

Kulbitsky and Kaltman. *Teacher's Dance Handbook No. 1.* Newark, N. J.: Folkraft, 1959.

LaSalle, Dorothy. *Rhythms and Dances for Elementary Schools.* New York: Ronald Press, 1951.

McIntosh, David S. *Singing Games and Dances.* New York: Association Press, 1957.

Metz, Louis L. *Action Songs and Rhythms for Children.* Minneapolis: T. S. Denison, 1962.

Murray, Ruth Lovell. *Dance in Elementary Education.* New York: Harper & Row, 1963.

Russell, Joan. *Creative Dance in the Primary School.* London: McDonald & Evans, Ltd., 1965.

Tobitt, Janet. *Red Book of Singing Games and Dances from the Americas.* Evanston, Ill.: Summy-Birchard, n.d.

———. *Yellow Book of Singing Games and Dances From Around the World.* Evanston, Ill.: Summy-Birchard, n.d.

5. STUNTS, TUMBLING, AND APPARATUS

Bailie, Sam, and Avelyn Bailie. *Elementary School Gymnastics.* St. Louis: Atlas Athletic Equipment Co., 1969.

Baley, James A. *Gymnastics in the Schools.* Boston: Allyn and Bacon, 1965.

Bedard, Irving. *Gymnastics for Boys.* Chicago: Follett, 1962.

Drehman, Vera L. *Head Over Heels.* New York: Harper & Row, 1970.

Harris, Rich. *Introducing Gymnastics.* Napa, Calif.: Physical Education Aids, 1964.

Keeney, Charles J. *Fundamental Tumbling Skills Illustrated.* New York: Ronald Press, 1966.

O'Quinn, Garland Jr. *Gymnastics for Elementary School Children.* Dubuque, Iowa: Wm. C. Brown, 1967.

Provansnik and Zabka. *Gymnastic Activities with Hand Apparatus for Girls and Boys.* Minneapolis: Burgess, 1965.

Orlick, Emanual and Jean Mosley. *Teacher's Illustrated Handbook of Stunts.* Englewood Cliffs, N. J.: Prentice-Hall, Inc.. 1963.

Szypula, G. *Tumbling and Balancing for All.* Dubuque, Iowa: Wm. C. Brown, 1957.

6. HEALTH, SAFETY, AND POSTURE

AAHPER. *Answers to Health Questions in Physical Education.* Washington, D. C., n.d.

———. *Health Appraisal of School Children.* Washington, D. C., 1969.

———. *Healthful School Environment.* Washington, D. C., 1969.

———. *Physical Growth Chart for Boys.* Washington, D. C., 1960.

———. *Physical Growth Chart for Girls.* Washington, D. C., 1960.

———. *Safety Education in Physical Education for the Classroom Teacher.* Washington, D. C., 1961.

———. *Suggested Safety Policies: Accident Prevention in Physical Education Athletics, and Recreation.* Washington, D. C., 1964.

———. *Teaching Safety in the Elementary School (Classroom Teachers Series).* Washington, D. C., 1962.

Darrow, May Goodall. *The Posture Problem Up To Date.* New York: Vantage Press, 1959.

Davies, Evelyn A. *The Elementary School Child and His Posture Patterns.* New York: Appleton-Century-Crofts, 1958.

Kelley, Ellen Davis. *Teaching Posture and Body Mechanics.* New York: Ronald Press, 1949.

Lowman, Charles, and Carl Haven Young. *Postural Fitness: Significance and Variances.* Philadelphia: Lea & Febiger, 1960.

Smith, Helen N. and Mary E. Wolverton. *Health Education in the Elementary School.* New York: Ronald Press, 1959.

Wells, Katherine F. *Posture Exercise Handbook.* New York: Ronald Press, 1963.

7. PERCEPTUAL-MOTOR DEVELOPMENT

AAHPER. *Approaches to Perceptual-Motor Experiences.* Washington, D. C., 1970.

———. *Motor Activity and Perceptual Development — Some Implications for Physical Educators.* Washington, D. C., 1968.

———. *Perceptual-Motor Foundations: A Multidisciplinary Concern.* Washington, D. C., 1969.

Braley, Konicki, and Leedy. *Daily Sensorimotor Training Activities.* Freeport, N. Y.:

Educational Activities, Inc., 1968.

Cratty, Bryant J. *Perceptual-Motor Behavior and Educational Processes.* Springfield, Ill.: C. C. Thomas, 1969.

Cratty, Bryant J., and Martin, Sister M. M. *Perceptual-Motor Efficiency in Children.* Philadelphia: Lea & Febiger, 1969.

Delacato, Carl W. *The Diagnosis and Treatment of Speech and Reading Problems.* Springfield, Ill.: C. C. Thomas, 1963.

————. *The Treatment and Prevention of Reading Problems.* Springfield, Ill.: C. C. Thomas, 1959.

Getman, G. N. *How to Develop Your Child's Intelligence.* Luverne, Minn., 1962.

Gillingham, Anna, and Bessie W. Stillman. *Remedial Training for Children with Specific Disability in Reading, Spelling, and Penmanship.* 6th Edition, 1960. Distributed by Anna Gillingham, 25 Parkview Avenue, Bronxville 8, N. Y.

Godfrey, Barbara, and N. C. Kephart. *Movement Patterns and Motor Education.* New York: Appleton-Century-Crofts, 1969.

Kephart, Newell C. *The Slow Learner in the Classroom.* Columbus, Ohio: Charles E. Merrill Books, 1960.

Portland Public Schools. *Improving Motor-Perceptual Skills.* Corvallis, Oregon: Continuing Education Publications, 1970.

Roach, Eugene, and Newell C. Kephart. *The Purdue Perceptual-Motor Survey.* Columbus, Ohio: Charles E. Merrill Books, 1966.

Rosborough, Pearl M. *Physical Fitness and the Child's Reading Problem.* New York: Exposition Press, 1963.

Stuart, Marion F. *Neurophysiological Insights into Teaching.* Palo Alto, Calif.: Pacific Books, 1963.

Van Whitsen, Betty. *Perceptual Training Activities Handbook.* New York: Teachers College Press, 1967.

8. CARD PACKETS FOR GAMES, RHYTHMS, AND STUNTS

Berger, H. Jean. *Program Activities for Camps.* Minneapolis: Burgess, 1961.

Fischer, Hugo, and Dean Shawbold. *Individual and Dual Stunts.* Minneapolis: Burgess, 1950.

Frederick, A. Bruce. *Gymnastic Action Cards.* Minneapolis: Burgess, 1965.

Harris, Jane A. *File O' Fun* (card file for social recreation), 2d ed. Minneapolis: Burgess, 1970.

Richardson, Hazel A. *Games for the Elementary School Grades.* Minneapolis: Burgess, 1951.

————. *Games for Junior and Senior High Schools.* Minneapolis: Burgess, 1957.

Stuart, Frances R., and John S. Ludlam. *Rhythmic Activities, Series I (K-3).* Minneapolis: Burgess, 1963.

————. *Rhythmic Activities, Series II (4-6).* Minneapolis: Burgess, 1963.

Vick, Marie, and Rosann McLaughlin Cox. *A Collection of Dances for Children.* Minneapolis: Burgess, 1970.

9. ENGLISH BOOKS ON MOVEMENT

Since much of the newer emphasis on movement has its origins in England, a selected list of English books is offered. These books may be secured from the Physical Education Association of Great Britain and Northern Ireland, which stocks all books and can provide information on other British books. The address is Ling Book Shop, 10 Nottingham Place, London, W.1, England. If only one book is desired, the author recommends the book by Bilbrough and Jones, which presents a middle-of-the-road approach of English methods.

Bilbrough, A. and P. Jones. *Physical Education in the Primary School.* London: London Press, Ltd., 1964.

Cameron, W. McD. and Peggy Pleasance. *Education in Movement.* Oxford: Basic, Blackwell, and Mott, Ltd. 1963.

Edmundson, Joseph. *Physical Education Teachers' Handbook for Primary Schools.* London: Evans Brothers Limited, 1960.

London City Council. *Educational Gymnastics.* London: London City Council, 1964.

Ministry of Education. *Physical Education in the Primary School.* Part 1, "Moving and Growing;" Part 2, "Planning the Programme." London: Her Majesty's Stationery Office, 1952.

Randall, Marjorie. *Basic Movement.* London: G. Bell and Sons, Ltd., 1963.

Sharpe, Julie. *Physical Education Teachers' Handbook for Infant Schools.* London: Evans Brothers, Ltd., 1959.

Note: The Infant School in England serves children 5 to 7 years of age. The Primary School is somewhat synonymous with our intermediate school.

10. GROWTH AND DEVELOPMENT; MISCELLANEOUS

AAHPER. *Adapted Education.* Washington, D. C., 1969.

_____. *Planning Areas and Facilities for Health, Physical Education, and Recreation.* Washington, D. C., 1965.

_____. *Preparing Teachers for a Changing Society.* Washington, D. C., 1970.

_____. *Professional Preparation of the Elementary School Education Teacher.* Washington, D. C., 1969.

Athletic Institute and AAHPER. *Equipment and Supplies for Athletics, Physical Education and Recreation.* Washington, D. C., 1960.

Baldwin, Alfred L. *Theories of Child Development.* New York: John Wiley and Sons, Inc., 1968.

Bell, Virginia Lee. *Sensorimotor Learning.* Pacific Palisades, Calif.: Goodyear, 1970.

Breckenridge, Marian E. and Margaret Nesbitt Murphy. *Growth and Development of the Young Child.* Philadelphia: W. B. Saunders Co., 1969.

Breckenridge, Marian E. and E. Lee Vincent. *Child Development — Physical and Psychological Growth Through Adolescence.* Philadelphia: W. B. Saunders Co., 1965.

Committee on Institutional Cooperation Conference. *Psychology of Motor Learning.* Chicago: The Athletic Institute, 1969.

Cratty, Bryant J. *Movement Behavior and Motor Learning.* Philadelphia: Lea & Febiger, 1964.

Doll, Edgar A. *Oseretsky Motor Proficiency Tests.* Minneapolis: American Guidance Services, 1946.

Ginsburg, Herbert and Sylvia Opper. *Piaget's Theory of Intellectual Development.* Englewood Cliffs, N. J.: Prentice-Hall, Inc., 1969.

Hartley, Ruth E. and Robert M. Goldenson. *The Complete Book of Children's Play.* New York: T. Y. Crowell, 1957.

Institute for the Development of Education Activities, Inc. Three Pamphlets. 1. Symposium on the Training of Teachers for Elementary Schools. 2. The British Infant School. 3. Innovations in the Elementary School. Melbourne, Fla., 1969.

Lawther, John D. *The Learning of Physical Skills.* Englewood Cliffs, N. J.: Prentice-Hall, 1968.

Sage, George H. *Introduction to Motor Behavior, A Neuropsychological Approach.* Reading, Mass.: Addison-Wesley Publishing Co., 1971.

Index

AAHPER Consultant, 5
AAHPER, 52
Abdominal exercises, 96
Accent, 236
Accident report, 45
Adapted program, 24
Administration — program, 18
Administration and the school, 40
Aim of education, 1
Aim of physical education, 1
Anatomical and physiological principles affecting posture, 54
Apparatus activities, 152
Arched ladders, 33
Arm-shoulder girdle exercises
Arranging for partners, 247
Art, integration with, 291
Assembly programs, 48
Attitudes, 25
Audio-visual aids, 75

Balance beam, 33, 34, 158
Balance beam benches, 33, 160
Balance boards, 34, 35, 123, 166
Balance in games, 207
Balance stunts, 178
Balance, types of, 86
Balloon Keep It Up, 124
Balls, 36, 38, 39
Balls, fleece, 36
Balls, yarn
Ball skills, 139
Ball skills to music, 242
Basic movement, 11, 50, 51, 102; factors for variety, 104; formations, 112; instructional procedures, 105; problem development, 108; processes in, 103
Basic principles important in movement experiences and skills, 70
Basic skills, 49, 50
Basic urges of children, 7
Basketball, 295
Basketball goals, 33
Beanbags, 36, 37
Beat (of music), 236
Behavior, ethical, 12
Behavioral objectives, 6
Benches, 33
Bench activities, 160
Bibliographical materials, 76
Blast-off launcher, 124
Blocks, 38
Body factors in movement, 105
Body management competency, 11, 12, 18, 49, 64, 74
Body position principle, 70
Bongo boards, 36
Boundary markers, 36

Bounding board, 34, 123, 167
Bowling pins, 38
Bowling skills, 143
Boxes, jumping, 35
Boy-girl relationships, 13
Bulletin boards, 75

Care and repair of equipment, 38
Card files, 76
Cart, supply, 35
Chalkboard work (training), 126
Characteristics of children, 8, 9
Characteristics of rhythmic background, 236
Characteristics of the slow learner, 120
Chinning bar, 34
Class size, 42
Classroom activities, 283, 285
Cleanliness of facilities, 44
Climatic factors, 18
Climbing frames, 33, 35
Climbing frames — English, 36
Climbing ropes, 33, 34
Climbing rope skills, 153
Climbing structures, portable, 34
Clubs, school, 18, 47
Coeducational activity, 13, 46
Combinations of movement, 117
Combination sets, 167
Community problems, 40
Competition in activities, 15
Conceptual understandings, 4
Concept formation, 2, 4, 15
Consultant in physical education, 40
Continuum of program development, 12
Coordination: body, 11; hand-eye, 11; foot-eye, 11
Creative rhythms, 236, 239, 243, 244; instructional procedures, 243
Creativity, 7
Culturally deprived children, 4
Cultural forces affecting physical education, 2

Dances: preschool, 248; kindergarten, 256; first grade, 260; second grade, 264; third grade, 269
Dance positions, 248
Deck tennis rings, 36, 38
Delacato, Carl, 4
Definition of physical education, 1
Demonstration in instruction, 71, 72
Demonstrations, 48
Depression years, 3
Developmental activity, lesson, 77, 79
Diagram of good posture, 56
Dignity of the individual, 1

Direct teaching approach, 6
Disadvantaged child, 4, 15
Disciplinary factors, 69
Displays, 76
Dramatic play, 134
Dramatic play, The Hike, 135
Dramatic play with poems, 130
Dramatization rhythms, 244
Draw step, 242
Dressing rooms, 18
Dualism in education, 2

Ear-shoulder method (posture), 59
Educational considerations, 65
Education forces affecting physical education, 2
Education frills, 3
Education Professions Development Act, 5
Elementary and Secondary Education Act, 5
Emergency care procedures, 45
Environment, healthful, 43
Equipment, 32
Equipment cart, 37
Ethical behavior, 12
European rhythmic running, 81
Evaluation, 73
Examination, health, 42
Excuses, 42
Exercise bar, 158
Exercises, old emphasis, 2
Exercises, 93; abdominal, 96; arm-shoulder girdle, 94; flexibility, 93; leg-agility, 97; posture, 60; trunk, 98
Exploration with games, 208

Facilities, 18, 31
Facilities, cleanliness, 44
Factors for securing variety of response, 104
Feedback in learning, 65
Feeling of good posture, 59
Film strips, 75
Finger plays, 129
First aid, 45
First grade program, 19, 20, 22; characteristics of children, 9; needs of children, 9; program needs, 9; program planning, 26
First grade activities: folk dance, 260; games, 213; relays, 260; singing games, 260; stunts and tumbling, 180
Fleece balls, 36
Flexibility exercises, 93
Flexibility, 86
Floor ladder activities, 125

321

322 INDEX

Flow, 104
Foreign influences, 2
Foreseeability (liability), 46
Folk dance, instructional procedures, 246
Folk dances, 236, 246, 248; first grade, 260; second grade, 265; third grade, 270
Follow through principle, 70
Foot-eye coordination, 11, 139
Foot-eye skills, 139
Formations: basic movement, 112; folk dance, 248; relays, 201; singing games, 248
Frills in education, 3
Fundamental movement patterns, 240
Fundamental rhythms, 236, 237

Games and sports emphasis, 2
Games, 205; beanbags, 139; exploration with, 208; instructional procedures, 207; introducing variations, 206; maintaining balance, 207; musical, 276; objectives of, 205; rhythmic, 276; safety suggestions, 206
Game lists: preschool, 208; kindergarten, 208; first grade, 213; second grade, 217; third grade, 224
Geographical factors, 18
Geography, integration with, 291
Geometric forms, 125
Goal of education, 1
Goal of physical education, 1
Grips: exercise bar, 158; paddle, 144; rope climbing, 155
Group interaction, 16
Guidelines, program planning, 17
Guides for conducting classroom and limited space activities, 284
Gym scooters, 36, 38, 167

Hammer grip, paddle, 144
Hampton (English) frame, 36
Hand-eye coordination, 11, 139
Hand-eye skills, 139
Handshake grip, paddle, 144
Hanson, Dr. Margie (AAHPER), 5
Head Start programs, 4
Health and safety, integration with, 292
Health and safety policies, 42
Health appraisal, 83
Health examination, 42, 44
Health instruction, 18
Health screening, 43
Healthful environment, 43
Hike, The (story), 135
History, integration with, 292
Hoop floor patterns, 151
Hoops, 36, 38, 150
Hopping, 116, 120, 122, 241
Horizontal bar, 33, 158
Horizontal ladder, 33, 157
How purposes can be attained, 16

Identification rhythms, 243
Indian clubs, 36, 38
Individual mats, 36, 38, 165
Inner tubes, 36
Inspection of facilities, equipment, 44
Instep squeeze, rope climbing, 156
Instruction, safety, 45

Instructional procedures, activities: balance beam, 158; balls, 140; basic movement, 105; basketball, 295; beanbags, 137; benches, 160; climbing frames, 157; creative rhythms, 243, 244; exercise bar, 158; folk dance, 246; fundamental movements to rhythm, 238; games, 207; hoops, 150; horizontal ladder, 156; individual mats, 165; jumping boxes, 163; magic ropes, 164; paddle and balls, 144; parachutes, 146; rope climbing, 153; soccer, 297; softball, 298; stunts and tumbling, 173; wands, 148
Instructional procedures, general, 66
Insurance, student, 46
Integration with other subjects, 291
Introductory activities, 77, 79, 81

Jack the Giant Killer (story), 128
Jumping, 116, 122, 241
Jumping boxes, 35, 163
Jump ropes, 36, 37
Jump-the-shot rope, 36, 38, 229

Kephart, 4
Kephart studies, 2
Klimraam-Holland climbing frame, 35
Kindergarten program, 19, 20, 21; characteristics of children, 9; needs of children, 9; program needs, 9
Kindergarten activities: games, 208; relays, 202; singing games, 256; stunts and tumbling, 171, 177
Kraus-Weber Tests, 3

Ladder, 33
Ladder, floor, 125
Ladder, horizontal, 33, 157
Language arts, integration with, 292
Lateral deviation, posture, 57
Laterality, 11, 126
Leadership experiences, 73
Leaping, 241
Learning, elements of, 63
Leg-ability exercises, 97
Legal responsibility, 46
Leg-around-rest, rope climbing, 155
Lesson planning, 77
Lesson, physical education, 77, 79
Liability, 46
Limited area activities, 283
Locomotor movements to rhythm, 240
Locomotor skills, 11, 12, 50
Long jump ropes, 36, 37, 280
Long rope jumping, 280
Low fitness programs, 25
Lummi sticks, 36

Magic (stretch) ropes, 36, 164
Manipulative activities, 11, 12, 13, 21, 22, 50
Manipulative activities to rhythm, 240, 242
Marking, 82
Marking equipment and supplies, 39
Mathematics, integration with, 293
Mats: care of, 39; individual, 165; tumbling, 34
Medicine chest, 46

Meter (of music), 236
Methods of teaching, 105
Mimetics, 71
Mixers, dance, 236
Motion pictures, use of, 75
Motivation in learning, 65
Motor learning, 11
Movement combinations, 117
Movement education, 3, 6, 49, 50
Movement excellence, 11
Movement exploration, 53
Movement suggestion box, 117
Multi-purpose room, 31
Musical games, 236, 276
Music, integration with, 292

National physical fitness test, 3
Needs of children, 8, 9; preschool, 8; kindergarten, 9; first grade, 9; second grade, 9; third grade, 9
Negligence (law), 46
Nongraded school, 5
Nonlocomotor movements to rhythm, 240, 242
Nonlocomotor skills, 11, 12, 50
Noon-hour play period, 47
Number concepts, integration with, 293
Nursery school program, 19, 20, 21; characteristics of children, 8; needs of children, 8; program needs, 8

Objectives: behavioral, 6; of games, 205; physical education, 6; physical fitness, 6
Obstacle courses for movement, 123
Ocular pursuit (perceptual-motor), 126
Opaque projector, 75
Outdoor areas, 32
Outdoor equipment, 32

Paddle and ball skills, 144
Paddles, 36, 38
Pads of the fingers, principle, 70
Pageants, 48
Parachute, 36, 145
Parachute play, 145
Parents-Teachers Association (PTA), 40, 47
Partners, arranging for (dancing), 247
Patterns of teaching responsibility, 40
Peer relationships, 1, 4, 13
Perceptual-motor activities, 118, 124
Perceptual-motor competency, 2, 4, 11, 21, 49, 51, 61, 118
Perceptual-motor team, 126
Personal and education values, 15, 74
Physical education, cultural forces affecting, 2
Physical education, educational forces affecting, 2
Physical education, general aim, 1
Physical education, definition, 1
Physical education lesson, 77, 79
Physical fitness, 2, 6, 85
Physical fitness (developmental) activities: astronaut drills, 101; circuit training, 99; exercises, 91; routines, grade 3, 90; movement experiences, 87

INDEX

Physical fitness: components, 85; definition, 85; emphasis, 3, 23; evaluation of, 74; goals, 10; guidelines for achieving, 85; and the handicapped child, 25; and motor learning, 11; objective, 6
Physicians and schools, 42, 43, 45
Planning facilities, 31
Playdays, 18, 47
Plumb line posture assessment, 59
Poems, 130
Policies, health and safety, 42
Policies, purchasing, 32
Portable climbing structures, 34
Posture and body mechanics, 49, 51, 54
Posture check sheet, 58
Posture, definition of, 56
Posture evaluation: ear-shoulder method, 59; plumb line method, 59
Posture exercises, 60
Posture, good walking, 58
Posture, lateral deviation of, 57
President's Council on Physical Fitness and Sports, 3
Preschool activities: games, 208; singing games, 248; stunts and tumbling, 171, 177
Preschool (nursery) program, 19, 20, 21; characteristics of children, 8; needs of children, 8; program needs, 8
Principal and the program, 41
Problem development in basic movement, 108
Processes in basic movement, 103
Program, adapted, 24
Program guides: preschool (nursery), 19, 21; kindergarten, 19, 20, 21; first grade, 19, 20, 22; second grade, 19, 20, 22; third grade, 19, 20, 23
Program, low-fit children, 25
Program needs, 8, 9; preschool (nursery), 8; kindergarten, 8; first grade, 9; second grade, 9; third grade, 9
Program, physically underdeveloped child, 25
Program planning: grade level emphasis, 19; guidelines for, 17; yearly percentages, 19
Program planning, year's program, 25
Program, swimming and water safety, 23
Program, year's program for third grade, 30
Projects, integration ideas, 293
Promotional ideas, 47
Proportional week scheduling, 26
Public relations, 47
Purchasing policies, 32
Purposes of physical education, 10; educational values, 15; movement excellence, 11; personal values, 15; physical fitness, 10; recreational values, 14; safety skills, 13; self-image, 14; social goals, 12

Qualities of movement, 104
Quality in movement, 112

Rabies, problem of, 46
Readiness to learn, 65
Readmittance after illness, 42
Rebound net, 124
Recess, 46
Record player, 34, 235
Records, 235
Records for rope jumping, 279
Recreation goal, 14
Recreational objective, 14, 74
Reinforcement of learning, 65
Relaxation principle, 70
Relays, 201; kindergarten, 202; first grade, 202; second grade, 202; third grade, 203
Repair policies, 38
Report, accident, 45
Resolution, American Medical Association, 5
Return activity, 153, 173
Rhymes for rope jumping, 280
Rhythm in movement, 8
Rhythmic accompaniment, 235
Rhythmic activities, 234
Rhythmic background, 236
Rhythmic ball skills, 242
Rhythmic beat repetition and reproduction, 237
Rhythmic running, 81
Role of the teacher, 63
Rope climbing, 153
Rope jumping, 279
Rope jumping, long, 280
Rope jumping rhymes, 280
Rope jumping to music, 236, 274
Ropes, climbing, 33, 34
Ropes, jump, 36, 37
Running, 116, 241
Running, rhythmic, 81

Safe environment, 44
Safe teaching place, 44
Safety education, 45
Safety: evaluation of, 74; in games, 206; in instruction, 72; instruction, 45; integration with, 292; procedures, 44; skills, 13; softball, 298; stunts and tumbling, 170; water, 14, 23
Schedule: daily, 42; proportional weekly, 26; weekly unit, 26
School board responsibility, 5
Scissors grip, rope climbing, 155
Scoops, 143
Scooters, gym, 167
Screening, health, 43
Second grade activities: dances, 264; games, 217; relays, 202; stunts and tumbling, 188
Second grade program, 19, 20, 22; characteristics of children, 9; needs of children, 9; program needs, 9
Self-concept, 4, 14, 74
Self-image, 4, 14, 74
Showering, 18
Simple balance stunts, 178
Singing games, 236, 245
Singing games, formations, 248
Singing games, instructional procedures, 245
Singing games, grade level placement: preschool, 248; kindergarten, 256; first grade, 260; second grade, 264
Sitting posture, 58
Skill achievement and social adjustment, 13
Skill types: locomotor, 11, 12, 50; manipulative, 11, 12, 21, 22, 80; nonlocomotor, 11, 12, 50; special, 11, 12, 50; sports, 11, 12, 23
Skills: activities: balls, 139; basketball, 295; bowling, 143; paddle and ball, 142; soccer, 297; softball, 299; basic, 11, 12, 49, 50; evaluation of, 74; instructional program, 51, 53; safety, 13; useful, 11
Skipping, 120, 242
Sliding, 242
Slow learner: characteristics of, 120; testing for, 120
Soccer, 297
Social goals, 12, 74
Softball, 298; backstops, 33; equipment, 36, 38; rules, 299
Space factors, 104
Special programs, handicapped, 5
Specialist in physical education, 5, 6, 40
Special skills, 11, 12, 49
Sports: skills, 11, 12, 23, 294; units, 294
Squad organization, 66
Start-and-expand technique, 71, 137, 153
Stepping stone patterns, 125
Stilts, 36
Stirrup descent, rope climbing, 156
Storage of equipment and supplies, 36, 37, 39
Storage facilities, 31
Story games, 127
Story — Jack the Giant Killer, 128
Stretch (magic) ropes, 36, 164
Structured movement, 106, 115
Student insurance, 46
Stunts and tumbling, 169; preschool emphasis, 171, 177; kindergarten, 171, 177; first grade, 180; second grade, 188; third grade, 193
Supplies, 32
Supply cart, 35
Supervised play period, 46
Supervision of play period, 46
Supervisor in physical education, 40, 44
Swim program, 14, 23

Tambourine directed activity, 82
Tape recorder, 235
Targets for beanbags, 139
Teacher, role of, 63
Teacher-training program, 5
Temperature of play areas, 43
Tempo, 236
Tetherball, 33, 36, 281
Third grade activities: basketball, 294; dances, 269; games, 224; relays, 203; soccer, 297; softball, 298; stunts and tumbling, 193

324 INDEX

Third grade program, 19, 20, 23; characteristics of children, 9; needs of children, 9; program needs, 9
Third grade, suggested year's program, 30
Time factors (movement), 104
Torque, development of, principle, 70
Total body coordination principle, 70
Trunk exercises, 98
Tumbling mats, 34
Turning bars, 158

Unstructured movement, 106, 114
Urges of children, 7
U. S. Office of Education, 5

Variations in games, 206
Ventilation, 43
Visual concentration principle, 70
Visualization principle, 70
Vocal side of teaching, 68

Walking, 46, 116, 240
Walking posture, 57
Wands, 148
Water safety programs, 14, 23
Weekly unit schedule, 26
Weight transfer principle, 70
What is physical education, 1
Whistle, use of, 67
World War I effects, 2
World War II effects, 3

Yarn balls, 36, 38, 139
Year's program planning, 25
Year's program, suggested, 30

EXERCISES

Arm Circling, 95
Bend and Stretch, 93
Body Circles, 99
Crab Kicking, 95
Curl-Up, 60
Curl-Up, Partial, 60
Curl-Up with Twist, 61
Floor Scratching, 61
Foot Carry, 61
Head and Shoulder Curl, 96
Hurdle Stretch, 94
Knee Raise, 97
Knot Tying (Rope), with Feet, 61
Leg Extension, 97
Marble Transfer, 61
Push-Ups, 94
Rowing, 61
Running in Place, 97
Side Flex, 98
Side Straddle Hop, 97
Sitting Stretch, 94
Swan, 60
Tailor, 60
Treadmill, 98
Trunk Twister, 98
Turn and Bounce, 99
Wing Stretcher, 96

FINGER PLAY RHYMES

Grandmother's Glasses, 129
Hickory, Dickory, Dock, 129
Jack and Jill, 129
Little Miss Muffet, 130
My Fingers, 130

GAMES

Add and Subtract, 285
Animal Chase, 218
Animal Tag, 213
Around the Row, 285
Automobiles, 218
Back-to-Back, 213
Balance Dodgeball, 230
Ball Passing, 216
Ball Toss, 217
Balloon Volleyball, 286
Basketball Bounce, 286
Bat Ball, 230
Beanbag Horseshoes, 139
Beanbag Pitch, 286
Beanbag Target Toss, 230
Bear and Keeper, 229
Beat-Ball Throw Softball, 300
Bicycle Race, 286
Birds Fly, 289
Black and White, 226
Blind Man's Buff, 209
Blue, Black, and Baloney, 226
Boiler Burst, 286
Bounce Ball, 231
Bowling (Classroom), 286
Bowling One-Step, 224
Bronco Tag, 225
Busy Bee, 225
Caged Lion, 218
Call Ball, 217
Cat and Mice, 218
Cat and Mice (Classroom), 286
Cat and Rat, 213
Catch the Cane, 217
Chair Quoits, 287
Change Seats, 287
Charlie Over the Water, 214
Charlie Over the Water — Ball Version, 218
Circle Kick Ball, 298
Circle Straddle Ball, 223
Circle Team Dodgeball, 231
Circus Master, 214
Club Guard, 231, 232
Colors, 209
Competitive Circle Contests, 232
Corner Ball, 297
Couple Tag, 225
Cross Over, 226
Crows and Cranes, 226
Do This, Do That, 287
Duck, Duck, Goose, 215
Eagles and Sparrows, 226
End Ball, 296
Exchange Dodgeball, 223
Fireman, 209
Floor Ping Pong, 287
Flowers and Wind, 219
Fly Trap, 227
Flying Dutchman, 227
Follow Me, 227
Footsie Dodgeball, 230
Forest Ranger, 219
Free Throw End Ball, 296
Frog in the Sea, 227
Frozen Tag, 216
Gallop Tag, 214
Galloping Lizzie, 228
Geronimo, 287
Guess the Leader, 210
Hill Dill, 219
Hopscotch, 281
Hot Potatoes, 220
Hound and Rabbit, 220
Hunter, 220
Hunter, Gun, Rabbit, 288
I Can Do What You Can, 220
Imitation, 288
I'm Very, Very Tall, 210
Individual Dodgeball, 232
In the Creek, 221
Jump the Shot, 229
Kick Shuffle, 282
King's Land, 218
Kneeling Tag, 210
Last Couple Out, 221
Leader Ball, 216
Leap the Brook, 221
Locomotor Tag, 216
Lost Children, 288
Magic Fountain, 210
Marching Ponies, 211
May I Chase You?, 222
Maze Tag, 228
Midnight, 215
Mother, May I?, 211
Mouse Trap, 222
Newcomb, 232
Old Man (Old Lady), 215
O'Leary, 282
One Step, 232
One Step — Bowling, 224
One Two, Button My Shoe, 215
Poison Circle, 228
Popcorn, 211
Put Hands, 288
Red Light, 222
Right Face, Left Face, 228
Roll Dodgeball, 223
Run for Your Supper, 215
Scarecrow and Crows, 211
Shapes, 212
Simon Says, 289
Slap Jack, 214
Snap, 289
Squirrel in the Trees, 216
Statues, 212
Steal the Treasure, 229
Stop and Start, 223
Straddle Bowling, 224
Streets and Alleys, 228
Tag Games, 210, 216, 225
Teacher Ball, 217
Ten, Ten, Double Ten, 289
Tetherball, 281
Three Deep, 229
Three Strikes (Softball), 300
Through the Tunnel Race, 229
Throw It and Run, 300
Tommy Tucker's Land, 212
Toss Target Ball, 233
Touch Ball, 232
Triple Change, 229
Two Deep, 223
Two Pitch Softball, 300
Underleg Throw Softball, 300

INDEX

Weathervane, 230
Where's My Partner, 216
Where, Oh Where?, 289
Who Am I?, 212
Who's Leading (Classroom), 290
Zoo, 290

POEMS

Elephant, 130
Giant, 130
Giants and Dwarfs, 131
Hippity Hop, 131
How to Make a Happy Day, 132
Jack Be Nimble, 132
Little Jack Horner, 131
Pat-A-Cake, 132
Ripe Apples, 132
Three Blind Mice, 133
Wallaby Kangaroo, 134
Wind, 133

RELAYS

Ball Pass, 202
Bench, 204
Beanbag Pass, 202
Bounce Ball, 203
Bowl, 204
Circle Pass, 203
Cross Over, 203
Lane, 202, 203
Locomotor, 204
Overhead, 288
Partner, 203
Pass the Buck, 204
Snowball, 203
Stoop and Stretch, 204

RHYTHMIC GAMES

Arches, 278
Circle Stoop, 276
Follow Me, 277
Freeze, 277
Partner Stoop, 277
Right Angle, 278
Whistle March, 278

RHYTHMS

Ach Ya, 267
A Hunting We Will Go, 267
Around We Go, 249
Baa Baa Blacksheep (Preschool), 250
Baa Baa Blacksheep (Kindergarten), 257
Bleking, 272
Bluebird, 258
Bow-Wow-Wow, 250
Broom Dance, 268
Brother John, 251
Carrousel, 271
Children's Polka, 271
Chimes of Dunkirk, 264
Chested Hen, 272
Csebogar, 274
Cuckoo Clock, 251
Dance of Greeting, 264
Did You Ever See a Lassle, 265
Diddle, Diddle Dumpling, 251
Donkey, 252
Down the Mississippi, 265
Eency Weency Spider, 252
Farmer in the Dell, 257
Farmer in the Wheat, 260
Good Morning, 253
Go Round and Round the Village, 265
Gustaf's Skoal, 273
Hansel and Gretel, 273
Hickory, Dickory Dock, 264
How D'Ye Do My Partner, 267
I See You, 263
Jack Be Nimble, 253
Jolly is the Miller, 266
Jump Jim Joe, 271
Kinderpolka, 271
Let Your Feet Go Tap, Tap, Tap, 258
Little Boy Blue, 253
London Bridge, 261
Looby Loo, 262
Mary Had a Little Lamb, 254
Muffin Man, 261
Mulberry Bush, 258
Oats, Peas, Beans, and Barley Grow, 261
Oh Where, Oh Where Has My Little Dog Gone, 254
Paw Paw Patch, 270
Pease Porridge Hot, 259
Popcorn Man, 269
Pussy Cat, 262
Rig-A-Jig-Jig, 268
Ring Around the Rosie, 254
Rock-A-Bye Baby, 255
Shoemaker's Dance, 266
Shoo Fly, 266
Sing a Song of Sixpence, 263
Snowball, 259
Ten Little Indians, 258
Thread Follows the Needle, 262
Three Blind Mice, 270
Touch Your Shoulders, 259
Trot, My Pony, Trot, 255
Twinkle, Twinkle, Little Star, 257
Who's That Knocking on My Door, 255
Yankee Doodle (Preschool), 256
Yankee Doodle (Third Grade), 270

STUNTS AND TUMBLING

Alligator, 179
Back Roller, 178, 186
Backward Curl, 191
Backward Roll, 192, 194
Backward Roll — Hand Clasped Position, 187
Balance Touch, 185
Bear Walk, 181
Bouncing Ball, 182
Chinese Get-Up, 200
Climb Up, 190
Coffee Grinder, 195
Crab Walk, 186
Crazy Walk, 191
Cricket Walk, 184
Crossed Legged Stand, 179
Curl-Up, 196
Directional Walk, 179
Double Lame Dog, 197
Double Top, 200
Elbow Crawl, 188
Elephant Walk, 181
Elevator, 179
Fluttering Leaf, 179
Forward Roll, 178, 184, 188, 193
Frog Handstand, 194
Frog Jump, 188
Gorilla Walk, 183
Hand and Knee Balance, 193
Head Balance, 182
Head Touch, 178
Headstand, 198
Heel Click, 185
Heel Slap, 189
Heel Stand, 194
Hip Walk, 146, 197
Jump Turns, 181
Kangaroo, 180
Lame Dog Walk, 183
Leg Balances, 190
Line Walking, 179
Long Bridge, 197
Lowering the Boom, 186
Measuring Worm, 190
Monkey Run, 181
Mule Kick, 196
One Leg Balance Reverse, 196
One Legged Balance Stands, 183
Partner Hopping, 199
Partner Pull-Up, 200
Pogo Stick, 189
Puppy Dog Run, 180
Rabbit Jump, 181
Reach Under, 195
Reverse Seal Crawl, 188
Rising Sun, 185
Rolling Log, 186
Russian Dance, 194
Scooter, 146, 197
Seal Crawl, 185
Seal Crawl Variations, 188
Seat Circle, 192
See Saw, 180
Side Roll, 178
Single Knee Balance, 193
Squat Thrust, 194
Staff Man Bend, 195
Thread the Needle, 187
Three Point Tip-Up, 190
Tightrope Walk, 182
Tip-Up, 194
Top, 189
Tummy Balance, 196
Turk Stand, 190
Turn Over, 186
Turtle, 197
Twister, 199
Walking in Place, 180
Walrus Walk, 195
Wicket Walk, 189
Wring the Dishrag, 187

WAND ACTIVITIES

Back Scratcher, 149
Grapevine, 149
Jump Stick, 150
Partner Catch, 150
Partner Change, 150
Thread the Needle — Standing, 149
Thread the Needle — V Seat, 148
Twist Under, 149
Wand Catch, 148
Wand Juggle, 150
Wand Whirl, 149